A CARLETON CONTEMPORARY

ABORIGINAL PEOPLES AND GOVERNMENT RESPONSIBILITY

Exploring Federal And Provincial Roles

Edited By

David C. Hawkes

Carleton University Press
Ottawa, Canada

 CARLETON UNIVERSITY PRESS

© Carleton University Press Inc. (1989), 1995

ISBN 0-88629-090-2 (paperback)

Printed and bound in Canada

Carleton Contemporary #12

Canadian Cataloguing in Publication Data

Hawkes, David C. (David Craig), 1947-
 Aboriginal Peoples and Government responsibility

ISBN 0-88629-090-2 (paperback)
ISBN 0-88629-098-8 (casebound)

 1. Indians of North America—Canada—Government relations
—1951-   . 2. Inuit—Canada—Government   relations.
3. Métis—Government relations. 4. Indians of North America—
Canada—Legal status, laws, etc. 5. Inuit—Canada—Legal status,
laws, etc. 6. Métis—Legal   status,   laws,   etc. 7. Federal
government—Canada. I. Title.

 E92.H379 1989   323.1'197'071   C89-090314-X

Distributed by: Oxford University Press Canada
          70 Wynford Drive,
          Don Mills, Ontario.
          Canada. M3C 1J9
          (416) 441-2941

Cover Design: Aerographics Ottawa

Acknowledgement

Carleton University Press gratefully acknowledges the support extended to its publishing programme by the Canada Council and
the Ontario Arts Council.

CONTENTS

ACKNOWLEDGEMENTS

I wish to acknowledge the arm's length financial support of the Native Affairs Directorate of the Government of Ontario, as well as the assistance—financial, substantive and administrative—of the School of Public Administration at Carleton University.

Both the School's Director, Gene Swimmer and the Administrator, Martha Clark, deserve special mention, since their interest and attention to this project went far beyond the call of duty.

I am indebted, as well, to my colleagues Frances Abele and Allan Maslove in the School of Public Administration, who read earlier versions of the first and final chapters. I am grateful to the graduate students from the School who took notes for me from the various conference sessions and who assisted in the arrangements for the conference. I wish to thank Jocelyn Beairsto, Alex Ker, Jean Flowers, and Paula Isaac for their assistance in this regard.

David C. Hawkes
Ottawa
June 1989

CHAPTER 1
INTRODUCTION
David C. Hawkes

During the past decade, attention in the field of aboriginal affairs has been riveted upon issues of aboriginal rights and constitutional reform, and in particular on the subject of entrenching the right to aboriginal self-government in the *Constitution Act, 1982*. While the focus is understandable, given the importance of the exercise (both symbolic and real), nevertheless it has shifted the attention away from other worthy issues. Some of these are less ethereal in character, such as the delivery of services in aboriginal communities, while others, such as federal/provincial responsibility, affect issues of both constitutional reform *and* service delivery. Because of the broad importance of federal/provincial responsibility for aboriginal peoples, and because it has received scant attention in the recent past, it is now time for a more comprehensive examination of emerging federal and provincial roles and responsibilities with respect to aboriginal peoples. This volume is intended to take some initial steps down this path.

This publication is the final part of a larger project undertaken by the School of Public Administration at Carleton University in Ottawa on aboriginal peoples and federal/provincial responsibility. Each of the chapters was specially commissioned for a conference on this topic, which was held in the Senate Room of Carleton University on October 4th and 5th, 1988. The conference brought together approximately 100 aboriginal people, senior federal and provincial government officials, and scholars and experts in the field.

The main themes which emerged from the conference are reported in the conclusion of this book. They are summarized here in point form:

- With respect to government roles and responsibilities, it is important to distinguish between government jurisdiction and government responsibility.
- For many reasons, provincial governments are becoming increasingly important in the lives of aboriginal peoples.
- Although the federal government has jurisdiction over aboriginal peoples, both federal and provincial governments have responsibilities toward them.
- The drive for constitutionally-based aboriginal self-government at the national level, and the provision of meaningful programs and services to aboriginal peoples at the community level, ought to be viewed as complementary rather than contending objectives.
- A debate is now raging across Canada as to whether a third level of government—aboriginal self-government—is now emerging in the Canadian federal system.
- At times, it appears that the interpretation of what is the source of power for aboriginal governments is more of a barrier to agreement than the range of such powers.
- Aboriginal self-government will be meaningless without a secure fiscal base, which both responds to the need for fiscal independence while at the same time providing a supportive national and provincial framework.

The studies which formed part of the larger project were commissioned for three purposes: to provide a conceptual or analytic framework for examining matters concerning aboriginal peoples and federal/provincial responsibility; to explore what responsibilities federal and provincial governments are actually accepting in this area; and to provide thought-provoking background reading for the then upcoming conference. This volume is organized into three parts to reflect this approach.

The first chapter in Part I is the most expansive in character. Alan Pratt, in his chapter entitled "Federalism in the Era of Aboriginal Self-Government," develops a conceptual framework for determining federal and provincial responsibilities for programs and services delivered to aboriginal peoples. In conducting his examination, he notes that this is fundamentally a political question, rather than one of legal liability.

The trust relationship of governments to aboriginal people, in his analysis, binds both the federal government (through s.91(24), "Indians and the lands reserved for the Indians") and provincial governments in their respective fields of jurisdiction, although the federal government has primary responsibility. Aboriginal peoples are provincial residents, as well as within a special federal category. Therefore, Pratt goes on to argue, there is no basis for denying aboriginal persons equal access to provincial programs and services. Equality and other individually focused *Charter* rights apply to aboriginal peoples, but cannot nullify the collective rights of minorities which are entrenched through political compromise, and which authorize legal regimes which treat those minorities in a preferential fashion.

In his conclusion, Alan Pratt finds that an older notion—that of "citizens plus"—is helpful in describing the appropriate federal and provincial roles. The federal government is responsible for the "plus"; that is, for "aboriginality" or the aboriginal-specific portion. This entails support for the preservation, enhancement and development of "aboriginality." Provincial governments are responsible for the "citizens"; that is, equity of service, equal to that enjoyed by others. This entails treating all individuals equally, without regard to race. Moreover, provincial governments have an obligation to tailor programs and services to meet the particular needs and circumstances of aboriginal peoples.

The second chapter in Part I, by Brad Morse, examines "Government Obligations, Aboriginal Peoples and Section 91(24) of the *Constitution Act, 1867*." He canvasses a range of aspects relating to the scope of s.91(24) ("Indians and lands reserved for the Indians") and its impact upon federal, provincial and aboriginal views of their common relationship. He conducts this review within the context of the debate over the "magic words" of "jurisdiction" and "responsibility." His elaboration of the different meanings of the two terms provides the basis for a more thorough exploration of federal and provincial government obligations toward aboriginal peoples.

Brad Morse concludes, as does Alan Pratt, that the trust obligation can be shared between federal and provincial governments, although the precise duties of governments in this regard may differ. He also argues that s.35 of the *Constitution Act, 1982* (affirming existing aboriginal and treaty rights) may have an impact upon

11

s.91(24) to create a more proactive obligation on the Government of Canada, in which it must seek to "affirm" aboriginal and treaty rights through suitable means. This may have the effect of limiting federal government discretionary power with respect to s.91(24). As a result of this development, Morse further concludes that the Supreme Court could direct the federal government to take executive action to remedy a breach of the trust obligation, although he thinks it unlikely that the Court would impose legislative action.

In the final chapter in Part I, entitled "Fiscal Arrangements for Aboriginal Self-Government," Allan Maslove and I explore the relationship between fiscal arrangements negotiated between governments and aboriginal communities, and the emerging arrangements for aboriginal self-government. Since fiscal arrangements imply forms of self-government, and vice-versa, the chapter seeks to develop a policy framework to link the two. In our view, three sets of considerations should be linked: (1) the aboriginal self-government arrangement or model, especially the amount of local autonomy involved; (2) the form of fiscal arrangement which should support and be consistent with the self-government provisions; and (3) the level of community development (in economic, political and administrative terms) into which these arrangements are to be introduced.

These three variables—governmental autonomy, fiscal autonomy and community development—should all be positively correlated. As aboriginal communities become more self-governing, their fiscal arrangements should become less conditional. Greater political autonomy and greater fiscal autonomy go hand in hand. Likewise, community development and self-government should grow together, so that greater political autonomy is accompanied by greater self-sufficiency in economic and administrative terms. Unfortunately, in reviewing existing fiscal arrangements for aboriginal self-government, we find little relationship between the autonomy of the aboriginal governments and the automony of their accompanying fiscal arrangements.

Part II of this volume explores the existing roles and responsibilities of federal and provincial governments regarding aboriginal peoples. Given the immense size of the area, it was not possible to examine the situation in every province, even if the data were available (which they are not!). Thus, some chapters examine the situations with respect to some existing aboriginal government arrangements (those which appeared most interesting), while one provides a partial comparison of Alberta and Manitoba in this regard. Although these two provinces took very different positions on entrenching the right to aboriginal self-government in the Constitution, it remains unknown if they differ significantly in terms of programming and services to aboriginal peoples.

The comparative chapter is Chapter 5, which Frances Abele and Katherine Graham have entitled "High Politics is Not Enough: Policies and Programs for Aboriginal Peoples in Alberta and Ontario." In their opinion, it is necessary to complement the "high politics" of constitutional reform at the national level with more practical matters of administration and service delivery in aboriginal communities at the local level. Because of this, relations between aboriginal peoples and provincial governments have become more important. Moreover, for the realization of aboriginal self-determination, questions of administration and implementation are just as important as constitutional and legal issues.

From their examination of aboriginal-provincial relations in Alberta and Ontario, Abele and Graham believe that there is some basis for optimism about the potential for progress toward self-government, even in the absence of constitutional negotiations. From their review of actual programs, "aboriginal self-government" in Ontario is effectively the same as "aboriginal self-administration" in Alberta. Their major policy prescription is the transfer of service delivery responsibilities to local aboriginal authorities, together with adequate funding and flexibility in implementation.

In Chapter 6, "Federal and Provincial Responsibilities for the Cree, Naskapi and Inuit Under the James Bay and Northern Quebec, and Northeastern Quebec Agreements," Evelyn Peters studies what are arguably the most complex relations among aboriginal, federal and provincial governments. The James Bay Agreement and the Northeast Quebec Agreement, concluded in 1975 and 1978 respectively, were the first modern land claims agreements negotiated under the new federal policy of addressing outstanding aboriginal land rights.

Evelyn Peters sets two objectives: first, to delineate the structure of federal and provincial government responsibilities regarding these two initiatives; and second, to describe and evaluate the processes of implementing these responsibilities. She examines federal and provincial policy responsibilities in the areas of: local and regional government; harvesting and environmental regimes; compensation and economic development and administration of local services. She finds the agreements to be inherently dynamic, and that responsibilities have evolved, and continue to evolve over time. If negotiating aboriginal self-government agreements and fiscal arrangements is half the battle, she concludes, then the implemetation of such agreements is the other half.

In Chapter 7, Fred Martin writes on "Federal and Provincial Responsibility in the Metis Settlements of Alberta." The Metis settlements in northern Alberta, established by the Government of Alberta in 1938, are the only lands held and "governed" by Metis peoples in Canada. The eight Metis settlements, equal in size to Prince Edward Island, are home to about 5 000 Metis. These settlements have been noted for their pragmatic leadership, which has focused on results rather than on rights.

In July of 1988, legislation was tabled in the Alberta Legislature which would achieve two Metis objectives: to provide self-government and to protect the Metis homeland. Fred Martin reviews the proposed *Metis Settlements Act*, which provides for self-government and by-law making powers for settlement councils, and the proposed *Metis Settlements Land Act*, which transfers surface rights and lands to the Metis General Council, a central land- and trust-fund holding body representing the eight settlements. Finally, he describes the proposed constitutional amendment to the *Alberta Act, 1982* (*Constitution Act, 1982*), which would prevent the Government of Alberta from expropriating settlement land, from amending the *Metis Settlements Land Act*, or from dissolving the Metis General Council without the agreement of that council.

In Chapter 8, John Taylor and Gary Paget look at a more recent development in "Federal/Provincial Responsibility and the Sechelt." The Sechelt people of British Columbia have embarked upon a unique, and very public experiment in aboriginal self-government. This chapter, which focuses on the federal and provincial context, as well as the legislative, political, administrative, financial and service structure implications, is the first to document developments pertaining to this experiment.

The *Sechelt Indian Band Self-Government Act* gives the Sechelt people control and ownership of band lands and resources, the flexibility to negotiate block grants, and the legislative framework for self-government, all without abrogating or derogating from any aboriginal or treaty rights, including land claims. In an interesting *quid pro quo*, the band can tax both Indian and non-Indian occupants of band lands, but other "normal" municipal taxes, such as school and hospital levies, apply to both Indians and non-Indians. The Sechelt Indian Band Constitution, which is developed and ratified by the band, is approved by the federal Cabinet. It gives band by-laws the status of federal laws.

The *Sechelt Indian Government District Enabling Act*, a British Columbia Act, recognizes Sechelt government jurisdiction over non-band occupiers of Indian lands, as well as band members. The Act enables the District to use provincial statutes (such as the *Municipal Act*), and treats the District as a municipality with respect to receiving provincial benefits and programs, including grants from the provincial revenue-sharing program.

Taylor and Paget view the Sechelt experiment as primarily a federal artifact, wherein provincial laws apply only insofar as they are inconsistent with federal legislation, the band constitution, or band by-laws. The powers of the Band Council go well beyond the conventional powers of a municipality, or in some cases, they assert, beyond the powers of a provincial government. It could be argued, they add, that the Sechelt experiment represents a "third level of government."

Part III of this collection attempts to bring together the challenges facing governments and aboriginal peoples, together with some conclusions which emerge from the previous analyses.

Chapter 9 is the transcript of the address of the Honourable Ian G. Scott, Minister Responsible for Native Affairs and the Attorney-General for the Government of Ontario, to the conference which formed a part of this project. His remarks focussed on the respective responsibilities and roles of the federal and provincial governments in their dealings with the aboriginal peoples of Canada. In his view, this issue in its broadest context—federal/provincial jurisdiction, responsibility and funding—gets in the way of attempts to solve the problems which aboriginal peoples face, and contributes to the lack of progress in this area. The problems are getting worse, he adds, due to fiscal restraint.

He suggests a new approach, based on the concept of aboriginal peoples as "citizens plus." Aboriginal peoples have a special place in society in *addition* to enjoying the basic rights of all Canadians. Aboriginal peoples are Canadians, with the full rights, freedoms and responsibilities of citizenship, including access to all provincial programs and services. They have the right to retain and develop their own communities, free from pressures to assimilate. The obligation of federal and provincial governments is to support the social, political and economic development of aboriginal communities in accordance with aboriginal aspirations.

Scott suggests a new vision of the federal government role in this regard; he believes that the federal government should provide ongoing support and enhancement of those features of aboriginal life which are uniquely aboriginal—the social, economic and political development of aboriginal communities, on and off reserve—in order to create greater self-reliance and autonomy within Canadian society.

The final chapter, the Conclusion, brings together the themes which emerge from these previous chapters, as well as the main lines of argument which dominated the conference in October of 1988.

PART I
CONCEPTUAL AND ANALYTICAL FRAMEWORKS

CHAPTER 2

FEDERALISM IN THE ERA OF ABORIGINAL SELF-GOVERNMENT

Alan Pratt

INTRODUCTION

It is clear that aboriginal communities and institutions will remain dependent upon government programs, services and transfer payments for the foreseeable future, even as they develop toward greater self-government and self-reliance. However, recent experience has reaffirmed that uncertainties regarding the roles of the provincial and federal governments in program and service provision are undermining progress toward the shared goal of aboriginal development.

This chapter examines the conceptual framework for determining federal and provincial responsibilities for programs and services delivered to aboriginal people. It is assumed that these responsibilities will continue to govern their respective roles in providing ongoing transfer-funding and program supports in an era of evolving aboriginal self-government.

This chapter uses, as a point of departure, principles of constitutional law, and attempts where possible to trace the broad patterns of non-legal responsibilities which give shape to legal rights. Statutory distinctions which have become deeply entrenched in practice (and which may embody fundamental Crown policies) are also considered. The focus on legal principles does not, however, imply that the resolution of these questions can be addressed in a legal (as opposed to a political) forum.

On the contrary, this discussion assumes that issues of responsibility for the provision of government services cannot be reduced to an analysis of legal liability, but are fundamentally political questions requiring a political resolution.

The terms "aboriginal," "native" and "Indian" are used here interchangeably to refer to persons and communities of aboriginal origin, including status and non-status Indians, Metis and Inuit people. For the purposes of this discussion it is assumed that the term "Indians" as used in s.91(24) of the *Constitution Act, 1867*[1] includes status and non-status Indians, Inuit and those Metis people who continue to identify themselves as aboriginal people.[2] Thus the analysis of principles of constitutional law in relation to "Indians" as used in s.91(24) is not intended to exclude their application to other aboriginal peoples. However, these distinctions will be of considerable importance in applying constitutional principles to the final study of responsibility, primarily where Parliament has created important distinctions (i.e., status and non-status Indians; or on-reserve and off-reserve Indians) within constitutional categories.

The questions which this chapter tackles are unique in the constitutional law and the public policy of Canada. No other group of people is listed in the Constitution as the exclusive object of special laws of Parliament. (Although, as will be discussed later, other minority groups are referred to for specific purposes related to their language, religious and education rights, which were secured as part of the "Confederation bargain" which constituted Canada.) No other group of people in Canadian society has been the subject of comprehensive race-specific laws and policies, which have obscured their place within Canada and their rights as Canadians.

The issues in this chapter raise the fundamental questions:

- What is the relationship between the aboriginal people and other Canadians?
- To what extent does the special character of aboriginal people alter their enjoyment of the rights and privileges of other Canadians, and their subjection to the obligations of other Canadians?
- How are the answers to these questions accommodated by Canada's federal structure?

Discussion of the "responsibility" of the federal or the provincial government is often simply a convenient but misleading way of referring to legislative powers. Usually it refers to the obligation to pay for certain programs or services provided by government pursuant to statute or to governments' discretion to spend public monies.

In general, the law does not impose obligations on governments. The Crown, historically, was immune from the obligations of ordinary persons, and legislative bodies were supreme. And even within the increasing exposure of the Crown to various types of liability, its obligations under public law and private law have essentially remained separate.

In Ontario at present, general programs and services are often extended to aboriginal people pursuant to a complex set of arrangements, with the federal government paying some or all of the cost of delivery to a part of the aboriginal population (usually to status Indians ordinarily residing on reserve).

The present regime has arisen since World War II through practical and *ad hoc* arrangements rather than through the explicit acceptance of broad principles of the federal and provincial governments' roles in providing and paying for programs and services to aboriginal people. These arrangements do, however, reflect some underlying assumptions about those roles.

The Federal Government View

Generally, the federal government argues that it has a power, but not a responsibility, to provide special legal regimes for some aboriginal people. Thus, Parliament can determine who has "status" for the purposes of eligibility of special treatment in federal law. Parliament has decided that the on-reserve aboriginal population is the proper concern of special federal laws and programs, but not the off-reserve population.

The federal government takes the position that these legislative distinctions are combined with a general and untrammelled spending power and a complete discretion to make spending distinctions on the basis of federal policy. Thus, federal aboriginal-specific programs are largely confined to the status Indian population ordinarily residing on reserve. There is, however, in the view of the federal government, no legal compulsion to continue any of these programs. Programs provided pursuant to legislation can end or change through legislative amendment. "Discretionary" programs, which are not founded in legislation, can be ended or changed by executive decision.

The Provincial Government View

Generally, the governments of the provinces have argued that aboriginal people have a special relationship with the Crown in right of Canada, and that this relationship is now expressed in unwritten constitutional conventions which create a political role of guardian or fiduciary. In the view of the province, this relationship gives rise to a federal obligation to pay for most or all programs and services for on-reserve status Indians, with the province often acting as a paid delivery agent. The approach to off-reserve aboriginal people has been to include them in normal provincial programs and services, acknowledging the difficulty of distinguishing these persons from the general provincial population. Occasionally, the provincial view is expressed in relation to the exemption of "Indians" and their lands from many forms of taxation, arguing that to the extent "Indians" are removed from the normal wealth-collection system of the provincial government, they should also be removed from the distributive side of the equation.

The Need For a New Arrangement

While present program and service provisions conform (somewhat uneasily) to the underlying assumptions of both governments, the differences between these assumptions will result in dramatic differences in financial responsibility if major shifts occur through new self-government arrangements or through unilateral alterations in federal or provincial policy regarding programs and services to aboriginal people.

These negotiated rearrangements may vest in aboriginal communities a substantial degree of autonomy in relation to many service sectors. Such governmental activities will ideally be financed through revenues generated by the communities themselves, but in the near future, they will continue to rely on transfer payments from the federal and provincial governments.

At present it appears that the Government of Canada is attempting to control its rapidly escalating expenditures for many programs that it traditionally provides to the aboriginal population, particularly on-reserve Indian people. According to the federal government's views, such reductions may be imposed with legal impunity. The inevitable result is of course either the denial of essential social programs or a dramatic increase in the provincial burden for them. Fear of such uncontrolled increases may prevent needed provincial initiatives.

At the same time, aboriginal groups continue to demand that the federal government maintain its traditional "special relationship" with them, which they argue includes financial responsibility for many special programs which counter the assimilationist tendencies inherent in being subject to programs of general application.

This chapter analyzes the meaning of s.91(24) of the *Constitution Act, 1867*, as the only provision of the Constitution which directly allocates federal and provincial roles relating to aboriginal people. There will be three components of this review:

- First, s.91(24) as an embodiment of the "special relationship" between the Crown and the aboriginal peoples;
- Second, s.91(24) as the provision which allocates legislative powers between Parliament and the provincial legislatures; and
- Third, the relationship between s.91(24) and the rights of equality and non-discrimination found in the *Canadian Charter of Rights and Freedoms*.

This discussion synthesizes these disparate subjects within a constitutional, political and historical context, with a view to suggesting a principled approach to the federal-provincial relationship.

Finally, the synthesis is applied to the existing system of financing of social programs, in order to examine the relative roles of the two levels of government in program and service provision to aboriginal people in the province.

THE SPECIAL RELATIONSHIP

Section 91(24) is the only part of the *Constitution Act, 1867* which refers specifically to aboriginal peoples and lands. Aboriginal people often argue that it is the source, or at least the embodiment, of a "special relationship" between them and the Crown in right of Canada, which gives rise to legal and political obligations of protection and trust. Often, it is used as a defence of special protections required against the assimilating effects of ordinary provincial laws, programs and services. Many judicial decisions make reference to a "special relationship" between aboriginal people and the federal Crown.

This elusive notion has, however, an uncertain legal content. Even in the amorphous realm of policy it is of uncertain scope. Indeed, there is no doubt that aboriginal policy has a way of becoming common law, and even fundamental constitutional law. As Professor Brian Slattery writes:

> The Crown's historical dealings with Indian peoples were based on legal principles suggested by the actual circumstances of life in North America, the attitudes and practices of Indian societies, broad rules of equity and convenience, and imperial policy. These principles gradually crystallized as part of the special branch of British law that governed the Crown's relations with its overseas dominions, commonly termed "colonial law", or more accurately "imperial constitutional law".[3]

The Special Relationship Before *Guerin*

The historical dimensions of the special relationship (both in Canada and the United States) can be traced back to the *Royal Proclamation of 1763*,[4] which has been termed by the Supreme Court of Canada as "the Indian Bill of Rights."[5] In this document, the Crown undertook a policy of protection of the lands of "the several nations or tribes of Indians with whom we are connected, and who live under our protection." It is recognized as having the force of a special fundamental statute.[6]

Throughout the nineteenth century it was recognized in the British colonies which were to become Canada that:

> ... as long as the Indian Tribes continue to require the special protection and guidance of the Government they should remain under the immediate control of the Representative of the Crown within the Province, and not under that of the Provincial Authorities.[7];

This policy was plainly based upon a fear that the provincial administrations would have too local a focus and too short-term an interest to honour the Crown's duties of protection. It also assumed that this protection was something which might one day end (i.e., when Indians became civilized and assimilated into the broader society).

In 1867, the allocation of exclusive legislative power to Parliament in s.91(24) continued what had become fundamental imperial policy. From 1868 Parliament enacted comprehensive legislation governing virtually every aspect of life on Indian reserves, including the determination of Indian status and the subjecting of Indians to a regime where their civil rights were indeed limited. They were, until 1960, unable to vote in federal elections;[8] at an earlier time there were restrictions on their movements, their ability to perform religious and political customs, to raise money for claims, and so on.

The present *Indian Act* is recognizable as the successor of the *Indian Acts* of the nineteenth century, despite a major revision of its underlying principles in 1951. From that time on, the most blatant limitations on civil rights were gradually removed; and at roughly the same time, the provinces began to include Indians in their general programs and services, in recognition that they were, in addition to being a special class of "federal" people, residents of the provinces too. Most often, the federal government paid for or subsidized these programs when they were extended to the reserve population.

Early judicial descriptions of the special relationship took into account the limitations on Indians' civil rights, equating it with wardship. For example, in 1950, it was stated by the Supreme Court of Canada that:

> The language of the [*Indian Act*] embodies the accepted view that these aborigines are, in effect, wards of the state, whose care and welfare are a political trust of the highest obligation. For that reason, every such dealing with their privileges must bear the imprint of Governmental approval, and it would be beyond the power of the Governor in Council to transfer that responsibility to the Superintendent General.[9]

In the previous year, the same court had discussed the "limited civil rights of the Indians."[10] The description of aboriginal people as "wards" with "limited civil rights" raises the possibility of a trust-like fiduciary relationship with the Crown. And, while it is a political relationship, it is now clear that important legal rights flow from the relationship."[11]

Chief Justice Marshall of the Supreme Court of the United States wrote the first comprehensive judicial description of this relationship in 1831 in *Cherokee Nation v. State of Georgia*:

> The condition of the Indians in relation to the United States is perhaps unlike any other two people in existence. In general, nations not owing a common allegiance are foreign to each other. The term foreign nation is, with strict propriety, applicable to the other. But the relation of the

> Indians to the United States is marked by peculiar and cardinal distinctions which exist no where else. [12]

After describing the "unquestioned right to the lands they occupy" and the protection extended by the United States by treaties, Marshall concluded:

> They occupy a territory to which we assert a title independent of their will, which must take effect in point of possession when their right of possession ceases. Meanwhile they are in a state of pupilage. Their relation to the United States resembles that of a ward to his guardian. [13]

Cherokee is one of a trilogy of seminal U.S. Supreme Court cases on aboriginal rights often referred to as the "Marshall cases," the others being *Johnson v. M'Intosh*[14] and *Worcester v. State of Georgia*[15]. In addition to describing the Indians' wardship, the Marshall cases established in U.S. federal common law the nature of aboriginal title, the aboriginal right to self-government and the general exemption of Indian lands from state laws.

In *Calder v. A.-G. British Columbia*[16] the Supreme Court of Canada paid homage to the trilogy. The focus in *Calder* was aboriginal title, and its source in the Indians' rights of occupancy which were recognized and protected on the assumption of sovereignty by the Crown. Although subsequent Canadian courts[17] have reaffirmed the persuasiveness of the Marshall cases, the aspects of the trilogy which deal with the trust, or wardship, relationship have not been exhaustively discussed by Canadian courts.

In the United States, the Marshall trilogy has given rise to a comprehensive, though not always consistent, theory[18] of a trust relationship between Indians and the United States. This relationship requires that government dealings with Indians be judged by "the most exacting fiduciary standards,"[19] gives rise to canons of construction favourable to Indians[20] and creates legal trust liability when the government assumes elaborate control over property belonging to Indians.[21] The Marshall judgments are expressly founded upon the policies established in the *Royal Proclamation*, which the United States continued to respect following the American Revolution.

Guerin and the Special Relationship

In 1984, in *Guerin v. The Queen*, the Supreme Court of Canada took a major step toward giving legal meaning and force to the

Crown's special relationship with aboriginal people. The case involved the liability of the Crown in right of Canada for its failure in 1957 to secure a lease of reserve lands in the terms which a band had sought. Instead, a much less favourable lease was entered into which was concealed from the band for several years. The trial judge had found in favour of the band in breach of trust. [22] Although the Federal Court of Appeal found that any liability of the federal government in managing a lease of reserve land was "a matter of governmental discretion, not legal or equitable obligation," [23] the Supreme Court restored the trial verdict against the Crown through a variety of legal theories.

Mr. Justice Estey found that the Crown acted as the statutory agent of the Indian band in arranging a lease. He recognized the special rights of aboriginal peoples by concluding that the *Royal Proclamation of 1763*, various pre-confederation laws and the *Indian Act* "all reflect a strong sense of awareness of the community interest in protecting the rights of the aboriginal population in those lands to which they had a longstanding connection." [24]

Madam Justice Wilson, on behalf of three members of the Court, described the Crown's liability in terms of breach of a trust. She found that the *Indian Act*'s provisions did not create a fiduciary obligation in relation to reserves, but the Act "recognizes the existence of such an obligation." [25] She went on:

> It is my view, therefore, that while the Crown does not hold reserve land under s.18 of the Act in trust for the bands because the bands' interests are limited by the nature of Indian title, it does hold the lands subject to a fiduciary obligation to protect and preserve the bands' interests from invasion or destruction. [26]

Mr. Justice Dickson, speaking for four members of an eight-judge panel, took a broader view. He concluded that the Crown's obligation in relation to the lease was of a fiduciary nature, but was of a *sui generis* (i.e., unique) nature, neither a trust nor an agency, though it had aspects of both. This was based upon the nature of aboriginal title as described in the Marshall trilogy and upon its inalienability except by surrender to the Crown. This latter element is the key to the existence of the fiduciary relationship.

Mr. Justice Dickson, proceeding from first principles, examined the nature of fiduciary obligations, summarizing:

> ... where by statute, agreement, or perhaps by unilateral undertaking, one party has an obligation to act for the benefit of another, and

> that obligation carries with it a discretionary power, the party thus empowered becomes a fiduciary. Equity will then supervise that relationship by holding him to the fiduciary's strict standard of conduct. [27]

The existence of Indian title as an independent legal interest in land predating the *Royal Proclamation of 1763*, combined with the Crown's undertaking in the Proclamation (and in subsequent legislation) of a responsibility to protect the Indian interest from exploitation gives rise to the fiduciary relationships in relation to land dealings. The general tone of the discussion leaves the fiduciary doctrine wide open to further elaboration in the aboriginal context.

Mr. Justice Dickson describes the Crown's fiduciary relationship to the Indians in the following sweeping terms:

> It should be noted that fiduciary duties generally arise only with regard to obligations originating in a private law context. Public law duties, the performance of which requires the exercise of discretion, do not typically give rise to a fiduciary relationship. As the "political trust" cases indicate, the Crown is not normally viewed as a fiduciary in the exercise of its legislative or administrative function. The mere fact, however, that it is the Crown which is obligated to act on the Indians' behalf does not of itself remove the Crown's obligation from the scope of the fiduciary principle. As was pointed out earlier, the Indians' interest in land is an independent legal interest. It is not a creation of either the legislative or executive branches of government. The Crown's obligation to the Indians with respect to that interest is therefore not a public law duty. While it is not a private law duty in the strict sense either, it is none the less in the nature of a private law duty. Therefore, in this *sui generis* relationship, it is not improper to regard the Crown as a fiduciary. [28]

This passage appears to be the creation of a new branch of law, spanning public and private law, to which familiar principles apply only by analogy. It places in the realm of law at least part of a relationship which has previously been described as political. It thus provides a context and a rationale for canons of construction [29] favourable to aboriginal people, just as the U.S. trust doctrine does.

In the present context, it is most important to consider the symbolism of the fiduciary doctrine as outlined in the judgment. To Mr. Justice Dickson, the Crown's self-imposed duty to hold the Indian interest is not a true trust, though it is "trust-like in character." [30] Nor is the Crown an agent, because the band is not a party to the ultimate sale or lease. [31] The Crown is, rather, a unique fiduciary whose discretion to act on behalf of the band is confined not only by statute and the formal instructions of the band membership through a surrender vote, but by the oral terms which the band understood would be embodied in the lease agreed to by the band membership. Upon the Crown's failure to negotiate such a lease, it had the obligation to return to the band to receive "counsel on how to proceed." [32]

While this last point may suggest classic agency principles, even Madam Justice Wilson (who saw the case in trust terms) agreed that the Crown was obliged to return to the band after the surrender to advise that the band's instructions could not be fulfilled. [33] Presumably, the band would remain competent to vary the terms of the trust, even though it had crystallized at the time of the surrender.

All three judgments in *Guerin* deal with a fiduciary relationship which is fundamentally different from earlier descriptions of "wardship." Unlike a ward, the band was not an incompetent at the mercy of its guardian's discretion, but a body capable of directing and confining that discretion.

Gradually, since 1951, the most glaring limitations upon the civil rights of status Indians have been removed, as they have been accorded the rights and privileges of full citizenship. (In a later section, this chapter will discuss the conceptual place of the converse of this, the continued exemption of Indians and their lands from most forms of taxation. [34]) The assessment of claims from earlier times must, however, take into account the limitations of those rights from time to time. At present, the principal limitations on Indians' freedom to act are in relation to their jointly-held lands. The Royal Proclamation, as partly codified in statute, continues to apply. But it does not seem to be a significant extension of *Guerin* to predict that many actions taken by Indian agents and other federal officials under the previous statutory regimes (conferring on them great power and discretion) will give rise to the application of fiduciary principles.

Future cases will determine whether the special fiduciary relationship of the Crown extends beyond land rights, and also the relevance of that relationship to "existing aboriginal and treaty rights" which are recognized and affirmed by s.35 of the *Constitution Act, 1982*.

It is also becoming clear that the fiduciary principles enunciated in *Guerin* cannot be applied to *all* aspects of the relationship between the Crown and aboriginal peoples. For example, in a recent decision of the Federal Court, Trial Division which held that the Department of Indian Affairs and Northern Development had been in breach of its fiduciary obligations relating to a surrender of a reserve, Mr. Justice Addy commented:

> The Indian Act was passed pursuant to the exclusive jurisdiction to do so granted to the Parliament of Canada by section 91(24) of the Constitution Act, 1867. This does not carry with it the legal *obligation* to legislate or to carry out programs for the benefit of indians [*sic*] anymore [*sic*] than the existence of various disadvantaged groups in society creates a general legally enforceable duty on the part of governments to care for those groups although there is of course a moral and political duty to do so in a democratic society where the welfare of the individual is regarded as paramount.[35]

For present purposes it is sufficient to note that, as Professor Brian Slattery has written, "... in *Guerin* the Supreme Court shows a willingness to consider the topic of aboriginal rights afresh, and to initiate a dialogue concerning the broad principles that alone can make sense of the subject."[36]

On the question of the federal-provincial aspects of the *Guerin* fiduciary theory, Slattery writes:

> The Crown's general fiduciary duty binds both the federal Crown and the various provincial Crowns within the limits of their respective jurisdictions. The federal Crown has primary responsibility toward native peoples under section 91(24) of the Constitution Act, 1867, and thus bears the main burden of the fiduciary trust. But insofar as provincial Crowns have the power to affect native peoples, they also share in the trust.[37]

This conclusion, while perhaps unsettling to provinces, may prove to be accurate, considering that the fiduciary duty is created by the coexistence of power and discretion. If the legal fiduciary duty is the tip of a larger political fiduciary iceberg, as this discussion suggests, the shifting scope of federal and provincial aboriginal policies will establish the parallel scope of political duties, within the Crown's general obligation of good faith and trust.

LEGISLATIVE COMPETENCE

Section 91(24) is conventionally viewed (certainly by the federal government) as a mere power-granting provision. The following is a review of the cases which consider this aspect.

It is now possible to summarize in a fairly comprehensive way the legislative competence of Parliament and the provincial legislatures in relation to "Indians, and Lands reserved for the Indians." This analysis can provide vital clues on the question of responsibility, but cannot answer it, any more than it can determine the scope of federal and provincial "spending power,"[38] a highly political issue. Section 91 of the *Constitution Act, 1867* lists a number of matters within the "exclusive authority" of the Parliament of Canada. There, in a miscellaneous list that includes such items as the "Postal Service," "Currency and Coinage" and "The Criminal Law," is clause 24: "Indians, and Lands reserved for the Indians."

The "Enclave" Theory

Clause 24 has long been recognized as a source of plenary federal authority to implement federal Indian policy, even concerning matters which normally fall within the provincial authority in relation to property and civil rights.[39] Indians as persons have, however, been considered subject to certain provincial laws since at least 1907.[40]

Until 1973, it was possible to consider that s.91(24) insulated Indian reserve lands from *all* provincial laws. This was one of the consequences of the Marshall trilogy in the U.S.,[41] and it is remarkable that in Canada the question remained unresolved for so long, an indication perhaps of the low priority of the subject and the general immaturity of Canadian constitutional theory relating to aboriginal rights. This belief, in one form or another, probably underlay much of the severe division between the on-reserve and off-reserve aboriginal populations in federal and provincial dealings with them. In *Cardinal v. The Queen*,[42] however, this theory was rejected by the Supreme Court of Canada, and a new era of rationalizing the federal and provincial governments' relationship to aboriginal people began. Mr. Justice Laskin, in dissent, described the "enclave theory" in terms similar to the U.S. position:

> Indian reserves are enclaves which, so long as they exist as Reserves, are withdrawn from provincial regulatory power. If provincial legislation is applicable at all, it is only by referential incorporation by the Parliament of Canada.[43]

Mr. Justice Martland, for the majority, contrarily stated:

> A Provincial Legislature could not enact legislation in relation to Indians, or in relation to Indian Reserves, but this is far from saying that the effect of s.91(24) of the *British North America Act, 1867,* was to create enclaves within a Province within the boundaries of which Provincial legislation could have no application. ... My point is that s.91(24) enumerates classes of subjects over which the Federal Parliament has the exclusive power to legislate, but it does not purport to define areas within a Province within which the power of a Province to enact legislation, otherwise within its powers, is to be excluded.[44]

In *Four B Manufacturing v. United Garment Workers,*[45] the application of provincial laws (here in relation to labour relations) on reserve was confirmed, "as long as such laws do not single out Indians nor purport to regulate them *qua* Indians."[46]

Basis of Application of Provincial Laws

It remained uncertain whether provincial laws applied to Indians and reserves of their own force, or as a consequence of the referential incorporation by s.88 of the *Indian Act* which reads as follows:

> Subject to the terms of any treaty and any other Act of the Parliament of Canada, all laws of general application from time to time in force in any province are applicable to and in respect of Indians in the province, except to the extent that such laws are inconsistent with this Act or any order, rule, regulation or by-law made thereunder, and except to the extent that such laws make provision for any matter for which provision is made by or under this Act.[47]

In 1985, in *Dick v. The Queen,*[48] Mr. Justice Beetz, for a unanimous panel of the Supreme Court, stated:

> I believe that a distinction should be drawn between two categories of provincial laws. There are, on the one hand, provincial laws which can be applied to Indians without touching their Indianness, like traffic regulation; there are on the other hand, provincial laws which cannot apply to Indians without regulating them *qua* Indians.
>
> Laws of the first category, in my opinion, continue to apply to Indians *ex proprio vigore* as they always did before the enactment of s.88 in 1951 ... and quite apart from s.88.

In the result, s.88 of the *Indian Act* has the effect of incorporating by reference certain provincial laws of general application which *do* touch on "Indianness." The important point is, however, that many provincial laws apply to Indians and Indian reserves of their own force. *Dick* is thus the final nail in the coffin of an "enclave theory" since it makes it clear that even if s.88 of the *Indian Act* were repealed, many—even most—provincial laws would continue to apply to Indians and reserves by virtue of the constitutional distribution of powers.

Most recently, the Supreme Court of Canada reaffirmed the inapplicability of the "enclave" theory in a case where provincial highway traffic laws were held to apply on an Indian reserve, notwithstanding federal regulations governing similar matters on reserve.[49]

"Indians, and Lands reserved for the Indians" has thus been construed strictly in accordance with classical Canadian constitutional law relating to the distribution of powers. The notion of "Indianness" referred to in *Dick* is an example of the traditional exercise of characterizing the "pith and substance" of laws. An Indian may for some purposes be amenable to provincial law *qua* resident of the province. In his capacity of "Indian," however, he may be insulated from some provincial laws by virtue of constitutional law (although federal legislation may deem that some of those laws apply).[50]

What is "Indianness"?

In *Natural Parents v. Superintendent of Child Welfare,*[51] the Supreme Court considered the application of a provincial adoption statute to an Indian child. Chief Justice Laskin stated that for the provincial statute to apply (and thus remove the child's Indian status) "would be to touch 'Indianness,' to strike at a relationship integral to a matter outside of provincial competence."[52]

In *Four B*, Mr. Justice Beetz may well have been defining "Indianness" when he pointed out that in applying a provincial labour relations statute on reserve:

> ... neither Indian status is at stake nor rights so closely connected with Indian status such for instance as registrability, membership in a band, the right to participate in the election of chiefs and band councils, reserve privileges, etc.[53]

The aspect of reserve lands which are immune from provincial laws was recently described by the Supreme Court of Canada in *Derrickson v. Derrickson* as follows:

> The right to possession of lands on an Indian reserve is manifestly of the very essence of the federal exclusive legislative power under s-s.91(24) of the *Constitution Act, 1867*. It follows that provincial legislation cannot apply to the right of possession of Indian reserve lands.[54]

Accordingly, a provincial family law statute was "read down" so as to be inapplicable to rights of possession of reserve lands.

Thus, Indians have multiple "aspects" for the purposes of characterizing laws which may affect them. "Indianness" is an aspect that is insulated from provincial laws, and is based on existing authorities, probably confined to the central features and privileges of Indian status and band membership. Reserve lands are not territories exempt from provincial laws, but like Indian persons, have a core of "Indianness" which defines their protection from provincial law.

While it is still debatable whether "Indians, and Lands reserved for the Indians" constitutes one or two legislative subject matters, the case-law which construes s.91(24) in terms of legislative competence seems to consider the determination of the Indianness of persons and of lands as being conceptually similar.

Although this chapter does not deal directly with the complex issues of aboriginal land rights, it may be useful to note here that the balancing between s.91(24) and s.92 as sources of law-making power has a parallel in the relationship between the aboriginal interest in lands (subject to s.91(24) protection) and the underlying provincial Crown title (granted to the province in s.109 of the *Constitution Act, 1867,* subject to "other interests" including that of aboriginal peoples.)[55] Legislatively, the provincial powers set out in s.92 are complete, subject to the core of "Indianness."

As Mr. Justice Dickson put it in *Nowegijick v. The Queen* in 1983:

> Indians are citizens and, in affairs of life not governed by treaties or the *Indian Act,* they are subject to all the responsibilities, including payment of taxes, of other Canadian citizens.[56]

This, of course, represents a remarkably different picture of the constitutional place of Indians than that of "wards" or persons with "limited civil rights." Thus, under that part of the Constitution which allocates legislative powers, aboriginal people have come to be conceptually part of the provincial population as well as being conceptually aboriginal and thus within a special federal category. This analysis will have a profound impact upon the ultimate allocation of governmental responsibilities.

EQUALITY RIGHTS AND COLLECTIVE RIGHTS

The present position of aboriginal peoples being "citizens" as well as "Indians" has come in large measure through the extension of egalitarian measures, such as the conferring of the vote in federal elections in 1960 and in the same year the enactment of the *Canadian Bill of Rights*. The *Constitution Act, 1982* has subsequently constitutionally entrenched rights of equality but also includes a number of provisions touching on the special collective rights of the aboriginal peoples of Canada.

The Canadian Bill of Rights

Section 1(b) of the *Canadian Bill of Rights*[57] provides:

> 1. It is hereby recognized and declared that in Canada there have existed and shall continue to exist without discrimination by reason of race, national origin, colour, religion or sex, the following rights and fundamental freedoms, namely,
> ...
> (b) the right of the individual to equality before the law and the protection of the law;

In the celebrated case of *R. v. Drybones*,[58] s.1(b) was found to render inoperative a section of the *Indian Act* which made it an offence for an Indian to be intoxicated off a reserve on the basis that:

> ... an individual is denied equality before the law if it is made an offence punishable at law, on account of his race, for him to do something which his fellow Canadians are free to do without having committed any offence or having been made subject to any penalty.[59]

In 1973, in *A.-G. Canada v. Lavell*[60] the infamous s.12 (1)(b) of the *Indian Act* came under attack on the basis of *Drybones*. This section clearly discriminated on the basis of sex, by causing an Indian woman who married a non-Indian to lose her status, while an Indian man marrying a non-Indian kept his (and in fact the Act conferred status on his non-Indian wife). Mr. Justice Ritchie (who had written the judgment of the majority in *Drybones*) now distinguished that case by stating that the *Bill of Rights* injunction against inequality before the law required only equality in the *administration* of the law, but did not reach the *substance* of the law. This unsatisfactory reasoning led to a somewhat scornful dissent by Chief Justice Laskin, who could not see the basis for distinguishing *Drybones*.

The *Lavell* court may well have been influenced by strong representations on behalf of Indian political organizations who argued that the section should survive a *Bill of Rights* attack, fearing that the entire *Indian Act* could fall under the onslaught of equality. To these intervenors, equality was not simply an unquestioned right of all members of an enlightened and liberal society; it was a profound threat to their distinct existence as Indians as preserved in the *Indian Act*.

In *A.-G. v. Canard*,[61] the equality debate took a new turn as Mr. Justice Ritchie upheld the *Indian Act*'s succession law provisions for Indians on the basis that s.91(24)

> ... clearly vests in the Parliament of Canada the authority to pass laws concerning Indians which are different from the laws which the provincial legislatures may enact concerning the citizens of the various provinces.
>
> If the provisions of the *Indian Act* and the regulations made thereunder are to be declared as offending the guarantee provided by s.1(b) of the *Bill of Rights* wherever they have the effect of treating Indians differently from other Canadians, then it seems to me to follow that eventually all such differences will be eradicated and Indians will in all respects be treated in the same way as their fellow citizens under the law. I cannot believe that the special Indian status so clearly recognized in the *British North America Act* is to be whittled away without express legislation being passed by the Parliament of Canada to that effect.[62]

In a dissenting judgment, Chief Justice Laskin took the view that because the *Indian Act* did not envisage that an Indian could administer a deceased Indian's estate, there was a denial of equality before the law. In his judgment, the *Indian Act* scheme was not to be rendered wholly inoperative as a separate system of succession law, but only to the extent it excluded Indians from eligibility to be administrators of the estates of deceased Indians. On the more general question of the relationship between the constitutional class of s.91(24) and the rights of equality, he added:

> It seems to me patent that no grant of legislative power, as a mere vehicle for legislation, should be viewed as necessarily carrying with it a built-in exclusion of the mandates of the *Canadian Bill of Rights*.[63]

The judgments of Mr. Justice Martland and Mr. Justice Beetz, concurring with the majority, contained what Professor Peter Hogg terms "the seeds of more subtle ideas of equality."[64] Mr. Justice Martland applied the test of "valid federal objective" which had ear-

36

lier been articulated in *The Queen v. Burnshine*[65] to conclude that "there are legitimate reasons of policy for the enactment of such provisions in relation to the estate assets of deceased Indians ordinarily resident on reserves."[66] Mr. Justice Beetz dealt with the issue by interpreting *Lavell* as follows:

> ... I understand *Lavell* to have primarily decided that Parliament must not be deemed to have subjected to the *Canadian Bill of Rights* the authority vested upon it under s.91(24) of the *British North America Act, 1867* exclusively to make laws for "Indians, and Lands reserved for the Indians", in so far as this authority, being of a special nature, could not be effectively exercised without the necessarily implied power to define who is and who is not an Indian and how Indian status is acquired or lost. In so defining Indian status, Parliament could, without producing conflict with the *Canadian Bill of Rights*, establish between various sorts of intermarriages, such distinctions as could reasonably be regarded to be inspired by a legitimate legislative purpose in the light for instance of long and uninterrupted history.[67]

The "valid federal objective approach" of *Burnshine* was refined in *MacKay v. The Queen*,[68] which considered the validity of a provision of the *National Defence Act* which required members of the armed forces to be tried by a military tribunal for criminal offences. In a judgment which has been described as a "model of judicial reasoning"[69] and which has been referred to often in *Charter* cases, Mr. Justice McIntyre required that any legislative inequality affecting a special class be "rationally based and acceptable as a necessary variation from the general principle of universal application of law to meet social conditions and to attain a necessary and desirable social objective."[70] He added:

> ... as a minimum it would be necessary to inquire whether any inequality ... has been created rationally in the sense that it is not arbitrary or capricious and not based upon any ulterior motive or motives offensive to the provisions of the *Canadian Bill of Rights*, and whether it is a necessary departure from the general principle of universal application of the law for the attainment of some necessary and desirable social objective. Inequalities created for such purposes may well be acceptable under the *Canadian Bill of Rights*.[71]

At this point, the *Canadian Charter of Rights and Freedoms* was enacted as part of the *Constitution Act, 1982*.

The *Constitution Act, 1982*

Unlike the *Canadian Bill of Rights*, the *Charter* is of course a truly constitutional enactment, limiting and binding the provincial legislatures as well as Parliament, and applying to executive action[72] as well as legislation.

The equality rights section of the *Charter*, s.15, is much broader than s.1(b) of the *Canadian Bill of Rights*. It reads:

> 15. (1) Every individual is equal before and under the law and has the right to the equal protection and equal benefit of the law without discrimination and, in particular, without discrimination based on race, national or ethnic origin, colour, religion, sex, age or mental or physical disability.
>
> (2) Subsection (1) does not preclude any law, program or activity that has as its object the amelioration of conditions of disadvantaged individuals or groups including those that are disadvantaged because of race, national or ethnic origin, colour, religion, sex, age or mental or physical disability.

The effect of s.15, only in force since April 1985, is not yet settled. Already, however, it is becoming clear that s.15 does not preclude *any* discrimination (in the sense of merely "singling out" persons for differential treatment by law), but rather is aimed at discrimination which places persons at some unjustifiable disadvantage by virtue of distinctions between individuals based upon human attributes or characteristics.[73] The reasoning of *MacKay* and other *Bill of Rights* cases is proving to be persuasive not only in justifying a breach of an equality right under s.1 of the *Charter* but in determining whether a legal distinction constitutes discrimination.

A recent decision of the Supreme Court of Canada in relation to constitutional and political problems—almost as old as those of the responsibilities for aboriginal matters—appears to shed some light. The vexing problem is that of public funding of separate school systems for religious minorities, and the case is *Reference re Bill 30*.[74] This discussion cannot of course do justice to the Bill 30 case, nor to the complexity of the legal, moral and political issues which underlie it. The value of Bill 30 rests mainly in its dealing with constitutional problems of comparable complexity to those of aboriginal rights. It is a different problem, but it provides strong assistance.

Bill 30 proposed amendments to the Ontario *Education Act* which would, among other things, extend full public funding for Roman Catholic separate schools. The Attorney General of Ontario referred the constitutional validity of Bill 30 to the Court of Appeal. The difficulty lay partly in the imposition of the *Charter*'s new constitutional rights of equality and freedom of religion upon the provisions of s.93 of the *Constitution Act, 1867*, which permitted the provinces to legislate *unequally* in order to give effect to the "powers, privileges and duties" of separate schools at the time of Confederation.

The Court of Appeal by a majority upheld the Bill.[75] The Supreme Court of Canada unanimously affirmed this decision. In the Court of Appeal, the majority drew upon the analogy to s.91(24) as follows:

> Although legislation with respect to Indians, enacted pursuant to Parliament's jurisdiction under s.91(24), may have to meet the test of *R. v. Drybones*, that "no individual or group of individuals is to be treated more harshly than another," the mere fact of Parliament legislating in respect to Indians and not everyone else cannot, *per se*, be held to be inconsistent with s.15 of the Charter.[76]

The majority immediately went on to generalize:

> The Constitution of Canada, of which the Charter is now a part has from the beginning provided for group collective rights in ss. 93 and 133 of the *Constitution Act, 1867*. ... The provisions of this "small bill of rights," now expanded as to the language rights of s. 133 by ss. 16 to 23 of the Charter, constitute a major difference from a bill of rights such as that of the United States, which is based on individual rights. Collective or group rights, such as those concerning languages and those concerning certain denominations to separate schools, are asserted by individuals or groups of individuals *because of* their membership in the protected group. Individual rights are asserted equally by everyone *despite* membership in certain ascertainable groups. Collective rights protect certain groups and not others. To that extent, they are an exception from the equality rights provided equally to everyone.[77]

The reference to the "small bill of rights" parallels the earlier description of the *Royal Proclamation of 1763* by the Supreme Court of Canada as the "Indian Bill of Rights."[78]

The source of these exceptional minority rights in relation to education is described thus:

> To apply this to s.93, it is necessary to recognize that the provision for the rights of Protestants and Roman Catholics to separate schools became part of "a small bill of rights" as a basic compact of Confederation. As Chief Justice Duff expressed it, in *Reference re Adoption Act, etc.*,[1938] S.C.R. 398 at p. 402, [1938] 3 D.L.R. 497, 71 C.C.C. 110:
>> "... section 93 (as is well known) embodies one of the cardinal terms of the Confederation arrangement."[79]

The majority of the Court of Appeal thus concluded that the special rights of the Ontario Catholic minority were immune from abrogation by the new equality rights. In reviewing the majority's description of the effect of this conclusion, one might well consider substituting "Indian" or "aboriginal" for "Catholic," and "band" for "separate school" and "Catholic school board":

> This conclusion does not mean, and must not be taken to mean that separate schools are exempt from the law or the Constitution. Laws and the Constitution, particularly the Charter, are excluded from application to separate schools only to the extent they derogate from such schools as Catholic (or in Quebec, Protestant) institutions. It is this essential Catholic nature which is preserved and protected by s.93 of the *Constitution Act, 1867* and s.29 of the Charter. The courts must strike a balance, on a case-by-case basis, between conduct essential to the proper functioning of a Catholic school and conduct which contravenes such Charter rights as those of equality in s.15 or of conscience and religion in s.2(a). Thus, the right of a Catholic school board to dismiss Catholic members of its teaching staff for marrying in a civil ceremony, or for marrying divorced persons, has been upheld as permissible conduct for a separate school board, but would the same protection be afforded a board which refused to hire women or discriminated on the basis of race, national or ethnic origin, age or disability?[80]

The Supreme Court of Canada, in affirming the Court of Appeal decision, also largely affirmed the reasoning of the majority. The judgment of Madam Justice Wilson represented the views of five of the seven-judge panel, giving great importance to the purpose and history of s.93 as part of the "basic compact of Confederation," and concluding:

> It was never intended, in my opinion, that the *Charter* could be used to invalidate other provisions of the Constitution, particularly a provision such as s.93 which represented a fundamental part of the Confederation compromise.[81]

Madame Justice Wilson, in amplifying the special nature of the religious minority education rights of s.93, adopted the words of Mr. Justice Beetz in *La Société des Acadiens v. Association of Parents*:

> Unlike language rights which are based on political compromise, legal rights tend to be seminal in nature because they are rooted in principle. Some of them, such as the one expressed in s.7 of the *Charter*, are so broad as to call for frequent judicial determination.
>
> Language rights, on the other hand, although some of them have been enlarged and incorporated into the *Charter*, remain nonetheless founded on political compromise.

> This essential difference between the two types of rights dictates a distinct judicial approach with respect to each. More particularly, the courts should pause before they decide to act as instruments of change with respect to language rights. This is not to say that language rights provisions are cast in stone and should remain immune altogether from judicial interpretation. But, in my opinion, the courts should approach them with more restraint than they would in construing legal rights. [82]

Mr. Justice Estey in a concurring judgment drew specific attention to the parallel with aboriginal issues. He described the "real contest" in the appeal as "clearly between the operation of the *Charter* in its entirety and the integrity of s.93." [83] He went on to say:

> Once s.93 is examined as a grant of power to the province, similar to the heads of power found in s.92, it is apparent that the purpose of this grant of power is to provide the province with the jurisdiction to legislate in a *prima facie* selective and distinguishing manner with respect to education whether or not some segments of the community might consider the result to be discriminatory. In this sense, s.93 is a provincial counterpart of s.91(24) (Indians and Indian land) which authorizes the Parliament of Canada to legislate for the benefit of the Indian population in a preferential, discriminatory, or distinctive fashion *vis-a-vis* others.
>
> ... Although the *Charter* is intended to constrain the exercise of legislative power conferred under the *Constitution Act, 1867* where the delineated rights of individual members of the community are adversely affected, it cannot be interpreted as rendering unconstitutional distinctions that are expressly permitted by the *Constitution Act, 1867*. [84]

If it is kept in mind that the rights of aboriginal peoples are specifically dealt with in the *Charter* itself, this reasoning makes it clear that the rights in the *Charter* cannot abrogate the federal power to enact laws specific to "Indians." Further, however, it is of great interest to consider the court analyzing the "purpose of [a] grant of power" to determine the relationship of that grant of power to the rights under the *Charter*. Finally, the characterization of s.91(24) as an authorization to "legislate for the benefit of the Indian population in a preferential, discriminatory, or distinctive fashion" is strongly suggestive that s.91(24) does *not* authorize legislative discrimination which harms Indians, only that which is preferential to them.

The Bill 30 case thus provides a powerful affirmation of group or collective rights against their dilution by liberal egalitarianism. It assists not only in giving effect to the aboriginal-specific provisions of the *Constitution Act, 1982*, but it provides a new way of understanding s.91(24) itself.

A SYNTHESIS OF FEDERAL
AND PROVINCIAL ROLES

Section 91(24) is a grant of legislative power *sui generis*, to echo the words of Chief Justice Dickson in *Guerin* and *Simon*. Like the other powers listed in s.91 and s.92, it describes a "matter" for legislation, but unlike them it also represents a political and legal relationship of trust and honour, uniquely applicable to the federal Crown. It also draws a distinction based on race and is thus a unique exception to the constitutional requirements of equality.

The allocation of federal and provincial government responsibilities must take into account each of the three aspects of this clause:

- What are the obligations of each level of government under the political (and legal) fiduciary relationship?

    Both appear to be subject to the Crown's overall duty, but the federal government's duty is primary. The scope and nature of the fiduciary doctrine is uncertain (and may be confined to dealings with land), but it appears to contain aspects of the agency and trust relationships.

- To what extent do the laws of Parliament and the provincial legislatures apply to aboriginal peoples and lands?

    Parliament can enact laws dealing with any aspect of aboriginal affairs (subject to the limits imposed by "existing aboriginal and treaty rights"). The laws of the provincial legislatures apply of their own force until they begin to impair or sterilize "Indianness."

- What is the impact of the *Charter*'s guarantees of legal equality?

    Equality and other individually focused *Charter* rights apply to aboriginal people but cannot nullify the collective rights of minorities which are entrenched through political compromise and which authorize legal regimes which treat those minorities in a preferential fashion.

The full significance of s.91(24) must be considered in the light of its history. It cannot be doubted that in 1867 (and perhaps until the defeat of the federal government White Paper in the early 1970s) it was unquestioned that the federal government assumed a trusteeship of peoples who, in the fullness of time would become "civilized," and the need for special legislation in relation to them would disappear. This would result in s.91(24) becoming, like many other provisions of the *Constitution Act, 1867* "spent" once its usefulness was over.

The 1969 White Paper

The federal government White Paper[85] of 1969 attempted to implement the final phase of an historical process of assimilation. In a spirit of egalitarianism, it proposed a federal policy which would permanently terminate the special arrangements under s.91(24); this policy included the transfer of title to reserve land to Indian people on an individual basis, and the transfer of service responsibilities to the provinces (accompanied by the transfer of federal funds to the provinces). This led to an outraged reaction by Indian political associations which by 1973 compelled the federal government to retract the White Paper in its entirety.

Since then, public policy in relation to aboriginal people has undergone a remarkable shift toward the acceptance of a right to remain distinct within Canadian society. This led, in 1982, to the inclusion of the aboriginal provisions of the *Constitution Act, 1982*.

It is now clear that aboriginal peoples will not tolerate their gradual assimilation, against their will, into the broader society. Their right to be different is exemplified by their unique constitutional place. They have a right, of course, to consent to the termination of this status. As individuals they are free to do so. As peoples, they are free to do so.

The Constitution Act, 1982

Section 25 of the *Charter* reads:

> 25.   The guarantee in this Charter of certain rights and freedoms shall not be construed so as to abrogate or derogate from any aboriginal, treaty or other rights or freedoms that pertain to the aboriginal peoples of Canada including
>
> (a)   any rights or freedoms that have been recognized and affirmed by the Royal Proclamation of October 7, 1763; and
>
> (b)   any rights or freedoms that now exist by way of land claims agreements or may be so acquired.

This section provides limits on *Charter* rights where they would have a harmful effect on the special rights of aboriginal peoples. It is, in effect, a constitutional recognition of the ambiguous and dangerous potential of equality (as well as other individual rights) when applied to aboriginal peoples.

It does not purport, however, to deprive aboriginal people of the *benefit* of *Charter* rights. Among aboriginal people, s.25 is generally viewed as an acknowledgement of their special collective rights which are vulnerable to erosion in favour of individually focused *Charter* rights, while the benefit of individual *Charter* rights pertain to them as individuals.

Section 25, along with the provisions of Part II of the *Constitution Act, 1982* which immediately follow the *Charter*, is plainly a recognition of the special place of aboriginal peoples in the fabric of Canada. Section 35 recognizes and affirms "the existing aboriginal and treaty rights" of "the aboriginal peoples of Canada," who are defined as including the "Indian, Inuit and Metis peoples of Canada." [86]

Section 35.1 requires a constitutional conference before any amendment is made to Part II or to s.91(24), and further requires the Prime Minister to invite "representatives of the aboriginal peoples of Canada" to such a conference.

Parts IV (s.37) and IV.1 (s.37.1) of the *Constitution Act, 1982* (now spent) required a series of constitutional conferences on "constitutional matters that directly affect the aboriginal peoples of Canada, including the identification and definition of the rights of those peoples to be included in the Constitution of Canada." As with s.35.1, the Prime Minister was required to, and did, invite representatives of the aboriginal peoples of Canada to these conferences, which were held in 1983, 1984, 1985 and 1987. These conferences ultimately concentrated upon an attempt to amend the *Constitution Act, 1982* to entrench some right of aboriginal self-government.

The constitutional position of aboriginal people after 1982 requires an examination not only of the relationship between s.91(24) and the rights in the *Charter* (an extension of the vexing questions explored in the *Bill of Rights* cases) but also the impact of Parts II, IV and IV.1 of the *Constitution Act* upon both the *Charter* and s.91(24). This background is vital in understanding the evolving place of aboriginal people as a political fact in Canada. Unlike the special rights relating to minority education, which were discussed in Bill 30, the present understanding of the aboriginal factor on Canada as a permanent, distinctive feature of Canadian life is relatively new.

To place this view in the purview of the analysis of Mr. Justice Beetz in the *Acadiens* case (as adopted by Madam Justice Wilson in Bill 30), the aboriginal "political compromise" giving rise to their distinct minority rights occurred in 1982 and 1983, rather than in 1867. The clearest indication that the constitutional events of the early 1980s had an impact on s.91(24) is the new (1983) requirement of a constitutional conference in s.35.1 before s.91(24) can be amended. The necessity of including aboriginal representatives clearly implies that this grant of legislative power has a broader significance (although it falls short of explicitly providing an aboriginal veto over amendments).

There is a clear implication that s.91(24) is, at least in one aspect, a provision which confers benefits upon the peoples to whom it refers, for it is not to be changed without their participation. There is also a clear implication that the new status of s.91(24), as a provision guaranteeing a *federal* role in relation to aboriginal matters, appears to end any argument that it is a mere grant of power which can be applied (or not applied) purely in accordance with federal government policy. It now symbolizes the primary federal "special relationship."

Until 1985, when a constitutional requirement of equality came into force, there was little doubt that as a matter of constitutional law, s.91(24) gave to Parliament the supreme power, if it so chose, to treat "Indians" as wards, to limit their civil rights, to regulate their movements and their religious and political practices. There was no constitutional rule limiting the scope of laws which in pith and substance were in relation to "Indians" and their lands.

The *Bill of Rights* cases of *Drybones*, *Lavell* and *Canard* eloquently demonstrate the difficulty (and for our courts, the novelty) of considering the relationship between "Indianness" as an issue of legislative power, and equality as a liberal ideal. By the time of *Canard*, members of the Supreme Court were openly considering "legitimate reasons of policy" and "valid federal objectives" underlying various provisions of the *Indian Act*, weighing the opposing demands of "Indianness" and equality against each other.

In the post-1982 era, the courts are compelled to consider not only the scope but the *purpose* of a grant of power to Parliament, just as they are compelled to consider the purpose of *Charter* provisions in order to determine their meaning and scope.[87] This is clear from the Bill 30 case.[88] The *Charter*, egalitarian and individualistic in thrust, is subject to the various rights of the aboriginal peoples, and s.91(24), is clearly not diminished by the new provisions. It is in fact elevated in stature by the requirement of s.35.1.

Certain things are clear:

- Section 91(24) can no longer be used to deprive "Indians" of civil rights, including the fundamental rights and freedoms set out in the *Charter.*

Section 15 confers on aboriginal people, as individuals, a broad guarantee of equality in the eyes of the law, but their collective rights (embodying their fundamental core of "Indianness," or "aboriginality") remain preserved. These rights, described by s.25 of the *Charter*, are broader than the "existing aboriginal and treaty rights" described in s.35, and appear almost certainly to include legal rights flowing from Parliament's authority in s.91(24). This core is what distinguishes them as the proper subjects of special federal laws. But this power must now be understood as being a purely benign one, a power to enact "preferential" laws for their benefit, in the words of Mr. Justice Estey in Bill 30.[89] It is also a power that is rooted in the special political relationship between the Crown and aboriginal peoples.

- The provinces have the obligation under s.15 of the *Charter* to ensure that aboriginal individuals in the province are not deprived of the equal benefit of provincial law.

Thus, to the extent provincial laws apply of their own force to aboriginal individuals and lands, there is no basis for denying equal access to provincial programs and services, although regulatory laws which threaten "Indianness" will not apply unless Parliament determines otherwise. Canadian constitutional law no longer creates "watertight compartments"[90] of federal and provincial power, but permits substantial overlap between them. Section 91(24) thus does not remove "Indians and Lands reserved for the Indians" from the provinces. In this Canada clearly departs from the U.S. theory outlined by Chief Justice Marshall in the 1830s.[91]

An understanding of the division between these two sets of obligations requires an examination of aboriginal people and the taxation system, which follows.

ABORIGINAL PEOPLE, SOCIAL SERVICES AND THE TAX BASE

The foregoing analysis describes the right of aboriginal peoples to be treated equally yet as a special component of our society. In particular, it describes in some detail the meaning of the term "citizens plus"[92] as it has often been applied to them (even if that term has often had an ironic sound when applied to their actual circumstances). The gradual acceptance of the idea that aboriginal people possess the *rights* of citizenship has not, however, been accompanied by an equivalent theory of their *obligations* as citizens.

Just as the primary right of every citizen may be the right to vote for a government of his or her choice, the equivalent primary obligation may be that of paying taxes. In the history of the *Indian Act*, the franchise and liability to taxation were, until 1960, inexorably linked. Status Indians were not entitled to vote, but neither were they required to pay tax. Indians who were enfranchised, by contrast, became subject to tax. In 1951, the franchise was extended to those Indians who executed a waiver of their *Indian Act* taxation exemptions.[93] It was not until 1960 that the franchise was granted to all Indians without conditions.[94]

The role of the federal and provincial governments in relation to social services for aboriginal peoples depends on the basis on which these services are supplied to Canadians and provincial residents generally. The underlying assumption of our social service system is the collection of wealth through the taxation system and its redistribution in the form of social services. Even the poor pay taxes (or they are at least within the purview of the tax system and are potentially liable to pay tax when their incomes are sufficient).

Despite the observation of Chief Justice Dickson in *Nowegijick*[95] that Indians are citizens and as such subject to the responsibilities of citizens, including the payment of taxes, on-reserve Indians are to a large extent *not* within the purview of the tax system. Section 87 of the *Indian Act* reads, in part, as follows:

> 87. Notwithstanding any other Act of the Parliament of Canada or any Act of the legislature of a province, but subject to section 83, the following property is exempt from taxation, namely:
>
> (a) the interest of an Indian or a band in reserve or surrendered lands; and
>
> (b) the personal property of an Indian or band situated on a reserve;

and no Indian or band is subject to taxation in respect of the ownership, occupation, possession or use of any property mentioned in paragraph (a) or (b) or is otherwise subject to taxation in respect of any such property ... .

Thus, as a matter of federal law, on-reserve real and personal property (including income payable on reserve)[96] is removed from the federal and provincial taxation base. Provincial legislation provides similar, essentially complementary, exemptions.[97] It is, however, federal law which provides the basic exemption.

Section 83 of the *Indian Act* provides for the designation by Cabinet of bands which have "reached an advanced state of development," resulting in the grant of additional governmental powers, including taxation of reserve lands by band councils.

The question arises: if on-reserve Indians are removed wholesale from the wealth collection process of the state, on what basis are they eligible for the benefits of the social services that are provided as the result of wealth distribution? To put it another way: if on-reserve Indians are eligible for the benefits of social services, what replaces the taxation system as a basis for paying for those services?

To comprehend these issues, it is necessary to understand the full meaning of the exemption from taxation. While s.87 of the *Indian Act* is in one sense merely ordinary federal legislation, it is clear that it, like the land-surrender provisions of the *Act* which were discussed in *Guerin*, is in fact the embodiment of a long-standing feature of federal Indian policy, which may have acquired the status of a central feature of the political special relationship. The exemption from taxation dates from at least 1850, when the Province of Canada enacted a statute which provided:

That no taxes shall be levied or assessed upon any Indian or any person intermarried with any Indian for or in respect of any of the said Indian lands, nor shall any taxes or assessments whatsoever be levied or imposed upon any Indian or any person intermarried with any Indian so long as he, she or they shall reside on Indian lands not ceded to the Crown, or which having been so ceded may have been again set apart by the Crown for the occupation of Indians.[98]

The *Indian Act* of 1876 then provided:

64.   No Indian or non-treaty Indian shall be liable to be taxed for any real or personal property, unless he holds real estate under lease or in fee simple, or personal property, outside of the reserve or special reserve, in which case he shall be liable to be taxed for such real or

> personal property at the same rate as other persons in the locality in which it is situated.
>
> 65.   All land vested in the Crown, or in any person or body corporate, in trust for or for the use of any Indian or non-treaty Indian, or any band or irregular band of Indians or non-treaty Indians shall be exempt from taxation.[99]

The *Indian Act* included variations of these provisions until 1951, when the present s.87 was enacted.

As Chief Justice Dickson pointed out in *Nowegijick*, the *Indian Act* exemption from taxation predated significantly the imposition of income tax in 1917 as a "temporary wartime measure."[100] Similarly, the contemporary panoply of publicly funded social services was clearly not in the contemplation of legislators when the *Indian Act*'s exemptions from taxation were introduced.

However, the taxation exemption provisions continue to hold vital meaning for the special relationship between the Crown and aboriginal peoples (at least those who are on-reserve status Indians). No Indian treaty specifically refers to an exemption from taxation, but the *Indian Act* itself links treaty benefits and the taxation exemption by providing in s.90:

> 90. (1) For the purposes of sections 87 and 89, personal property that was
>
> (a)   purchased by Her Majesty with Indian moneys appropriated by Parliament for the use and benefit of Indians or bands, or
> (b)   given to Indians or to a band under a treaty or agreement between a band and her Majesty, shall be deemed to be situated on a reserve.

Historically, the issue of taxation arose in the negotiation of treaties. The Treaty Commissioner for Treaty No. 8 was compelled to assure Indian negotiators that the treaty would not open the way to the imposition of any tax, in response to repeated concerns that the signing the treaty would lead to taxation.[101] The benefits of treaties, as s.90 of the *Indian Act* makes clear, are to be received free of taxation.[102]

The exemption from taxation of on-reserve property is clearly a fundamental component of the special relationship. Furthermore, unlike s.91(24) of the *Constitution Act* discussed earlier, it does draw a stark distinction between those whose residence is on reserve and those whose residence is off reserve.

This study has suggested that Indian reserve life may be a special feature of "aboriginality" and thus on-reserve activities may be the legitimate object of special federal law, despite the gradual erosion of the "enclave" theory. At an earlier time in federal Indian policy, the reserves were considered as temporary expedients toward an enfranchised Indian population of small fee-simple landholders.

It is now clear that, like Indian status itself, reserves are a permanent feature of Canadian life and public policy. The exemption from taxation of property and activities on reserves have, it would appear, become permanent and fundamental features of federal Indian policy. This is not, of course, inconsistent with taxation by aboriginal governmental institutions.

This leaves the provinces in a difficult dilemma. They are required to provide the equal benefits of provincial social services to all provincial residents, including Indians residing on reserve. They are also precluded from generating revenue from reserve-based Indian people through the taxation system.[103]

How can governments ensure, then, that the financing of services to be provided on reserve respect the fundamental characteristic of aboriginal policy which is embodied in s.87 of the *Indian Act*? If provinces are to deliver services on reserve, they should receive transfer payments from the federal government sufficient to compensate for the loss of revenue occasioned by the policy of s.87. The additional costs of services on reserve (resulting from the frequent remoteness of reserve communities and their high demand for many services) should also be borne by the federal government, as a cost occasioned by the "aboriginality," or "Indianness," of reserve communities.

In addition, the federal government should make transfer payments to provinces which deliver services to aboriginal people residing off reserve to compensate for the additional special costs of tailoring services to the requirements of aboriginality of those people. The principle is much like that of federal-provincial equalization payments, now embodied in s.36 of the *Constitution Act, 1982*:

> 36 (1) Without altering the legislative authority of Parliament or of the provincial legislatures, or the rights of any of them with respect to the exercise of their legislative authority, Parliament and the legislatures, along with the government of Canada and the provincial governments, are committed to
>
> (a) promoting equal opportunities for the well-being of Canadians;
> (b) furthering economic development to reduce disparity in opportunities; and
> (c) providing essential public services of reasonable quality to all Canadians.

> (2) Parliament and the government of Canada are committed to the principle of making equalization payments to ensure that provincial governments have sufficient revenues to provide reasonably comparable levels of public services at reasonably comparable levels of taxation.

In practice, provinces do not provide all services to the aboriginal population. The federal government and, to an increasing degree the aboriginal peoples themselves, deliver services both on and off reserve. In an era of aboriginal self-government, more and more responsibility will be assumed by aboriginal government agencies of different types. While both federal and provincial governments will make transfer payments to aboriginal governments and agencies, the arguments of this chapter will continue to be valid in the area of federal-provincial financial responsibility, regardless of the delivery agency.

It is a matter for the courts to decide whether the federal government has a legal duty to contribute to service costs relating to reserves and to the special requirements of "aboriginality" off reserve. But there are compelling reasons in policy for such a contribution.

A SUMMARY OF FEDERAL AND PROVINCIAL ROLES

The essential underlying constitutional rationale for federal and provincial governments in providing services to aboriginal people is now becoming clear. It boils down to the old but profound idea of "citizens plus" and to the division of that idea into its two principal components.

The Federal Role: Aboriginality ("The Plus")

The federal role, exemplified by the grant of power in s.91(24) of the *Constitution Act*, is the preservation and enhancement of "Indianness" or more generally, "aboriginality." This includes the definition and protection of the incidents of the special status of aboriginal persons, communities, institutions and lands, as well as specific legal protections as set out primarily in the *Indian Act*. Possibly, much more than this is included in the special federal role—the enhancement of self-government powers, economic

51

development and the integration of aboriginal economies into the broader economy.

There is no reason to confine such special status to those residing on reserve lands, since s.91(24) applies to Indians as persons and communities wherever they are. It is true, however, that the reserves represent the purest expression of "aboriginality," and that the preservation and development of reserve communities require the most direct special treatment under federal law.

Translated into responsibility for programs and services, the federal government must acknowledge a responsibility for those programs and services which are required by the special needs of "aboriginality." The special (and temporary) requirements of *protection* are now being supplanted with the special (and permanent) needs of *development*.

Reserve communities in particular must be accorded those programs and services which are required to preserve and strengthen their ways of life, their cultures and their economic viability. Aboriginal peoples off reserve likewise require the benefits of special federal development programs and services to preserve and strengthen their "aboriginality." The requirements of "aboriginality" might include the following:

- support for institutions of aboriginal social, cultural and political life;
- specific fiduciary responsibilities for aboriginal lands and other assets;
- the making of transfer payments or supplements to compensate for the exemptions from taxation of aboriginal lands and activities on those lands.
- economic, social and political development of aboriginal peoples generally.

The Provincial Role: Equity of Services ("Citizens")

The provincial role is to treat all individuals equally, without regard to race. In this context, a group must not be deprived of the benefit of provincial residence by virtue of race, but may in specific instances require some inequality of treatment. [104] Inequality, in the broader and non-pejorative sense of drawing beneficial distinctions to support the collective rights of aboriginal peoples, is *not* prohibited by s.15, particularly when read with s.25. Further, when s.91(24) is understood in light of its underlying purpose, there would appear to be no prohibition against provincial laws which *preferentially* single out aboriginal persons or institutions. Indeed, the classical constitutional law decisions which discuss the prohibition against "singling out" almost invariably use the term in the sense of impairing or sterilizing the status of the subject.[105] There is no reason, for example, why a provincial statute in relation to an aspect of property and civil rights could not apply differentially to aboriginal institutions and persons, if that differentiation did not impair their status (which of course must be defined in accordance with federal law).

For their part, the provinces must acknowledge aboriginal peoples as being fully part of the provincial population. The benefits and privileges of provincial residence must be available to all aboriginal persons, on and off reserve. The programs and services which give effect to these benefits and privileges must also be tailored to the needs, circumstances and rights of the aboriginal population, without fear that a beneficial "singling out" will render *ultra vires* an otherwise valid and proper legislative regime.

When these two responsibilities overlap, there is no clear answer to their resolution. Each level of government has an independent constitutional role and responsibility. These have different sources: the federal role is aboriginal-specific; the provincial role is based on equity to all residents. Both are, however, subject to the demands of the honour of the Crown,[106] and this must mean, at a minimum, that the aboriginal people to whom the Crown in all its emanations owes an obligation of protection and development, must not lose the benefit of that obligation because of federal-provincial jurisdictional uncertainty.

In conclusion, an entitlement to social services is, in public policy if not in law, a right of all Canadians. The special and evolving place of aboriginal peoples in the Canadian federation requires an ongoing and rigorous review of the social service needs of those peoples. This review must take into account the special rights of aboriginal peoples and the unique relationship that they have with the Crown.

The co-ordination and fulfilment of federal and provincial responsibilities will require political compromise through co-operative federalism. These issues, so fundamental to the Crown's honour, cannot be resolved through acrimonious litigation, but only through consensus and compromise.

Notes

1. "Indians, and Lands reserved for the Indians."
2. This appears to be justifiable on the basis of the broad reading of the term "Indians" in *Reference re Eskimos*, [1939] S.C.R. 104. The application of the term to Metis people remains contentious, however.
3. Brian Slattery, "Understanding Aboriginal Rights," 66 *Can. Bar Rev.* 727, (1987) pp.736-737.
4. R.S.C. 1970, Appendix II, No. 1.
5. *St. Catherines' Milling & Lumber Co. v. The Queen* (1887) 13 S.C.R. 577, p. 652, per Gwynne, J.
6. For example, see *Calder v. A.-G. B.C.* (1973) 34 D.L.R. (3d) 145 (S.C.C.), p. 203, per Hall, J., who stated: "Its force as a statute is analogous to the status of the Magna Carta which has always been considered to be the law throughout the Empire."
7. Canada, *Report on the Affairs of the Indians in Canada*, (*Journals*, Legislative Assembly), 1847, Appendix T, p. 360.
8. S.C. 1960, c.39 extended the vote to Indians; in 1954 (S.O. 1954, c.25, s.5) Ontario had extended to Indians the right to vote in provincial elections.
9. *St. Ann's Island Shooting & Fishing Club v. The King* (1950) 2 D.L.R. 266 (S.C.C.), p. 232, per Rand, J.
10. *Miller v. The King* (1950) 1 D.L.R. 513 (S.C.C.), p. 525. See also *Francis v. The Queen*, [1956] S.C.R. 618, where at p. 629 Rand, J. began a sentence: "Appreciating fully the obligation of good faith toward these wards of the state..."
11. *Guerin v. The Queen* (1984) 13 D.L.R. (4th) 321 (S.C.C.). *Guerin* will be more fully discussed later in this chapter.
12. *Cherokee Nation v. State of Georgia*, [1831], Peters 1 at p. 16.
13. *Ibid.*
14. *Johnson v. M'Intosh*, [1823], 8 Wheaton 543.
15. *Worcester v. State of Georgia*, [1832], 6 Peters 515.
16. *Supra*, note 6, p. 151, per Judson, J.; p. 169 and pp. 193-196, per Hall, J.
17. Most notably *Guerin, supra*, note 11. But see also *Hamlet of Baker Lake v. Minister of Indian Affairs* (1979) 107 D.L.R. (3d) 513 (F.C.T.D.), pp. 541-542.
18. Notes: "Rethinking the Trust Doctrine in Federal Indian Law," *Harv.L.R.*, Vol. 98, No. 2 (1984), 422-440.
19. *Seminole Nation v. U.S.*, [1942] 316 U.S. 286, pp. 296-297.
20. *Choctaw Nation v. U.S.*, [1943] 318 U.S. 432, pp. 431-432; *Oneida County v. Oneida Indian Nation*, [1985] 105 S.Ct. 1245, p. 1258.
21. *U.S. v. Mitchell*, [1983] 103 S.Ct. 2961, p. 2972.
22. *Guerin v. The Queen* (1981) 10 E.T.R. 61 (F.C.T.D.).
23. 143 D.L.R. (3d) 416 (Fed.C.A.), p. 469, per LeDain J.
24. *Supra*, note 11, p. 346.
25. *Ibid.*, p. 356.
26. *Ibid.*, p. 357
27. *Ibid.*, p. 358.
28. *Ibid.*
29. See *Nowegijick v. The Queen* (1983) 144 D.L.R. (4th) 193 (S.C.C.), p. 198; and see *Simon v. The Queen* (1985) 24 D.L.R. (4th) 390 (S.C.C.), p. 402. In *Simon*,

p. 404, Chief Justice Dickson describes an Indian treaty as "an agreement *sui generis*," in a clear echo of the language used in *Guerin* to describe both Indian title and the Crown-Indian fiduciary relationship.

30. *Guerin, supra* note 11, p. 342.
31. *Ibid.*, p. 343.
32. *Ibid.*, p. 344.
33. *Ibid.*, p. 361.
34. See below in this chapter, Equality Rights and Collective Rights.
35. *Apsassin v. The Queen in Right of Canada* (1988) 1 C.N.L.R. 73 (F.C.T.D.), p. 93. The Indian plaintiffs lost the action because of a successful limitations defence by the Crown.
36. Slattery, *op. cit*, note 3, p. 731.
37. *Ibid.*, p. 755.
38. The power to spend of the federal and probably the provincial governments is unrestrained by the limits of legislative competence. See P. Hogg, *Constitutional Law of Canada* (2nd ed., Toronto: Carswell, 1985), pp. 123-131. And see 1987 *Constitutional Accord*, June 1987, proposing a new s.106A, implicitly recognizing a federal spending power in areas of provincial legislative competence.
39. Sucession law provisions of the *Indian Act* were assumed to be valid for this reason in *A.-G. Canada v. Canard*, [1976] 1 S.C.R. 170.
40. *R. v. Hill* (1907) 15 O.L.R. 406 (Ont.C.A.), applying provincial law licensing physicians.
41. In *Worcester, supra*, note 14, p. 557, Chief Justice Marshall, after recognizing the national character of the Cherokees and their right to self-government, added: "The treaties and laws of the United States contemplate the Indian territory as completely separated from that of the states; and provide that all intercourse with them shall be carried on exclusively by the government of the Union."
42. *Cardinal v. The Queen*, [1974] S.C.R. 695.
43. *Ibid.*, p. 716.
44. *Ibid.*, p. 703.
45. *Four B Manufacturing v. United Garment Workers* (1979) 102 D.L.R. (3d) 385 (S.C.C.).
46. *Ibid.*, p. 398, per Beetz, J.
47. R.S.C. 1970, c.C-8.
48. *Dick v. The Queen* (1985) 23 D.L.R. (4th) 33 (S.C.C.), pp. 59-60.
49. *Francis v. The Queen* (Supreme Court of Canada, unreported at time of writing, May 26, 1988).
50. The approach is identical to that articulated in *Bank of Toronto v. Lambe* (1887), 12 App. Cas. 575 where the Privy Council upheld a provincial taxation law which applied to a bank (within exclusive federal authority) because it was "in pith and substance" a taxation measure *affecting* banks, but not *in relation to* banks and banking. Thus were banks (listed as an exclusive legislative subject of Parliament) rendered subject to provincial law.
51. *Natural Parents v. Superintendent of Child Welfare*, [1976] 2 S.C.R. 751.
52. *Ibid.*, pp. 760-761.
53. *Four B Manufacturing, supra*, note 45, p. 397.

54. *Derrickson v. Derrickson* (1986) 26 D.L.R. (4th) 175 (S.C.C.), p. 184, per Beetz, J.
55. See *St. Catherines' Milling and Lumber Co v. The Queen* (1888) 14 App. Cas 46; *Smith v. The Queen* (1983) 147 D.L.R. (3d) 237 (S.C.C.).
56. *Nowegijick, supra,* note 29, p. 198.
57. *Canadian Bill of Rights,* S.C. 1960, c.44, R.S.C. 1970, Appendix III.
58. *R. v. Drybones,* [1970] S.C.R. 282.
59. *Ibid.,* p. 297. In *R. v. Hayden* (1983), 8 C.C.C. (3d) 33, the Manitoba Court of Appeal applied *Drybones* to render inoperative a provision of the *Indian Act* making it an offence for a person to be intoxicated on a reserve, since it is aimed at Indians, who are the predominant residents of reserves. The Supreme Court of Canada refused leave to appeal.
60. *A.-G. Canada v. Lavell,* [1974] S.C.R. 1349.
61. *Canard, supra,* note 39.
62. *Ibid.,* pp. 191-192.
63. *Ibid.,* p. 184.
64. Hogg, *op. cit.,* note 38, p. 789.
65. *The Queen v. Burnshine,* [1975] S.C.R. 693.
66. *Canard, supra,* note 39, p. 189.
67. *Ibid.,* p. 206.
68. *MacKay v. The Queen,* [1980] 2 S.C.R. 370.
69. Hogg, *op. cit.,* note 38, p. 792.
70. *MacKay, supra,* note 68, p. 406
71. *Ibid.,* p. 407.
72. This is clear from s.32 of the *Charter.* And see *Operation Dismantle v. The Queen,* [1985] 1 S.C.R. 441.
73. See for example the Ontario Court of Appeal decisions in *R. v. Ertel,* [1987] 35 C.C.C. (3d) 398, *R. v. Ramos,* [1987] 58 O.R. (2d) 737 and *Re McDonald and The Queen,* [1985] 51 O.R. (2d) 745, leave to appeal refused by the Supreme Court of Canada [1985], 52 O.R. (2d) 688.
74. *Reference re Bill 30* (1987) 40 D.L.R. (4th) 18 (S.C.C.).
75. *Reference re Bill 30 (1986), 53 O.R. (2d) 513.*
76. *Ibid.,* p. 566.
77. *Ibid.,* p. 566.
78. See *St. Catherines' Milling, supra,* note 5.
79. *Bill 30* (C.A.), *supra,* note 75, p. 567.
80. *Ibid.,* p. 576.
81. *Supra,* note 74, per Wilson J., p. 60.
82. *La Société des Acadiens v. Association of Parents,* [1986] 1 S.C.R. 549, p. 578.
83. *Supra,* note 74, per Estey, J., p. 27.
84. *Ibid.,* pp. 27-28.
85. Canada: *Statement of the Government of Canada on Indian Policy,* House of Commons, June 25, 1969.
86. A discussion of "existing aboriginal and treaty rights" is beyond the scope of this chapter, but the phrase is generally understood to refer to rights to occupy and use land in various ways, as well as to the specific rights secured through treaties. These constitutionally entrenched rights do not address general issues of service provision.

87. *Hunter v. Southam Inc.* (1984) 11 D.L.R. (4th) 641, (S.C.C.), pp. 650-651, per Dickson, J.
88. *Supra*, note 74.
89. *Supra*, note 84.
90. *A.-G. Canada v. A.-G. Ontario (Labour Conventions case*, [1937] A.C. 326, p. 354, per Lord Atkin.
91. *Supra*, note 41.
92. See the discussion in the Report of the Hawthorne Commission. H.B. Hawthorne (ed), *A Survey of the Contemporary Indians of Canada.* Vols. I and II (Ottawa: Quenn's Printer 1967).
93. *Indian Act*, S.C. 1951, c.29, s.86 (2).
94. *Canada Elections Act*, S.C. 1960, c.18, s.1; and S.C. 1960, c.39.
95. *Supra*, note 29.
96. *Nowegijick, supra*, note 29.
97. For example, the *Assessment Act*, R.S.O. 1980, c.31, s.3(2); *Retail Sales Tax Act*, R.S.O. 1980, c.454, s.5(1)(69); *Provincial Land Tax Act*, R.S,O. 1980, c.399, s.3(1)(2).
98. *An Act for the protection of the Indians in Upper Canada from imposition, and the property occupied or enjoyed by them from trespass or injury,* 13 and 14 Vict., c.74, s.IV.
99. S.C. 1876, c.18.
100. *Supra*, note 29, p. 196.
101. See generally Bartlett, "Taxation" in B. Morse, *Aboriginal Peoples and the Law* (Ottawa: Carleton University Press, (1985), pp. 579-616.
102. See also *Greyeyes v. The Queen* (1978) 84 D.L.R. (3d) 196 (Fed. Ct. T. D.), where it was held that a scholarship paid to an Indian in accordance with a treaty obligation to provide an education and to attend a university not on reserve was exempt from tax.
103. Although other laws of general application can provide for the assessment of provincial taxes on reserve, if s.87 of the *Indian Act* is not contravened: see *Re Hill and Minister of Revenue* (1985) 50 O.R. (2d) 765 (H.C.J.) and *Re Loeb Inc. and Minister of Revenue* (1987) 59 O.R. (2d) 737 (H.C.J.), both in relation to the Ontario *Tobacco Tax Act.*
104. See *Big M Drug Mart v. The Queen* (1985), D.L.R. (4th) 321 (S.C.C.), p. 362, per Dickson, J.
105. See generally Hogg, *supra*, note 38, pp. 315-316, which lists many instances of provincial laws which single out federal persons or institutions and which have been found to be valid. This conclusion is supported by the recent case *O.P.S.E.U. v. A.-G. Ont.* (1987) 41 D.L.R. (4th) 1 (S.C.C.), which upheld a provincial statute even though it specifically singled out political activity relating to a federal election.
106. For example, see *R. v. Taylor and Willams* (1981) 34 O.R. (2d) 360 (C.A.), p. 367, per McKinnin, A.C.J.O.: "In approaching the terms of a treaty … the honour of the Crown is always involved and no appearance of 'sharp dealing' should be sanctioned." See also *R. v. Agawa* (Ontario Court of Appeal, unreported at time of writing, August 3, 1988).

CHAPTER 3

GOVERNMENT OBLIGATIONS, ABORIGINAL PEOPLES AND SECTION 91(24) OF THE *CONSTITUTION ACT, 1867*

Bradford Morse

INTRODUCTION

This chapter canvasses a range of aspects relating to the scope of s.91(24) of the *Constitution Act, 1867* and its impact upon federal, provincial and aboriginal views of their common relationship within the context of the debate over the magic words "jurisdiction" and "responsibility." Following a definition of these terms, the discussion examines the attitudes of the three parties over the decades. The heart of this contribution is to consider the developments in the doctrine of fiduciary obligations since the pivotal court case of *Guerin v. The Queen*[1] as well as to explore the potential ramifications of this new judicial initiative in light of the provisions of the *Constitution Act, 1982*[2] and the drive by aboriginal people for recognition of their right to self-government.

"JURISDICTION" VERSUS "RESPONSIBILITY"

Both these terms were bandied about with great regularity throughout the five-year-long process of First Ministers'

Conferences on Aboriginal Constitutional Matters (hereinafter referred to as FMC or FMCs). Similar to the more dramatic word "self-government," speakers from all 17 delegations frequently used the words "jurisdiction" and "responsibility" in a way which imported different meanings. Although aboriginal groups were often questioned as to what they meant or wanted when they spoke of "self-government," no common definition of the term among all parties was achieved. Curiously, little attention was devoted to exploring the divergent usages of "jurisdiction" and "responsibility." Because almost no effort was given to achieving a common understanding of the terms, a great deal of misunderstanding occurred as listeners inferred their own meaning to the terms which may not have coincided with the speaker's meaning.

The *Oxford Universal Dictionary* (3rd ed.) defines "jurisdiction" in this way:

1. Administration of justice; exercise of judicial authority, or of the functions of a judge or legal tribunal; legal authority or power.
2. Power or authority in general; administration, rule, control.
3. The range of judicial or administrative power; the territory over which such power extends.
4. A judicial organization; a judicature; a court, or series of courts, of justice.

The same dictionary gives the following meanings to "responsibility":

1. The state or fact of being responsible.
2a. Wish. A charge, trust, or duty, for which one is responsible.
2b. A person or thing for which one is responsible.

The *Oxford Universal Dictionary* also defines the root word "responsible" as follows:

1. Correspondent or answering to something.
2a. Answerable, accountable (to another for something); liable to be called to account.
2b. Morally accountable for one's actions; capable of rational conduct.
3. Answerable to a charge.
4a. Capable of fulfilling an obligation or trust; reliable, trustworthy; of good credit and repute.
4b. Of respectable appearance.
5. Involving responsibility or obligation.

However, many speakers throughout the years of debate have used these key terms in more specific senses that were politically charged and influenced by their backgrounds. Lawyers are comfortable with the concept of jurisdiction since they use it with great frequency in various legal contexts. *Black's Law Dictionary* (rev. 4th ed.) defines "jurisdiction" in part as follows:

> The word is a term of large and comprehensive import, and embraces every kind of judicial action. It is the authority by which courts and judicial officers take cognizance of and decide cases; the legal right by which judges exercise their authority. It exists when court has cognizance of class of cases involved, proper parties are present, and point to be decided is within issues. It is the authority, capacity, power or right to act... It is of three kinds, of the subject-matter, of the person, and to render particular judgement which was given...

This excerpt of a definition that runs almost two full pages, poses an interesting counterpoint to the complete yet brief statement describing "responsibility" as: "The obligation to answer for an act done, and to repair any injury it may have caused."

These dictionary definitions demonstrate that the law and the legal profession concentrate solely upon "jurisdiction," which is a term of art within the law, and merely use the word "responsibility" from time to time in its everyday sense. Some other disciplines, however, use the terms interchangeably while still others focus upon the latter and virtually ignore the former.

As both a witness to and a participant in the FMC process, I was continually struck by the misunderstanding that occurred through the usages of these terms and the concomitant lack of commonality in their meanings. In my view, the word "jurisdiction" was most often used as meaning: "The legal power or authority to act in a particular way (for example, in the sense of courts, tribunals or statutory officers) or to legislate." Some people, however, confused simple jurisdiction with sovereign, or inherent jurisdiction. I add these modifiers to denote that the latter expression indicates a particular category within the broader concept of jurisdiction in which the wielder of the power derives authority not from a supervisory body (e.g., Parliament, a legislature or a particular statute) but from a superior law (e.g., a constitution that allocates jurisdiction to sovereign entities) or from a supreme being (e.g., God or the Great Spirit) or from the ultimate sovereign directly in a manner that cannot be withdrawn (e.g., irrevocable grants of authority from the monarch as has been the case with the royal courts and their descendants in Canada as the superior or s.96 courts of the *Constitution Act, 1867*).[3]

This distinction is vital in the context of the aboriginal self-government debate as certain individuals would talk of the jurisdiction of aboriginal governments in terms of powers to be delegated by federal and provincial governments, while others were discussing powers that would be derived from the Canadian Constitution itself, such that they would form governments with sovereign status, or a third level of government within Canada. In addition, various aboriginal leaders would also be speaking in terms of obtaining constitutional recognition for powers that were derived from the original sovereign status of the aboriginal nations, such that the source would remain outside the national Constitution with only specified aspects of it receiving the Constitution's formal acknowledgement.

The other key word under consideration, "responsibility," has been used in a variety of manners. Some speakers kept referring to responsibility as something that should be done by one or another of the parties—a moral obligation to act. Other participants used it in more of its political-science meaning regarding ministerial responsibility to Parliament and/or Treasury Board. This arose especially concerning the duty of the federal government to account for how aboriginal groups spent federal funds allocated to them. A third usage, also common, reflected a belief that there was a legal obligation requiring certain conduct, particularly to do with the Government of Canada's special relationship with Indians and the financial consequences thereof. A further tendency was, as previously mentioned, to use the word "responsibility" as a synonym for "jurisdiction." The resulting confusion, which was never resolved, created a further obstacle to consensus on the language for an amendment or even a climate conducive to fostering such agreement.

The participants in the FMC process cannot truly be faulted for this lack of precision. Despite the frequent use of these terms by all 17 parties and in governmental circles generally, little attention appears to be devoted by anyone to seeking common understandings regarding terminology. I have searched extensively and in vain for months to locate any case law or learned legal commentary that discusses these two concepts in relation to each other. Not only is the jurisprudence missing, but I have also been unable to uncover any analysis from the political science and public administration communities that examines the connection between these two fundamental ideas.

The legal profession has concentrated its attention solely on the jurisdictional question in the context of various distinct fields. Within constitutional law, the basic theory focuses upon the power or authority to enact legislation by Parliament or the provincial legislatures, which also includes the law-making mandates of subordinate governments and other statutory entities created by these sovereign governments. Our courts and legal theorists have blithely restated the basic Diceyan principles time and again that parliamentary supremacy involves the ability to pass statutes at the will of the lawmakers. The decision to act, or not to act, is exclusively within the hands of the parliamentarians and cannot be reviewed by the courts. Likewise, the wisdom or folly evident in the statutes duly and properly enacted is for the voters to decide rather than for the judiciary to assess. Thus, the Canadian jurisprudence ignores any moral, political or legal tenets regarding the matter of responsibility or obligation toward pursuing certain conduct. There is no such obligation in the eyes of the law.

The sole issue for consideration in a federal system is which of the two standard levels of government has the power—or jurisdiction—to exercise its dominion over a specific subject or field. The assumption always prevailing was that one of the two must have the jurisdiction to legislate no matter what the contents might be, except if it invaded the inherent jurisdiction of the superior courts. The courts would then assert their own exclusive right to serve as referee when disputes arose concerning alleged infringements by one sovereign government of the domain properly the preserve of another. Traditionally, the federal power was considered paramount, where both levels of government are properly acting within the scope of their respective jurisdiction yet in a way that was contradictory. Federal-provincial tensions have been lessened by the emergence of the post-World War II theory of co-operative federalism which demonstrated a greater sensitivity by the Canadian judiciary than the Judicial Committee of the Privy Council had previously displayed.

The advent of the *Charter of Rights and Freedoms* has ushered us into a new era in which the courts have been directed by our lawmakers *qua* constitution builders to adopt a broader role. Although the judiciary is still not authorized to second guess the intelligence of our legislators, the judges are required to examine the content of laws beyond the division of powers question. They must determine if otherwise valid legislation is unconstitutional by reason of its conflict with provisions of the *Charter*. The same mandate has been presented to our judges concerning Part II of the *Constitution Act, 1982*, even though there is no equivalent to s.24(1). It is also worth noting that s.35 is unencumbered by the saving clause in s.1 of the Charter.

This dramatic change in the function of our constitutional umpires has not been lost on the public or on governmental officials. It has given further credence to the notion of a governmental responsibility to take action in certain spheres. However, it is too early to see if the legal community will come to grips with this far more nebulous, subjective and slippery concept which until now, it has successfully ignored.

DIVERGENT PERCEPTIONS OF THE FEDERAL GOVERNMENT'S CONSTITUTIONAL MANDATE

This segment summarizes the development of federal, provincial and aboriginal perspectives on the import of s.91(24) within the context of "jurisdiction" and "responsibility."

The Traditional View

The federal and provincial interpretations of s.91(24) were relatively straightforward for the first hundred years after Confederation, although shifts in opinion did occur. The Government of Canada believed that s.91(24) provided Parliament with exclusive jurisdiction to enact laws and play an administrative role relating to "Indians" as well as to "Lands reserved for the Indians." Initially, this meant that the Government of Canada acquired those obligations formerly accruing to the colonial governments under pre-Confederation treaties, along with responsibility for all existing Indian reserves whether created by the Crown or otherwise. The newly created Cabinet post of Secretary of State for the Provinces immediately attempted to absorb the Indian affairs bureaucracy, and spearheaded enabling legislation in 1868[4] based upon the models previously in force in the Province of Canada.[5]

In addition to dealing with existing reserves, the Government of Canada undertook that portion of the royal prerogative to negotiate new treaties with the First Nations so as to maintain and promote peaceful relations, while obtaining cessions of large tracts of land that could be made available for non-aboriginal settlement or exploitation. This was viewed as an exclusive federal mandate in which provincial governments had no involvement. Although the provinces might encourage treaty-making, they were not seen as having any authority to negotiate treaties on their own behalf with aboriginal nations resident within their new borders. Nor were tripartite discussions deemed necessary. The Ontario government subsequently obtained a guaranteed role in such negotiations, first with Treaty No. 9 and its adhesions as well as in the Williams Treaty of 1923. However, this was not truly due to any constitutional imperative, but rather it reflected a federal willingness to include the province and a desire to shift some of the financial burdens onto Ontario's shoulders.

The Government of Canada originally thought that it would acquire the primary benefits from treaty-making, that the surrender of aboriginal title would transfer the fee simple interest of the Indian Nations to the Crown in right of Canada free from s.92(5) and s.109 of the *Constitution Act, 1867*. The Judicial Committee of the Privy Council ultimately rejected a legal argument founded on this supposition in *St. Catherines' Milling and Lumber Co. v. The Queen*[6] by concluding that land cession treaties had the effect simply of removing the aboriginal burden on provincial Crown title but passed nothing to the federal signatory. In doing so, the Court declared that the original inhabitants of Canada were not its owners, but merely possessed limited rights to use the land. These rights evaporated upon their surrender by treaty so that the underlying provincial Crown title became complete. Ironically, the Privy Council also later concluded that the provinces bore none of the costs for providing treaty annuities.[7]

The Government of Canada further believed that the legislative power embodied in s.91(24) permitted Parliament to do what it wished regarding all aspects of the lives of the indigenous population. Ancient governmental systems could be abolished by the stroke of the lawmakers' pen and replaced by an allegedly democratic model in which women and young men were disenfranchised and non-Indians could be elected chief.[8] Traditional religious practices were outlawed while Christian denominations received frequently exclusive domain over particular Indian communities. A pass system was established whereby the approval of the local Indian agent was necessary to obtain permission to leave a reserve for employment, food gathering or any other purpose. A scheme was created through which children would be forcibly sent to residential schools far away from their homes. Aboriginal languages were suppressed, customary laws ignored and longstanding cultural practices undermined. Even membership in the community, with all incidents of that position, was regulated by statute with little regard for the wishes of, and impacts upon, the people involved. All of these restraints and impositions were debated and selected by Parliamentarians for whom the people directly affected had no electoral voice. Indian people were treated as if they were children or mentally incompetent wards who required a guardian to make all decisions.[9]

This federal authority carried with it the ability to create divergent approaches in various regions of the country and to treat groups differently. Although the courts have yet to declare conclusively what is the proper definition of the term "Indians" within Class 24 of s.91, the Fathers of Confederation likely intended the expression to encompass all of the indigenous population as a whole. Thus, the early legislation[10] dealt with "Indians" and "halfbreeds" without reference to specific racial, cultural or blood criteria. Sometimes the Metis people were treated the same as Indians when they were members of Indian communities. On other occasions they were given the choice of taking treaty, (thereby being treated the same as treaty Indians) or taking scrip. Under the *Manitoba Act,1870*,[11] the federal government pursued a distinctive policy for the numerous Metis population in which their "Indian title" was extinguished by s.31 in return for 1.4 million acres of land. Despite these differences in treatment, it was still the Government of Canada making these decisions. At the same time, the Inuit (then universally called the Eskimos or Esquimaux) were being ignored both legislatively and administratively not for the lack of any federal authority, but because there was little interest in them or their lands and resources.

The provinces were largely content to see the federal government assume all authority and obligation for aboriginal peoples. Although provincial governments occasionally denounced specific federal policies, particularly concerning the creation of reserves, resistance was not grounded upon a constitutional challenge designed to limit the scope of s.91(24). The provincial governments generally conceded that it was the federal government's mandate both to negotiate treaties as well as to decide if any were to be concluded. Likewise, the provinces looked to the Government of Canada as the deliverer and financier of all programs and services to the aboriginal population.

Provincial legislatures did not attempt to enact their own laws explicitly for Indians, Inuit or Metis peoples as such until the Government of Alberta passed *The Metis Population Betterment Act*[12] just over 50 years ago. It was passed after several years of study, including failed efforts to involve the federal government in its remedial efforts to address the impact of the Depression upon Metis peoples living in road allowance lands.[13] No other provincial government, before or since, has enacted special legislation of any form that is directed toward aboriginal people *per se* except as part of a co-ordinated initiative with Parliament,[14] or in fulfilment of a comprehensive land-claim settlement.[15] The provinces also did not enact laws directed toward Indian reserves except as part of a joint scheme.

On the other hand, provincial governments assumed that the prevailing law would govern all aboriginal people even when living off reserve, in the absence of federal law to the contrary. Thus, an Indian could be elected a reeve like anyone else.[16] In addition, the courts on rare occasions stated that general provincial statutes could apply on reserve.[17]

In addition, provincial legislation did single out Indians in particular so as to impose disabilities regarding provincial institutions. For example, it was common to deny Indians explicitly the right to vote in provincial elections.[18] It is important to realize, however, that these instances were limited both in number and in nature. They involved usually one small provision or reference within an overall statutory scheme that was otherwise clearly within the provincial sphere.

The aboriginal perspective throughout this first century of Canada is not as well documented nor as clearly understood. Not surprisingly, there are very few recorded instances of aboriginal people litigating either to obtain clarity in the constitutional division of powers or to foster direct provincial action. This lack of use of the courts was in part induced by a statutory prohibition that existed for some time within the *Indian Act*,[19] as well as by the negative experiences before the Canadian judicial system as defendants in criminal and wildlife harvesting proceedings. It is most commonly suggested that the aboriginal people largely remained apart from federal-provincial struggles while attempting as best they could to retain their lifestyle, economy, values, beliefs and communities intact under their own governments and laws.

When external aid or intervention was sought, the requests were directed toward awa or England. Without relying upon s.91(24) and constitutional principles per se, it was the federal government that was seen as the treaty-maker. It was considered responsible for the policies, programs and functionaries that most directly affected the lives of aboriginal people. The Crown in right of Canada was supposed to be the protector of their land and their well-being. It was thus to the Queen or her representatives, such as the Governor General, that delegations, petitions, memorials and urgent appeals were dispatched. On the other hand, provincial governments were the source of pressure on their lands or in regulating the exercise of the traditional economy. The provincial governments were more likely to be viewed as representing the non-aboriginal society, while the Government of Canada was the self-proclaimed trustee that was expected to serve as the intermediary between these two worlds.

From the aboriginal perspective, the federal government generally failed miserably at meeting its mandate. It also was thoroughly unsuccessful in meeting the objectives of assimilation or integration that held sway for so many decades once the threat of armed insurrection disappeared. Yet its dominant presence went largely unchallenged until the last 25 years. Thus, its broad authority under s.91(24) was not the subject of dispute until the 1960s.

The Modern View

The decade of the 1960s was a turning point in the history of the relationship between aboriginal people and the rest of Canada in so many ways and for so many reasons. The decade began with Prime Minister Diefenbaker's bold new initiative of prodding Parliament to pass the *Canadian Bill of Rights*.[20] A new age was to have dawned in which equality of opportunity for all was to be a political and legal guarantee for Canadians. The civil rights movement in the United States starting in the 1950s was forcing Canada to examine its own prejudices discretely, while nightly television news coverage brought marches and sit-ins south of the border into living rooms across the nation.

Somehow the second-class treatment and position of aboriginal people in Canada rang a false note in the symphony that was to accompany the Bill of Rights. Mr. Diefenbaker also moved then to extend the right to vote in federal elections to all aboriginal people.[21] There was, however, far more to be done. Mr. Diefenbaker also raised the profile of the North as our last great frontier. Both the Indian Affairs Branch and Northern Development were later upgraded to form a ministry. Major studies on Indian policies and the position of aboriginal people in conflict with the law were initiated by the minister of the new department. The Walpole Island First Nation evicted its Indian agent on a one-year trial basis in 1965, thereby proving that band councils could govern community affairs on their own.[22]

Indian residential schools were closed across the country resulting in the sudden return of thousands of children to their families. This generated major repercussions that are particularly relevant to this study. Few communities possessed residential schools which could be transformed into their own educational systems. Many others did not receive schools either because of lack of funding or because they were too small. As a result, local public schools were called upon to accept large numbers of children from families who did not pay school taxes. Federal-provincial agreements became the primary mechanism through which the Government of Canada provided money to pay tuition costs.

Another ramification of shutting down residential schools was that many families were unable to cope with the return of their children. With the large numbers of Indian children and youth on reserve, provincial social service agencies now had cause to apply their standards of acceptable home life. As a result, thousands of Indian children were apprehended by social workers and brought within the child welfare system. This naturally increased costs to provincial treasuries such that pressure was placed on the Department of Indian Affairs and Northern Development to reimburse for all expenses relating to status Indians. Certain provinces flatly refused to provide child welfare services to reserve residents other than in life and death situations, either because of the absence of federal funds or because they saw this as a federal responsibility. Federal-provincial agreements or commitments through exchanges of letters ultimately obligated the Department to cover most or all of the costs involved in delivering these services. However, resistance and dissatisfaction continued.[23]

The federal view of s.91(24) throughout the 1960s and 1970s was like looking down a long tunnel toward the light cast by the magnitude of this piece of jurisdiction—a light that seemed to shrink but in fact was not changing at all.

During this period the federal government felt that it possessed only a discretionary power to legislate and to provide non-statutory benefits that were withdrawable at will. The *Department of Indian Affairs and Northern Development Act*[24] gave a mandate to the Minister to govern the Yukon and Northwest Territories as well as to implement all obligations undertaken through the terms of the *Indian Act*. The White Paper of 1969[25] demonstrated clearly the perception that the Government of Canada could abolish its statutory obligations by repealing the *Indian Act* and terminating all non-statutory benefits and services it provided directly or through third parties.

The Supreme Court of Canada had, on several occasions,[26] rejected any residue of the federal enclave theory. The general judicial abhorrence of a legal vacuum was evident as the Court concluded that provincial legislation could apply to registered Indians both on and off reserves in the absence of federal law to the contrary. Section 88 of the *Indian Act* facilitated this reasoning by expressly opening the door for provincial laws of general application to apply to status Indians, although subject to several limitations (nor did they apply in reference to reserve land itself). This section, which was introduced as part of the major overhaul of the *Indian Act* implemented in 1951, reads as follows:

> 88.   Subject to the terms of any treaty and any other Act of the Parliament of Canada, all laws of general application from time to time in force in any province are applicable to and in respect of Indians in the province, except to the extent that such laws are inconsistent with this Act or any order, rule, regulation or by-law made thereunder, and except to the extent that such laws make provision for any matter for which provision is made by or under this Act.

The federal government defined a much larger role for the provinces. Not only were they to be the primary service delivery agent for reserve residents, but they were to be prodded to pay part of the costs. The Ontario and Quebec governments were the most willing to adopt an active role, including the absorption of a significant share of the total expenditures. Certain other provinces (e.g., Manitoba, Saskatchewan and British Columbia) were far less responsive to federal entreaties. The federal government also believed that its obligations were generally limited to reserve borders. Any federal activities beyond these territorial limits were defined as *ex gratia* and restricted to band members still residing on reserve and those temporarily absent or in the process of changing their domicile. Thus, all expenditures and responsibilities for off-reserve residents (other than for specified time periods, or in the context of specific programs such as post-secondary education, or those with physical or mental handicaps requiring specialized assistance) were left to the provinces. Most provincial and territorial governments responded by treating off-reserve status Indians the same as all other provincial residents, supplemented by the occasional special program or small funding agency (e.g., the Native Citizens Branch of the Ontario Ministry of Culture and Recreation or the First Citizens Fund of the Government of British Columbia).

The federal view regarding the parameters of s.91(24) in relation to Metis and non-status Indians also hardened. These groups were defined officially as falling outside federal authority other than in the territories. Ironically, they could and did receive special attention as disadvantaged, migrating or multicultural peoples through the Secretary of State and the Canada Mortgage and Housing Corporation. This was implemented as part of a broad federal initiative designed to alleviate suffering and promote a more "Just Society," rather than as an aspect of even a discretionary authority pursuant to s.91(24) regarding "constitutional Indians." The earlier decision of the Supreme Court of Canada in *Reference re Eskimos*[27] was interpreted narrowly so as to address solely the position of the Inuit. This conservative approach, however, was not uniformly followed as the non-status Innu in Labrador were brought within the terms of the Canada-Newfoundland-Native Peoples Agreements as early as 1954, thereby assuring the provision of community infrastructure needs by the province. The federal government usually paid 90 per cent of the cost.

The great expansion in the public sector undertaken by all provincial governments in the 1960s increased the capacity of provincial programs and services to accommodate aboriginal people, and fostered a general desire to incorporate aboriginal residents within these enhanced agencies. Although not all provinces were eager to extend provincial programs to on-reserve residents, all were amenable to treating off-reserve registered Indians the same as other classes of aboriginal people. Special initiatives regarding this distinct population began to be implemented by the early 1970s through unilateral provincial action or by virtue of federal-provincial agreements. This occurred not only in the areas of education and child welfare, but also in other fields, such as arts and crafts;

criminal justice (primarily through native court worker or court communicator services along with a few legal service clinics, justices of the peace and prison programs); some limited cultural and oral history projects; drug and alcohol abuse efforts; special urban assistance programs; and occasional employment training initiatives.

Attitudes also changed regarding the enforcement of provincial laws. Although there was a sprinkling of court decisions before the 1960s making it clear that provincial legislation could apply to all aboriginal people off Indian reserves, and that some statutes were applicable on reserve, efforts to enforce non-criminal laws were sporadic. The decision to enforce provincial laws systematically, especially concerning wildlife harvesting, represented a significant departure from past practice. The previous *laissez-faire* attitude was jettisoned in favour of vigorous application of the law to make clear that all people were being treated equally. Protecting provincial jurisdiction came to be seen as a political imperative, while longstanding assimilative impulses were recast as positive efforts to promote fairness for all.

The reaction of aboriginal people reflected concern and discord. While the 1960s began with efforts to bring together Indian, Inuit and Metis peoples into a common cause along with white sympathizers, dissension and distrust was rampant by the end of the decade. The fight to repulse the 1969 White Paper provided a catalyst for the development of organizations within each province and territory to represent the objectives and aspirations of reserve residents, articulated in Ottawa by the National Indian Brotherhood. The speedy success demonstrated by the withdrawal of the proposed federal policy was exhilarating and empowering for the Indian leadership. Federal funding was provided at a heretofore unprecedented scale for these organizations to meet, conduct research, file land claims and lobby for change in federal policies, programs and laws. [28]

This experience also fostered intense competition. Conflicts developed over land claimed by different groups; organizations fought over obtaining federal funds; power struggles ensued for control over these new associations; jealousies erupted over staffing decisions; differences of political perspective (both in terms of mainstream parties and organizational demands) flared. Due to numerous internal reasons and the terms of federal funding criteria, a clear dividing line was drawn between groups representing First Nations (then exclusively called bands) and the rest of the aboriginal population. The Department of Secretary of State later developed a special branch to provide core funding for an association to pursue the goals of the Inuit as well as for Metis and non-status Indian associations in each province and territory. (Newfoundland was unique in not having any registered Indians or reserves; initially only one group in that province was created for the non-Inuit aboriginal population). The funding rules required each organization to represent all Metis and non-status Indians within that province or territory, thereby lumping together people that shared a common disadvantaged position but that sometimes had quite different objectives. This difficulty would later be the partial cause of a split within the Native Council of Canada and give birth to the Metis National Council. Off-reserve status Indians were ignored altogether as it was assumed that they would be represented by the band-based associations, since they were virtually all members of a band somewhere. The fact that they may have lived away from their home community for many years or that they may even live in another province was of no import.

The development of the federal claims process in 1969 regarding specific claims, and in 1973 for comprehensive claims further magnified the boundaries separating the groups.[29] The Inuit were recognized as possessing aboriginal title and were accepted as coming within the federal sphere as s.91(24) Indians. Thus, they were shifted to the same side of the line as the First Nations. The Metis and non-status Indians were excluded from pursuing both kinds of claims, although the policy was later redefined in practice to allow the Metis in the Northwest Territories and non-status Indians in the Yukon to participate in the resolution of aboriginal title claims as long as they joined with the relevant band-based organization. Suddenly, the federal interpretation of its constitutional sphere had even more considerable consequences.

As the decade progressed, the anger of First Nations over the under-utilization of the federal legislative power grew. This sense of dissatisfaction was fanned by the ever-increasing role of the provinces, which was seen as a threat to the special relationship of registered Indians with the Queen as represented by the Government of Canada. The refusal of federal policy-makers to extend the same treatment to Metis and non-status Indians caused them to turn to the rising level of interest displayed by provincial governments. The response of the Inuit depended upon their specific circumstances.

The Inuit of northern Quebec welcomed that province's willingness to settle land claims and provide special legislation, services and funding. The Inuit in the Northwest Territories were unaffected by an expanding provincial role in aboriginal affairs, while the Inuit in Labrador had been the beneficiaries of just such a provincial attitude since 1954. The differences in reaction, especially between the southern First Nations on the one hand and non-status Indian and Metis organizations on the other, tended to foster further dissension.

Prime Minister Trudeau's bold plan to patriate the Constitution represented a turning point in the relationships among aboriginal groups, as well as in the federal-provincial-aboriginal triangle.[30]

POST 1982—IS THIS A NEW WORLD?

The political and legal situation has been altered dramatically, and perhaps irreversibly, by the *Constitution Act, 1982.* However, it has been exceedingly difficult for the non-aboriginal population and their governments to respond to the fundamental changes wrought by the new Constitution. Aboriginal issues have moved from the periphery to one of the feature side stages in both the public eye and the political arena. Although the First Ministers' Conference (FMC) process on aboriginal constitutional matters generated few results in the final analysis (despite the concentrated energy and heat from 1982 to 1987), the elevation in media attention to aboriginal issues during this period and subsequently has been unparalleled in this century. The presence of aboriginal leaders at an oval table surrounded by Minsters and First Minsters, with an image of a rough parity in importance, significantly revised the perceptions of both aboriginal and non-aboriginal people in Canada.

The former now expect and demand the attention of the country's senior political representatives as negotiators on subjects pressed upon them by Indian, Inuit and Metis associations. The general public has also shifted its attitudes away from favouring pure integration, and from seeing aboriginal peoples as simply another ethnic group within the cultural mosaic of Canada—a perception which would only permit aboriginal people to retain their heritage for artistic reasons and public display. Instead, popular opinion supports the concepts of self-government and land rights for this distinct society within Canada. Rather than attacking the legitimacy of aboriginal demands and even their place alongside First Ministers, or suggesting that this would lead the nation on the road to Balkanization, setting a dangerous precedent for which all other racial, religious and ethnic minority groups would clamber, the general reaction has been to accept the unique status of the original inhabitants of this country and pillory the federal and provincial governments for their unwillingness to be more forthcoming.

Although virtually all Ministers were critical of the longstanding unofficial FMC process being opened up to include aboriginal representatives, their beliefs as individuals were affected considerably by this five-year experience. During a matter of a few years, incredulity shifted to resistance, which moved to guarded support on the issue of aboriginal self-government. This development in thinking gave rise to the adoption of modest differences in approach regarding the ongoing programs and services which governments continued to deliver to aboriginal people on a daily basis. A new receptiveness existed for special initiatives in limited areas, as is evident by the creation of Indian child and family service agencies in many parts of the country.

On the issue of s.91(24), however, little changed. If anything, the FMC experience heightened provincial concerns about the dilution of the federal mandate. The subject became heavily influenced by a general strategy of the Government of Canada to restrain the growth of the federal deficit through reducing the size of transfer payments to the provinces in a variety of social service, post-secondary education and economic development areas.

The federal position regarding s.91(24) has been extensively revised since 1982 because of a number of influencing factors. The scope for legislative action has now been declared to be narrow, such that provincial co-operation is deemed to be required. The rationale for this new theory has not been clearly articulated. Although some might suggest that the *Charter of Rights and Freedoms* was the cause for this reduction in power, it appears that the prevailing interpretation is that s.25 of the Charter will likely blunt a full frontal attack on Parliament's legislative authority and the judiciary would endorse the basic reasoning of the Supreme Court of Canada a decade and a half ago in the *Lavell* case.[31]

Another explanation would be the effect of s.35(1) itself (i.e., that the recognition and affirmation of "existing aboriginal and treaty rights" reduce the room for federal action since Parliament cannot enact statutes that in any way conflict with these rights). The federal

Department of Justice, however, regularly asserts before Canadian courts that s.35 has no such effect. A more likely answer may be found as part of the generally enhanced desire for more amicable relations with the provinces. The development of an expanded base for delegated local government legislation for the Sechelt Band in British Columbia demonstrates the change in federal philosophy under the Mulroney Government; the legislation passed by Parliament[32] provided more limited powers than those granted by the *Cree-Naskapi (of Quebec) Act*[33] and those for all First Nations proposed in the *Indian Self-Government Act* of 1984.[34] The *Sechelt Act* was also designed in a way expressly to permit the legislature of British Columbia to enact a compatible statute to which the Sechelt Government could opt in, so as to obtain further municipal powers.[35] Part of the theory underlying this dual statute approach reflects a restrictive opinion of s.91(24).

Another subtle change occurred in treaty-making. The comprehensive claims policy inaugurated in 1973 did not truly demand the participation of willing provinces to negotiate aboriginal title settlements. However, the current ownership of most unoccupied land by the Crown in right of the province under s.109 of the *Constitution Act, 1867*, by virtue of the *Constitution Act, 1930*, or through specific Terms of Union, did suggest that provincial co-operation was necessary. With the advent of s.35, and especially after the amendment adding ss.(3), the Government of Canada argued that active provincial participation was essential in the negotiations and in ratification of any agreements reached. The basis for this argument was the assertion that final settlements generated rights that obtain constitutional affirmation, if not entrenchment, such that they indirectly had the effect of amending the Constitution. Federal officials argued that the government could not, and at the very least would not, create new treaty rights operating within any province without the express involvement and agreement of that provincial government. Thus, the political agreement reached in Ontario regarding treaty negotiations in the late 1800s had become national in scope and imperative in nature by the mid-1980s.

Tripartite action has become a major tenet in federal policy concerning all aboriginal people, although differences still remain. The Prime Minister announced during the 1985 FMC that he wished to embark upon self-government arrangements for the Metis and non-status Indians using a "bottom-up" approach. The subsequent articulation of this policy required the provincial government to initiate the negotiations by making a written request to the Minister of Justice. In addition, it was up to the province to set the budget for the participation of the aboriginal group, and the federal government would match the provincial contribution.

Tripartitism is not limited to the Metis and non-status Indians, as the Government of Canada has actively sought provincial involvement in issues affecting on-reserve Indians and the Inuit. At one stage the federal Minister declared in effect that provincial participation was essential concerning the Inuit south of the 60th parallel, as well as for status Indians off-reserve as they were outside exclusive federal responsibility. Although this statement was later revised, and provincial participation has not been compulsory, the thrust of federal policy in policing, child welfare, education, treaty land entitlement and other areas has concentrated upon achieving tripartite agreements in which the province would bear a share of the burden.

One aspect of the federal position has softened concerning non-status Indians. Major changes were introduced to the registration criteria through amendments to the *Indian Act* in 1985[36] that may result in over 100 000 people of Indian ancestry moving across into the status side of the dividing line. Although the reasons for this dramatic move included the coming into force of the *Charter* and Canada's international reputation being tarnished by the United Nations Human Rights Committee's decision in the *Lovelace* case,[37] the constitutional basis for the legislation was grounded in s.91(24). In other words, the Government of Canada asserted that it had the jurisdiction to expand the definition of what constituted a legal Indian because of its authority over constitutional Indians. The Metis, however, remained beyond the pale—as did many thousands of non-status Indians who still could not fit themselves within the "new and improved" registration criteria.[38]

A final variable, which will be discussed in more detail below, is the reluctant acceptance of a fiduciary role imposed upon the Minister of Indian and Northern Affairs by the Supreme Court of Canada in *Guerin v. The Queen*.[39] The initial federal reaction to the Court's decision in late 1984 was panic. This was replaced within a few months by a belief that the Department of Indian Affairs and Northern Development had to intensify governmental control over accountability demands from First Nations in order to prevent new instances in which the Crown's agents were breaching this fiduciary obligation. At the same time, the official policy favoured Indian self-government, the transfer of more responsibility directly to First Nations, and the downsizing of the Department of Indian Affairs and Northern Development so as to reduce federal expenditures and comply with the overall policy platform of the Conservative Party regarding the size of the public service as a whole.

The provinces' perspectives became more diverse on several facets of this field. Concerns over federal cost-cutting and off-loading began to dominate provincial thinking more and more during the 1980s. It became financially attractive to assert ever more vigorously that the federal government had a broad mandate under s.91(24) and that this authority encompassed all aboriginal people. Alberta stood alone in maintaining that the Metis were not subjects for federal power, in order to defend that province's authority over the remaining Metis settlements. Quebec was also not anxious to see any expansion in federal influence within its provincial borders; however, it generally preferred not to partake of these debates.

In practice, the provinces pursued a less homogeneous philosophy. The habits and beliefs of the 1970s have proved to be quite enduring. The on-reserve/off-reserve dichotomy has remained very much a driving force in provincial thinking. Some provinces continue to argue that they have no authority whatsoever on-reserve in their own right, but merely can be involved upon request on a fee-for-service basis. Other provinces suggest that they have a rightful role to play, but solely by virtue of the existence of s.88 and the exercise of their own discretionary power. A few believe that they share a responsibility to on-reserve communities with the Government of Canada.

In the off-reserve setting, no provincial government has suggested that it is without power or jurisdiction. The debate has ranged between one position—that suggests the provinces have exclusive legislative jurisdiction with the federal government bearing financial obligations, the magnitude of which is the subject of negotiation—to an assertion that the entire field should be shared both in terms of legislative and financial responsibilities.

There has been nothing approaching a uniform position on the aboriginal side, although there have been striking instances of solidarity among almost all groups. The drive for self-determination minimized the calls for federal legislative action in a substantive sense. First Nations and tribal councils instead began to seek a federal occupation of the field followed by a withdrawal. The concept underlying this strategy is that traditional or contemporized Indian law would fill the so-called legal vacuum, thereby expanding the authority of the First Nations' governments. In effect, the federal enclave theory would be revamped and restored such that provincial law would be effectively ousted by the federal presence in specific subject areas, and could not re-enter in the wake of the federal withdrawal.

A more satisfactory approach for some is to achieve a constitutional amendment recognizing the inherent right of self-government as a continuing vestige of the sovereign status of the original rulers of the land. This, of course, requires support from Parliament as well as seven of 10 provincial legislatures. Not only is this anathema to some of the First Ministers, but many of the Indian supporters of this objective reject any role for the provinces in the amendment formula when it comes to approving this right. Other Indian leaders who favour constitutional recognition of the inherent right to self-government are prepared to take a long-term perspective, in which they will continue their efforts to persuade a sufficient number of First Ministers to endorse such an amendment.

While virtually all First Nations regularly reaffirm the special relationship they possess with the Crown in right of Canada, there is a clear division of views regarding the proper role for the provinces. While a few wish no contact whatsoever, many are entering into tripartite arrangements. A growing number of First Nations are also negotiating straight bilateral agreements with provinces as well as "double bilateral" ones, in which the First Nation has a direct agreement with the provincial government and a separate yet compatible one with the federal Department of Indian Affairs and Northern Development.

The drive for expanded autonomy has generated a concomitant lessening of the desire to define the Department of Indian Affairs and Northern Development as guardian and trustee. On the other hand, the *Guerin* case has raised the profile of the fiduciary obligation in the political arena in a way that may appear to contradict a push for enhanced self-determination. It has become an added club in the arsenal that consisted of aboriginal and treaty rights before, and is used to pressure the federal government to act in accordance with policies promoted by First Nations' leaders. The actual resolution of this contradiction remains below the surface of the debate and as of yet, can only be dimly seen.

The other aboriginal groups do not have as many cards to play in this high-stakes poker game. They have yet to be accepted by the Government of Canada as being the beneficiaries of either a special relationship or a fiduciary obligation. They also do not possess a significant faction that might be labelled "hardliners" when it comes to dealing with provincial governments or in aggressively pursuing a sovereignty position. Therefore, they willingly solicit bilateral arrangements with provinces and tripartite agreements including the federal government.

SECTION 91(24) AND THE FIDUCIARY OBLIGATION

The fiduciary concept is closely related to the law of trusts, although there are some important distinctions.[40] One becomes a fiduciary in relation to another person by holding a special expertise (e.g., as a stockbroker, financial advisor or lawyer); or through acquiring property of another subject to particular obligations (e.g., for its protection); or because of a special relationship between the parties. The essential concept has been described by Professor Weinrib in these terms:

> [Where there is a fiduciary obligation] there is a relation in which the principal's interests can be affected by, and are therefore dependent on, the manner in which the fiduciary uses the discretion which has been delegated to him. The fiduciary obligation is the law's blunt tool for the control of this discretion.[41]

Later he states that "the hallmark of a fiduciary relation is that the relative legal positions are such that one party is at the mercy of the other's discretion."[42] After quoting these passages, Mr. Justice Dickson went on to say in *Guerin v. The Queen*:

> I make no comment upon whether this description is broad enough to embrace all fiduciary obligations. I do agree, however, that where by statute, agreement, or perhaps by unilateral undertaking, one party has an obligation to act for the benefit of another, and that obligation carries with it a discretionary power, the party thus empowered becomes a fiduciary. Equity will then supervise the relationship by holding him to the fiduciary's strict standard of conduct.[43]

The courts have only been articulating this doctrine over the past two decades (although its roots are centuries old), and in so doing they have been drawing a distinction between it and the position of express and constructive trustees, who form a particular class of fiduciaries. Analogous to the doctrine of unjust enrichment, the judiciary has stated that neither the list of fiduciaries is closed nor the scope of the obligations incurred. The law has intentionally evolved in a way that has placed a premium upon maintaining flexibility in the application of fiduciary obligations, so as to accommodate new situations that arise in the pursuit of achieving equity and justice.

When it comes to applying this concept in relation to aboriginal people, many uncertainties arise. The Supreme Court of Canada was divided in the *Guerin* case on several points. Due to illness, Chief Justice Laskin did not participate in the decision, leaving a bench of eight to render judgment. Mr. Justice Estey wrote a decision in which he concurred in the result but did so relying on agency principles with only minimal comments upon the contents of the other judgments. Mr. Justice Dickson wrote the leading decision on behalf of three other justices; however, it did not truly reflect a majority opinion (i.e., for it represented the opinion of four of eight judges only). It was he who concluded that the Crown undertook a fiduciary obligation which was actionable when it was breached. Madam Justice Wilson (on behalf of two concurring judges) asserted that a trust had been created, the terms of which had been violated by the conduct of the Department of Indian Affairs and Northern Development officials in handling the conditional surrender of on-reserve land for a golf course by the Musqueum Band of Vancouver.

Although the Dickson view has received most of the scholarly comment[44] and has been accepted as the prevailing law in subsequent cases,[45] one should realize that the Supreme Court has not resolved this conflict. The Wilson position can also still be argued to be a correct statement of the law. The subtleties of this debate, and the precise reasoning of the Court in the *Guerin* case, go beyond the scope of this chapter. Instead, it will be used as the point of departure to identify a number of questions left unresolved by the courts to date, and as a source of speculation for possible developments in the future.

Although we now know that a fiduciary obligation (or trust) exists, we are unsure who qualifies as beneficiaries under this relationship. It is obvious that bands recognized under the *Indian Act* are in this position as collective entities, but does the relationship also extend to individual band members? A strong argument could be made that they do so benefit, at least concerning trust account funds held for them personally and administered by the Department of Indian Affairs and Northern Development. Could individuals also sue the Crown in right of Canada for their personal losses as members of a band when its collective proprietary assets are improperly diminished? Does the relationship extend to encompass services, as opposed to personalty or realty, provided to band members on an individual basis, for example, regarding health care or post-secondary education? We also do not yet know if the federal government has fiduciary obligations in relation to unrecognized Indian bands, to the Inuit, the Metis or non-status Indians.

The majority of the Supreme Court does appear to have endorsed the view expressed by Mr. Justice Dickson that the "interest of an Indian band in a reserve rather than with unrecognized aboriginal title in traditional tribal lands ... is the same in both cases."[46] Thus, he observed that the Indian "interest in their lands is a pre-existing legal right not created by Royal Proclamation, by s.18(1) of the *Indian Act*, or by any other executive order or legislative provision."[47] This approach views aboriginal title at common law as equivalent to the Indian interest in reserve lands, although certain special benefits are attached to reserve lands which are also subject to a separate management scheme pursuant to the terms of the *Indian Act*.[48] This position can give rise to an argument that the fiduciary obligation extends to other aboriginal groups.

Dickson and Wilson JJ. both rejected the existence of an *enforceable* trust with respect to unsurrendered reserve lands. It appears arguable, however, that some other form of equitable obligation may exist. Madam Justice Wilson spoke of a fiduciary obligation existing over reserve lands that is not crystallized until a surrender is made to the Crown. Mr. Justice Dickson is at some pains to declare that aboriginal title alone is insufficient to create this special relationship. He puts it this way:

> The fiduciary relationship between the Crown and the Indians has its roots in the concept of aboriginal, native or Indian title. The fact that Indian bands have a certain interest in lands does not, however, in itself give rise to a fiduciary relationship between the Indians and the Crown. The conclusion that the Crown is a fiduciary depends upon a further proposition that the Indian interest in the land is inalienable except upon surrender to the Crown.[49]

The restraint on the alienability of aboriginal title is thus a central element to his reasoning. This restriction has been developed by the common law and elaborated in all instances in which aboriginal title has been discussed regarding a specific group. Inalienability has been held to apply as well to the Inuit interest in land,[50] and would presumably be present in any case in which a Metis or non-status Indian group was declared to possess aboriginal title.

Although both Dickson and Wilson JJ. fastened upon the surrender provisions of the *Indian Act*, the former suggests that this is a descendant of a responsibility first taken upon itself by the Crown in the *Royal Proclamation of 1763*. It would be possible for a court to conclude in the future that traditional lands of any aboriginal group that are subject to aboriginal title will give rise to fiduciary duties on the Crown when the lands are surrendered pursuant to the Royal Proclamation procedure (if it still exists after the Ontario Court of Appeal decision in the *Temagami* case[51]), or through some other mechanism such as the comprehensive claims procedure. It is possible that the relationship may exist in general, but not create enforceable duties until aboriginal rights are being surrendered, expropriated, extinguished or otherwise violated.

Thus, we are unsure as to who benefits, when the obligation becomes operational, precisely how it arises, and what lands or other objects fall within its net. We are also uncertain as to who is the fiduciary. The initial assumption was that s.91(24) did not create any fiduciary obligations but served merely to designate the Government of Canada as the fiduciary. Even this early belief did not answer the question as to whether it was the Minister of Indian and Northern Affairs who obtained this fortunate position alone, or if he or she shared it with the other members of the Executive Branch.

Professor Bartlett has argued that the obligation attaches to the Crown rather than to any individual minister, which is a view that I share. He also stated that:

> It is suggested that the Crown in right of Canada and in right of the Province may both be liable for breach of the fiduciary obligation in the event of the non-fulfillment of conditions attached to a surrender. Liability vests, of course, in the Crown, *not* merely the Crown in right of Canada or Crown in right of the Province. The liability of the Crown in right of Canada arises per se from the non-fulfillment of the conditions attached to the surrender in spite of the assurances and promises made by the Crown in right of Canada. The liability of the Crown in right of the Province arises upon its failure to perform its fiduciary obligation, by ensuring that the conditions of surrender are met.[52]

Although he provides no explanation for this statement, he is probably relying upon the fact that it is the provincial Crown which benefits from the surrender, at least when the land is for sale, in that its underlying title becomes complete with the disappearance of the burden of the Indian interest. Although there is no case law on this point, and the Supreme Court in *Guerin* was only dealing with a claim against the federal government, the judgments do not imply a limitation of the duty to the Crown in right of Canada alone. It is perhaps easier to understand this shared responsibility when it is recalled that the Court did not distinguish between reserve and non-reserve lands such that the fiduciary obligation could crystallize upon the surrender of either.

The Supreme Court has also left us wondering what is the scope of remedies available when a duty has been breached by a fiduciary. Damages clearly can lie, as the Court restored the trial judgment of $10 million plus post-judgment interest. Presumably, a declaratory order would also always be available. Does a wronged beneficiary have the ability to obtain an injunction to block an anticipated breach? Can an accounting be demanded for the proceeds of the sale or lease of any assets? Can the fiduciary be ordered to return assets still in the Crown's possession or purchase equivalent ones? The sole guidance one can glean from the *Guerin* decision emanates from Mr. Justice Dickson's references to the validity of making analogies with the principles of trust law on several occasions. This suggests that all remedies available against a private trustee who is in breach should exist in favour of the aboriginal beneficiary. It is hard to imagine, however, that our courts would direct a fiduciary who is also a lawmaker to legislate in a certain way to avoid making, or to rectify a breach of such an obligation.

It must also be remembered that the Supreme Court was dealing with a conditional surrender that was conducted in 1957. As such, the impact of the *Constitution Act, 1982* was not an issue even though the Court delivered its judgment in late 1984. Has the new Constitution altered this legal position? I think that it has. Far from eliminating this fiduciary obligation, it is possible to assert that this duty has been recognized as a component of "existing aboriginal and treaty rights" within s.35(1). The language of the judgment grounding this obligation in aboriginal title and its inalienability except to the Crown suggests that it is an aspect of aboriginal rights that clearly "existed" in 1982. It is also possible that many treaties are analogous to the surrender that was before the Supreme Court, at least when they involve land cessions, such that the Crown has undertaken to act as a fiduciary in fulfilling the promises made in these treaties. The position of peace and friendship treaties is less certain, in that the commitments made by the Crown are less susceptible to being characterized as fiduciary obligations.

It would also logically follow that this relationship would come within the parameters of the shield created by s.25 in reference to the rest of the *Charter of Rights and Freedoms*. It could again be characterized as an aboriginal right, a treaty right, or as falling within the undefined category of "other rights and freedoms" within s.25. This position is further buttressed by the import placed on the *Royal Proclamation of 1763*, which is specifically identified in s.25(a), by Mr. Justice Dickson in the *Guerin* case.

There is, of course, a contrary view that would suggest that no fiduciary obligation has any legal significance, if it even exists at all, until it is crystallized by a surrender pursuant to the terms of the *Indian Act*. This opinion would hold that the duty is not an aspect of aboriginal title or aboriginal rights per se, but rather is created in recognition of that special interest in land. In other words, it flows from aboriginal title but is not an incident of that proprietary interest. Furthermore, it only comes to fruition when the Crown makes particular commitments pursuant to the terms of a specific surrender, such that the fiduciary obligation is not captured by any of the language used in either s.25 or s.35(1).

The decisions of Dickson and Wilson JJ. do not give clear direction on this point. There are passages that could be cited which provide ammunition for each position. It is clear, however, that the Crown cannot seek to defend its position by relying solely upon the precise terms of any surrender, as Mr. Justice Dickson stated:

> While the existence of the fiduciary obligation which the Crown owes to the Indians is dependent on the nature of the surrender process, the standard of conduct which the obligation imports is both more general and more exacting than the terms of any particular surrender.[53]

If the fiduciary relationship has been "recognized and affirmed" as "existing aboriginal and treaty rights" within s.35(1), then what are the possible implications? It would likely mean that any attempt expressly to eliminate fiduciary obligations by statute would be unconstitutional. Further, any attempt to amend s.25 or s.35(1) so as to exclude this obligation from their scope would be legally possible, although perhaps not attractive in political terms. Such a move would also obviously trigger s.35.1, resulting in the need for the Prime Minister to convene a FMC to debate the draft resolution.

Whether Parliament may amend the *Indian Act* so as to alter provisions that have an impact on this duty depends on the ultimate judicial interpretation of the impact of s.35(1). The question is whether this section only recognizes the status quo in which Parliament is free to revise the *Indian Act* at will, while overriding aboriginal and treaty rights through general legislation; or does Part II signal an alteration of the prior jurisprudence such that, at the very least, it protects those rights which have survived from further diminution or regulation, if s.35 does not restore them to their original vigour. We must await the outcome of cases like *Sparrow v. The Queen*[54] before we have any final judicial guidance on this point.

Can the federal government transfer this fiduciary obligation to the provinces? My initial reaction is negative, based on analogies with the private law of trusts and fiduciaries, in the absence of express consent by the beneficiaries of the obligation. However, this may be possible because of the unique nature of the relationship. The obligation attaches to the Crown directly such that it could be argued that a transfer from one sovereign representative of the Queen to another generates no change in substance to the content of the obligation nor to the nature of any remedies for its breach, so that the position of the beneficiary is unaffected. After all, this situation is *sui generis*, and it would be difficult to imagine that the Canadian judiciary would wish to assert the right to sanction such a transfer as they do when a sole trustee retires or dies without an express power of choosing a successor.

Can the federal government share this fiduciary obligation with a province? I agree with Professor Bartlett in concluding that in certain circumstances both the Crown in right of Canada and the Crown in right of the Province are fiduciaries, although their precise duties may differ.

Can the Government of Canada eliminate its role as a fiduciary with the consent of its aboriginal beneficiaries? I would again draw a parallel with the common law and conclude that this is possible. Any trust or fiduciary obligation can be terminated when the beneficiary agrees, so long as this party has full knowledge of the consequences of this action. One aspect of the private law which may give rise to some concern is that termination cannot occur without judicial approval when the rights or interests of infants and the unborn are involved. Since aboriginal people usually acquire their participation in collective rights upon birth, it is possible that a court might conclude some day that adults are unable to consent to the extinguishment of this fiduciary relationship on behalf of their minor children and generations yet to come into existence.

The uncertainty surrounding these questions indicates that one can expect significantly more litigation. The U.S. courts have been elaborating a federal-Indian trust doctrine for over a century and a half, yet there are still many unresolved issues. We can hardly expect to settle them all in one or a handful of lawsuits.

It is also possible that the fiduciary relationship in conjunction with s.35 may have an impact upon s.91(24). It may create a more proactive obligation on the Government of Canada in which it must seek to "affirm" aboriginal and treaty rights through suitable means. Although legislative action may not be imposed, executive action might take place. For example, a court might declare that it is a violation of s.91(24) responsibility and a breach of a fiduciary obligation for the Department of Indian Affairs and Northern Development to refuse to negotiate comprehensive land claims with more than six aboriginal groups at a time, thereby causing a backlog for decades. Likewise, it could be a similar violation to fail to resolve expeditiously the presence of hundreds if not thousands of specific claims regarding reserve lands.

This intersection of two constitutional provisions and a private law concept derived from equity could result in a more proactive fiduciary obligation on the federal government to deal more extensively with the needs of Metis and non-status Indian people. Is it a breach of a fiduciary obligation for the Government of Canada to refuse to protect even the alleged rights to land of the Metis, if they are in fact beneficiaries of such a relationship? Would it be a violation of duty for the Attorney General of Canada to intervene to oppose a land claim of an aboriginal group that is brought only against a provincial government?

In other words, even if s.91(24) provided a discretionary power to legislate prior to 1982, it still possessed within it a restraint not to violate aboriginal interests as part of mandatory fiduciary duties once those duties had become concrete in a given situation. It is conceivable that as a result of the *Constitution Act, 1982*, the former discretionary authority has been slightly transformed so as to be subject to some active duties. The nature of these obligations might be similar to those imposed upon a trustee regarding the necessity to take action to preserve and protect trust assets, as well as to maintain the beneficiary at an appropriate standard of living.

Could it ever extend further to include an obligation to legislate? Such a proposition would be idiocy bordering on heresy within a Diceyan view of parliamentary supremacy. Nevertheless, our world, including our constitutional law and structure, has fundamentally changed in a way that we could not have ever imagined only 20 years ago. It is thus unwise to preclude the possibility of further dramatic and surprising changes in our jurisprudence in the future.

Finally, what of the Charter itself? Section 15 is already having a significant effect upon our legislation and on societal thinking. It probably will not obstruct special federal and provincial legislation or programs as long as they can be defined as reaffirming the identity and promoting the advancement of aboriginal people.

In addition, s.15(1) imposes obligations on governments of a non-fiduciary nature that cannot be ignored. This could require provinces, such as Saskatchewan, to deliver services on reserves that have been previously refused on the basis that it was a federal responsibility. This could create an interesting new possibility for a federal government anxious to offload some of its financial burdens. The Department of Indian Affairs and Northern Development could reduce its contribution or refuse to pay at all for programs and services provided on reserves, and then turn around and sue the provinces for failing to provide equal benefits to those available for other provincial residents. Perhaps it will be the provincial governments that will argue for a broad interpretation of fiduciary obligations regarding aboriginal people. Odder things have happened. After all, 100 years ago the Government of Canada was in court asserting that aboriginal title was the same as the fee simple interest in property law, while the troops left Toronto to crush the Riel Rebellion. Politics uses law as a tool in making strange bedfellows.

Thus, we can anticipate much uncertainty, extensive arguments, frequent litigation and unusual developments in these issues over the next few years. The future will not be dull.

Notes

1. *Guerin v. The Queen*, [1984] 2 S.C.R. 335, (1984) 13 D.L.R. (4th) 321 (S.C.C.).
2. Enacted by the *Canada Act*, 1982 (U.K.) c.11, Sched. B.
3. R.S.C. 1985; formerly *British North America Act* (1867) c.3 (U.K.) 30-31 Vic.
4. *An Act providing for the Organisation of the Department of the Secretary of State of Canada, and for the management of Indian and Ordinance Lands*, S.C. 1868, c.42, 31 Vict.
5. *An Act for the Better Protection of the Lands and Property of the Indians in Lower Canada*, S.C. 1850, c.42, 13 and 14 Vic; and *An Act for the protection of Indians in Upper Canada from imposition, and the property occupied or enjoyed by them from trespass and injury*, S.C. 1850, c.74, 13 and 14 Vic.
6. *St. Catherines' Milling and Lumber Co. v. The Queen* (1889) 14 A.C. 46 (J.C.P.C.), aff'g. (1887) 13 S.C.R. 577.
7. *Dominion of Canada v. Province of Ontario* (1910), A.C. 637 (J.C.P.C.). See also *Attorney General for Canada v. Attorney General for Ontario* (1897), A.C. 199 (J.C.P.C.).
8. One still does not have to be a band member or a registered Indian to be eligible to be elected as chief, *Indian Act*, R.S.C. 1970, c.I-6, s.75(2).
9. See, e.g., Canada: *The Historical Development of the Indian Act* (Ottawa: Department of Indian Affairs and Northern Development, 1978).
10. See, e.g., *Indian Act*, S.C. 1876, c.18; *Indian Act*, R.S.C. 1886, c.43; and notes 4 and 5, *supra*.
11. Formerly, *An Act to amend and continue the Act 32-33 Victoria Charter 3; and to establish and provide for the Government of the Province of Manitoba*, 1870, c.3 (Can.) 33 Vic.
12. *The Metis Population Betterment Act*, S.A. 1938, c.6
13. For further information see J. Sawchuck, Sawchuk and Ferguson, *Metis Land Rights in Alberta: A Political History* (Edmonton: Metis Association of Alberta, 1981) and F. Martin, "Federal and Provincial Responsibility in the Metis Settlements of Alberta," elsewhere in this book.
14. See, e.g., *An Act for the settlement of certain questions between the Governments of Canada and Ontario respecting Indian Reserve Lands*, S.C. 1924, c.48 and *The Indian Lands Act, 1924*, S.O. 1924, c.15.
15. See, e.g., *An Act respecting hunting and fishing rights in the James Bay and New Quebec Territories*, S.Q. 1978, c.92.
16. *Rex rel. Gibb v. White* (1870) 5 P.R. 315 (Ont).
17. *R. v. Hill* (1907) 15 O.L.R. 11 (C.A.).
18. For a detailed discussion of electoral laws see R.H. Bartlett, "Citizens Minus: Indians and The Right to Vote," (1979) 44 Sask. L.R. 163.
19. *Indian Act*, S.C. 1927, c.32, s.6 consolidated as R.S.C. 1927, c.98, s.141 made it an offence to receive, request or solicit funds for "the prosecution of any claim" for the benefit of the band. This provision was repealed in 1951.
20. *Canadian Bill of Rights*, R.S.C. 1960, c.44; R.S.C. 1970, Appendix III.
21. Note 18, *supra*.
22. For a thorough description of this development see, Nin.Da.Waab.Jig, *Walpole Island: The Struggle for Self-Sufficiency*, Occasional Paper No. 3, (1984); and Nin.Da.Waab.Jig, *Walpole Island: The Soul of Indian Territory*, (Walpole Island, 1987).

23. For an excellent discussion of this area see, Patrick Johnston, *Native children and the child welfare system* (Toronto: Canadian Council on Social Development in association with James Lorimar & Co., 1983).

24. *The Department of Indian Affairs and Northern Development Act*, R.S.C. 1970, c.1-7.

25. Canada: *Statement of the Government of Canada on Indian Policy,* (Ottawa, 1969).

26. See, e.g., *Cardinal v. Attorney General of Alberta*, [1974] S.C.R. 695; and *Four B Manufacturing v. United Garment Workers* (1979) 102 D.L.R. (3d) 385 (S.C.C.).

27. *Reference re Eskimos*, [1939] S.C.R. 104; 2 D.L.R. 417.

28. For an excellent discussion of the White Paper and its aftermath see, R. Gibbins and R. Ponting, *Out of Irrelevance: A Social Political Introduction to Indian Affairs in Canada* (Toronto: Butterworths, 1980); and S. Weaver, *Making Canadian Indian Policy: The Hidden Agenda 1968-1970* (Toronto: University of Toronto Press, 1981).

29. *Calder et al v. Attorney General of British Columbia*, [1973] S.C.R. 313.

30. For a discussion of the patriation fight see, M. Valpy, *The National Deal: The Fight for a Canadian Constitution.* (Toronto: Fleet Books, 1982); and K. Banting and R. Simeon (eds.) *And No One Cheered: Federalism, Democracy and the Constitution Act* (Toronto: Methuen, 1982).

31. *Lavell v. Attorney General of Canada* and *Isaac v. Bedard* (1974) 38 D.L.R. (3d) 481 (S.C.C.).

32. *Sechelt Indian Band Self-Government Act*, S.C. 1986, c.27.

33. *Cree-Naskapi (of Quebec) Act*, S.C. 1984, c.18.

34. Bill C-47.

35. *Sechelt Indian Government District Enabling Act*, S.B.C. 1987. See, also, the chapter by John Taylor and Gary Paget in this book.

36. *An Act to Amend the Indian Act*, S.C. 1985, c.27, still largely known as Bill C-31.

37. *Lovelace v. Canada*, [1981] 1 Canadian Human Rights Y. B. 305.

38. For an elaboration of the many issues involved see Bradford Morse and Robert Groves, "Canada's Forgotten Peoples: The Aboriginal Rights of Metis and Non-Status Indians" 2 *Law & Anthropology* (1987) 139.

39. Note 1, *supra*.

40. For a general review of these discussions see, D. W. M. Waters, *The Law of Trusts in Canada*, 2d ed. (Agincourt, Ont: Carswell Co., 1984); M. Ellis, *Fiduciary Duties in Canada* (Don Mills, Ontario: De Boo Ltd., 1988); and J. C. Shepherd, *The Law of Fiduciaries* (Toronto: Carswell, 1981).

41. E. Weinrib, "The Fiduciary Obligation," 25 U.T.L.J. (1975) 1 at p. 4.

42. *Ibid.* at p. 7.

43. Note 1, *supra*, at p. 341.

44. See, e.g., D. Johnston, "A Theory of Crown Trust Towards Aboriginal Peoples," 18 . L.R. (1986) 307; R. Bartlett, "You Can't Trust the Crown: The Fiduciary Obligation of the Crown to the Indians: *Guerin v. The Queen*," 49 Sask. L.R. (1984-1985) 367.

45. *Kruger et al. v. The Queen* (1985) 17 D.L.R. (4th) 591 (F.C.A.); and *Apsassin et al v. The Queen in Right of Canada* (1987) 37 D.L.R. (4th) 257 (F.C.T.D.).

46. Note 1, *supra*, at p. 337.

47. *Ibid*, at p. 336.

48. See Bartlett, note 44, *supra*, for an attack on the inappropriateness of this aspect of the judgment.

49. Note 1, *supra*, at p. 334.

50. *Hamlet of Baker Lake v. Minister of Indian Affairs and Northern Development* (1979) 107 D.L.R. (3d) 513 (F.C.T.D.).

51. *Bear Island Foundation v. Attorney General of Ontario et al.*, as of yet unreported, February 27, 1989.

52. Note 44, *supra*, at p.374.

53. Note 1, *supra*, at p. 344.

54. *Sparrow v. The Queen* (1987) 36 D.L.R. (4th) 246; appeal and cross-appeal argued before the Supreme Court of Canada on November 3, 1988 and decision reserved at the time of writing.

CHAPTER 4
FISCAL ARRANGEMENTS FOR ABORIGINAL SELF-GOVERNMENT

David C. Hawkes
Allan M. Maslove

INTRODUCTION

Fiscal arrangements for aboriginal self-government are not hypothetical or abstract matters. At this very moment, negotiations are proceeding with regard to the appropriate type of fiscal arrangement for different forms of self-government. Fiscal arrangements are already in place for the James Bay Cree and Naskapi, for the Northeastern Quebec Inuit, as well as for the Sechelt peoples in British Columbia. In addition, alternative funding agreements continue to be negotiated between the Department of Indian Affairs and Northern Development and Indian band governments. Community self-government negotiations, which are now at the framework-proposal and agreement stage, are underway in over forty communities. In the next few years a sustained effort is anticipated to achieve constitutional recognition for aboriginal self-government; as a result, policy development with respect to the accompanying fiscal arrangements is required now.

Federal negotiations to date appear to have been driven largely by considerations of the specific public functions in question and by the constraints of ministerial responsibility. Block funding to band governments has fallen into non-federal financial areas or where federal interests are more relaxed. However, such an approach lacks an appreciation of the forms of aboriginal self-government that will be implied by these arrangements. This chapter provides the necessary perspective from which to view fiscal negotiations. It also develops a policy framework to link fiscal arrangements negotiated between the governments and aboriginal communities to the emerging arrangements for aboriginal self-government.

The underlying premise of the essay is that three sets of considerations are (or should be) linked in exploring these issues. The first is the aboriginal self-government arrangement or model, specifically the amount of local autonomy the arrangement embodies. The second is the form of the fiscal arrangements which must support and be consistent with the self-government provisions. The third set of factors, which is more in the nature of a background consideration or constraint, is the level of community development (economic and political or administrative) into which these arrangements are to be introduced.

The chapter is divided into seven main sections. Following this introduction, we discuss several important aspects of government-aboriginal relations that condition both self-government and fiscal arrangements, including constitutional issues and the question of ministerial responsibility. The third section deals with the respective responsibilities of the federal and provincial governments to the aboriginal peoples, and with their intergovernmental relations. The fourth section presents a conceptual framework for the design of fiscal arrangements and offers typologies of the three basic sets of considerations. In the fifth section, the principles for fiscal arrangements are elaborated, as are the interrelationships (trade-offs) among them. The sixth section applies the framework to self-government without a land base. The final section develops some of the major conclusions that emerge from the analysis. In the Appendix, several existing and proposed self-governing arrangements are briefly summarized within the context of the three sets of primary considerations discussed in the chapter.

FEDERAL-ABORIGINAL AND PROVINCIAL-ABORIGINAL RELATIONS

To develop a policy framework for fiscal arrangements and aboriginal self-government, it is important to place the topic in its larger context—the Canadian federal system. Key aspects of the relationship between aboriginal peoples and Canadian governments, aspects which bear upon this policy framework, are legal, constitutional and intergovernmental. It is impossible to understand the fiduciary, or trust, relationship, and its impact upon ministerial responsibility, without knowledge of aboriginal rights and the Crown. Recent constitutional changes, such as the newly entrenched Canadian *Charter of Rights and Freedoms*, affect the obligations of federal and provincial governments toward aboriginal peoples. These obligations, in turn, are brought to bear upon the roles and responsibilities of federal and provincial governments, a situation which leads to the crucial subject of federal and provincial financing of programs and services for aboriginal peoples in Canada. It is to this larger context that we now turn.

Aboriginal Rights and the Crown

The legal root of aboriginal rights lies in the right of aboriginal title, the relationship to land of the indigenous inhabitants of this country. The existence of aboriginal title as an independent legal interest in land predates the *Royal Proclamation of 1763* (aboriginal lands were not taken in conquest nor, except through the treaty process, voluntarily surrendered). This, combined with the British Crown's undertaking in the Proclamation (and in subsequent legislation) of a responsibility to protect Indian interests from exploitation, gives rise to the fiduciary relationship (that of trust, as in a guardian or a trustee) in relation to land dealings. It is important to note in this regard that the Indian interest in land is an independent legal interest, and not a creation of either the legislative or the executive branches of government.

This is the import of the Supreme Court decision in the *Guerin* case in 1984.[1] The Court found the Crown liable if it fails in its performance of its fiduciary duties (the case involved the lease of reserve lands). Brian Slattery commented upon the implications of the decision for federal and provincial governments. Since aboriginal title is a legal right that can be extinguished only by native consent (or, in Slattery's view, by legislation although this appears to be clearly at odds with the main thrust of the *Guerin* decision), the burden of proof shifts to federal and provincial governments. They must show that aboriginal land rights were lawfully extinguished in the past, or acknowledge their continuing existence. Where the rights were wiped out by legislation, the decision implies that compensation should have been paid. [2]

In reviewing the Crown's historical relationship with aboriginal peoples, Slattery provides the following summary. The Crown, in offering its protection to aboriginal peoples, accepted that they would retain their lands, as well as their political and cultural institutions and customary laws, unless the terms of treaty ruled this out or legislation was enacted to the contrary. Aboriginal groups would retain a measure of internal autonomy, allowing them to govern themselves, subject to the overriding authority of Parliament. [3] Local law was held to remain in force in the absence of Acts to the contrary. In return, aboriginal peoples renounced the use of force to defend themselves and were required to maintain allegiance to the Crown, to abide by her laws and to keep the peace.

It should be noted that opinion on the interpretation of the *Guerin* decision is not unanimous and that some would disagree with Slattery's analysis. In a sense, the Slattery interpretation presents a worst-case scenario with respect to the decision's impact upon aboriginal self-government and ministerial responsibility. For purposes of argument, however, temporarily adopting Slattery's interpretation should not cause the reader any problem since the *Guerin* decision appears to have had no negative consequences regarding ministerial responsibility, self-government and fiscal arrangements.

Ministerial Responsibility

Concern has been expressed that the trust responsibility could limit the federal government's options with respect to self-government and fiscal arrangements. The worry is about the relationship among the fiduciary responsibility, ministerial responsibility and financial accountability, and flows, in part, from a particular interpretation of the *Guerin* decision. The more autonomous that self-government arrangements and Indian-federal government fiscal arrangements become, the less influence and control the minister and department will have over the conduct of Indian government programs and services. The fear is that this system could leave the minister and the department exposed to a *Guerin*-style challenge, should the newly self-governing Indian communities fumble their new responsibilities. If, in the unlikely situation that an Indian government goes bankrupt, or is unable to deliver basic services after becoming self-governing, is the minister or federal government responsible, or has the minister defaulted in his fiduciary duty?

Those who answer these questions in the affirmative, base their argument on the *Guerin* case in which the Minister was found to be negligent in fulfiling his fiduciary responsibility with respect to the lease of Indian lands in British Columbia. Officials from the Department of Indian Affairs and Northern Development, in their capacity as trustee of Indian lands, entered into a lease arrangement with a third party which was economically disadvantageous to the Indian band in question. Although aware of the negotiations, the Indian band was not informed or involved in the negotiation of the lease arrangement and discovered only later that they had been poorly served by their trustees. The court action was initiated thereafter.

In our view, the *Guerin* situation is not analogous to that which would prevail with Indian self-government and the corollary fiscal arrangements. The situations are different in several respects. First, these arrangements will be entered into with the consent of the Indian people concerned and will require community ratification. Second, these arrangements are being requested by Indian people and are designed to provide a greater measure of self-determination to Indian people. This, arguably, is the proper exercise of the fiduciary responsibility of the federal government. Finally, in entering into self-government and fiscal agreements, the minister is devolving such responsibilities as are covered by the agreements to the people themselves. With self-government comes responsibility and accountability to the community.

This is not to say that if a disaster occurs, the minister will not receive a call. But, in a sense, it would be "politics as usual" in such a case. It would be similar to a situation in a single industry town where the only industry closes (e.g., Uranium City in Saskatchewan) or to a situation in which an entire community is flooded. In these situations, the federal government has responded, although the discretion to do so rests with the government.

The Impact of the Canadian *Charter of Rights and Freedoms*

The impact of the *Charter* on aboriginal peoples and federal-provincial relations is only now beginning to become clear. Oddly enough, much of the clarity has come not through the discrete issue of aboriginal rights, but through a court case involving the public funding of separate schools in Ontario. Bill 30 proposed amendments to the Ontario *Education Act* which, among other effects, would extend full public funding for Roman Catholic separate schools. At issue was the application of the *Charter*'s new constitutional rights of equality and freedom of religion upon the provisions of s.93 of the Constitution, which permitted provinces to legislate *unequally* in order to give effect to the "powers, privileges and duties" of separate schools at the time of Confederation.[4]

In its ruling on the case, the Supreme Court rendered a decision which spoke to the relationship between individual and collective rights, and how they *do* co-exist in Canada.

> Collective or group rights, such as those concerning languages and those concerning certain denominations of separate schools, are asserted by individuals or groups of individuals *because* of their membership in the protected group. Individual rights are asserted equally by everyone *despite* membership in certain ascertainable groups. To that extent, they are an exception from the equality rights provided equally to everyone.[5] [Emphasis added]

> It was never intended...that the *Charter* could be used to invalidate other provisions of the constitution, particularly a provision such as section 93 which represented a fundamental part of the Confederation compromise.[6]

Moreover, the Court drew an analogy between s.93 and s.91(24), the section of the Constitution relating to "Indians and lands reserved for the Indians".

> In this sense, section 93 is a provincial counterpart of section 91(24) (Indians and Indian land) which authorizes the Parliament of Canada to legislate for the benefit of the Indian population in a *preferential*, discriminatory, or distinctive fashion vis-à-vis others.[7] [Emphasis added]

The implication of this interpretation is that s.91(24) does *not* authorize legislative discrimination which harms Indians, but only that which is preferential to them.[8]

The Bill 30 case sheds light on two aspects of the relationship between aboriginal peoples and Canadian governments. First, it provides support for the view that some group or collective rights have protection from an attack by liberal individualism. Second, it strengthens an interpretation of s.91(24) as a political and legal relationship of trust and honour (further arguments supporting this interpretation are made in the next section). It notes that this section draws a distinction based on race, and that it is a unique exception to the constitutional requirements of equality.[9]

To summarize the relationship between aboriginal peoples and federal and provincial governments, both levels of government are bound by the Crown's fiduciary or trust duty, although the federal government has primacy. Parliament can legislate with respect to any aspect of aboriginal affairs, subject to the limits imposed by the "existing aboriginal and treaty rights" clause in s.35 of the Constitution. Laws of provincial legislatures apply of their own force until they begin to impair "Indianness" or "aboriginality."[10]

Moreover, we would suggest that the individual and equality rights guaranteed in the *Charter* cannot override the collective rights of minorities which are entrenched through political compromise (such as denominational schools), and which permit treatment of those minorities in a preferential fashion. This supports s.25 of the Constitution, which guarantees that the *Charter* will not

> ...abrogate or derogate from any aboriginal treaty or other rights or freedoms that pertain to the aboriginal peoples of Canada, including:
>
> (a) any rights or freedoms that have been recognized by the Royal Proclamation of October 7, 1763; and
>
> (b) any rights or freedoms that may be acquired by the aboriginal peoples of Canada by way of land claims settlements.

At the same time, aboriginal people continue to enjoy the benefit of *Charter* rights which apply to them as individuals. This perspective is in no way contradictory and, as this chapter seeks to demonstrate, is a truer characterization of the new relationship between aboriginal peoples and Canadian governments.

Aboriginal peoples have a guarantee of equality under s.15 of the *Charter*, but their collective rights (and the core of their "aboriginality") remain preserved. Section 91(24) of the *Constitution Act 1867* is now a power to enact preferential laws for the benefit of aboriginal peoples, and a power rooted in the special relationship between the Crown and aboriginal peoples.[11]

Provincial governments have an obligation under s.15 of the *Charter* (the equality clause) to ensure that individuals in the province are not deprived of the equal benefit of provincial law. Therefore, to the extent that provincial laws of general application apply, there is no basis for denying aboriginal persons equal access to provincial programs and services. Provincial laws which impair or threaten "Indianness," or "aboriginality," will not apply.

It is interesting to note that s.91(24) was included in the Meech Lake non-derogation clause. Since non-derogation clauses are designed to protect the rights of certain peoples or governments, this measure supports the new interpretation of s.91(24) as a provision which confers benefits upon aboriginal peoples. It also supports a view of s.91(24) as an authorization to legislate for Indian peoples, but only in a way that is preferential to them. In a sense, s.91(24) is being treated as an aboriginal right.

FEDERAL-PROVINCIAL RELATIONS: RESPONSIBILITIES, ROLES AND FINANCING

Federal-Provincial Responsibility

It is also important to note that the Crown's fiduciary duty binds both the federal Crown and the provincial Crowns within the limits of their respective jurisdictions.

> The federal Crown has the primary responsibility toward Indian peoples under section 91(24) and thus bears the main burden of the fiduciary trust. But insofar as provincial Crowns have power to affect aboriginal peoples, they also share in the trust. [13]

Thus, although "Indians and the lands reserved for the Indians" of s.91(24) of the *Constitution Act 1867* provides the federal government with jurisdiction, many provincial laws apply to Indians and Indian reserves of their own force, by virtue of the constitutional distribution of powers. [14] Thus Indians may be subject, for some purposes, to provincial law as is any resident of the province. In their capacity as "Indians," however, they may be insulated from some provincial laws by virtue of constitutional law (although federal legislation may deem that some of those provincial laws apply).

Indians are citizens, and in the affairs of life not governed by treaties or the *Indian Act*, they are subject to all the responsibilities of other Canadian citizens. Therefore, in terms of existing constitutional interpretation, aboriginal peoples have come to be part of the provincial population, as well as being Indian and thus within a special federal category.

Federal and Provincial Government Roles

The role of the federal government vis-à-vis aboriginal peoples concerns the preservation and enhancement of "Indianness" or, more generally, "aboriginality." This includes the definition and protection of the special status of aboriginal persons, institutions and land. There is no reason to confine such special status to those residing on reserve lands, since s.91(24) applies to Indians as persons and communities wherever they are. This is not to say that the preservation and development of reserve communities does not warrant concerted federal attention. Indeed, they require the most direct special treatment under federal law. [16]

It follows that the federal government must acknowledge a *responsibility* for those programs and services which are required by the special needs of "aboriginality." Aboriginal peoples living on Indian reserves require programs and services to preserve and strengthen their ways of life, culture and economic viability. For those living off Indian reserves, special federal development programs and services are required to preserve and strengthen those persons' "aboriginality."

The role of provincial governments vis-à-vis aboriginal peoples is to treat all individuals equally, without regard to race. Equality requires that a group not be deprived of provincial residence by virtue of race. Moreover, in specific instances, *inequality* of treatment may be required—inequality in the broad and non-pejorative sense of drawing beneficial distinctions to support the collective rights of aboriginal peoples. Therefore, there should be no prohibition against provincial laws which *preferentially* single out aboriginal persons or institutions. In other words, s.91(24) is not a barrier to provincial action and should not be used as a shield to defend the absence of provincial initiative. [17]

It follows that provincial governments must acknowledge aboriginal peoples as fully part of the provincial population. The benefits and privileges of provincial residence must be available to all aboriginal persons, on and off reserve. In addition, programs and services which deliver these benefits must be tailored to the needs, circumstances and rights of the aboriginal population, without fear that this beneficial singling out will render *ultra vires* an otherwise valid and proper legislative regime.

Federal and Provincial Financing

The roles of federal and provincial governments have always been tied to the matter of which level of government will provide or finance the services required.

A key issue in this perhaps thorniest of intergovernmental problems is the position of aboriginal peoples with regard to taxation. From an examination of the historical treatment of Indian peoples by the Crown, beginning with the *Royal Proclamation of 1763*, the exemption from taxation of on-reserve property is clearly a fundamental component of the special relationship between aboriginal peoples and Canadian governments. Any weakening of these taxation exemptions could be viewed as a breach of the fiduciary or trust duty. It would seem that taxation exemptions of Indian reserves are a permanent and fundamental aspect of Indian policy. [18]

Some observers are of the view that this leaves provincial governments in a difficult spot. They are required by the Constitution to provide equal benefits to all provincial residents, including Indians on reserve. But they are also precluded from generating revenue from reserve-based Indian people through the taxation system. It would seem only fair, the argument goes, that the federal government should compensate provincial governments for:

- additional costs of services on reserves (due to remoteness or high demand) and foregone revenues; and
- additional special costs of tailoring services to aboriginal peoples off reserve (to accommodate their "aboriginality"). [19]

We do not find this line of reasoning persuasive for several reasons. First, each order of government shares in the fiduciary or trust responsibility toward aboriginal peoples within their respective spheres of jurisdiction. It follows that, as residents of a province, aboriginal peoples are entitled to the same services as non-aboriginal residents. If provincial governments are required by their trust responsibility to tailor programs and services to meet the needs of aboriginal peoples, it is a result of that relationship. Second, both federal and provincial governments are precluded from taxing Indians on reservations. In this respect, the provincial governments are no more disadvantaged than the federal government. The case for special compensation is difficult to sustain.

A clarification of federal and provincial jurisdiction, responsibility and financing would assist greatly in clearing the way for concerted action on the part of both orders of government.

A POLICY FRAMEWORK

Typology of Self-Government

A fundamental part of the context for negotiations on fiscal arrangements will be the form of arrangements for aboriginal self-government which the community has adopted. We suggest that there are four critical parameters to the definition of aboriginal self-government. These are:

- whether the government (or self-governing institution) has a land base;
- whether the government (or institution) is public or ethnic;
- whether the government (or institution) is local, regional or national in scope; and
- the source, amount and type of power exercised by the government (or institution).

There are two or three options within each of these key parameters.

Land-based versus Landless

There are only two alternatives to this dimension of aboriginal self-government—government and institutions based on land, and government and institutions based on membership in an aboriginal community (a community of interest). While land-based forms of self-government are well known, forms of self-determination off a land base are still developing. The former include band government, tribal government, municipal government, federal government and so forth. The latter include self-governing societies, institutions, and local, provincial and national organizations.

Public versus Ethnic Government

There are two main options here—government based on ethnicity, and government based on territory. In ethnic government, membership (citizenship or residency) is determined by an ethnic criterion. Mere residence (without meeting the ethnic criterion) on lands under the jurisdiction of an ethnic government would not necessarily provide entitlement to citizenship rights and government services. In public government, every individual residing within the boundaries of that government is under its jurisdiction, and entitled to its rights and services. This distinction is meaningful only to self-government on a land base, since self-governing institutions off a land base would be ethnic by definition.[20]

Scope of Government

There are three clear options with respect to the scope of aboriginal self-government and self-governing institutions—national, regional and community/local. At issue is where the locus of decision-making resides. At the national level, one can conceive of self-governing institutions representing aboriginal communities of interest (the Canadian National Aboriginal University or the Aboriginal Institute for Legal Research). Regional government could encompass tribal territories (e.g., Gitskan Wet'suwet'en) or share jurisdiction with local governments (e.g., Cree Regional Authority). Community/local government would be based in the particular aboriginal community.

Government Powers

There are two distinct aspects of the powers to be exercised by aboriginal governments and institutions. The first relates to the source of powers: the legal status of an aboriginal government or institution—that is, whether it is embedded in the Constitution or in legislation—determines the source of its powers. If its powers are enumerated in the Constitution, it can enact laws in its own right within its fields of jurisdiction (as is the case with the federal and provincial governments). If it is the product of federal or provincial legislation, it can exercise only those powers delegated to it by the relevant order of government (as is the case with municipal governments). Whether a government or institution is autonomous or dependent is a reflection of that relationship.[21]

The second aspect relates to the distribution of powers between aboriginal governments and institutions and other Canadian governments and institutions, and to the types of powers that a government or institution exercises. These powers might be legislative, adjudicative, administrative or some combination thereof. Three broad options emerge within this parameter. An aboriginal government or institution could be autonomous, with legislative and adjudicative powers. It could be dependent, with administrative powers. Or, it could be semi-autonomous, exercising some mixture of legislative, adjudicative and administrative powers. Each of these options has a direct impact on what types of fiscal arrangements are most appropriate, since some forms of self-government (e.g., autonomous with legislative powers) are quite incompatible with some forms of fiscal arrangement (e.g., funded only by conditional grants).

Community Characteristics

The second set of factors that fiscal arrangements must take into account are the economic and political characteristics of the aboriginal communities. The existence of a land base is a parameter in determining models of self-government; there is an important distinction between aboriginal communities that possess a land base (for the most part, but not exclusively, reserves) and those that do not (again, mostly but not exclusively, urban communities). The discussion that follows refers to land-based communities, although some brief comments on the latter communities are also included.

One recent examination of the economic status of Indian communities highlighted many of the commonly recognized problems, including their small size (the average reserve band includes less that 500 people), their mostly rural, often isolated locations offering no proximity to goods markets and employment opportunities, low levels of education compared to the non-Indian community, low incomes and low employment rates.[22] The study also noted that transfer payments from government typically make up a very high proportion of monetary income. However, the study also suggested that the economic potential of many of these communities was quite good. The agricultural potential of reserve lands is on average as promising as other land—many areas possess wildlife and forestry potential, and many reserves also have considerable mineral resource potential. Of course, having these potentials in physical terms and bringing them to reality in economic terms can often be very different.

The relevant political characteristics of the aboriginal communities centre on two issues. The first involves the existence or development of accountability mechanisms between the aboriginal leadership and the community. In what fashion are the aboriginal governments to be responsive to the needs and demands of their populations? To express this in non-aboriginal governmental terms, what is the budgetary process through which funds will be allocated to functions, and how will these allocations be adjusted over time in light of changing circumstances and popular demands?

Secondly, assistance is required to assure that aboriginal leaders and officials will possess the administrative capacity for financial management, planning and budgeting. These factors directly affect the community's ability to use funds effectively and to deliver services in forms that may be different but not appreciably more inefficient than other governments in Canada.

The economic and political circumstances change for non-land-based, urban communities. These groups are much more likely to participate in the mainstream urban economy of which they are a part (although this is not to say that they participate as equals alongside their non-aboriginal counterparts). Political structures and relationships are also likely to differ, approaching something more like an ethnic community association and less like a conventional government. Accordingly, funding arrangements might be expected to address a narrower range of functional areas than would arrangements with land-based communities. There may also be different administrative requirements for arrangements not involving a land base.

Fiscal Arrangement Typology

There are several existing fiscal arrangement and transfer programs which could serve as models for a system of fiscal arrangements with aboriginal peoples. These range from federal-provincial transfer programs, to provincial-municipal and provincial-school board programs, to arrangements with quasi-independent institutions such as provincial funding arrangements for universities and hospitals. Public funding for interest groups (e.g., Consumer's Association of Canada) and community associations may also be relevant.

Our objective here is to specify parameters, each of which may take two or more values, to categorize this variety of programs. One can then examine which of these parameter values are consistent with various conceptions of aboriginal self-government, and in this fashion, identify a relatively small number of possible arrangements for further detailed analysis. At this stage, our framework includes a much broader range of possibilities than the fiscal arrangements that have emerged thus far in negotiations between governments and aboriginal peoples.

There are three basic issues that all arrangements must address:

- What is the legal framework of the arrangement? It may be written into the Constitution (as equalization payments now are); it may be the result of an agreement or contract between the donor and recipient governments; or it may be based on legislation passed by the donor government. Clearly as one moves from the first to the third of these possibilities, the degree of the recipients' dependence increases.
- What is the source of funds? There may be a cash transfer from the general revenues of the granting government, or the arrangement may call for the recipients to have direct access to certain tax bases (either regional or national), or a blend of both. Indian governments may gain access to a tax base by being granted the right to the revenues produced by "x" percentage points levied on a specified tax base(s) with the federal government acting as the collection agency.
- What is the basis for receipt of funding? Arrangements could grant funds to aboriginal governments as a matter of entitlement (e.g., as an aboriginal right and/or as part of a land claims settlement), through an unconditional grant program (e.g., provincial equalization), through a program conditional transfer (e.g., Established Programs Financing), or through a spending (and program) conditional transfer (e.g., Canada Assistance Plan). The first of these options implies a high level of autonomy for the aboriginal governments; the successive options may imply that these governments are strictly administrative or program delivery agencies.

The categorization of existing federal and provincial fiscal programs, using these parameters, is presented in Table 1.

In addition to these three basic parameters there are a number of more technical program design parameters, including:

- Determinacy—whether the fiscal formula itself determines what a government unit will receive, or whether the formula defines a share of a global sum determined elsewhere. Most federal transfers to the provinces are examples of the former, while Ontario's arrangements for its universities is an example of the latter. In the second case, the provincial government determines, as part of its normal budget process, the global amount of its grant to

107

TABLE 1

Fiscal Parameters of Federal and Provincial Fiscal Programs

Fiscal Parameter	Equalization	EPF	CAP	Ontario University
Legal framework	constitutional (unilateral pre-1982)	unilateral (informal contract)	unilateral	unilateral
Source of funds	cash	cash and tax	cash	cash
Basis of funding	provincial entitlement based on fiscal capacity	program cond.	spending cond.	program cond.
Determinacy	unique to recipient	unique to recipient	unique to recipient	province sets global amount
Redistributive	yes—up to relative measure	no—not directly	no	no
Adjustment	determined in five-years legislation	GNP growth rate	cost of service	unilateral— donor disc.
Accountability	no	no	yes	yes
Term of Agreement	indefinite but with five-years commitments on formula	five years	indefinite	annual

universities, which is allocated among the institutions according to predetermined formulas. (This is an oversimplification, but is essentially correct). Presumably, if aboriginal governments are viewed as autonomous within certain domains, both in relation to the federal and provincial governments and each other, some of their funding must be determined following the first approach. On the other hand, if in part they are regarded as delivery agencies for a government program, then that government may determine its total spending on the program independently of a formula devised to distribute the funds.

• Redistributive—whether the fiscal arrangement incorporates an explicit equalization factor. If so, then two approaches to equalization may be adopted. The first relies upon a relative measure

108

to determine eligibility and the level of support; the federal equalization program is of this type, with the standard being defined by the fiscal capacity of a group of provinces. The alternative approach is to specify an absolute standard, and to attempt to bring each recipient up to that level; an example would be a standard funding sufficient to provide objectively defined levels of public services.

- Adjustment—the criteria used to determined growth (or change) over time: first, funding may vary with some aggregate measure of economic production such as GNP. Second, funding might increase according to cost measures, which may be general in nature (e.g., Consumer Price Index) or specific to a particular type of service. Third, the growth factor may be pre-defined as part of the legal basis on which the fiscal arrangement is established (e.g., in a bilateral contract or in legislation). Finally, the adjustment may be entirely at the discretion of the funding authority; this would be the case if the program was simply a discretionary budget item of the funding government. In moving from the first to the last of these possibilities, one is roughly moving from greater to lesser notions of autonomy of the recipient units.

- Accountability—whether the recipient is accountable to, and subject to, audit by the donor government. (We assume that any self-government arrangement will involve accountability of the aboriginal government to its own citizens. The question here is whether there is accountability to the donor government for the transfer, or in Bish's terms whether ministerial responsibility applies.)[23] Obviously an arrangement not subject to audit in this sense implies more autonomy than one that is.

- Term—whether the agreement is indefinite or determined for a fixed number of years, and the length of that term. A longer term implies greater planning, predictability and autonomy.

The application of this typology of fiscal arrangements to existing aboriginal self-government agreements is presented in Table 2.

Given all the values that these parameters may assume, the possible combinations that exists are daunting. However, some are clearly non-starters because choices on one parameter rule out options on others, or because certain parameter combinations do not come together comfortably. In the next section we develop the few combinations that, in our view, are viable and politically realistic, and analyze their self-government implications.

TABLE 2

Fiscal Parameters of Existing Aboriginal Self-Government Agreements*

Fiscal Parameter	Self-Government Agreement						
	Band Govt.	Sechelt	Cree/ Naskapi	Kativik	Gabriel Dumont	Indian College	Cree Schl. Bd.
Legal framework	donor legis.	contract	donor legis. & contract	donor legis.	donor legis.	donor legis.	contract
Source of funds	cash	cash	cash	cash	cash	cash	cash
Basis of funding	spending	program	entitlement	spending	spending	spending	entitlement
Determinacy	unique	unique	unique	unique	unique	unique	unique
Redistributive	no	n/a	no	no	n/a	n/a	no
Adjustment	donor disc.	cost	cost	donor disc.	donor disc.	negotiated disc.	cost
Accountability	yes	no	no	yes	yes	yes	yes
Term of Agreement	one to five years (AFA)	five years with annual adjust.	five years with annual adjust.	one year	one year	five years	one year

* See Appendix for further details.

PRINCIPLES FOR FISCAL ARRANGEMENTS

There are several key principles in designing fiscal arrangements for aboriginal self-government, foremost being the relationships among three primary dimensions: governmental autonomy, fiscal autonomy and community development (both economic and political/administrative). These relationships, among others, are expressed in the following five principles which provide a policy framework for designing systems of fiscal arrangements.

- **The fiscal arrangement regime should be compatible with the model of self-government that it accompanies.**

The primary relationship of concern here is between the degree of autonomy in the self-government arrangement, and the basis for receipt of funding. In this instance, we are not referring to autonomous self-government in terms of legal authority, but rather in terms of *de facto* discretionary decision-making powers of a government. To be effective, increased political autonomy (e.g., power to decide the character and levels of programs within the allocated areas; power to tax) must be accompanied by increased levels of unconditional funding.

One can see the relationship between the form of self-government and the fiscal transfer by first focusing on the extremes. If the transfer is composed of only conditional funds, the recipient government would have no meaningful autonomous powers to determine policy. Issues such as priorities and program design are, in effect, determined by the donor government when it sets the eligibility conditions and the rate at which grants match program spending. While the recipient government may have some influence when the fiscal arrangements are negotiated, it is essentially in the position of being an administrator of the funds for the donor government.

The other extreme is a system in which all funds are transferred unconditionally. The recipient government in this situation is provided access to a revenue source that does not constrain the uses to which these revenues are allocated. The recipient therefore has the autonomy to decide what programs to provide, at what levels, under what conditions, and what prices (if any) it should charge its own constituents. Decisions on any of these would not affect its grant. (Strictly speaking, this unconditionality would apply only in the short run. Future adjustments in the transfer may occur, depending on how these decisions affect the economic circumstances of the community. This point is discussed in terms of the next funding criterion.)

Between these extremes, a variety of compatible combinations of self-government and fiscal arrangements are possible. The key issue is to ensure that the fiscal transfer regime incorporates a sufficient degree of non-conditionality to reflect and support the degree of autonomy in the self-government arrangements. This does not mean that all funds transferred to an aboriginal community be granted under the same conditions. It does imply a broader range of transfer mechanisms than has been the case to date. It may be desirable, for example, to ensure that the local community adheres to standards (e.g., national or provincial) established for the larger population for specific programs (e.g., public health); accordingly a grant based on a carefully defined set of conditions could be established to fund these programs. At the same time, other funds could be transferred to the community giving it the flexibility to carry out its mandate in areas where it has been accorded autonomous decision-making authority.

It is difficult to specify the proportion of a community's total transfer that must be unconditional in order to ensure its discretionary decision-making capacity. Judging by the budgetary behaviour of provincial, territorial and municipal governments as it relates to their dependence on transfers of various types, a magic threshold proportion does not exist. However, a clear inverse relationship exists between the size of conditional grants (relative to total revenues) and budgetary discretion. [24] Ultimately there must be a policy determination and a negotiated compromise as to what level of unconditional funding is required to afford a community the desired scope for discretionary action. This point is further discussed under the fifth principle below.

Other choices of fiscal design emerge from the central relationship between the grant structure and self-government. For example, the requirements for reporting/audit from the community government to the federal government would presumably be related to the conditionality of the transfer. Spending (and program) conditional transfers would require accountability procedures sufficiently rigorous to enable the federal government to ensure that all conditions were being met. Less constrained funding should have less stringent reporting standards associated with it. Similarly, more autonomous transfer programs should be established for longer terms. There are at least two reasons for this: first, longer terms provide the recipient government with an assurance of funding that enables it to plan rationally and efficiently, thereby enhancing the operation of the self-government arrangement. Second, depending on the type and length of program, short-term arrangements can become another way to impose conditions upon the recipient that are incompatible with the level of autonomy in the self-government arrangement.

- **The fiscal arrangement should be compatible with the economic circumstances of the recipient community.**

As a consequence of the generally lower level of economic development, aboriginal communities will be restricted with respect to the levels of revenues they can raise from their own sources. (Ultimately, virtually all tax bases of governments in Canada are related, over the long term, to the level of economic development and the wealth of the community.) Having lower capacity to raise revenues from their own citizens, aboriginal community governments will, on average, have to rely on higher funding levels (relative to expenditure levels) from other governments. This fact raises questions about the form of self-government itself, specifically concerning the level of effective autonomy that aboriginal governments can assume. If a government is heavily dependent upon another for its revenues, it may be that its autonomy is compromised even if all the funds it receives are nominally unconditional. This suggests that questions of self-government and financial arrangements cannot be considered in the abstract without taking into account the level of, and prospects for, economic development of the recipient community.

The other aspect of community circumstances relevant for our purposes concerns accountability links internal to the recipient community. If a high proportion of total revenues are provided by an external authority, can the accountability link between the aboriginal government and its citizens be as strong and effective as in situations in which the community itself is the major source of government revenues? The link between the effectiveness of local control and the local contribution to financing is an important issue in public finance. It has been argued that significant local financing is a prerequisite for effective accountability of a government to its people, and is necessary to prevent decision-making powers from shifting to the government that is the source of external funds.[25] This question again highlights the link between community circumstances, self-government arrangements and fiscal transfers.

- **The fiscal arrangements should encourage the recipient government to move towards greater reliance on its own revenue-raising efforts.**

This criterion should be interpreted as creating incentives for the local community to pursue its own economic development, whether through manufacturing enterprises, agriculture, tourism, resource industries or other forms of economic activity that would create employment, raise individual incomes and create an increased fiscal capacity to fund public services within the community. Economic development should also include promotion of traditional activities. A good example of the latter is the support offered through the Income Security Program for Cree hunters and trappers. A similar program exists for Inuit hunters, trappers and fishers.[26]

113

A useful way to characterize the incentive factor is in terms of a "marginal tax rate" or "transfer reduction rate" (TRR). The TRR can be defined as the aggregate change in the fiscal transfer divided by the change in the fiscal capacity of the local community. The definition of fiscal capacity, in turn, is based on the federal-to-provincial Fiscal Equalization Program, that is, the revenue that the local tax base would produce at national average tax rates. The local tax base would include those revenue sources in which the aboriginal government has been given jurisdiction to assess levies; for example, property taxes, user fees and perhaps the sale of goods and services. National average tax rates and fiscal capacity benchmarks could be determined by assembling a sample of aboriginal and non-aboriginal communities comparable in terms of jurisdictional authority and economic circumstances.

It is useful to conceptualize the TRR as a continuum of incentive structures. At the negative extreme is a system of transfers that declined as the community's fiscal capacity grew on a one-to-one basis or more (TRR$\geq$1.00). This would mean that as the community succeeded in promoting its own development, the aboriginal government would be required to raise taxes from its own population at national average rates just to maintain its aggregate revenues at the same level. While there would still presumably be net benefits to the community as a result of the increased development, the disincentive for the aboriginal government to pursue economic advancement is very strong.

A negative TRR is the other extreme. In this case the local community would be doubly rewarded by economic growth, because its transfer would actually increase as its fiscal capacity grew. A strong positive incentive to pursue economic growth would thus be incorporated into the fiscal transfer system. The cross-over point in this spectrum would be where TRR equals zero; the size of the transfer would be unaffected by the economic growth of the local community. While this is a neutral point in a mathematical sense, it still represents a positive incentive in an economic sense.

Between the extremes, of course, a range of values exists. For example, the TRR could be positive but considerably less than one. Taking into account both political realism and economic desirability, it would seem that an arrangement in which the TRR is between zero and a small positive number (certainly <1.0, probably ≤ 0.5) should be attempted. This would meet the incentive criteria in that both the community and the fiscal position of its government would benefit from economic development. Further, a positive TRR would actually create some incentive for the aboriginal government to increase its reliance on own revenue sources.

One method to effect TRR adjustments is through the negotiation process itself. That is, rather than write explicit TRR provisions into a fiscal transfer agreement, it may be preferable to take the approach that these adjustments, in light of changing economic circumstances and fiscal capacities, would be subject to discussion when agreements are renegotiated. Since the agreement periods are unlikely to extend much beyond five years, it might be argued that this provides a sufficient opportunity for adjustment since economic development is unlikely to change a community's situation dramatically within that period of time. Even in this process, however, it would still be important to ensure that the effective TRRs that emerge from the renegotiations would incorporate the desired incentive effects discussed above. We note that the five-year Sechelt agreement contains no specific provision for reducing federal funds in response to increased band revenues; if such adjustments become part of the renegotiation, the Sechelt agreement would, in effect, be following this option.

- **The fiscal arrangements should incorporate appropriate equity properties.**

Equity, in this context, must be viewed across two dimensions: among aboriginal communities and between aboriginal communities as a group and non-aboriginal communities. In addition to the direct concern for equity itself, this criterion is important in its contribution to the viability of the aboriginal communities. Aboriginal communities in which governments cannot afford to deliver public services are in danger of disintegration, as individuals leave in search of better opportunities and services elsewhere. These events can quickly develop into a vicious circle, if community disintegration further impairs the financial capacity of the government. Therefore, equitable funding to these communities can strengthen the forces keeping them together.

As we suggested earlier in this chapter, there are (at least) two methods by which this criterion could be applied. The first might be described as the "adequacy variant," the second as the "relative standard variant."

The adequacy variant is based on the actual costs of delivering the services for which the community government is responsible.

It would achieve inter-community equity in fiscal arrangements by providing each aboriginal government with the fiscal resources needed to supply the set of defined services at specified levels. This does not imply that each service must be funded separately and conditionally; it does require that the total transfer (the sum of all the components) be sufficient to enable the recipient to provide the services up to their specified levels, if it wishes to do so. The actual allocation of funds would depend upon factors such as the conditionality of transfer components and the priorities of the aboriginal government.

The relative standard variant would focus on the fiscal capacities of the community governments rather than on the cost of service provision directly. This approach would be analogous to that taken in the federal Fiscal Equalization Program. Either a national or a regional standard could be adopted, based on a set of relevant revenue sources. The total transfers to the aboriginal governments would then be adjusted to bring each of them up to the average of the communities included in the standard. While this approach would require the maintenance of a data set on government revenue sources (e.g., property values, volumes of activities subject to user fees, sales of services), it would need much less data than the first option which requires analysis of the costs of delivering services. Because this approach is based on fiscal capacity rather than on costs of services directly, it avoids many of the difficulties of the adequacy variant.

The formula-funding agreements between the federal government and the territorial governments are sophisticated versions of this model. Expenditure requirements are determined by adjusting a base expenditure level by the growth of a provincial-local expenditure escalator. From this amount is subtracted the eligible revenues of the territorial government (which includes other federal transfers such as the Established Programs Financing program). The difference is the amount of the formula grant. Adapting this model to self-government financing would require the development of a new expenditure escalator to reflect the narrower range of public services that are likely to be involved. In fact, given the diverse situations of the aboriginal communities, a single escalator may not be appropriate. It may also require an adjustment to provide a stronger incentive for aboriginal governments to develop their own revenue bases; in our terms, the territorial agreements essentially involve a $TRR = 1$.

It should be noted that, in either of these approaches to the equity criterion, there are administrative implications for aboriginal governments. The construction and maintenance of data bases may require training in the aboriginal communities to ensure the administrative capacity to operate the systems of fiscal arrangements.

- **The design of the components of the overall fiscal transfer should reflect the characteristics of the relevant public services.**

Specifically, the level of conditionality attached to the various components should be related to the attributes of the corresponding service areas. In cases where the services have an impact well beyond the local community, as in the case of public health, a government may want to ensure that these responsibilities are met in quite specific ways and at particular levels. In other words, there may be a strong national interest in the program, and the federal government should act as the agent of that national interest. Spending conditional grants would be appropriate in these cases. Grants of this type would also be appropriate in cases of "one time" programs (e.g., job creation initiatives, capital projects); however, here the federal payment should be considered as the result of an agreement on a specific joint project. In this sense, it would be analogous to a federal contribution to a province or municipality for a special purpose.

Where there is a general national interest in the design of programs, but not a strong national interest with respect to their levels, program conditional grants would be appropriate. The model for these transfers is the Established Programs Financing (EPF) program. Payments would be conditional upon the program having certain characteristics—for example, no direct user fees on medical services—but they would not be tied to the level of spending decided upon by the aboriginal government.

Finally, all functions which are purely local in nature, such as recreation or road maintenance, would be supported from funds provided unconditionally. In these instances purely local preferences should prevail, and no federal direction is warranted. Note that this principle implies an alternative procedure for adjusting fiscal transfers to that of the incentive principle. In this case, if a community's economy expanded and its fiscal transfer was reduced, this criterion argues that the adjustment should occur in unconditional funding, because spending conditional programs are determined by externality considerations.

In general, as aboriginal communities become more self-governing, the fiscal arrangements should become less conditional. Greater political autonomy and greater fiscal autonomy go hand in hand. It follows that the system of fiscal accountability will (or should) be related to the self-government arrangements. Some programming will likely remain spending conditional (as in shared-cost programs), some program conditional (as in EPF), while other portions could (or should) become unconditional (as in equalization). As aboriginal communities become more self-governing, they will (or should) become more accountable to community members for the expenditures of their funds. As with any government, an audit is required when public funds are expended. With increasing self-government, however, the minister and the department will (or should) exercise less influence and control over these expenditures. While a departmental "veto" over Indian band expenditures may be appropriate for fully conditional programs, it would most certainly be inappropriate for more autonomous fiscal arrangements, such as EPF.

A partial precedent for this type of fiscal arrangement is the Established Programs Financing (EPF) agreement between the federal and provincial governments, which is set out in federal legislation. The EPF program provides for federal contributions, through a combination of tax point transfer and cash payment, to provincial governments ostensibly in support of health care and post-secondary education. The federal contributions in support of health care, for example, are not dependent upon provincial governments offering particular services to their residents (such as sports medicine facilities), but on provincial adherence to more general principles (such as accessibility, portability, public adminstration or, as more recently set out in the *Canada Health Act*, a penalty for extra billing by physicians). This enables the provincial governments to have more flexibility in health care policy, which is a field of exclusive provincial jurisdiction. For example, one province may choose to allocate more resources to preventative health care, while another may focus greater attention on long-term care, with each responding to its unique demographic characteristics and policy preferences.

Such arrangements, in place since 1977, have not greatly offended principles of ministerial or financial accountability within the federal government nor, in our view, would similar fiscal arrangements between relatively autonomous aboriginal governments and the federal government.

Trade-offs Among Criteria

It is obvious that the five primary principles discussed above are not independent. Decisions taken in pursuit of one criterion will usually have implications for at least one other. Where these inter-relationships take the form of goal conflicts, trade-offs must be made.

Perhaps the most obvious of these trade-offs is between the goals of creating the desired incentive structure and achieving equity. Bluntly stated, it is impossible to ensure that the fiscal arrangement does not penalize a community for its successes in achieving economic development and, at the same time, ensure that the arrangement recognizes differences in wealth or income (the level of economic development) across communities. As a community's income increases, its fiscal transfer must be adjusted in order to attain, at least partially, the equity criterion. The costs of moving too quickly or too slowly are recognizable from considering the principles themselves.

A trade-off also may exist between the goals of making the fiscal arrangements compatible with the degree of autonomy embodied in the self-government arrangement on the one hand, and matching conditionality to service characteristics on the other. This problem would also arise if the total transfer is adjusted downward as a consequence of increased wealth of the community (as the equity goal would require). Since the more rigidly conditional portions of the transfer presumably reflect some national interest, adjustments would occur in the unconditional components of the transfer. However, this may result in an emerging inconsistency between the fiscal discretion available to the community and its level of autonomous self-government.

ADAPTING THE FRAMEWORK TO ABORIGINAL SELF-GOVERNMENT WITHOUT A LAND BASE

Aboriginal self-government without a land base, sometimes termed "self-administration," can take several forms. One is "institutional autonomy," which involves the creation or expansion of specialized, autonomous, aboriginal institutions and agencies in different areas of service delivery. A second is "political autonomy," which involves the creation of central aboriginal policy-making bodies, which administer service delivery institutions and agencies as part of a larger function of political representation.[27] A third form is that of an aboriginal society, based on the model of a professional society (as in law and medicine).[28]

The "institutional autonomy" form, represented by single purpose institutions such as training institutes, child welfare agencies and economic development corporations, is usually managed by a board, which is elected by aboriginal people in the area served by the institution, who become members of the organization. The board sets policy for the development and delivery of programs, and for hiring and managing staff.

For the "political autonomy" form, aboriginal councils at the local, regional and provincial levels appear to be the most appropriate structure. An example is AMNSIS, the former Association of Metis and Non-Status Indians of Saskatchewan. Through membership in an aboriginal provincial association, aboriginal people participate in local and regional units of the organization. While voting at the local level, aboriginal persons directly elect local councilors, as well as regional councilors and provincial executive officers. The provincial council serves as the political voice of aboriginal peoples off a land base, articulating objectives and needs, formulating policy for dealing with government, and designing and managing programs and services. (This last function is shared by the "institutional autonomy" form.) Members of the executive committee hold various portfolios in areas of social policy, economic policy and so forth, and are responsible for the design and delivery of programs and the management of institutions.

With the professional society model, aboriginal persons living off a land base could become self-governing in the same way that the medical and legal professions are self-governing. They determine rules of membership and govern the activities of members within a limited sphere of activity—the professional sphere. If this approach were applied to aboriginal peoples, the society could govern the "aboriginal sphere." In this instance, aboriginal societies could negotiate administrative arrangements to deliver services to aboriginal peoples who claimed aboriginal status, and were accepted as members by others in the aboriginal society.

Perhaps the most serious constraint of such an approach—that is, one without a land base—is that aboriginal peoples can easily "opt out" of the arrangement, and take advantage of the substitute municipal, provincial or federal program or service. If they were dissatisfied with the aboriginal health clinic, they could always opt for other services in the area.[29] There is also the matter of negotiating the delegation of authority from, at times, both the federal and provincial orders of government.

Fiscal provisions for aboriginal self-governing institutions should be adapted to reflect the degree of autonomy which these institutions have. As with land-based governing bodies, these too should be accountable to their members for their expenditures before significant movement toward unconditional grants.

An example of aboriginal self-government without a land base could be an aboriginal school board in centres which have a significant number of aboriginal peoples, as in cities such as Regina, Winnipeg, Calgary, Toronto, Vancouver, Prince Albert, Medicine Hat, etc. An aboriginal school board, elected by aboriginal persons in such centres, could operate primary and secondary schools for aboriginal students. The aboriginal schools could be financed in several ways. Taxes could be levied upon users, and/or a portion of the public and separate school levy could be allocated to the aboriginal schools. Special arrangements could be made with the federal and provincial governments to aid in the development of aboriginal curricular materials (e.g., language, history, culture), and to promote aboriginal teacher education. This would enable aboriginal people living off a land base to have some control over the education of their children. In addition, it could increase the prospects, which are currently very grim, for aboriginal children to graduate from high school. Such an arrangement is possible at the present time within the framework of Canadian federalism.

There are already self-governing aboriginal institutions, without a land base, in existence. The Saskatchewan Indian Federated College and the Gabriel Dumont Institute in Saskatchewan are cases in point (although the former is a product of land-based status Indians). Both institutions are controlled by Indians and Metis and non-status Indians respectively, and are accountable to their peoples for their actions. Their financial arrangements with governments are described in the Appendix. Both institutions offer ongoing service delivery programs in Regina and Saskatoon, as well as in local communities throughout Saskatchewan. Thus, long-term funding would be desirable, to enable planning and development of curriculum, courses and programs. Only the Federated College has been somewhat successful in this regard.

In addition, if these institutions are to do developmental work, and are to have the capacity to respond to the wishes of their people—that is, to have some policy-making capacity—their funding cannot be purely spending and program conditional. Some expenditures must be at the discretion of the aboriginal institution, if the institution is to be self-governing in any meaningful sense. Again, the College has made more, if still somewhat limited, progress in this regard.

To sum up, the policy framework for fiscal arrangements and aboriginal self-government developed in this chapter can be adapted to situations without a land base. Most of the same principles and trade-offs would apply in both instances.

MAJOR CONCLUSIONS

A policy framework for fiscal arrangements and aboriginal self-government has been elaborated throughout this chapter. The principles for matching the appropriate fiscal arrangements to the appropriate self-government arrangement, and to do so while at the same time considering the community's economic, political and administrative characteristics, have been developed. The next step in policy development is to design a set of guidelines for self-government negotiations, based on this policy framework (assuming that this framework is an acceptable basis for government policy).

The key policy decisions revolve around the trade-offs among the (at times) competing principles for fiscal arrangements. The actual choices depend on the weight attached to each principle. These are fundamental policy decisions, and it would be inappropriate for us to speculate on what weight should be given to each principle.

There would appear to be several considerations in designing fiscal arrangements for aboriginal self-government. Perhaps foremost among these is the relationship among governmental autonomy, fiscal autonomy and community development (both economic and political/administrative).

All three variables should be positively correlated. That is, as aboriginal self-governments become more autonomous, their fiscal arrangements should become less conditional (and more autonomous). Governmental autonomy is also related to economic development and political/administrative capacity. A government with a very limited economic base cannot be truly autonomous, insofar as it receives the major portion of its revenues from another government. Economic development and self-government should grow together.

Perhaps the most overwhelming conclusion is the yawning gap between what these fiscal arrangements *ought* to be, given our principles, and what they are. In existing fiscal arrangements for aboriginal self-government (several of which are summarized in Table 2 and in the Appendix), there is little relationship between the autonomy of the aboriginal government and the autonomy of its fiscal arrangement. At the present time, as aboriginal governments become more autonomous, their fiscal arrangements tend not to— they tend to remain short term, spending and program conditional, and at the discretion of the federal government. There has been some progress with respect to making these fiscal arrangements less conditional (e.g., with the Cree-Naskapi, and, to a lesser extent, with the Sechelt), but the federal government has to travel much further down this road if aboriginal self-government is to have any real meaning.

A second conclusion relates to economic development for aboriginal peoples. Fiscal arrangements should contribute to economic development for aboriginal people, rather than act as disincentives, as many of the current arrangements now do (e.g., short-term, spending conditional, no incentives). Fiscal arrangements can do more than express the financial relationship between the federal government and aboriginal people. They can also be a policy instrument in the economic development field.

A third conclusion is with respect to political development and administrative capacity. If aboriginal governments are to become more politically autonomous, more economically developed and enjoy more fiscal autonomy, they will also have to become better developed in political and administrative terms. This means further developing accountability relationships between aboriginal leaders and their communities. The communities should participate in the policy-making process and be consulted in the design of programs and services. The leaders should be accountable to the community for the expenditure of government funds. It also means that the administrative capacity of aboriginal government will have to be further developed. The tasks of more autonomous aboriginal governments, be they the administration of sophisticated fiscal arrangements or the negotiation of complex intergovernmental agreements, require more highly trained public servants. We are concerned that, to date, there is too little effort being made on this front. It would be counterproductive to have a federal government policy which promoted autonomous—but inept—aboriginal governments.

Our fourth conclusion bears on the issue of ministerial responsibility. We see no conflict between increased autonomy for aboriginal peoples, as represented in both self-government and fiscal arrangements, and ministerial responsibility. The fiduciary, or trust, responsibility does not prevent greater self-determination for aboriginal peoples—it demands it.

Fifth, with respect to the matter of federal and provincial responsibility, we are of the view that there is a responsibility and a role for each order of government. We have outlined what we believe these responsibilities are, the roles each order of government should play, and how this relates to federal and provincial government financing. That there is a provincial government role is undeniable.

Finally, a suggestion with regard to the design and negotiation of fiscal arrangements with aboriginal governments: serious consideration should be given to restricting adjustments during the term of the fiscal arrangement to technical criteria (such as changes in population and costs), and to making more fundamental adjustments (emerging from the incentive and equity principles) during the renegotiation of the fiscal arrangement. Presumably, this would occur about every five years. If such a suggestion were implemented, it would be important for the federal government to elaborate publicly the principles which would apply to the renegotiation before the initial agreement is concluded. This would give both parties a full and prior understanding of the rules governing renegotiation, and demonstrate that the federal government intends to pursue its policy of more autonomy—both governmental and fiscal—for aboriginal peoples.

Acknowledgements

The authors wish to acknowledge the helpful comments of Professor Robert Bish of the School of Public Administration at the Uni-

124

versity of Victoria, and those of our colleagues Frances Abele and Katherine Graham of the School of Public Administration at Carleton University.

Notes

1. *Guerin v. The Queen*, [1984] 2 S.C.R. 335, (1984) 13 D.L.R. (4th) 321 (S.C.C.).
2. Brian Slattery, "Understanding Aboriginal Rights," 66 *Canadian Bar Review*, (1987) p. 731.
3. *Ibid.*, p. 736.
4. For a more complete analysis of the impact of the Bill 30 case, see Alan Pratt, "Federalism in the Era of Aboriginal Self-Government," elsewhere in this volume.
5. Supreme Court decision on Bill 30, 1987, 40 D.L.R. (4th) 18 (S.C.C.), p. 566.
6. Justice Wilson in Supreme Court decision on Bill 30, 1987, *Ibid.*, p. 48.
7. Justice Estey in Supreme Court decision on Bill 30, 1987, *Ibid.*, p. 9.
8. Pratt, *op. cit.*, note 4.
9. *Ibid.* The distinction is actually based on aboriginal or treaty status.
10. *Ibid.*
11. *Ibid.*
12. *Ibid.*
13. Slattery, *op. cit.*, note 2, p. 755.
14. Supreme Court decision in *Dick*, 1985.
15. *Nowegijick v. The Queen*, [1983], 144 D.L.R. (4th) p. 193 (S.C.C.).
16. Pratt, *op. cit.*, note 4.
17. *Ibid.*
18. *Ibid.* In a sense, exemption from taxation is an element of "retained sovereignty."
19. *Ibid.*
20. See David C. Hawkes, *Aboriginal Self-Government: What Does It Mean?* (Kingston: Queen's University, Institute of Intergovernmental Relations 1985). In practice, this dimension is more complex, since governments exercise extra-territoriality, and have authority over some aspects of their citizens' lives even if they reside elsewhere.
21. The amount of power exercised by a government *could* be identical, regardless of its source, except in the power to make changes. For example, an aboriginal government could have the same powers under either the Constitution or federal legislation, although with the former it could make changes itself, while the latter would require Parliamentary approval.
22. J.P. Nicholson and Paul Macmillan, *An Overview of Economic Circumstances of Registered Indians in Canada* (Ottawa, Indian and Northern Affairs Canada, 1986).
23. Robert L. Bish, *Financing Indian Self-Government: Practice and Principles* (Ottawa: Institute for Research on Public Policy, March 1987).
24. See Allan M. Maslove (ed.) *Budgeting in the Provinces*, (especially chapter 6) (Ottawa: Institute of Public Administration of Canada, 1989).
25. For a discussion of this point with respect to education, see Jerry Paquette, *Aboriginal Self-Government and Education in Canada*, Background Paper No. 10 (Kingston: Queen's University, Institute of Intergovernmental Relations, 1986).
26. See R.F. Salisbury, *A Homeland for the Cree: Regional Development in James Bay, 1971-1981* (Kingston and Montreal: McGill-Queen's University Press, 1986).

27. See John Wienstein, *Aboriginal Government Off A Land Base*, Background Paper No. 8 (Kingston: Queen's University, Institute of Intergovernmental Relations, 1986).
28. See William Reeves, "Native Societies: The Professions as a Model of Self-Determination for Urban Natives," in J. Rick Ponting (ed.) *Arduous Journey: Canadian Indians and Decolonization* (Toronto: McClelland and Stewart Limited, 1986).
29. Opting out of some activities (e.g., child custody or tribal inheritance) would likely also require renouncing aboriginal status.

APPENDIX

EXISTING ARRANGEMENTS AND PROPOSALS: A SELECTED SUMMARY

Cree-Naskapi

- *Form of Self-Government*

Under this arrangement, aboriginal self-government is land-based and is ethnic in character. The scope of government is regional while its basis of power is the result of legislation (the *Cree/Naskapi of Quebec Act*). Government powers are semi-autonomous.

- *Fiscal Arrangements*

The legal framework for fiscal arrangements is the result of legislation (the *Cree/Naskapi of Quebec Act*). Funds are provided through cash transfers; in addition, band corporations have powers of taxation. The basis for receipt of funding is through subsidies in the form of unconditional grants and entitlement payments from the Cree and Naskapi land claims settlement. Fiscal arrangements do not incorporate fiscal equalization factors. Funding levels are determined by a fiscal formula which considers population increases and inflation as well as special circumstances. The Cree/Naskapi must maintain accounting, reporting, audit and financial systems conforming to Part IV of the Act. The minister can appoint an administrator if the band's financial affairs are in disorder and can also inspect financial records or appoint an auditor. This arrangement is for five years with annual adjustments.

- *Community Characteristics (Economic and Political)*

While the level of economic development allows for some own-revenues, cash transfers are the main source of funding. The Cree/Naskapi do have powers of taxation. In terms of incentives, the Cree/Naskapi have instituted programs whereby Cree hunters and trappers pursuing subsistence activities are provided with a degree of income security. Under this model, bands are accountable to their memberships for their own financial affairs. Records must be kept for federal and non-federal funds. Ministers have financial accountability for the general well-being of the corporations, but not in determining funding for local government priorities. Clearly some capacity exists in the communities for financial management, planning and budgeting.

Kativik Regional Government

- *Form of Self-Government*

This model of aboriginal self-government is land-based and public in character. Its scope is regional while its semi-autonomous government powers are the result of legislation.

- *Fiscal Arrangements*

The legal framework for fiscal arrangements is the result of provincial legislation (the *Act concerning Northern Villages and the Kativik Regional Government*), which provides Kativik with the legal status of a municipal corporation. Funds for Kativik come from tax revenues and external financing from seven Quebec departments. The funding is in the form of spending conditional transfers. The adjustment of funds is at the discretion of the donor (the Quebec government). Ministers of the seven Quebec departments retain final word over funding proposals. Kativik does an audit and provides the results to the Quebec government. Kativik must negotiate annually with the seven Quebec departments for its external funds.

- *Community Characteristics (Economic and Political)*

Municipalities have taxation powers over businesses, stock in trade, rental property and can issue both building permits and business licenses. It is uncertain whether fiscal transfers are aimed explicitly at establishing equity between aboriginal communities and the rest of the population. Kativik has income support programs for individuals engaging in hunting, fishing and trapping. With respect to accountability, municipalities must submit their budgets to Kativik and in turn Kativik must submit its budget proposals to the appropriate provincial ministries.

Indian Band Government

• *Form of Self-Government*

This model of aboriginal self-government is land-based and is ethnic in character. The government is local and its basis of authority is derived from legislation (the *Indian Act*). Government powers are dependent/administrative, with legislative authority on some matters.

• *Fiscal Arrangements*

The legal framework for fiscal arrangements is through legislation (the *Indian Act*). Funds are provided through cash transfers, and in addition bands have power of taxation. The cash transfers are spending conditional. There is no clear model that determines funding to all bands, and the funding arrangements do not incorporate explicit equalization factors. Funding is adjusted at the donor's discretion. Chiefs and councils must negotiate annually on every item in the band's operating budget. Bands are accountable to the minister.

• *Community Characteristics (Economic and Political)*

The degree of economic development for the majority of bands is low. Thus, cash transfers are the primary source of revenues. It is uncertain whether fiscal arrangements are aimed at establishing some degree of equity between aboriginal communities and the rest of the population. There does not seem to be any consideration of incentives under this arrangement since bands are purely administrative for the most part, and have no say in decision making, planning and budgeting. The accountability of the band council to its members is diverse. The degree of administrative capacity for financial management, planning and budgeting is varied.

• *Alternative Funding Arrangements*

Alternative Funding Arrangements (AFA) are available to some Indian bands. The arrangements, which cover a wide range of services, offer somewhat greater certainty since they can be for a five-year term (subject to annual Parliamentary appropriation). They also offer more flexibility in that unused funds can be reallocated to other sectors, although conditions attached to the funds are still very strict (service standards, program audits, administrative procedures).

Penner Report Proposals

• *Form of Self-Government*

The Penner Report proposal for aboriginal self-government is land-based and ethnic in character. It is local/community in scope and its basis of powers would be constitutional. Government powers would be autonomous in nature.

• *Fiscal Arrangements*

The legal framework for fiscal arrangements would be constitutional. Funds would be paid through a combination of cash transfers and tax revenues. The basis for receipt of funding would be claims settlements as well as direct grants to all recognized Indian First Nations. Funding would be based on a per capita formula. Global amounts of funding would be determined by federal and First Nation representatives. The fiscal arrangement would also incorporate an explicit equalization factor. Adjustment would be by formula (not stated); in addition, funding for exceptional needs would be provided. Accountability to the minister would cease; however, an independent office to monitor and report to Parliament on official actions affecting Indian First Nations would be established. The term for funding would be five years.

• *Community Characteristics (Economic and Political)*

Fiscal arrangements would be aimed at achieving both equity within aboriginal communities and with the non-Indian population (equalization payments). The fiscal arrangements could potentially incorporate strong incentives for development since Indians would have control over budgeting, planning and program design. Indian First Nation governments would be accountable to their own people. A Minister of State for Indian First Nation Relations would be established to promote the interests of First Nations. A strong administrative capacity would be required since First Nations would be responsible for formulation, implementation and delivery of services.

Cree School Board

• *Form of Self-Government*

The Cree School Board is land-based and was created under the James Bay and Northern Quebec Agreement which was signed by Ottawa, Quebec and representatives of the Cree nation. This school board falls under Quebec jurisdiction. However, it retains special powers and a mandate to provide culturally relevant programs.

• *Fiscal Arrangements*

The legal framework for fiscal arrangements is contained in s.16.0.28 of the James Bay and Northern Quebec Agreement. Quebec provides 25 per cent of the board's funds while the Department of Indian Affairs and Northern Development contributes the remainder. The basis for receipt of funding is entitlement; funding is determined by a formula. Adjustments are made to accommodate cost increases. The degree of the board's accountability to both levels of government is uncertain. Funding is on an annual basis.

• *Community Characteristics (Economic and Political)*

Administrative capacity is relatively high; the board manages a system of 190 teachers and 260 administrative support and professional staff.

Saskatchewan Indian Federated College

• *Form of Self-Government*

The Saskatchewan Federated College is not directly land-based. The college is under the jurisdiction of the Saskatchewan Indian First Nations (an organization representing status Indians in the province) and is federated with the University of Regina.

• *Fiscal Arrangements*

The funds are provided through cash transfers authorized in legislation by the donor governments. Funding is spending conditional. Adjustments in funding are at the donor's discretion. The degree of accountability to both levels of government is unclear. The college is financed through five-year agreements with the federal and provincial governments.

- *Community Characteristics (Economic and Political)*

This dimension is not directly comparable to the other arrangements. The college is independent from the University of Regina.

Gabriel Dumont Institute of Native Studies and Applied Research

- *Form of Self-Government*

This is not a land-based model. The institute is incorporated as a non-profit corporation. Programs offered are for teacher education and technical training. The institute conducts research in curriculum development and Metis culture and history.

- *Fiscal Arrangements*

Funds are provided by the Saskatchewan departments of Education and Advanced Education and Manpower. Supplementary funding for certain programs is available from the Secretary of State and from Employment and Immigration Canada. The funding is spending conditional. Adjustments are at the donor's discretion. The degree of accountability is uncertain. However, the curriculum must be fully accredited and recognized. Funding is negotiated on an annual basis.

- *Community Characteristics (Economic and Political)*

As in this previous instance, this dimension is not directly relevant. However, administrative capacity is relatively high; the institute designs and supervises activities and programs.

Denendeh (Dene-Metis proposal)

- *Form of Self-Government*

The Dene-Metis model for aboriginal self-government is land-based and public in character. The scope of the government would be regional and its power would be based on legislation. Government powers would be semi-autonomous.

• Fiscal Arrangements

The legal framework for fiscal arrangements would be by means of an agreement. Funds would be provided through cash transfers and tax revenues. The funding arrangements would be part of a land claims settlement. Other aspects such as equity, adjustment mechanisms, accountability and the term of the fiscal arrangements are uncertain.

• Community Characteristics (Economic and Political)

The degrees of economic development, and administrative capacity are varied.

Sechelt Band Government

• Form of Self-Government

The Sechelt model of aboriginal self-government is land-based and is ethnic in character. It is regional in scope (consists of 33 reserves) and its basis of power is federal legislation (*Sechelt Self-Government Act*). Provincial legislation (*Sechelt Indian Government District Enabling Act*) also confers the comparable legal status of a municipality. Government powers are semi-autonomous.

• Fiscal Arrangements

The legal framework of the arrangement is federal legislation, based on a government-aboriginal agreement. Funds are in the form of cash transfers; revenues may also be raised through local taxes. Additional financing between the band and the federal government can also be arranged in the form of conditional grants. Funding is determined by a fiscal formula. It is uncertain whether this fiscal arrangement incorporates an explicit equalization factor. Funding is adjusted in response to cost increases and includes a population index. Bands must provide audited consolidated financial statements to the minister. The funding period is for a five-year term, and the level of funding in any year is determined by the formula.

• Community Characteristics (Economic and Political)

In relative terms the level of economic development is advanced; administration, logging and fishing are key economic activities. The council is financially accountable to members of the Band. The administrative capacity for financial management, planning and budgeting is relatively strong.

Nunavut Proposal

• *Form of Self-Government*

This proposal is land-based and public in character. The scope of government would be regional. Government powers would be semi-autonomous.

• *Fiscal Arrangements*

The legal framework for fiscal arrangements would be the result of legislation. Funds would be a combination of cash transfers and tax revenues. Block grants are favoured by the Inuit. Funding determinacy, the redistributive aspects, adjustment mechanisms, accountability and term are unspecified.

• *Community Characteristics (Economic and Political)*

The Nunavut government would be accountable to its own people. However, the degree of accountability to the federal minister is uncertain. Administrative capacity under this model would be high.

BIBLIOGRAPHY

Bish, Robert L. *Financing Indian Self-Government: Practice and Principles*. Ottawa: Institute for Research on Public Policy, 1987.

Canada. Supply and Services Canada. Report of the Special Committee (Penner Report), *Indian Self-Government in Canada*. Ottawa, 1983.

Hawkes, David C. *Aboriginal Self-Government: What Does It Mean?* Kingston: Queen's University, Institute of Intergovernmental Relations, 1985.

Malone, M. *Financing Aboriginal Self-Government in Canada*, Background Paper No. 9. Kingston: Queen's University, Institute of Intergovernmental Relations, 1986.

Maslove, Allan M. (ed.) *Budgeting in the Provinces*. Ottawa: Institute of Public Administration of Canada, 1989.

Nicholson, J.P. and Paul Macmillan. *An Overview of Economic Circumstances of Registered Indians in Canada*. Ottawa: Indian and Northern Affairs Canada, 1986.

Paquette, Jerry. *Aboriginal Self-Government and Education in Canada*, Background Paper No. 10. Kingston: Queen's University, Institute of Intergovernmental Relations, 1986.

Peters, Evelyn J. *Aboriginal Self-Government Arrangements in Canada*, Background Paper No. 15. Kingston: Queen's University, Institute of Intergovernmental Relations, 1987.

Pratt, Alan. "Federalism in the Era of Aboriginal Self-Government," this volume.

Reeves, William. "Native Societies: The Professions as a Model of Self-Determination for Urban Natives" in J. Rick Ponting (ed.), *Arduous Journey: Canadian Indians and Decolonization*. Toronto: McClelland and Stewart Limited, 1986.

Salisbury, R.F. *A Homeland for the Cree: Regional Development in James Bay, 1971-1981*. Kingston and Montreal: McGill-Queen's University Press, 1986.

Slattery, Brian. "Understanding Aboriginal Rights." (1986) 66 *Canadian Bar Review*, pp. 727-783.

Weinstein, John. *Aboriginal Government Off A Land Base*, Background Paper No. 8. Kingston: Queen's University, Institute of Intergovernmental Relations, 1986.

PART II
EXISTING FEDERAL AND PROVINCIAL RESPONSIBILITIES

CHAPTER 5

HIGH POLITICS IS NOT ENOUGH: POLICIES AND PROGRAMS FOR ABORIGINAL PEOPLES IN ALBERTA AND ONTARIO

Frances Abele and Katherine Graham

INTRODUCTION

The long process of political mobilization and national organization begun by aboriginal peoples[1] in the mid-1960s culminated in a series of First Ministers' Conferences (FMCs) on Aboriginal Constitutional Matters in the 1980s. Canada's newly patriated and amended Constitution entrenched "existing aboriginal and treaty rights" and set in motion the series of highly publicized meetings of federal, provincial and aboriginal leaders.[2] Although the FMCs concluded without resolution of what became the focal issue—constitutional entrenchment of aboriginal peoples' inherent right to self-government—the participants in the process may count many victories, including the constitutional amendment itself, increased public awareness of, and respect for, aboriginal peoples' concerns, and the precedent of dealing with these concerns at the highest possible level of negotiation.

A secondary, and arguably less positive effect of the First Ministers' Conferences was the direction of leaders' and activists' attention towards the high politics of executive federalism and away from issues of administration and service delivery in native communities. This chapter begins with the observation that attention to these practical matters is an essential *complement* to high-level negotiation and political activism at the national level. As a consequence, particularly now that the First Ministers' Conferences have concluded, relations between aboriginal peoples and the governments of the provinces where they live have become more important. Not only do provincial governments contest control of some of the land and resources that figure largely in some aboriginal peoples' plans for their future, but more important for our purposes here, provinces also possess the constitutional mandate, expertise and administrative systems in program and service delivery central to most visions of aboriginal self-government. For the realization of self-determination, questions of administration and implementation are just as important as constitutional and legal issues— though they are not *more* important.

The first section of this chapter outlines the reasoning that led us to consider aboriginal-provincial relations. Then we turn our attention to aboriginal-provincial relations in two provinces, Alberta and Ontario. The circumstances of aboriginal people in Alberta and Ontario are briefly described, and then some preliminary observations about aboriginal-provincial relations in each province are offered, with a view to exploring the complex prospect that now faces aboriginal peoples in the aftermath of the FMC process. Recent developments in programming and program agreements provide some basis for optimism about the potential for progress towards self-government even in the absence of high-level nation-to-nation negotiations. Noting that the process of policy and program development in each case is very different and reflects the political and administrative cultures of the two provinces, we argue that in each situation there are opportunities for aboriginal peoples to realize benefits that extend beyond those that could have been realized through unitary negotiations at the aboriginal-federal-provincial bargaining table.

WHY HIGH POLITICS IS NOT ENOUGH

The FMCs created and concluded a period of principled debate and vigorous political struggle, dominated by aboriginal, provincial and federal leaders, activists, organizers, researchers, lawyers and constitutional advisors who found their grandest stage in the high politics of nationally televised conferences. Preparation for, and participation in, the FMCs occupied a great deal of the attention of many (though not all) aboriginal political leaders and their staffs. The high stakes at the constitutional table and prospect of registering permanent gains in the legal system that governs aboriginal peoples' relations with the rest of society compelled such a concentration of effort. Also, while the FMCs were in progress, there was a tendency for non-constitutional issues to be placed on hold, or at least to be resolved only on a provisional basis, to ensure that victories at the constitutional table would not be undercut by concessions at other levels. And, as is often the case, scholarly attention was attracted by the importance and energy of constitutional political struggle, with the result that relatively scant attention has been paid to other questions.[3]

Yet there are other important aspects to aboriginal peoples' struggle for their rights. These include traditionally *provincial* policy fields which impinge upon local or community social and economic development, language preservation and cultural development, and aboriginal control in policing and in social service delivery. Victories achieved in the high politics of constitutional negotiation and in legal battles are very important, but without progress in policy and programming in these other areas, the constitutional victories will be hollow. Self-government is a *practice*, as well as a condition. Under any constitutional regime, administrative systems and suitably trained personnel, as well as procedures through which agencies co-operate with the communities they are serving, must be developed along lines complementary to the goal of aboriginal self-government. The development of all these capacities by aboriginal-controlled organizations is bound to require experimentation and to take some time.

As the statistics we review later in this paper indicate, the social and economic circumstances in most aboriginal communities in Canada mean that the people who live there have less chance than most non-aboriginal Canadians to live fully satisfying lives. Though this situation is a consequence of historical injustices and errors not of their own making, it is only aboriginal people themselves who can sustain the process of change to better conditions. What they require from non-aboriginal people and governments are the room and the resources to develop their communities. In doing this, most aboriginal peoples in Canada will have to deal with both provincial and federal governments, although the extent and specific areas of involvement will vary. For treaty Indians living on reserves, federal obligations are relatively clear-cut and protected by the precedents set by earlier interpretations of the treaties. However, there have been, and probably will continue to be, disputes about the adequacy of federal funding to on-reserve programs and certainly about any extension of federally-funded programming. For the Metis and the slowly diminishing number of non-status Indians, as well as for treaty Indians living off reserve, federal obligations are somewhat less clear.[4] Whatever is the case in legal principle, in practice it is evident that, as in the past, both federal and provincial participation will continue to be crucial for adequate provision of services to these groups. It is likely, too, that the political jousting about which level of government is responsible for specific services will continue.

For this reason among others, aboriginal organizations neither can nor should abandon their political advocacy roles or executive-level political negotiation. Aboriginal peoples' political organizations, *particularly* in their role as national representatives and collective voices, are crucial to the continuation of the process of national realignment that aboriginal peoples initiated over twenty years ago. Without their activities on the national scene, it is likely that very few changes would have been realized locally. Further, whatever the provinces may undertake, the federal role is still decisive. Federal leadership is still required to move discussions of self-government ahead, and federal funds are necessary, both legally and practically, for specific programs and services. Thus the federal stance on aboriginal issues sets the stage for provincial actions, as is evident from the somewhat contradictory effects of the current federal reluctance to deal with aboriginal issues creatively and energetically. Federal inaction both prompts pragmatic responses from provincial governments concerned with meeting their statutory obligations *and* constrains provincial actions by heightening uncertainty, particularly about the all-important legal and fiscal relationship between the Government of Canada and aboriginal peoples. Particularly in the aftermath of the First Ministers' Conferences on the Constitution, the necessary involvement of representative provincial, territorial and national aboriginal organizations in high politics will certainly continue, but it may be advisable to combine these efforts with a new openness to the provinces.

In a number of ways the research presented here is incomplete. We offer only a provocative contribution to what must be in the long run a very ambitious research project, best undertaken by numbers of researchers working in all provinces. It is not possible to do justice to the complexity and variety in the basket of initiatives for even the two provinces we have chosen; there is space here only for general observations, interesting examples and cautious conclusions. As well, our attention has been primarily upon *provincial* organization and initiatives, and upon *provincial* responses to aboriginal peoples' demands. Although we have considered what aboriginal peoples have had to say, we have not conducted a thorough community-based evaluation of the impact of provincial initiatives. Such an enterprise was well beyond our means; yet it is necessary before the complete picture will be available. Another limitation is that neither province's public accounts include a systematic record of programs designed primarily to serve aboriginal people, nor is it possible to develop for either province time-series data on levels of provincial spending for services to aboriginal people. Therefore, at this stage in our research it has not been possible to complement our administrative analysis with an accurate measure of either province's financial commitment to program goals.

ABORIGINAL PEOPLES IN ALBERTA AND ONTARIO

The single most evident characteristic of the aboriginal population of the two provinces is the diversity. It is most important to realize that this diversity applies when one examines the characteristics of the aboriginal population *within* each province. Generally, while aboriginal peoples are in poorer socio-economic circumstances than the rest of the population, the diversity of circumstance among urban and rural, and status and non-status Indians is striking. In some respects, aboriginal people living near or in urban settings in both provinces have more similarities with each other than they do with other aboriginal people who live in rural or remote areas of their respective province. Nonetheless, differences in heritage among aboriginal communities should not be minimized. These differences shape the relationships of particular aboriginal communities with each other and with their respective provincial governments.

Data from the 1986 census indicate that the total aboriginal population in Alberta was 103,930.[5] According to the Indian Register of the Department of Indian Affairs and Northern Development,[6] there were 48,706 registered Indians in Alberta in 1986 comprising about 13 per cent of the national total of registered Indians. This same year 72 per cent of all registered Indians in Alberta were living on a total of 90 reserves, with nearly 93 per cent of the reserve residents living within 350 kilometres of the nearest service centre accessible year-round.[7] Reserves in Alberta vary in size, but generally are larger than the national average. There is also great variation in economic prosperity, particularly between reserves with significant oil and gas production and those without revenue from this source.

According to the 1986 census data, the aboriginal population of Ontario was 167,375.[8] The Department of Indian Affairs and Northern Development reported 86,544 registered Indians in Ontario in 1986, or about 23 per cent of the registered Indians in Canada. In Ontario, 64 per cent of all registered Indians in Ontario were living on reserves. In 1981, there were 185 Indian reserves in Ontario, and as in Alberta, these were on average larger than reserves elsewhere in Canada.[9] Most of the aboriginal population lives in the southern more-developed parts of the province, but significant numbers live in the much smaller centres and more rural circumstances of northern Ontario. The Kenora area has the highest concentration of aboriginal people, with more than one-quarter (27 per cent) of the population in the region and almost 15 per cent of all aboriginals in the province. Another region with a significant concentration of aboriginal peoples is the area between Nipissing and Parry Sound (both northward and westward). Aboriginal people represent an important proportion of the local population in Brant County, and the districts of Cochrane, Rainy River and Manitoulin.

Recent demographic profiles of the status-Indian populations in the two provinces indicate some striking similarities. The Indian population is growing faster than the general population in both Alberta and Ontario, and is generally younger. This trend may be declining in Alberta but is expected to continue in Ontario. In both provinces, Indians have higher crude death rates and a significantly lower life expectancy than the rest of the population. Indians are less well-educated in both provinces than the general population.

Low educational attainment is most acute among Indians living in rural and remote areas. Younger Indians are achieving higher levels of education than their elders but still lag behind. Labour force participation and income among the Indian population is lower, while unemployment among Indians is generally higher than the rate of unemployment experienced by the rest of the population in both Alberta and Ontario. [10]

These patterns, while not reliable enough to provide precise measures, do in the aggregate establish that there are very significant social and economic needs among aboriginal people living in both provinces. By all social indicators, aboriginal peoples in both jurisdictions are in worse shape than the general population. The reasons for this differential lie in the history of relations between aboriginal and non-aboriginal people, in the occupation of aboriginal lands by non-aboriginals and in the policies that have governed aboriginal people's lives since Europeans arrived here. Aboriginal peoples have been working for decades in a number of different settings to establish the political and economic independence necessary for long-term solutions.

As this process has evolved in Alberta, distinctions among treaty and non-treaty Indians and Metis have had considerable political salience. Northern Alberta Metis have had a unique relationship with the provincial government, arising from the establishment of Metis settlements in northern Alberta under the *Metis Betterment Act* (1936). [11] The settlements are represented by the Alberta Federation of Metis Settlement Associations. Metis elsewhere in the province are represented principally by the Metis Association of Alberta (MAA) and a provincial office of the Native Council of Canada. [12] The Indian Association of Alberta represents Indians whose ancestors signed Treaties 6, 7 and 8.

Besides these major representative bodies, there are other aboriginal organizations which represent the interests of, for example, aboriginal women, or which have specific service roles. Besides the Alberta Native Women's Association, there are four other more specific bodies. [13] There are friendship centres in a province-wide network, and dozens of community-based or regional organizations in the areas of arts and crafts, culture, communications and education. Two important examples of aboriginal-controlled service-delivery organizations with a province-wide focus are the Native Counselling Services of Alberta, which provides a range of services in justice and corrections, and the Nechi Institute, devoted to rehabilitation of people with drug and alcohol problems. More recently, aboriginal people have also formed a number of co-operative councils, for example, in the area of economic development planning.

Within Ontario, a fairly complex network of organizations represents various segments of the aboriginal population. The variety of organizations carrying out a representational role beyond the band or community level reflects the diversity of the Ontario aboriginal population itself. The Chiefs of Ontario Office represents the four status-Indian associations to the Assembly of First Nations and is a vehicle for Ontario government/Indian consultation on matters pertinent to Indian people in Ontario. The office consists of the Association of Iroquois and Allied Indians (AIAI)—an umbrella organization representing the interests of eight bands (First Nations) in Southern Ontario; the Grand Council Treaty No. 3 which represents 25 Ojibway Nations reserves—the three main areas of the treaty being Kenora, Dryden and Fort Frances; the Nishnawbe-Aski Nation (NAN) which represents Treaty No. 9 people; and the Anishinabek Nation Union of Ontario Indians (UOI)—the oldest political aboriginal organization in Ontario, representing the interests of 38 First Nations along Lake Superior, Georgian Bay and in Southern Ontario.

The Ontario Metis and Non-Status Indian Association (OMNSIA) represents the interests of Metis and non-status Indians in Ontario. The province is administratively split into five zones. Membership is composed of residents of Ontario who are 18 years of age, of aboriginal descent, Metis or non-status Indian. The Metis Native Council has been active in Ontario as well.

The history of treaties in Ontario is long and varied. The conclusion of treaty agreements at various periods in the province's history has set the stage for current land claims disputes. Such disputes tend to occupy centre stage and gain the lion's share of public attention related to aboriginal politics in Ontario.

Treaties made between the British Crown or federal government and aboriginal people of Ontario generally were concluded during three periods: pre-Confederation, early Confederation and early twentieth century. After the United States War of Independence, the Crown concluded a number of land cession agreements with Indians in southern Ontario to assist in the settlement of the United Empire Loyalists and to fulfil promises of land grants made to its Iroquois allies in recognition of their military service.

In 1850 the Robinson-Superior Treaty and the Robinson-Huron Treaty (the Robinson treaties) were concluded, clearing aboriginal title to the area north of lakes Superior and Huron for the development of minerals.

Treaty No. 3 was signed in 1873 by the Canadian government and the Ojibway nations of what is now northwestern Ontario. The treaty cleared aboriginal title to lands from southeastern Manitoba. to east of Dryden, from the Canada/United States border to the 50th parallel. Treaty No. 9 was concluded in 1905-06 by the Canadian government, the Ontario government and the Cree-Ojibway nations in the area now known as northern Ontario. The Chippewa and Mississauga agreements were concluded in 1923, in an effort to resolve disputes and uncertainties concerning pre-Confederation land cessions in southern and central Ontario.

GOVERNING TRADITIONS IN ONTARIO AND ALBERTA

For many years, Alberta and Ontario have presented contrasting faces in national constitutional matters. Alberta has a national image as the haven of free-enterprise "buccaneer" capitalism, with a series of provincial governments dedicated to serving the interests of regional entrepreneurs. On aboriginal matters, Alberta is seen as one of the traditional "spoiler" provinces, stubbornly unwilling to recognize the legitimacy of aboriginal aspirations or to negotiate new principles. Ontario, on the other hand, has often displayed more openness and a cautious willingness to reach symbolically-important agreements on aboriginal matters, a stance compatible with Ontario's image as a rich but bland province whose leaders have assumed (with some degree of *noblesse oblige*) that what is good for Canada is good for Ontario, and vice versa.

While there is some basis in fact for these different images, they are also misleading: the practical reality beneath the public image in each province is more similar than different. Alberta's "red-neck" reputation is belied by many internal provincial initiatives, while Ontario's more "liberal" national face has not always been complemented by action (and fiscal commitment) in services.

First, despite the differences between the positions of the two provinces in national constitutional talks, neither has been particularly successful in addressing outstanding specific claims within their borders.[14] Second, despite the differences in the language used by politicians and officials to describe the process, neither province has displayed any indication that extension of powers to aboriginal collectivities will move beyond delegation of statutory authority in specific functional areas. The review of actual programming later in this discussion suggests that, to date, aboriginal self-government in Ontario has been effectively the same thing as what could be called aboriginal self-administration in Alberta.

Since the 1930s, Alberta has known a series of legislatures dominated by one party and faced with negligible opposition. This has led to a certain governing style, characterized by relatively inaccessible ministers, weak legislative committees and few central agencies. It has also produced some very interesting openings to popular participation at the administrative level. A system of special advisory committees and permanent advisory councils on matters ranging from arts and culture through northern development to senior citizens' affairs makes public participation in the policy process possible. The legislative branch in Alberta appears relatively impermeable to opposition forces, while the bureaucracy is unusually open. However odd this system appears when compared to the traditional Westminster model of democratic government, the practical consequences of the system are less undemocratic than might be expected. Some evidence for this is found in the province's relatively high levels of spending on health care, education and social services and in Albertans' willingness to elect, repeatedly, very large majority governments.[15]

Both the province's relative electoral unanimity and successive provincial governments' reluctance to entrench aboriginal self-government are related to Alberta's historical and current position in Confederation. Alberta is a recently formed "settler" province. Provincial control over Crown land (and thus the energy reserves upon which provincial prosperity is based) was not ceded by the federal government until 1930. While certainly energy-sector corporations exercise enormous economic and political power in Alberta (over governments, unions, parties and citizens' everyday life), Albertans' enduring support for "provincialist" strategies is more than a manifestation of the overriding influence of corporations. As successful politicians in the province have long recognized, these strategies are based upon an interpretation of reality that is still persuasive to the descendants of recent settlers. Significant proportions of the electorate, at least, may see themselves precariously established in a territory quite recently taken from aboriginal people, more recently yet secured against "colonial" administration by the federal government, and then confronted by federal governments led by parties responsive to the more populous provinces of central Canada.[16]

Taken together, these considerations shed some light on the overall approach to aboriginal affairs by successive Alberta governments. These have all been remarkably consistent on certain questions of principle: in particular, there will be no symbolic agreement to aboriginal self-government until there is a clear definition of the political, economic and administrative implications of such a step. On the other side, treaty Indians in Alberta insist upon the overwhelming importance of their treaties with the Crown, even where this emphasis interferes with the benefits that might arise from political solidarity with non-treaty aboriginal people in Alberta and nationally. For treaty Indians, the treaties are all there is between them and further displacement by the growing settler population. This has sustained a reluctance to deal directly with the provincial government which is often seen to represent only the interlopers.

Further, it is clear that provincial control over energy reserves and other resources will be carefully guarded, and that provincial authority and responsibility in other areas will be protected, even if this is expensive. Thus, while the province resists any contraction of federal fiscal responsibilities, there is a willingness to spend money on a made-in-Alberta solution. This willingness, taken together with relatively well-stocked provincial coffers and the permeability of the provincial bureaucracy, has created opportunities for aboriginal people in Alberta to make significant incremental breakthroughs. As will be clear from the examples in the next section, even treaty Indians have found a way to take advantage of these opportunities without sacrificing their principles. The 1980s have brought some stirrings towards pragmatic co-operation by all parties for a local resolution of significant problems.

Although Ontario's electoral history is somewhat more multidimensional than Alberta's, the dominance of the Progressive Conservative party in the provincial legislature from the Second World War to the early 1980s, combined with a general ethos toward secular modernity among the province's economic and political elite, shaped the administrative and political structures of the provincial government. Specifically, since the mid-1960s the dominance of rational planning and policy-making structures within the Government of Ontario has been a central characteristic of that province's operation. [17] Decisions may ultimately be made on a "big P" political basis; in fact, partisan political battles in Ontario have tended to be much more heated than in Alberta. However, the longevity of the Conservatives, perhaps to be followed by an equally impressive reign by the current Liberal government, has ensured the place of rational policy and program development structures to deal with broad issues. Inter-departmental committees of officials, up to the Deputy Minister level, grapple with such issues before passing on their findings and recommendations to "mirror committees" of Cabinet. At the bureaucratic level, the system is somewhat more closed than in Alberta. To be sure, external interests may be consulted; but they tend to be established interests rather than government-initiated groups. In short, the elements of a rational, technocratic system exist to channel the energies of Ontario politicians and bureaucrats as they grapple with complex and contentious issues, including aboriginal policy issues.

In contrast with Alberta, the current government in Ontario has embraced the principle and language of self-government without clear definition of the concept. Discussions with provincial officials suggest, however, that the evolution of self-government towards some form of municipal model is implicit in the province's acceptance of this term. Ontario's stance on self-government has had two, somewhat contradictory, results. On one level, its endorsement of the concept has led the bureaucracy to view developments in the aboriginal-affairs field entirely through the prism of self-government, thereby necessitating a "wait and see" approach in the context of deliberations by both aboriginal people and the federal government on the meaning of the concept as well as on the legal and fiscal arrangements which will result from its implementation. On another more pragmatic level, various provincial ministries are moving ahead. In some instances, such as the establishment of aboriginal children's services agencies, this is being done under the provisions of existing provincial legislation (the *Child and Family Services Act* to be exact). In other cases, initiatives are being undertaken in the context of a broader policy stance. For example, the province's Ministry of Correctional Services is now contracting out to various aboriginal organizations the provision of a variety of support services for aboriginal offenders. This is part of the implementation of that Ministry's overall corporate plan which establishes enhancement of services to aboriginal peoples as a priority.

There is another contrast in attitudes to the federal role. Alberta wants to ensure that the federal government meets its responsibilities, but is willing to spend money to provide an equal level of services to all Albertans, in which category they include aboriginal people. Because of historic mistrust of federal power, Alberta is committed to made-in-Alberta solutions. Ontario has a history of a more co-operative relationship with the federal government and has, therefore, been more reluctant to seek independent solutions. Although Ontario has a national image as a "fat cat" province, there are competing demands on the provincial treasury. The fact that significant amounts of the province's own resources have not been expended in innovative programs for aboriginal residents may indicate the weakness of aboriginal organizations relative to other claims on provincial resources.

During the last few years, both provinces have been working in an atmosphere of fiscal restraint. This may account for the fact that, although the political tables were turned in 1984 (putting the Tories in power in Alberta and Ottawa, while a new Liberal-NDP coalition and then a Liberal government in Ontario faced the Tories in Ottawa), each province stuck to its traditional approach. Although the elections of the 1980s may have eased Alberta-Ottawa relations somewhat, the province continued to seek made-in-Alberta solutions and apparently did not display much more reluctance to deploy provincial funds for this purpose. The table-turning elections (and restraint) have affected relations somewhat between Ontario and the federal government. For example, negotiations between Ontario and the federal government concerning funding for the Aboriginal Constable Program have been particularly vexatious for the province. In general, however, neither province has radically departed from their established approach.

There are some similarities between Alberta and Ontario as they grapple with aboriginal policy and program issues. Each province must deal with the reality that status Indians are a federal responsibility, and with federal interest in "off-loading" responsibilities to provincial governments. This concern is particularly acute as Bill C-31 increases the number of Indians entitled to services under the *Indian Act* and reduces the number of non-status Indian citizens. The larger population of Indians with a statutory right to services under the *Indian Act* makes both provinces understandably suspicious that they will have to pick up the slack as the federal government squeezes expenditures on aboriginal peoples. Each province has responded by resisting this trend.

In each province, status-Indian organizations are reluctant to deal directly with the province (both as a matter of principle and from fear that the federal government will reduce its commitment of funds), and in each province there is a history of political and legal conflict between aboriginal people and the provincial government. Both provinces have responded in the same way, by expressing a willingness to do business with communities and bands, individually and on matters in specific program areas. As well, both provinces have maintained a formally "reactive" stance, of waiting for bands to approach them. But they are not passive, since each has taken steps to ensure that doors will be open when bands approach. Alberta cleared the way with the 1978 Extension of Services Policy;[18] in Ontario, the Peterson government has adopted a comprehensive aboriginal policy which sets out the government's overall commitment to dealing with aboriginal issues and providing services to aboriginal people in a manner consistent with their needs and interests. This policy sets the broad framework within which specific ministries, such as Correctional Services, Community and Social Services and Education, operate. Ministry by ministry, more specific commitments to the province's overall goals have started to emerge.

These developments do not mean that each province has rushed willy-nilly into extensive program changes to respond to aboriginal aspirations for either self-government or autonomous program delivery. Indeed, each province shows concern about the capacity of aboriginal organizations to participate in detailed policy development. In some service areas, such as child welfare services and native policing, there is concern about accountability and for how the province will meet statutory responsibilities to ensure certain standards of care and service. The present emphasis in each province seems to be somewhat different, with Ontario most concerned with capacity and restraint, and Alberta currently emphasizing standards and oversight.

154

PROVINCIAL ARRANGEMENTS FOR ABORIGINAL POLICY AND PROGRAM DEVELOPMENT

Structures through which aboriginal policy is developed in each province differ, and (not surprisingly) reflect each province's general tradition of policy development. Over the last fifteen years, Ontario has gradually put in place a formal infrastructure of policy development bodies. The Ontario Native Affairs Directorate (ONAD) was established in the mid-1970s. Its original intent was to signal enhanced provincial-government awareness of aboriginal concerns and to co-ordinate the initiatives of various provincial ministries as they affected aboriginal people. The Directorate was something of a weak sister in its early period, partly reflecting the Conservative government's reluctance to take on aboriginal servicing issues in a major way. This was reflected, in part, by a 1977 Cabinet directive eliminating the provincial governments' involvement in delivering services on Indian reserves.

A considerable change occurred with the 1985 election of a minority Liberal government that held power by virtue of a formal accord with the New Democrats. In the new Cabinet, a high profile senior minister was made responsible for aboriginal affairs. A Cabinet committee on aboriginal affairs was struck, with membership from among the more prominent members of Cabinet. In the best Ontario government tradition, this committee has a corresponding committee of deputy ministers. Both committees meet regularly to deal with broad issues of aboriginal affairs policy as well as possible specific government initiatives. The committee of deputies also acts as an information forum, allowing individual ministries and other government agencies an opportunity to "show and tell" their particular initiatives affecting aboriginal peoples. Apparently both meetings are well attended and lively.

ONAD has also been beefed up under the Liberals. The status of its executive director has been upgraded to that of a deputy minister equivalent, and that person chairs the Committee of Deputy Ministers. The directorate played a lead role in developing the government's aboriginal affairs policy and acts as a central agency in seeing that individual ministries and agencies live up to the spirit and letter of the policy. The bureaucratic capacity for ONAD to carry out this policing/helping role has been enhanced by the recruitment from line ministries of individuals with considerable experience in dealing with aboriginal issues.

In Alberta, there is no Cabinet committee, but rather a system of issue-specific ad hoc advisory committees coupled with some more permanent institutional emphasis. The then-new Progressive Conservative government began the process in 1971,[19] with the establishment of the Alberta Indian and Metis Liaison Group (renamed the Alberta Native Secretariat in 1976 and, renamed again, the Alberta Native Affairs Secretariat in 1979). The Secretariat supported a minister, appointed in 1975 as the first provincial minister in Canada whose sole responsibility was aboriginal affairs. Early in 1986, as part of a general reorganization of a number of departments, the program elements of the native affairs secretariat were amalgamated with municipal affairs and incorporated as part of the Improvement District Operations Division. This new divisional structure was renamed the Improvement Districts and Native Services Division (IDNSD). There is no longer a minister with sole responsibility for aboriginal affairs, although this is not necessarily an indication of a diminishing provincial commitment to addressing aboriginal issues. Besides the officials in the IDNSD, there are now also quite highly-placed and specialized staff to deal with aboriginal matters in the departments of Education, Municipal Affairs and Social Services, among others, as well as an active Intergovernmental Committee on Native Employment.[20]

Committees and councils are used extensively in the Alberta policy-development process, both to promote interdepartmental coordination and to create opportunities for public participation in policy development. The councils tend to be somewhat independent of departments, often supported by their own secretariat and providing advice directly to ministers. Council recommendations are typically made public as well, increasing the likelihood that their message will be attended to by Cabinet. This pattern prevails equally for aboriginal participation on issues that affect them as Albertans (through, for example, the Arts and Culture Council and the Northern Alberta Development Council) and that affect them as aboriginal people specifically.

For specifically aboriginal affairs, ad hoc committees and councils have been used in a number of ways. Some, like the Working Committee on Native Child Welfare, were created as a means to open public participation deliberations on particularly sensitive issues. The Working Committee on Native Child Welfare was formed in the heated aftermath of the suicide of Richard Cardinal, a young Metis who had not been well cared for in the provincially-run foster care system, and other complaints across the prairie provinces about the placement of native children in non-native foster homes. The Alberta Native Child Welfare Committee brought together aboriginal people with expertise on child welfare issues and provincial bureaucrats in the same area.

In the two years it was active, the Working Committee proposed a comprehensive set of long-term strategies in a wide range of areas from legislation and service delivery to financing. These proposals add up to a fundamental change in the nature of aboriginal child welfare services. The principles of the 42 recommendations were threefold: that aboriginal child welfare services be aboriginal-specific, that they be community-based and controlled, and that the content and direction of the services be determined by aboriginal people.[21] Indications are that the Minister of Social Services will implement at least one important recommendation, the formation of a permanent advisory committee on aboriginal issues, although this has not yet occurred. Complementing the work of the Native Child Welfare Committee have been two international conferences on native child welfare, organized by provincial officials and native people concerned with this question.

Another important but somewhat less painful issue was addressed by the Working Group on Native Education, Training and Employment, which had both native and non-native members. This working group conducted research and regional workshops, to produce a final report that analyzed the needs of aboriginal Albertans in these areas and made recommendations for improvements in service. Key recommendations stressed the inter-relationship of education, training and employment with overall social, cultural and economic health in native communities, and the need for native people to have primary responsibility for their own development.[22] In the early 1980s, provincial funding also supported a series of regional seminars organized by the Metis Association of Alberta in 1984 to identify policy areas in need of attention, including education, employment and training, business assistance, social services, justice, recreation, land, housing hunting, trapping and fishing. The spirit of the recommendations emerging from this process are well captured by the title of the final report: *Our Children, Our Future, Our Community, Our Challenge.*[23]

157

Besides these initiatives towards public participation in policy development, the province has been receptive to approaches from bands and tribal councils interested in transferring responsibility for service delivery. This has happened in child welfare and corrections. In 1975 a trilateral agreement on child welfare was reached with the Blackfoot which delegated responsibility for child welfare services to the band. The federal government funds the programs, while the province retains both fiscal and statutory oversight responsibilities. The Blackfoot agreement has recently been renegotiated, and differently structured agreements with other aboriginal peoples have followed. This new generation of child welfare agreements makes use of "double bilateral" agreements, ingenious devices to establish the basis for delegated program delivery by aboriginal peoples that do not jeopardize the constitutional principles held by any of the parties. Establishment of the child welfare regimes on reserves require the agreement and co-operation of the federal and provincial governments and the relevant aboriginal reserve government(s). As noted earlier, treaty Indians in Alberta have been reluctant, for constitutional reasons, to deal directly and officially with the provincial government. Child welfare, however, is a provincial responsibility, which only the province has the power to delegate. The impasse was resolved by casting the necessarily tripartite arrangements in the form of two complementary *bilateral* agreements; one being between the federal government and the Indian authority, and the other between the Indian authority and the province. [24]

In the area of corrections, many services to aboriginal people are contracted out to Native Counselling Services of Alberta (NCSA), a native-controlled organization established in 1971. NCSA is a private non-profit organization devoted to developing and operating programs designed specifically to fill the gaps in legal and social services delivered to aboriginal people. Its programs and services, which are provided free of charge to clients, are directed towards fulfilling the following primary objective: "To gain fair and equitable treatment for aboriginal people involved in the legal system." This objective is achieved by directing program goals toward increasing the understanding of members of the legal system and the public at large about aboriginal involvement in the system, and making information available to aboriginal people about the legal and other systems. Emphasis continues to be mainly on the Criminal and Family Courtwork Programs, the founding programs of

NCSA. Other services also are provided to aboriginal young and adult offenders in the areas of liaison, probation, and parole, and there are also media services, educational workshops and training programs available. To meet local needs, NCSA offers among others a family-life improvement program, an elder's program, and minimum security forestry camps. An important secondary role for NCSA has been the training of aboriginal people for work in government and other agencies. [25]

More recently, some steps have been taken towards creating a more formal negotiating system through which aboriginal organizations may communicate directly with Alberta government officials. A framework agreement has been signed by Metis organizations and provincial officials, which outlines a comprehensive, staged process for communication and negotiation on a wide range of issues of mutual interest. Provincial officials are hopeful that a similar regularization of communication with organizations representing treaty Indians may be achieved. In both cases, the agreement provides certainty and direction to bureaucrats and has the potential to finesse the "large-P" political principles which often obstruct pragmatic co-operation on programs and services. Perhaps the most interesting feature of the existing agreement with the Metis is that it places aboriginal leaders on the same level as provincial Cabinet ministers in the communications protocol. In retrospect, this may be seen as the first tiny and tentative step taken by the Alberta government towards recognition of at least quasi-governmental status for aboriginal organizations; at a minimum, it suggests a means for opening badly needed channels of communication at the political level.

In Ontario, the pattern of interaction and involvement of aboriginal people with the province is somewhat different. There is a fairly extensive network of organizations representing aboriginal interests above the band or community level. Under current Ontario government policy, only three groups—the Ontario Federation of Indian Friendship Centres, the Chiefs of Ontario and the Ontario Native Women's Association—receive core funding, although discussions are underway to open eligibility for core-funding support to others. Other native groups receive funding from various provincial ministries on a negotiated basis. Depending on the issue, provincial politicians and bureaucrats interact with these different groups. The official stance of groups representing status Indians is that they would prefer not to deal with the provincial government. However, at a pragmatic level, discussions do occur and occasionally alliances are forged. [26] This is especially the case in areas subject to bipartite federal-provincial agreements which have aboriginal participation in the process of review and negotiation. For example, both aboriginal organizations and provincial representatives shared frustration over the federal government's nitty-gritty financial perspective on aboriginal policing. Both parties agree there are broader issues to be discussed.

The province also does not hesitate to deal with individual bands, aboriginal communities and special purpose organizations who make independent overtures. This has been the approach in concluding agreements for the provision of children's services and of correctional services to aboriginal offenders. It has also been used in the fields of aboriginal economic development and education.

For example, three Indian agencies have been designated by the Ministry of Community and Social Services as Children's Aid Societies, with all of the powers granted to CASs under the *Child and Family Services Act*. [27] The same Ministry also supports day-nursery programs operated by bands on reserves and by Indian CASs off reserves through agreements under the *Day Nurseries Act*. In this case the bands, treated like Ontario municipalities, are responsible for 20 per cent of the cost of their day nursery programs. (This 20 per cent is paid by the Department of Indian Affairs and Northern Development under the 1965 *Native Welfare Agreement*.)

One provincial-native program without a specific legislated base is the so-called "Li'l Beavers" program. This program, delivered through Indian friendship centres, is designed to take a holistic approach to deal with the culture shock and other problems that young natives may face when they move into an urban setting. It is funded entirely by the government of Ontario: no federal cost-sharing occurs.

The process of developing a positive working relationship between the province and aboriginal organizations and bands for the mounting of programs appropriate to aboriginal needs has not been easy. Negotiations between individual ministries and particular bands or other groups are often protracted, and there are problems in reaching agreement on issues of standards and aboriginal control. Nonetheless, there is evidence of interest and movement by both sides.

Although the Alberta government holds firmly to a position which precludes implementation of aboriginal self-government, at

160

the practical level a number of steps have been taken to increase participation by aboriginal people in the administration of both federally- and provincially-funded programs which affect them. In some cases this has involved delegation or contracting out of service delivery responsibilities. There have even been some tentative steps towards official acceptance of a quasi-governmental role for representative organizations. In Ontario, although the principle of aboriginal self-government is officially accepted, the instruments for consultation and co-operation hardly differ. Where differences do arise, they are more due to the technocratic policy process in Ontario, which gives all government-public interactions a distinct style.

In both provinces, one gets a particular sense from public servants in various ministries that there is a certain amount of excitement in the air. There seems to be at least an ideological commitment at the political level to tackle aboriginal issues, and this has stimulated what may have been an already interested bureaucracy. The open questions that remain concern how the provinces' politicians will be disposed to approach both thorny land claims and the need for increased program expenditures in a period of fiscal restraint. The answers to these two questions will ultimately determine the extent and nature of further microcosmic changes.

WHO IS RESPONSIBLE, AND WHO BENEFITS?

It is appropriate now to examine all these developments from a somewhat broader perspective. We began by asserting that victories at the level of high politics will not on their own produce the necessary improvements in the life circumstances of aboriginal peoples in Canada. Innovative policies and creative program initiatives, with a significant measure of *local* aboriginal control and influence, are also required. More to the point, we take the position that the formulation and delivery of programs appropriate to the needs and interests of aboriginal peoples represents the underside of the iceberg. Programs, regardless of their functional orientation, are the stuff of life for most people in Canada, and this extends to aboriginal Canadians. The backdrop of self-government and aboriginal-rights issues is all pervasive; but concrete needs and aspirations for community development and the enhancement of the condition of aboriginal people are pressing. This issue is particularly acute given

the current impasse at the constitutional level, but even with constitutional entrenchment of the inherent right of aboriginal peoples
to self-government, there will be a need for Aboriginal-federal-
provincial co-operation in the relocation of service delivery responsibilities, and in the development by aboriginal peoples of appropriate programming.

Recognition of the importance of programming has some critical
implications for aboriginal communities and their leaders. The fact
is that the most public programming in areas relevant to the needs
and interests of aboriginal peoples is now a provincial responsibility.
Constitutionally, and under the strictures of the *Indian Act*, this is
certainly true for non-status Indians and Metis, but the reality of
provincial involvement is becoming equally salient for status Indians
as well. The federal government is increasingly disinclined to offer
programs directly to status Indians. This suggests that whatever
capacity the federal bureaucracy had for direct programming in
areas such as education or social services is on the wane. At the
level of programming, federal strength appears to be further weakened by the terms of the Meech Lake Accord, especially in the area
of social policy, which is so crucial to aboriginal peoples.[28] This prospect of what is likely to emerge as our new federal system is ignored
by aboriginal peoples at their peril.

Acknowledgement of the importance of programming does not
deny the fundamental issue of self-government. Incremental
changes towards aboriginal-controlled social and economic services, even under the ideal conditions of steady incremental change
and adequate funding, will not eliminate the need for constitutional
amendment. Adoption of a conscious perspective on the development of programs to meet the needs and interests of aboriginal peoples, however, may help elaborate a concrete understanding of the
forms self-government might take. And in the meantime, it may
improve the relative level of self-determination practiced by aboriginal peoples living in the provinces. In conclusion, we offer some
suggestions about an approach to the development of programs to
meet aboriginal needs and interests. We also explore the implications of this approach for aboriginal communities, provincial governments, provincial/territorial organizations representing aboriginal people and the federal government.

One must begin with an understanding of the problem posed
by fragmented program planning and delivery. Everywhere in
Canada, the traditional model for government creates function-

specific offices, and often fragmented service-delivery units, each aimed at a particular problem. There are employment offices, training facilities, various economic-development support programs, and a variety of social services programs—ranging from transfer payments for individuals to various kinds of counselling and direct intervention. On Indian reserves and in rural settlements, the fragmentation is often compounded by jurisdictional divisions between federal and provincial governments.

Yet many aboriginal people live in small, relatively isolated communities, where this functional differentiation creates more problems than it solves. Frequently, services in these areas are delivered by one resident staff-person or by a shared staff-person who may be responsible for service delivery in several locations (and responsible to distant decision-makers). Professionals work without collegial contact and support and, frequently, without the authority to implement necessary program adjustments. Further, for residents of the communities, it is often difficult to make sense of program differentiation: when one is thinking of the well-being of perhaps 50 specific teenagers, how can their needs be sorted out into appropriate program areas, and how can the officials responsible for program delivery co-ordinate their efforts?

One obvious step in the right direction is to transfer service-delivery responsibilities to local authorities, with adequate funding and with sufficient room (in the terms of the funding) to permit recombination of service functions as appropriate in a particular area. An instance of just such a measure exists in Slave Lake, Alberta, where the federally-funded Young Offenders Program, the Department of Indian Affairs and Northern Development and the provincial social services department have co-operated with local people who wanted to establish a multi-purpose drop-in centre for the community's youth. In this example, the federal and provincial governments have begun to support a process of community-led development, guided by local perceptions of needs.

This apparently straightforward solution to the fragmentation problem may not have been so easy to achieve in Ontario, where the existence of a more formalized policy-process strengthens functional separations. Alberta's pragmatic approach, and the province's commitment (apparently even fiscal) to home-grown solutions, makes such ventures easier to achieve. In Ontario, the province's capacity to take pragmatic steps could be enhanced by assigning more programmatic responsibilities to ONAD—including the responsibility to work through, and with, service-delivery personnel in line ministries. Integrated policy development must be complemented by integrated program planning.

There is, of course, a corresponding danger associated with the advantages of the pragmatic, informal approach in Alberta. The province is willing to make arrangements with aboriginal communities and reserves on a piecemeal basis, working where possible around jurisdictional problems. From the point of view of aboriginal people in Alberta, there are risks associated with dealing with the province in this fashion. To the extent that the province can work with communities one by one, it will reduce the political effectiveness of aboriginal solidarity and collective pressure. Bad precedents, as well as useful ones, may be established.

This raises the need for involvement by provincial (and territorial)[29] aboriginal organizations on both the pragmatic and the political levels. At the political level, they have a continuing role to ensure that the federal government lives up to its responsibilities for funding programs for aboriginal people. The financial pressures stemming from implementation of Bill C-31 combined with the current federal penchant for putting the fiscal squeeze on funding for aboriginal peoples make this role extremely important.[30] At the more pragmatic level, provincial aboriginal organizations can facilitate communication among native communities about models of servicing. They can resist dilution of political impetus by seeking, cautiously, to develop mechanisms for higher level communication and negotiation between provincial and aboriginal politicians and officials. That such mechanisms can be developed without subversion of important legal and constitutional principles is suggested by the Framework Agreement negotiated by the Metis in Alberta, and at a lower level, by the "double bilateral" agreements developed in Alberta to facilitate transfer of child welfare responsibilities. It is early to judge the long-term impact of such arrangements, but it seems that they are at least as likely to reinforce aboriginal peoples' progress towards self-government in practice as they are to hinder this trend.

There are other roles that might be played by the province-wide aboriginal organizations. They can act as sources of expertise to provide interim support and training. In this way they can help individual communities overcome the capacity problems that are seen by some provincial and federal officials as roadblocks to permitting greater autonomy in the design and delivery of programs by aboriginal peoples. Aboriginal organizations may also assume a role as overseer to monitor and evaluate community-based programs. Although the organizations might have initial philosophical difficulties in taking on an oversight role, the reality of our Canadian political system is that someone will have to do it. Again, new approaches are needed.

Although considerable latitude can be negotiated concerning program funding, there are still constitutional responsibilities which must be satisfied. Both provinces interpret ministerial responsibility to include: oversight to ensure financial probity; guarantee of service delivery in the areas required by statute; and the guarantee of roughly comparable standards of care for all provincial citizens. While aboriginal people do not share these views, a way must be found on the provincial side for perceived responsibilities to be met in the context of new approaches to programming involving aboriginal peoples.

There would appear to be three sorts of tools available, all of which can be recorded in contractual agreements. Standard audit procedures should monitor financial probity. Independent program evaluations can be conducted to assess the adequacy of care and the level of service. Here, provincial and territorial aboriginal organizations may make a positive contribution in assisting individual aboriginal communities to meet negotiated audit and evaluation requirements. Where these measures are inappropriate, the Minister may retain the power to intervene on a crisis basis, acting on a previously specified trigger. This type of oversight implies the need for some basic standards of service in order to avoid direct harm to individuals caused by failure to provide adequate service. This type of ministerial action is most often precipitated by finding that someone or some group has "fallen between the cracks." Aboriginal communities and their more broadly based organizations will have to recognize that this type of ministerial oversight is a necessary accompaniment to the use of public funds by any group, including a federal or provincial government department. The practice of setting such standards is quite well established in Ontario and seems to be gaining currency in Alberta. If our small sample of two suggests that standard-setting is increasingly becoming part of government life in Canada, this implies that aboriginal communities must enter vigorously into debate about what standards are appropriate in the context of aboriginal cultures and patterns of life.

To summarize, the degree of effective aboriginal self-administration (as a necessary complement to constitutional self-government) can be understood as a matter to be negotiated with provinces, step by step, in one functional area after another. The focus must be on meeting the real needs of aboriginal communities, rather than on merely delegating to communities responsibility for delivering conventional provincial programs. This model has certain advantages. It envisions a long process through which local capacities could be developed, and local solutions invented, in a relatively secure, experimental atmosphere. As some autonomy is realized, negotiations could begin in other areas. For aboriginal people, this approach implies a need to build program capacity in individual communities and at the level of their provincial or territorial organizations. For provincial governments, it implies a central commitment to lateral thinking about new approaches to programming which may violate the traditional divisions of program and funding responsibilities. Whatever specific structural arrangements are put in place to achieve this commitment, considerable political and bureaucratic will is required.

Finally, this approach has implications for the federal role. It is increasingly clear that the federal government will continue to withdraw from direct service delivery even on Indian reserves. This is a benign trend, creating an opening for local control, *so long as funding is not correspondingly reduced*. The historic trust responsibility between the Minister of Indian and Northern Affairs and the country's status Indians does not, in our view, impede practical elaboration of this new provincial perspective. In fact, existence of the trust relationship may support good results from new program experiments if the federal-aboriginal relationship is re-oriented to emphasize federal assistance in capacity-building and in funding the process through which aboriginal communities may define their specific needs and interests. As is the case for all other citizens in Canada, the process of identifying needs, and ways to meet them, can be expected to involve experimentation and considerable evolution over time. Unlike what is the case for constitutional changes, there are no once-and-for-all answers to such questions.

Whatever the developments on this front, it is clear that, while the federal government has a moral and legal commitment to aboriginal people that it should not be permitted to shirk, the role of the provinces in meeting the program needs of aboriginal communities is now central and will be even more so in the era after Meech

Lake. If aboriginal communities, their representative organizations and individual provincial governments acknowledge this situation and play it right, programmatic innovation can occur that will meet the immediate needs of aboriginal peoples and may go some distance in contributing to resolution of the current impasse at the level of high politics in aboriginal affairs.

Acknowledgements

We are grateful to the aboriginal representatives and provincial officials in Ontario and Alberta who answered our questions thoughtfully and frankly, as well as to some of those officials and our editor David Hawkes for perceptive comments on an earlier draft. Nadine Changfoot and Bonita Neri provided most efficient research assistance.

Notes

1. In this paper, we follow what has come to be common practice by using the terms "aboriginal peoples" and "native people" to refer to the descendants of the original inhabitants of North America, including treaty and status Indians, non-status Indians, Metis and Inuit. These older terms reflect the process of colonization of Canada, and bear a mixture of juridical and ethnic meanings that do not reflect the real basis of aboriginal peoples' identities. In each group are many different nations, such as Cree, Blackfoot, Nishnabwe and Odawa, among many others.
2. David C. Hawkes, *Negotiating Aboriginal Self-Government* (Kingston: Queen's University, Institute of Intergovernmental Relations, 1985).
3. Academic work concerning aboriginal-provincial relations has barely begun. Major breakthroughs were the publication of Raymond Breton and Gail Grant, eds. *The Dynamics of Government Programs for Urban Indians in the Prairie Provinces* (Montreal: Institute for Research on Public Policy, 1984) and J. Anthony Long and Menno Boldt, eds. *Governments in Conflict? Provinces and Indian Nations in Canada* (Toronto: University of Toronto Press, 1988). The study by James Frideres, "Government Policies and Programs Relating to People of Indian Ancestry in Alberta," in Breton and Grant provides a thorough history of the evolution of policy on aboriginal matters in Alberta, and a detailed overview of programs in existence at the end of the 1970s. To our knowledge, no similar study has been published concerning Ontario.
4. On the question of federal-provincial buck-passing with respect to funding for treaty Indians living in urban centres, see all of the papers in Breton and Grant, *op. cit.*, and for Alberta, Joan Ryan, *Wall of Words: The Betrayal of the Urban Indian* (Toronto: Peter Martin Associates, 1978).
5. Statistics Canada, *Summary Tabulations of Ethnic and Aboriginal Origin, 1986* Census. Ottawa, December 1987, Table 3. This census data must be treated with caution for two reasons. First, as some reserves did not participate or provide complete responses there is a problem of missing data. Second, in this census the question about ethnicity encouraged multiple responses, so that particularly the categories of North American Indian, Metis and Inuit are not discrete. Thus, for example, the 103 930 total aboriginal population figure does not include an estimated population of over 9 000 residents of reserves who did not participate, while over half of census respondents reported multiple origins. See Statistics Canada, *Reference Census Canada 1986*. Ottawa, 1987, chapter 5 for a more complete treatment of these issues.

    More generally, even earlier census data for aboriginal people are notoriously unreliable, and probably always underestimate the total numbers of people in various categories. We have used the best available data from the 1981 and 1986 census surveys. See George K. Jarvis, *An Overview of Registered Indian Conditions in Alberta* (Ottawa: Indian and Northern Affairs Canada, 1987).
6. Canada, *Basic Departmental Data* (Ottawa: Indian and Northern Affairs Canada, December 1988), Table II, p. 15.
7. *Ibid.* p. 12.
8. Statistics Canada, *op. cit.* See note 3 above for qualification. For Ontario this total population excluded at least 11 800 residents of reserves.

9. See Katherine A. Graham, *An Overview of Registered Indian Conditions In Ontario* (Ottawa: Indian and Northern Affairs Canada, 1986).

10. See George Jarvis, *An Overview of Registered Indian Conditions in Alberta* (Ottawa: Indian and Northern Affairs Canada, 1987) and Katherine A. Graham, *op. cit.*

11. See Fred V. Martin, "Federal and Provincial Responsibility in the Metis Settlements of Alberta" in this volume.

12. The existence of both the MAA and the NCC at the provincial level is a consequence of changes at the level of national representation. In 1984, the Metis National Council was formed, removing the support of prairie Metis from the older Native Council of Canada (NCC). This led the NCC to establish offices in each of the prairie provinces.

13. The Advisory Council of Treaty Women, Indian Rights for Indian Women (Alberta), Metis Women's Council of Edmonton and the Women of the Metis Nation.

14. Here comparison of Alberta's behaviour with respect to the long-overdue creation of a reserve for the Lubicon band, and Ontario's concerning the similar case of the Temagami Indians in that province, is instructive. It would be difficult to show that Ontario has been either more successful or more forthcoming with provincially occupied lands than has been the Alberta government with lands to which the Lubicons are entitled. On the Lubicon case, see Frances Abele and Katherine Graham, "Plus Que Ca Change ... Northern and Native Policy," in Katherine A. Graham, ed. *How Ottawa Spends 1988-89: The Conservatives Heading Into the Stretch* (Ottawa: Carleton University Press, 1988), p. 114 and note 2; on the Temagami situation, "Temagami Indians Reject New Land Offer," *The Globe and Mail* [Toronto], March 2, 1989; "Ontario to Extend Temagami Logging Road" *The Ottawa Citizen* [Ottawa], March 4, 1989.

15. Alberta has for many years spent more per capita on social welfare programs than most other provinces. See Allan Moscovitch, "The Welfare State Since 1975," *Journal of Canadian Studies* 21(2) (Summer 1986).

16. Generalizations as bold as those we make here obviously obscure the heterogeneity of the Albertans' political views, reflected more in popular vote figures than in the results of elections. Increasingly, too, the classic "settler" ideology is being eroded by urbanization and other changes. For somewhat contrasting and much more complete recent analyses, see Larry Pratt and John Richards, *Prairie Capitalism: Power and Influence in the New West* (Toronto: McClelland and Stewart, 1979); Larry Pratt and Garth Stevenson, *Western Separatism: The Myths, Realities and Dangers* (Edmonton: Hurtig Publishers, 1981); Chuck Reasons, *Stampede City: Power and Politics in the West* (Toronto: Between the Lines, 1984); Larry Pratt, ed. *Socialism and Democracy in Alberta: Essays in Honour of Grant Notley* (Edmonton: NeWest Press, 1986).

17. For a further discussion of this point see Lionel D. Feldman and Katherine A. Graham, *Bargaining For Cities* (Montreal: Institute For Research on Public Policy, 1979) pp. 80-93.

18. On the conflicts that led to this measure, see Frideres, "Government Policies" in Breton and Grant, *Dynamics of Government*, pp. 343-344.

19. On provincial initiatives in the earlier period, see Frideres, "Government Policies" in Breton and Grant, *op. cit.*, note 3.

169

20. This committee began as an inter*departmental* committee, initiated apparently on the initiative of provincial officials with the blessing of the respective ministers. The committee became intergovernmental when federal civil servants with responsibilities in this area were drawn in. The committee is rather informally established, but meets regularly.

21. Alberta Social Services, *In the Interest of Native Child Welfare Services: Recommendations from the Working Committee on Native Child Welfare* (Edmonton, April 1987). The Indian Association of Alberta independently produced another analysis of these issues: *Child Welfare Needs: Assessment and Recommendations* (Edmonton, n.d. c. 1987). The Indian Association's study was produced in a broadly participatory process, involving an advisory board of elders and community-based researchers.

22. Alberta Municipal Affairs, Career Development and Employment, *Final Report: Working Group on Native Education, Training and Employment* (Edmonton, 1987).

23. Metis Association of Alberta, *Our Children, Our Future, Our Community, Our Challenge* (Edmonton, 1984).

24. The other side of the triangle (between the provincial and federal governments) is regularized by an overarching intergovernmental agreement on native social welfare arrangements, referred to as the Memorandum of Understanding between Indian Affairs and Northern Development and Alberta Social Services (1985). This memorandum formalized intergovernmental arrangements for a variety of social welfare areas in place since the 1960s.

    The first "double bilateral" agreement was negotiated by the Blood Indians of southern Alberta, while a somewhat different and so far less permanent arrangement has been made by the Yellowhead Tribal Council in north-central Alberta. The wording of the agreements appears to protect the aboriginal organizations' principle concern for constitutional precedent. It is quite likely that there will be other such agreements negotiated by other aboriginal peoples, varying according to local circumstances.

25. Native Counselling Services of Alberta, *Annual Report 1986-87* (Edmonton 1987); Canada. Department of Justice, *Criminal Courtworker: Native Counselling Services of Alberta: Program Review and Evaluation Assessment.* Prepared by Co-West Associates, (June 1981).

26. Ontario Aboriginal Council on Justice (ONJC) is an aboriginal body working in the area of judicial issues pertaining to aboriginal people. Membership is extended to those organizations of a regional or provincial base which address a range of policy, program and service issues. The aboriginal organizations which have two voting delegates on the council are as follows: Association of Iroquois and Allied Indians, Grand Council Treaty No. 3, Nishnawbe-Aski Nation, Ontario Federation of Indian Friendship Centres, Ontario Metis and Non-Status Indian Association, Ontario Aboriginal Women's Association and the Union of Ontario Indians.

27. Under this legislation, Children's Aid Societies are constituted as provincially funded and regulated non-governmental organizations with responsibilities for child welfare services (for all Ontarians) as governed by the Act. In Alberta, similar services are provided by Alberta Social Services, a government department.

28. See K. G. Banting, "Federalism, Social Reform and the Spending Power" and for a contrary view, T. J. Courchene, "Meech Lake and Socio-Economic Policy," both in *Canadian Public Policy* v. 14 supp. (September 1988).

29. The situation of aboriginal peoples living in the two territories are significantly different from that of aboriginal peoples in the provinces, requiring a separate discussion beyond the reach of the present paper.

30. Abele and Graham, *op. cit.*, note 14, pp. 113-138.

CHAPTER 6

FEDERAL AND PROVINCIAL RESPONSIBILITIES FOR THE CREE, NASKAPI AND INUIT UNDER THE JAMES BAY AND NORTHERN QUEBEC, AND NORTHEASTERN QUEBEC AGREEMENTS

Evelyn J. Peters

INTRODUCTION

The James Bay and Northern Quebec Agreement was signed in 1975, and the Northeastern Quebec Agreement was signed three years later. These agreements represented the settlement of native land claims in the James Bay area of northern Quebec, and formed the first modern land claims agreement under the new federal policy of addressing outstanding native land rights. Since that time, the Western Arctic Claim was signed with the Inuvialuit in 1984, and an agreement in principle was signed with the Dene and Metis of the Northwest Territories in the fall of 1988.

The Cree and the Inuit have described the difficulty of the negotiating process, due in part to the lack of precedents and the paucity of examples and models which they could compare and assess.[1] Although both native groups and governments have been quick to deny that the James Bay and the Northeastern Quebec agreements represent models for other settlements, there are, nevertheless, lessons which can be learned from them. These are lessons not only about structure and content, but also about implementation. In the thirteen years since the James Bay Agreement was signed and the decade since the signing of the Northeastern Quebec Agreement, the governments and the native parties have had considerable time to work out the practical implications.

While other studies have described in detail the structure and jurisdiction of the aboriginal governments emerging from the agreements, there has been less emphasis on delineating the structure of federal and provincial responsibilities. Similarly, while implementation issues have periodically been brought to public attention by the media, little exists in the way of a comprehensive history of this process. The issue of implementation is one of major importance: powers and jurisdiction on paper have little meaning if they are not put into practice. Accordingly, this chapter has two main objectives: to describe federal and provincial responsibilities for the Cree, Naskapi and Inuit under the James Bay and the Northeastern Quebec agreements; and to describe and evaluate the processes of implementing these responsibilities.

SIGNING THE AGREEMENTS

Because the circumstances surrounding the signing of the James Bay and Northern Quebec Agreement have been detailed in a number of places, they will only be described here very briefly.[2] In 1971 the Quebec government began to construct the James Bay hydro-electric project in an area not yet ceded by the native peoples and still used by them in their traditional hunting pursuits. The land in question was part of a tract that had been transferred by the federal government to Quebec under the 1912 *Boundary Extension Act*, with the condition that the province obtain surrender of native interests in the area before development. In May of 1972, when the province failed to negotiate, the Cree and Inuit instituted legal proceedings against Quebec and the James Bay Development Corporation in an attempt to secure an injunction against further hydro-electric development until the question of native rights had been dealt with. Mr. Justice Malouf of the Quebec Superior Court granted the Cree and Inuit a hearing and, after receiving the testimony of Inuit and Cree hunters about their continuing use and occupation of these lands, accorded an interlocutory injunction against further hydro-electric development. Shortly after the Malouf decision, Quebec began to negotiate for a settlement. Although the Malouf injunction was overturned by the Quebec Court of Appeal, a settlement was reached with the Cree and Inuit before the appeal court's decision was announced. The Naskapi signed the Northeastern Quebec Agreement, the first of the complementary agreements to the James Bay Agreement, in 1978.

The negotiations took place under unique historical, cultural and political circumstances which affected the content and structure of the agreement. First, the agreement was negotiated under the heavy pressure of rigid deadlines. The province was eager to proceed with hydro-electric development, the cessation of which was becoming increasingly expensive. The native parties, realizing that the decision of the Quebec Court of Appeals could go against them, believed they had little option but to settle before the decision was announced. As a result, there are a number of sections where provisions are vague, and where negotiators agreed to work out details later.

Secondly, these were the first settlements of their kind negotiated in Canada, and in the decade and a half since then, it has become evident that many of the implications were not clearly recognized at the time of signing. In particular, it seems clear that provincial and federal governments were not prepared either for the costs of implementing the agreement, or to create structures and mechanisms to ensure that its provisions were carried out. Nor were the native parties prepared for the implications of changing economic and policy climates on the willingness of both governments to implement specific provisions of the agreements. Their inexperience resulted in the failure to insist on guarantees and commitments that provisions would be implemented. Ted Moses, chief negotiator for the Crees in 1975, recently warned the Dene and the Metis of the Northwest Territories to insist on binding language, not to leave details to be worked out later and to obtain guarantees that the provisions would be implemented.[3]

Thirdly, the agreements reflect the very strong emphasis which the native people, and especially the Cree, placed on securing their traditional way of life based on harvesting activities. To this end, the agreements set out a detailed hunting regime, procedures to protect the traditional land base from environmental degradation resulting from new development projects and support programs for native hunters, fishers and trappers. The integrity of native cultures was also to be protected by special provisions concerning education and justice.

Finally, the agreements reflect Quebec's intention to affirm its presence and its jurisdiction over the territory. In his speech before the Quebec Parliamentary Committee convened to examine the agreement prior to its signing, the Honourable John Ciaccia explained the philosophy:

> The Agreement has enabled us to accomplish two great tasks to which the government committed itself. It enables us to fulfill our obligations to the native peoples who inhabit our North, and to affirm finally Quebec's presence throughout its entire territory.[4]

The province's intention to extend its sovereignty in the north probably affected its willingness to take on responsibilities for funding and administering services for the area's native peoples.

LAND AND GOVERNMENT SYSTEMS FOR THE NATIVE PARTIES

The agreements distinguish several main classes of land with respect to allocation of title, resources and interest in land. The Cree and Naskapi systems are similar, while the land regime for the Inuit varies marginally. The following is a simplified description: detailed information about the nature of jurisdiction over these lands can be found elsewhere.[5] Category I lands correspond to the location of Cree, Naskapi and Inuit villages and their peripheries, and have been set aside for the "exclusive use and benefit" of the native bands and communities. Category II lands are those adjoining Category I lands. They are lands under provincial jurisdiction, on which the Cree, Inuit and Naskapi have exclusive rights of hunting, trapping and fishing. Category III lands comprise the largest portion of the territory, and are public lands over which the native parties enjoy exclusive trapping rights as well as certain rights with respect to outfitting and other activities.

The local and regional government systems for the Cree, Naskapi and Inuit are also different. The Inuit are completely under provincial jurisdiction as far as the James Bay Agreement is concerned. Local communities are incorporated as municipalities under the

Quebec *Cities and Towns Act*, as is the regional government. Local and regional governments are not ethnic in character—all residents, aboriginal and non-aboriginal may vote, be elected and otherwise participate. However, over ninety per cent of the population in the area is Inuit and benefits under the James Bay Agreement. Administration of compensation monies under the agreement is the responsibility of Makivik Corporation which *is* an Inuit ethnic institution. Makivik's role is to ensure that the agreement is implemented so that its members, the Inuit beneficiaries, enjoy the cultural, political, social and economic rights and benefits provided for by the agreement.

The Cree and Naskapi have retained some federal jurisdiction by splitting their Category I lands. On Category IA lands, the "administration, management and control" is vested in Canada, while IB lands are under provincial jurisdiction. The James Bay Agreement provided for negotiations concerning Cree local government subsequent to signing, and in 1984 the *Cree-Naskapi (of Quebec) Act* was passed. This Act replaces the *Indian Act*, setting out the powers and jurisdiction of Cree local governments, which are ethnic in character. The Cree Regional Authority, incorporated in 1978, is the chief regional administrative body of the Crees and is responsible for giving valid consent on behalf of the Crees when required under the agreement. The Board of Compensation of the Cree Regional Authority is the legal entity to which Cree compensation monies were paid, and administers these monies for "the relief of poverty, the welfare and the advancement of education of the Crees." Naskapi local government is structured like that of the Crees but, because the Naskapi of Quebec are represented by only one band, they do not have any aboriginal regional governing bodies.

METHODOLOGY

The following outline of federal and provincial responsibilities under the agreements, and the process of their implementation, is based primarily on an analysis of the text of the agreements, on existing legislation enacting these agreements, and on written materials describing the implementation process. The Crees and the Inuit have made a number of submissions to various commissions and Parliamentary committees—these provide a good description of issues of concern to the native parties. The Annual Reports of the Cree Regional Authority, Kativik Regional Government, and the Makivik Corporation trace the development of negotiations on particular issues. The Department of Indian Affairs and Northern Development's Annual Report on the implementation of the James Bay and the Northeastern Quebec agreements, the 1982 federal review of the process (Tait Report), and Quebec's *Recontre*, a publication which describes aboriginal issues in the province, provide the government perspectives. In addition, information about recent developments was provided by several individuals involved with Cree and Inuit organizations. [6]

In the analysis which follows, policy areas are grouped into four main sections: local and regional governments; harvesting and environmental regimes; compensation and economic development; and the administration of local services. A fifth section addresses responsibilities for, and processes of, implementation. The analysis of each policy area begins with a description of provincial and federal responsibilities as outlined in the agreements, and then summarizes the implementation process. In conclusion, the final section draws out a number of implications of the agreements, and the attempts by governments and the native parties to have their provisions implemented.

The printed version of the James Bay and Northern Quebec Agreement is over 450 pages long, and at this time there are seven complementary agreements and more than twenty pieces of enacting legislation. This discussion, therefore, provides a very general overview of government responsibilities. A detailed summary of specific commitments is contained in the Appendix. The implementation process has been continuing for more than a decade for the Cree and the Inuit, and for about ten years for the Naskapi. This study does not attempt to provide a complete description of all the issues and events occurring during this process, but rather to highlight the more outstanding and significant incidents.

LOCAL AND REGIONAL GOVERNMENTS

The Cree and Naskapi governments are ethnic in character, and primarily under federal jurisdiction. Inuit governing institutions are public, under provincial jurisdiction. In terms of funding, both are heavily supported by transfer payments, although the source and nature of funding are different. Cree local governments receive federal support primarily, and the Cree have negotiated block funding for operations and maintenance. Negotiations for capital funding are now in process. The administrative responsibilities of the Cree Regional Authority are delegated and funded by the local bands. Funding for Inuit local and regional governments is negotiated with the province on a program-by-program basis. The following sections describe federal and provincial responsibilities with respect to local and regional government for the native groups in the James Bay area.

LOCAL GOVERNMENT

Sections 9 and 10 of the James Bay and Northern Quebec Agreement provide local government for the Cree on Category IA and IB land respectively. These sections are almost identical to s.7 and s.8 of the Northeastern Quebec Agreement, which deal with local government for the Naskapi. Section 12 of the James Bay Agreement provides for "Local Government North of the 55th Parallel;" s.7 gives Inuit landholding corporations specific powers.

The agreements provide very little detail about the content of local government legislation for the Cree and Naskapi—the sections combined take up about five pages each in the published versions of the agreements. The responsibilities of federal and provincial governments extend mainly to the introduction of legislation providing for local government. No time was specified, but these discussion were to take place "forthwith upon the execution of the Agreement." Sections 8 and 10 of the James Bay and Northeastern Quebec agreements respectively provide for the creation of eight Cree and one Naskapi village municipalities under provincial jurisdiction. The powers and responsibilities of these village municipalities are largely derived from the Quebec *Cities and Towns Act*, though the application of this law is modified to take into account the communal nature of land holding and the lack of local land-taxation power. The council is also granted powers not generally extended to municipalities, principally the right to affect environmental and social protection and the right to pass regulations regarding the protection and use of natural resources.

Section 12 of the James Bay Agreement is a draft of legislation providing for local government for the Inuit and other residents north of the 55th parallel. Under the terms of this section, Quebec undertook to submit to the National Assembly bills incorporating the 13 settlements of the area as northern village municipalities under provincial jurisdiction. Quebec also undertook to incorporate the Inuit landholding corporations to receive title to Category I land for Inuit community purposes. These purposes are not defined in the agreement other than to say that they "include the use of the lands ... for commercial, industrial, residential or other purposes."

Section 28.15 of the James Bay Agreement and s.18.19 of the Northeastern Quebec Agreement contain commitments by the federal government to provide core funding for Cree and Naskapi local governments on Category IA lands. There are no provisions for core funding for the northern, or Cree and Naskapi village municipalities — they come under Quebec jurisdiction and receive funds from the province for the type of expenditure usually covered by core funding.

Implementation

Quebec legislation creating village corporations was enacted on June 23, 1978, with *Bill 23: An Act concerning Northern villages and the Kativik Regional Government* (*Kativik Act*) and *Bill 24: The Cree Villages Act*. Bill 24 was amended to include the Naskapi on June 22, 1979, with *Bill 26: An Act respecting the legislation provided for in the Northeastern Quebec Agreement and amending other legislation*. Inuit landholding corporations were established on December 22, 1978, under *Bill 29: An Act respecting the land regime in the James Bay and New Quebec territories*. Federal legislation concerning local government for Cree and Naskapi on Category IA and IA-N lands was not enacted until nine years after the signing of the James Bay Agreement, with *Bill C-46: The Cree-Naskapi (of Quebec) Act*, assented to on July 3, 1984.

Before the agreement, each settlement in northern Quebec had its own Inuit community corporation, which was federally incorporated and locally elected. These corporations provided essential community services, such as water delivery, garbage collection and road maintenance under service contracts with the Department of Indian Affairs and Northern Development, and were almost totally funded by the Department. The corporations held no legislative or regulatory powers but could make recommendations to the Department of specific courses of action or for the fulfilment of particular local needs.[7] Under the *Kativik Act*, the settlements became northern village municipalities under provincial jurisdiction. Canada's core funding to the Inuit communities ceased in 1980-81.

The province's responsibilities for the northern village municipalities are like those for any municipality in the province. Part I of the Act, which deals with the village municipalities, is largely inspired by Quebec municipal law. Most of the provisions are borrowed or adapted from the *Municipal Code* and the *Cities and Towns Act*. Rostaing noted that the powers of the municipalities "do not differ substantially from those found in the *Municipal Code* and could therefore be claimed to afford a reasonable degree of autonomy to the northern communities."[8] He pointed out, though, that the economic conditions of the territory and the structures created through the James Bay Agreement significantly limited the level of local autonomy.

While the northern municipalities can technically collect taxes, Rostaing wrote "there is no tax base to speak of in any of the communities."[9] Other sources of funding—collecting a portion of rent, or imposing a real estate tax are not feasible alternatives. Massive subsidization means that the rent which northern residents pay is disproportionately low. Inuit landholding corporations hold most of the municipal lands, and a real estate tax would make these corporations the principal supporters of the municipal corporations. The landholding corporations, as ethnic entities, are not intended to provide public services, especially to non-ethnic municipal corporations. As a result, Rostaing argued: "the northern municipalities are more dependent on external assistance and subject to greater control and restrictions than municipalities in southern Quebec."[10]

The *Cree-Naskapi (of Quebec) Act* replaces the *Indian Act* for the Cree and Naskapi, and limits the responsibilities of the federal government in the day-to-day administration of band affairs and band lands. The general power of disallowance of by-laws has been abolished, and the Act indicates specific areas which Canada may regulate—local taxation, by-laws concerning hunting and trapping, elections, special band meetings and referenda, long-term borrowing, the land registry system, band expropriations, and fines and sentences for breaking band by-laws. With respect to band finances, the responsibility of the federal government is restricted to matters such as appointing an auditor if the band fails to do so, and appointing an administrator if the affairs of the band appear to be in serious disorder. Part XII of the Act established the Cree-Naskapi

Commission as an independent agency to monitor implementation of the Act. Funding for the Commission is a federal responsibility.

While Cree and Naskapi representatives were negotiating local government legislation, they were also negotiating arrangements by which financial resources were to be transferred from the federal government to the band corporations. The result was the "Statement of Understanding of Principal Points Agreed to by the *Cree-Naskapi (of Quebec) Act* Implementation Working Group," signed on August 9, 1984, by the then Minister of Indian Affairs and Northern Development (Douglas Frith), the then Grand Chief of the Crees (Billy Diamond), and the Chief of the Naskapi Band (Joseph Guanish). The statement contained a multi-year fiscal arrangement, funded through an unconditional transfer payment to the bands, with provision for annual adjustments determined by a formula with a set of six cost factors.

The Cree and Naskapi received funding in line with the statement for the 1984-85 fiscal year. Funding for subsequent years, however, was not in accordance with the annual adjustment formula negotiated with the Cree and Naskapi in the statement. The Cree-Naskapi Commission pointed out that, as a result:

> the difference over four years between the federal subsidy offered and what the Cree and Naskapi claim could be as high as 20% of total Cree-Naskapi budget levels for the period 1985-86 to 1988-89. [11]

In October 1986, the Department of Indian Affairs and Northern Development took the position that the statement of understanding was neither binding nor a legal obligation of Canada. [12] Based on an examination of the issue and the events surrounding the signing of the statement, and after seeking legal opinion, the Cree-Naskapi Commission concluded that Canada was:

> legally bound by the Statement and ... legally obligated to negotiate in good faith an adjustment formula for the federal subsidy which considers all the cost factors of the Statement. [13]

Cree-Canada negotiations over these financing issues broke down in 1986 and were not resumed until early 1988. In March of 1987 the Naskapi band signed off the statement of understanding. In 1987 the Crees instituted a lawsuit against Canada for failing to live up to its obligations. The Crees reported that the resumption of negotiations with the federal government was accompanied with considerable disagreement. [14] Nevertheless, an agreement for operations and maintenance funding for the period from April 1, 1984 to March 31, 1989, was reached in July of 1988.[15] The letter from the Honourable William McKnight to Grand Chief Coon Come commits the federal government to negotiate a further five-year agreement to cover operations and maintenance funding for the Crees for the period from April 1, 1989 to March 31, 1994. This agreement shall contain a base-year funding level and an annual adjustment formula, both of which will be negotiated between the Crees and the federal government. The government's letter also makes the federal government responsible for providing a specified level of operations and maintenance funding, should negotiations break down again.

REGIONAL GOVERNMENT

Sections 11 and 13 of the James Bay and Northern Quebec Agreement provided for the establishment of regional governments for the Cree and Inuit. Because only one band came under the agreement, there are no similar provisions for the Naskapi. Quebec was responsible for introducing legislation to create both the Cree Regional Authority and the Kativik regional government under these sections of the agreement.

The James Bay Agreement gives the Kativik regional government the powers of a northern village municipality over those parts of the territory which are not part of the village corporations, and regional powers over the whole territory including the municipalities. Kativik can make ordinances with respect to public health, it is legally qualified in matters of local administration, and it has the power to establish minimum standards for building and road construction, sanitary conditions, water pollution and sewerage. The Kativik regional government is also competent in local transportation and communications, regional police and manpower training and utilization. The agreement entrusts Kativik with the administration of the Inuit hunting, fishing and trapping support-program, and with the administration of general and provincial programs for economic development in the territory. The extent to which Kativik exercises these powers, then, can considerably reduce Quebec's administrative responsibility for residents in the area.

The Cree Regional Authority is a public corporation with its corporate seat in Cree Category I lands. Section 11A of the James Bay

Agreement gives the Cree Regional Authority powers to appoint representatives to various bodies created by the agreement, and to give consent on behalf of the Cree, when such consent is required by the agreement. Additional powers to co-ordinate and administer programs on Category I lands must be delegated to the Cree Regional Authority by the Cree bands.

Section 28.15 indicates that Canada will provide core funding for the Cree Regional Authority, for internal administration and for the administrative costs of delegated governmental programs, subject to departmental directives. No similar provisions exist for Kativik, although as a municipality under provincial jurisdiction it could expect to receive funding for administrative costs from the provincial government.

Implementation

The legislation for regional governments in the James Bay area was assented to on June 23, 1978. It included: *Bill 23: An Act concerning Northern villages and the Kativik Regional Government; Bill 25: An Act respecting the Cree Regional Authority*; and *Bill 26: An Act concerning the James Bay Regional Zone Council*. The legislation largely follows the provisions laid out in the James Bay Agreement. However, Bill 25 makes the Board of Compensation, a legal entity contemplated under s.26 of the agreement, part of the Cree Regional Authority.

With respect to the Inuit, because of the economic circumstances of the area, the actual day-to-day division of responsibilities between the province and Kativik may differ from that contemplated by the agreement. Under the *Kativik Act*, funds necessary for the regional government's operation are to be raised through its taxation powers on lands outside the northern village municipalities, a tax on each municipality equivalent to an aliquot share of a proportion of Kativik's expenses, and charges for services rendered. The absence of significant development in the territory means that the first source does not generate much revenue. The dependence of northern village municipalities on provincial subsidies means that taxes or service charges imposed are charges to the province. As a result:

> The KRG's budgetary proposals, which incorporate provisions for projects and activities perceived as priorities in the north, are submitted annually to the appropriate provincial ministries. They, in turn, review the proposals and act upon them according to their own perception

> and evaluation of northern priorities, the whole being subject to the
> provincial government's northern policies. [16]

In other words, because of its role in subsidizing Kativik, the province's responsibilities in policy-making and administration appear to be greater than that specified by the Act.

There is some indication that, with increased experience in writing proposals and negotiating procedures, Kativik administrators have become more successful at obtaining funding according to regional government priorities. [17] The 1986 Kativik Annual Report, however, maintained that the methods of financing resulted in only "conditional autonomy" for Kativik. At that time, Kativik recommended changes including a five-year plan with a single general subsidy, and statutory financing. The 1987 Annual Report indicated that financing negotiations with Quebec were continuing. In 1988 a five-year block-funding agreement was reached for municipal infrastructure, and Kativik regional government representatives were negotiating for block funding for manpower and all other services. [18]

The nature of the federal government's responsibility for core funding for the Cree Regional Authority has been the subject of a long-standing debate. The federal government's 1982 review of the implementation of the James Bay Agreement, the Tait Report, found that the Department of Indian Affairs and Northern Development maintained that the only type of core funding for which the Cree Regional Authority was eligible was that available to district councils under the provisions of the Department's D-2 program circular. This circular provided that district councils could receive a small start-up grant for only the first three years of operation. The Tait Report pointed out that, at the time of negotiations, Canada and the Crees expected the role of the Cree Regional Authority to be limited and costs to be minimal. The actual constitution and responsibilities of the Cree Regional Authority meant that its workload has been considerably higher than expected. The report concluded that:

> it appears clear that, although the original intention may have been
> to fund the CRA in accordance with the circular on funding district
> councils, subsequent events have made this position untenable. The
> review team is of the view that a special CRA CORE funding program
> is necessary. [19]

In response to the Tait Report, the Department of Indian Affairs and Northern Development announced on July 8, 1982, that an additional sum of $5.5 million would be provided to the Cree to cover their costs in negotiations concerning implementation of the James Bay Agreement. A sum of $2.9 million was made available to the Inuit for the same purpose.

THE HARVESTING AND ENVIRONMENTAL REGIMES

The regimes established by the agreements concerning native harvesting rights, environmental protection from new development and the income support programs for individuals engaged in harvesting activities, represent the Cree, Naskapi and Inuit's approach to protecting their traditional cultural base. The following sections outline federal and provincial responsibilities with respect to these aspects of the agreements.

Hunting, Fishing and Trapping Regime

Section 24 of the James Bay and Northern Quebec Agreement, and s.15 of the Northeastern Quebec Agreement establish a single, special hunting, fishing and trapping regime for the native beneficiaries. Federal and provincial governments are responsible for implementing this regime, each for areas under their jurisdiction. In the implementation and administration process they are required to participate on, and consult with, a co-ordinating committee with representatives from the three native groups who were signatories to the agreements. The province and the federal government retain responsibility for conservation and the protection of wildlife resources in the territory.

In addition to this broad assignment of responsibilities, s.24 of the James Bay Agreement also contains a number of specific commitments on the part of each level of government. Quebec is required to consult the co-ordinating committee before allowing nonnative trappers to trap in areas where natives have exclusive rights, and to give native applicants for outfitting operations on Category III land "right of first refusal." Both levels of government are committed to assist in establishing native trappers' associations and a native-operated trapping industry, and to train and hire native conservation officers.

186

Federal and provincial governments and the three native parties each pay their own members on the co-ordinating committee, while Quebec is responsible for funding the secretariat for the committee.

Implementation

Section 24 of the James Bay and Northern Quebec Agreement was enacted on December 22, 1978 in the Quebec National Assembly with *Bill 28: An Act respecting hunting and fishing rights in the James Bay and New Quebec territories.* Section 15 of the Northeastern Quebec Agreement was assented to on June 22, 1979 through *Bill 26: An Act respecting the legislation provided for in the Northeastern Quebec Agreement and amending other legislation.*

The 1981 Cree statement to the Standing Committee on Indian Affairs and Northern Development indicated that this section had been successfully implemented. Nevertheless, both the Crees and the Inuit reported continuing disagreement with Quebec over the right of first refusal concerning outfitting operations. [20] Following negotiations with the native parties and with Quebec, the co-ordinating committee adopted, on February 28, 1979, a procedure to implement this right. The Crees report that the provincial Minister of Recreation, Fish and Game rejected this procedure and adopted alternative administrative rules. Legal proceedings initiated by the Cree, Naskapi and Inuit parties resulted in a ruling that the procedural rules adopted by the Minister were "illegal, null and *ultra vires* ..." Quebec's initial decision to appeal this judgment was withdrawn May 3, 1985. On October 2, 1986, the native parties and Quebec came to an agreement concerning the rules governing the exercise of native peoples' right of first refusal under the James Bay and the Northeastern Quebec agreements. These issues will be part of Complementary Agreement 8, which outlines changes in the hunting, fishing and trapping regime for the Crees.

The Inuit maintain that the agreement had an underlying theme that the Inuit should be able increasingly to take over and manage their own affairs. Wildlife management and research, including the monitoring and control of subsistence hunting of marine animals and in-shore subsistence fishing, are areas in which the Inuit are strongly in favour of greater participation and control. [21] Federal and provincial responses to this issue appear to favour remaining within the existing consultative structures. [22] However, these issues continue to be the subject of negotiation between the Inuit and the federal and provincial governments.

Support Programs for Hunting, Fishing and Trapping

Sections 29 and 30 of the James Bay Agreement, and s.19 of the Northeastern Quebec Agreement describe income security programs for harvesting for the Inuit, Crees and Naskapi, respectively. While the programs vary for the native parties, Quebec is responsible for establishing and financing all of them.

The income security program for the Cree is administered by the Quebec Department of Social Affairs, and the Cree Regional Authority through a Cree hunters and trappers income security board. I. E. LaRusic writes that the program is "a rationalization of the social aid which hunters and trappers had been receiving over the past few decades."[23] Those Cree who receive benefits from the program, a guaranteed annual income scheme for those who spend more than four months in the bush in "harvesting" activities, are not entitled to combine these with benefits from "social aid, social assistance for Indians or Inuit or guaranteed annual income programs of general application existing from time to time in the Province of Quebec." Payments made pursuant to the income security program shall be offset against payments received from the programs listed above. Similar stipulations apply to the Naskapi. One effect of these programs, therefore, is to substitute provincial assistance under the income security program, for social assistance formerly provided by the federal government to status Indians.

The support program for Inuit hunting, fishing and trapping activities is administered and regulated by Kativik. The Inuit program is not an income security program. Instead it guarantees a supply of hunting, fishing and trapping produce to Inuit who are disadvantaged, improves the exchange of produce between Inuit communities, provides access to remote areas and facilitates search and rescue operations. The municipalities are responsible for hiring hunters to carry out the first objective above. Payments are not made directly to individuals, but specified levels of funding are paid to the regional government, indexed annually and based on population and administrative costs.

Implementation

The first legislation to allow for the establishment of a support program for Cree hunters and trappers was enacted almost immediately after the signing of the agreement with *Bill 40: An Act modifying the Act on social aid* assented to in 1976. LaRusic indicates that this legislation was passed to allow immediate payment under the program to begin, since there was no provincial legal machinery in place until 1979. [24] He writes that within ten months from the signing of the agreement, a transitional board was established, and staff secured from the Ministry of Social Affairs to design forms, program computers and work with the Cree on establishing eligibility lists and interviewing people in the communities.

> It was an impressive performance, the more so when it is considered that the whole operation was financed for $150,000 ... The smooth implementation can be attributed to very close cooperation between the government and the Cree. [25]

Legislation formally establishing the program was *Bill 12: An Act respecting Income Security for Cree Hunters and Trappers*, assented to on June 21, 1979. While the James Bay Agreement specified a "manday" limit of 150,000 per year, Bill 12 set that limit at 286,000. The 1987-88 Annual Report of the Grand Council of the Cree indicated that the Cree and Quebec had reached an agreement to increase of the person-day minimum to 350,000.

Section 29 was never implemented as drawn up in the James Bay Agreement. Researchers indicate that the Inuit negotiators did not have adequate time to consult with their constituents, who were not completely satisfied with the program as it was set out in the final agreement. [26] After further consultation it was decided to revise the program with Quebec. By late 1979, another agreement-in-principle had been reached, but the main accomplishment was the removal of the clause whereby only one per cent of the Inuit population, to a maximum of 65, could be employed as hunters, fishers and trappers. [27] The Inuit program received legislative approval on December 16, 1982, with *Bill 83: An Act respecting the support program for Inuit beneficiaries of the James Bay and Northern Quebec Agreement for their hunting, fishing and trapping activities*. The Bill specifies Quebec's responsibilities to fund the program through an annual indexed grant equal in 1982 dollars to:

- $17,410 per Inuit community;

- $17,419 per group of 100 beneficiaries or fraction thereof;
- $19.33 per beneficiary; and
- 15 per cent of the total for administrative costs.

In 1987 the amount of the subsidy totalled $2,468,611. [28]

Environmental Regime

Sections 22 and 23 of the James Bay and Northern Quebec Agreement, and s.14 of the Northeastern Quebec Agreement set out an environmental and social impact assessment review procedure for future developments on all categories of land in the James Bay area. Section 22 begins by outlining a range of principles to which the responsible governments are to give "due consideration" in making decisions about developments in the area, and then describes a series of consultative committees and administrative procedures under which they will act. Both levels of government have a responsibility, under the agreement, to participate on advisory committees which review and make recommendations concerning the environmental regime established, as well as about the statements on social and economic impact made by prospective developers. The respective native groups are to be represented on these committees. Administrators appointed by the native communities make final decisions about developments proposed for Cree and Naskapi Category I lands. The federal administrator makes final decisions about developments proposed for Inuit Category I lands.

In addition to the responsibilities outlined above, for matters under federal jurisdiction on Category II and III lands, the administrator (authorized by the Governor-in-Council) makes decisions about whether or not to assess development projects not automatically subject to assessment under the agreement, and whether and under what conditions developments should proceed. The agreement also provides for federal government participation on review panels—with Cree representatives in the south and with Kativik representatives in the north.

For matters under provincial jurisdiction in Cree Category II and III lands, the Quebec Director of the Environmental Protection Service decides whether or not to assess a development not automatically subject to assessment under the agreement, and whether and under what conditions developments should proceed. North of the 55th parallel, the Environmental Quality Commission makes these decisions. Four provincial representatives participate on this commission, along with four representatives from Kativik, two of whom must be Inuit or Naskapi. Section 23.3.21 specifies that if the Quebec Director of the Environmental Protection Services does not accept the decision of the commission, "he may only modify it, change it or decide otherwise with the prior approval of the Quebec Minister." The powers of the Environmental Quality Commission, then, may give the Inuit somewhat greater influence over future developments than that enjoyed by the Cree.

Quebec and Canada pay their own staff and members on the various advisory and administrative bodies created by the agreement, as well as some of the native members. Both levels of government fund equally the secretariats for the James Bay Advisory Committee on the Environment, the Evaluating Committee and the Kativik Environmental Advisory Committee.

Implementation

Quebec legislation enacting the environmental regime was *Bill 30: An Act to again amend the Environmental Quality Act*, assented to December 22, 1978. There appear to have been few problems with the implementation of these sections. In the Cree Statement to the Standing Committee on Indian and Northern Affairs in 1981, the establishment of the environmental regime was cited as an example of a section which had been relatively successfully implemented. Makivik however, has requested that application of a revised regime be extended to offshore areas around northern Quebec.[29]

COMPENSATION AND ECONOMIC DEVELOPMENT

Under s.24 and s.25 of the James Bay Agreement, and s.16 of the Northeastern Quebec Agreement, the Cree, Inuit and Naskapi received in total, $234 million compensation in addition to monies paid for their negotiation costs. In addition, federal and provincial responsibilities for economic development are addressed in s.28 and s.29 of the James Bay Agreement, and s.18 of the Northeastern Quebec Agreement.

All the native parties negotiated provisions under which they would continue to be eligible for federal and provincial programs, funding and assistance available to other Indians and Inuit. They also negotiated a general responsibility on the part of Canada and Quebec to "assist and promote" economic development efforts by the native people, as well as for joint federal and provincial responsibility to train native people for employment, to assist native entrepreneurs, and to participate on committees which review and make recommendations concerning economic development.

In addition, each native party obtained some specific commitments. Section 28, for example, contains a series of short sections which describe the pre-conditions for the establishment of associations to co-ordinate the Cree trapping industry, outfitting and handicrafts. LaRusic indicates that the Cree had sought specific assistance from the Department of Indian Affairs and Northern Development for the programs, but were unable to obtain commitments for funding.[30] Quebec was unwilling to commit funds without a cost-sharing agreement with the federal government. As a result, the provisions in the agreement call for a series of "feasibility studies" which, if positive, would lead to the negotiation of cost-sharing formulae in the areas of trapping, outfitting and handicrafts associations. In addition, s.28 provides for both governments to increase Cree employment in government positions, to establish Cree priority in employment and contracts, and to provide for each community an economic development agent. Quebec is responsible for establishing and funding a James Bay native development corporation.

Specific federal and provincial responsibilities for Naskapi economic development include establishing a development plan for Naskapi manpower, and assisting in establishing both a Naskapi handicrafts association and a commercial fishing operation. Under s.29, the Inuit negotiated a commitment on the part of both governments to develop a plan to train and employ Inuit staff in the bureaucracy of the territory north of the 55th parallel.

Few of the responsibilities outlined in these sections are defined with respect to time limits, particular employment objectives, levels of support or specific actions. Most of the responsibilities of governments are modified by phrases like "subject to budgetary restraints," "within the scope of services and facilities existing from time to time," "whenever possible" or "to the maximum extent possible." W. Moss indicates that while the native negotiators recognized that these sections set up uncertain standards of expected performance, they decided to sign the agreement anyway and try to obtain a more precise delineation afterward. She writes that:

> The reason for adopting this strategy was that both governments, but especially the federal government, were very much against having anything in the Agreement relating to socio-economic development; this appeared to be the only way to wring any promises out of them on this question.... The Cree negotiators remain convinced that the shorter time spent negotiating, the better the chances are of obtaining the best deal possible from government parties. [31]

Implementation

Legislation for the James Bay Native Development Corporation was passed on June 23, 1978 with *Bill 33: An Act to incorporate the James Bay Native Development Corporation*. No other legislation has been passed specifically to implement federal and provincial responsibilities under these sections.

The primary disagreement over federal and provincial responsibilities arising from this section is over the meaning of several subsections—s.28.1.2 and s.29.0.3 of the James Bay Agreement, and s.18.1.2 of the Northeastern Quebec Agreement. These subsections specify that Canada and Quebec will assist and promote the efforts of the native people, subject to the previous subsection. The previous subsections (28.1.1 and 29.0.2 JBNQA and 18.1.1 NEQA) specify that the native parties continue to be eligible for federal and provincial programs for native people in Quebec and Canada. The federal government has generally interpreted these sections to mean that Cree, Naskapi and Inuit projects had to fit into existing programs and compete for limited economic development funds with other Indian and Inuit communities.

In contrast, a series of briefs and submissions from the native parties argue that the agreements "in spirit and letter" obligate Canada and Quebec to encourage and promote their economic development initiatives beyond the limits of existing programs. They maintain that a strict legal interpretation of provisions does not meet federal and provincial responsibilities. The Tait Report appears to support this position, suggesting that it is difficult to understand to what the commitment for promotion of the economic development efforts (s.28.1.2 and s.29.0.3 JBNQA and s.18.1.2 NEQA) actually entitles the native parties, if it is subject to existing programs for which the native parties are already eligible. The Tait Report concluded that the issue could not simply be ignored and that:

> although Sections like 28.11 may not contain precise legal commitments, they imply an intention by Canada to make its "best efforts" to assist in the accomplishment of the goals referred to in the Agreement. [32]

As a result of this disagreement, the Cree statement to the Standing Committee of Indian Affairs and Northern Development, March 26, 1981, indicated that the implementation of s.28 had been an unqualified failure. Makivik's submission to the MacDonald Commission reiterated the view that s.29 called for the establishment of new programs for economic development. [33] The Inuit especially have focused on the issue of economic development [34] because, without block funding commitments, the limited economic base in the north has constrained their ability to be self-governing.

Federal and provincial expenditures for economic development stand in contrast to the emphasis of the native parties. In its 1980 analysis of Department of Indian Affairs and Northern Development expenditures for the James Bay Cree, Peat Marwick commented that the Department's definition of economic development (reflected in its funding policies) included feasibility studies, management assistance and technical assistance in the form of grants and loans. Five per cent of the total departmental expenditures for 1978-79 were directed toward economic development for the Crees, and Peat Marwick concluded: "Economic development is not a priority area to the Department based on its percentage share of the total budget." [35]

Amounts spent on economic development in 1987 suggest this area is still not a priority. The expenditures reported in the Department of Indian Affairs and Northern Development's 1987 Annual Report on the James Bay and Northeastern Quebec agreements showed that 2.4 per cent of departmental spending was directed toward economic development for the Cree, Naskapi and Inuit of northern Quebec. Of the total expenditures of $104 million by all federal government departments in the area, $34 million (5.8 per cent) was focused on economic development. D. Axford's analysis of provincial expenditure for the Inuit from 1983 to 1986, suggests that the proportion of provincial government spending on economic development is similar to that of the federal government. [36]

The Cree and the Inuit also criticize both governments for failing to develop a comprehensive economic development plan for the region as recommended in the Tait Report.[37] The native parties have engaged in extensive lobbying for an Economic and Regional Development Agreement (ERDA) to provide for federal- provincial co-operation and planning for economic development in northern Quebec.[38] While no such agreement has been forthcoming, a memorandum of understanding between Quebec and the federal government was signed on September 30, 1987, to set up a structure for the two governments to co-operate on native economic development in northern Quebec. In fairness to federal and provincial governments, it must be noted that some of the commitments for Inuit economic development are subject to proposals from the regional government. Presently, Kativik appears to be in the final stages of formulating its regional economic development plan.[39]

However, the experience with economic development may have changed the negotiators' evaluation of appropriate strategies in signing the agreements. By 1988 Ted Moses, chief negotiator for the James Bay and Northern Quebec Agreement, had this advice for the Dene and Metis of the Northwest Territories:

> My advice is to insist on language which binds the government ...
> During the next months you will constantly be asked to trust the negotiators for Canada, to be patient and understanding, and to permit language which gives them a way out. They will tell you that stronger more specific language "would never be approved in the system" ...
> Sooner or later Canada will look at your agreement and decide it also costs too much. There is only one answer. Use binding language. You need protection from the government's abuse of power.[40]

ADMINISTRATION OF LOCAL SERVICES

The agreements contain four detailed sections concerning health and social services, educational services, the establishment of new police forces and the administration of justice. Provisions for housing and municipal services are included in the section on economic development. Under the James Bay and the Northeastern Quebec agreements, these services fell almost entirely under provincial jurisdiction.

LaRusic points out that the provisions in these sections reflect a general policy, already well-established before negotiations began, for involving native people in the administration of local services, and for provincial assumption of responsibility for services formerly provided by the federal government.[41] However, Quebec's intention to extend its presence over its northern region must have had an impact on the province's willingness to assume these responsibilities.

Health and Social Services

Sections 14 and 15 of the James Bay and Northern Quebec Agreement and s.10 of the Northeastern Quebec Agreement shift responsibility for health and social services to provincial jurisdiction, transferring all health centres and nursing stations to Quebec in order to provide the basis of a system of health facilities.

South of the 55th parallel, a Cree board delivers health and social services to the Cree beneficiaries on Category IA and IB lands. The Crees negotiated the provision that Quebec should deliver these services "to the maximum extent possible" through the Cree board. In the northern area of the James Bay region, the regional Kativik Health and Social Services Council administers these services. Quebec delivers health services directly for the Naskapi, but the agreement specifies that a Naskapi Health and Social Services Consultative Committee must be consulted before modifying any programs related to health and social services.

Both the James Bay and the Northeastern Quebec agreements outline a provincial responsibility to provide employment to native people in health and social services, and to take into account in budgeting, the implications of a northern location. Levels and criteria for evaluating whether these objectives are being met were not specified. The Crees, Inuit and Naskapi continue to be eligible for special programs for native people, both federal and provincial, and each section specifies that the transfer shall not mean a reduction in health or social services. In addition, the Inuit obtained a number of specific commitments, from both levels of government, for improvements in health services in particular communities.

The Mercury Agreement, signed by the Cree, Quebec, Hydro-Québec, and the Société d'Énergie de la Baie James, created additional responsibilities for the province in the area of health. The mercury committee is responsible for studying the presence of mercury in the environment and its effects on Cree health and socio-economic activities. Quebec's responsibilities include participation in committees, and funding for some of the administrative costs as well as aspects of the program relating to health.

Implementation

Sections 14 and 15 of the James Bay Agreement were enacted on November 17, 1977, with *Bill 10: An Act to amend the Act respecting health services and social services*. While health care to native communities in northern Quebec is considered by the federal government to be a provincial responsibility pursuant to the agreements, there are some exceptions relating to medical services undertaken by the federal governments after the agreements were signed. [42] The most important of these, the National Native Alcohol and Drug Abuse Probram and the Indian and Inuit Professional Health Career Program, continue to be funded and administered by the federal government.

Both the James Bay and the Northeastern Quebec agreements provide for joint funding and delivery of health programs during a transitional period, with provisions for the transfer of facilities, equipment and responsibility to Quebec. With respect to the Inuit, s.15 specified that the transfer to provincial jurisdiction and the Kativik Council should be completed within five years of the execution of the agreement. Section 14 is not as clear with respect to the date by which the transfer of Cree health services should be completed. The 1982 federal review of the implementation process (Tait Report) indicated that federal lawyers held the opinion that the agreement required the transfer to provincial jurisdiction of health and social services. The process took place in stages, with the final transfer on March 31, 1981. The Northeastern Quebec Agreement specifies that health services should be transferred once the Naskapi were established on their permanent residence on Category IA-N lands.

The transfer to provincial jurisdiction did not create major problems for the Inuit and other residents north of the 55th parallel. However, the Crees did experience enough difficulty to attempt to obtain an injunction preventing the transfer of health services to the province in March of 1981. In their brief to the Standing Committee on Health, Welfare and Social Affairs (May 19, 1981), and the Standing Committee on Indian Affairs and Northern Development (March 26, 1981), the Crees pointed out that the lack of essential sanitation services had contributed to serious health problems in some communities, including a gastroenteritis epidemic in which a number of Cree infants died. The Crees argued that, pursuant to s.91(24) of the *BNA Act*, the federal government was ultimately responsible as a guarantor of health for the Crees and that the federal withdrawal of services represented an abrogation of this responsibility. Moreover, attempts to implement health services as specified in the agreement had not gone smoothly: the Cree launched legal proceedings against the province, and Quebec put the Cree Health Board under provisional administration.

The 1982 Tait Report stated that problems in the Cree health care system had resulted in a loss of confidence by both Cree individuals and communities in the ability of the board to provide adequate health care. The report attributed the crisis to disputes between Quebec and the board over the board's mandate and budget, to disagreement about Canada's role in health care and to internal board management problems. While the Tait Report did not question the federal government's transfer of Cree health and social services, it did indicate that the issue of improved sanitation facilities was of major importance. The report also noted a number of initiatives to resolve the continuing difficulties, including a reorganization of the management of the Cree Health Board, and fruitful budget negotiations between the board and the province.

In response to the Tait Report, the Department of Indian Affairs and Northern Development paid the Cree $26.3 million for a number of capital projects including accelerated construction of essential sanitation. The 1984-85 Annual Report of the Grand Council and the Cree Regional Authority indicated that:

> There had been considerable progress in relation to the identification of needs. The Department of Social Affairs and the Cree Board of Health ... are in substantial agreement on the operating and capital budgets required for the Board.[43]

While the report indicated that there were still a number of outstanding problems, most difficulties associated with implementation appeared to be solved.

EDUCATION

Under s.16 and s.17 of the James Bay and Northern Quebec Agreement, and s.11 of the Northeastern Quebec Agreement, ed-

198

ucation was transferred to provincial jurisdiction. Education programs for the Inuit are administered through the Kativik School Board, which provides these programs to all residents of the territory north of the 55th parallel. On the other hand, the Cree School Board, which has special powers and a mandate to ensure that educational programs are culturally relevant, provides educational services only for Cree beneficiaries of the agreement. The Naskapi school is for the Naskapi beneficiaries of the Northeastern Quebec Agreement residing on Category IA-N lands. The duties and powers of the Naskapi Education Committee also ensure cultural relevance and survival. Various clauses make certain that the levels of educational services are maintained despite the transfer to provincial jurisdiction.

There are some additional differences between native groups in terms of the negotiated responsibilities of federal and provincial governments. The Crees negotiated provisions that Canada and Quebec consult the Cree School Board regarding funding formulae, and that unique features of both geography and student needs be taken into account in setting funding levels. For the Naskapi, Quebec has a responsibility to make available special funding to qualify Naskapi beneficiaries as teachers. Finally, Canada is responsible for 75 per cent of educational funding for the Crees and the Naskapi, while Quebec pays the remaining 25 per cent. For the Inuit, the proportions are reversed—Canada pays 25 per cent and Quebec, the remainder.

Implementation

Sections 16 and 17 of the James Bay Agreement were enacted on June 18, 1978 with *Bill 2: An Act to amend the Education Act*. The education provisions of the Northeastern Quebec Agreement were assented to June 22, 1979 in *Bill 26: An Act respecting the legislation provided for in the Northeastern Quebec Agreement and amending other legislation*. The James Bay Agreement outlines the steps for a two-year transition period for Cree education; the transition period for the Kativik School Board was set at a minimum of two years, with no specific steps outlined. Section 11.6 of the Northeastern Quebec Agreement establishes a provisional Naskapi Education Committee, and s.11.5 and s.11.10 provide for an education committee and the building of a school, once the Naskapi have established permanent residence on their Category IA-N lands.

The process of transfer appears to have gone relatively smoothly for all the native groups. However, both the Crees and the Inuit in their 1981 submissions to the House of Commons Standing Committee on Indian Affairs and Northern Development, indicated that levels of funding available for school boards made it impossible for these boards to fulfil their mandates, especially with respect to the development of curriculum and the establishment of teaching materials based on the Cree or Inuit language.

The 1982 Tait Report noted these complaints, but pointed out that, according to the agreement, the role of the federal government in managing Cree and Inuit education was limited. The report, however, stated that:

> On the basis of the overall review, it is clear that the success of the education system is critical to the successful implementation of almost all aspects of the Agreement. It is essential that all the parties to the Agreement cooperate to ensure that the legitimate educational goals of the native parties are achieved. [44]

In a 1987 paper, Billy Diamond, Chair of the Cree School Board indicated that the board's funding problems had not been ameliorated: both the provincial and the federal government considered the Cree School Board a provincial school board and had not recognized the special mandate and unique circumstances under which it operated, in funding decisions. Specifically, the capital assets, which the Cree School Board inherited at the time of transfer of jurisdiction, were inadequate to provide the quality of education available to residents in other parts of the province. [45] Funding to remedy this situation was not forthcoming from either Quebec or Canada, and the Cree School Board had to dip into its educational operating funds to improve the school infrastructure. In addition, the operating budget of the Cree School Board did not enable it to administer or develop policies or programs to fulfil its mandate under the agreement to provide culturally relevant curriculum materials. Nor did Cree school board budgets recognize the expense of operating in a northern and isolated environment, or the necessity for developing curriculum in three languages. [46] Finally, Cree School Board representatives had never participated in negotiations over the funding formula for annual operating budgets. Budget negotiations had been bilateral, and H.A. McCue, Director of Education for the Cree School Board in 1986, argued:

> Because the Crees have been shut out of the process which establishes
> the budget of the CSB, the CSB is dependant entirely on the perception
> of others, namely Federal and Provincial officials as to the needs of
> Cree education. Furthermore, this exclusion ensures that any effort
> by the Crees to determine who to lobby in an effort to obtain more
> money will result in fruitless frustration.[47]

The result was that the board had to take resources normally allocated for other purposes to fulfil its education mandate, and to
operate at a deficit. Diamond's paper also argued that:

> The result is that the support and administrative activities of the board
> suffer in order to provide some resources, however minimal, for these
> other major concerns. The governments seem intent on perpetuating
> the inherited problems of the board and working against the attain-
> ment of the objectives set forth in section 16.[48]

POLICING

Sections 19 and 21 of the James Bay Agreement, and s.13 of the
Northeastern Quebec Agreement address the issue of policing in
the James Bay area. All of these sections place policing under provincial jurisdiction, subject to the laws of Quebec, and governed
by the Quebec *Police Act*. In the area north of the 55th parallel, the
Kativik Regional Government is primarily responsible for establishing and administering a regional police force for all residents of the
territory. Kativik may also appoint special constables for the municipalities as well as establish and maintain a police school.
Quebec's responsibilities for the Inuit in particular, separate from
its responsibilities for the entire population of the area, consist of
consulting with Kativik about by-laws made by the Quebec Police
Commission respecting the qualifications required by Inuit members.

Quebec is more involved in the day-to-day administration of policing for the Cree and Naskapi. The province is responsible for
training a specified number of Cree as members of the provincial
police force, and establishing them in Cree communities. Quebec
is also responsible for training Cree special constables, appointed
by Cree village municipalities, for Cree Category I lands, following
special Quebec legislation allowing the municipalities this power.
Finally, the James Bay Agreement provides for the establishment,
by Quebec, of a police advisory committee.

The Northeastern Quebec Agreement has arrangements similar to those of the Crees for the policing of Naskapi IA-N lands. Quebec is responsible for legislation to allow for the appointment of Naskapi special constables by the Naskapi village corporation, as well as for the cost of their training. Section 13.1.5.1 of the Northeastern Quebec Agreement also provides for a Naskapi representative (for Naskapi matters) on the police advisory committee.

The agreements specify that Quebec pay the costs of police training, although the federal and provincial governments will negotiate cost-sharing arrangements for direct policing services for the Cree and the Naskapi, while no funding arrangements are specified for the Kativik Regional Police Force.

Implementation

Policing is one of the areas under the competence of the regional government in *Bill 23: An Act concerning Northern villages and the Kativik Regional Government*, assented to on June 23, 1978. The Quebec *Police Act* was amended by *Bill 38: An Act respecting the police force of Cree villages and of the Naskapi village*, allowing Cree and Naskapi village municipalities to establish and maintain special constables. Bill 38 also allowed Quebec to create an advisory board to advise on "the maintenance of peace, order and public safety in a Cree environment." The budget for the municipal police force must be submitted for approval to the provincial attorney general.

The Cree brief in response to the first report on the implementation of the James Bay Agreement tabled in the House of Commons indicates that, although the implementation of this section had been delayed because of disagreements between the federal and provincial governments about financing, the police forces were now functioning well. [49]

The 1984-85 Annual Report of the Grand Council and the Cree Regional Authority showed that a serious problem existed respecting the number of Cree police required, and that although Quebec recognized Cree requests, "the main problem seems to be budgets." [50] Following hearings in each of the Cree communities, the 1986 Cree-Naskapi Commission reported that the financial resources of the band councils were inadequate to hire and train sufficient numbers of constables to provide satisfactory policing in many communities, and that band councils hesitated to make by-laws for some of the areas under their jurisdiction since there were no police available to enforce these by-laws once they were passed.[51] These issues, however, appear to be largely outside the scope of the implementation of the agreements.

JUSTICE

The responsibilities of Canada and Quebec with respect to the justice system under the James Bay Agreement and the Northeastern Quebec Agreement, are similar for the Crees, the Naskapi and the Inuit. The administration of justice was placed under provincial jurisdiction. Under the agreement, Quebec undertook to adapt the administration of justice to native culture in several ways. First, non-native persons working in the justice system should be cognizant of Cree, Inuit and Naskapi culture and ways of life. Secondly, aspects of the legal system were to be available in all the native languages, although the Crees and Naskapi appear to have negotiated more extensive rights in this area than the Inuit. Third, Quebec agreed to modify eligibility criteria for legal aid services to take into consideration the situation of native people in the northern environment. Fourth, court procedures and sentencing were to take account of native culture and circumstances. Finally, Quebec was responsible for programs to train native people for employment in the justice system, to hire as many native people as possible and to provide information about that system to local communities.

Both levels of government were responsible for establishing detention centres in the James Bay area. Both levels of government also agreed to amend legislation to adapt it to native cultures and to the circumstances of the northern environment. Quebec undertook to amend its *Code of Civil Procedures*; Canada undertook to amend the *Criminal Code* and the *Canada Evidence Act*.

The Crees negotiated for the establishment of a judicial advisory committee with representatives from the Crees and the province, as well as various specialists, to "advise on a permanent basis the authorities with respect to the administration of justice respecting the Crees" (s.18.0.37). No such committee was established for the Inuit, but there are provisions which call for consultation with Kativik on almost every aspect of the justice system. Similarly in the Northeastern Quebec Agreement, approval is required from the Naskapi local authority for many undertakings.

Implementation

The 1981 Cree Brief to the Standing Committee on Indian Affairs and Northern Development cited this section as one which had been quite successfully implemented. However, Makivik's 1985 report on the implementation of the agreement indicated that, in spite of the pressing nature of the problem of implementing justice in the area, the commitments of the section on justice had not been kept. The report stated:

> the actual court personnel is [sic] very ignorant of Inuit customs... Inuit training programs have never received the support needed to be delivered ... no action has been taken to fulfill the commitments to reform legal aid legislation and to establish detention institutions in the North. [52]

By 1986 other difficulties with the justice system had been identified by the Crees and Naskapi as well. After its hearings in the communities, the Cree-Naskapi Commission reported that although bands had powers to make by-laws which dealt with matters such as hunting, fishing, trapping, access to and residence on IA and IA-N lands, health and hygiene, public order and safety, and the protection of the environment, many were reluctant to make these by-laws because of the lack of resources for enforcement. [53] The local justice system consisted of an itinerant provincial court without a regular schedule, and provincial Crown prosecutors were not available to prosecute band by-laws. At the time of the hearings, many bands did not have the financial resources to retain a lawyer to conduct prosecutions on their behalf. According to one band, this and other problems with the justice system "... carry the potential to cause serious harm to the respect our people would otherwise hold for a justice system that is quite foreign to us to begin with." [54]

To date the implementation of provisions with respect to justice has not been a major focus of the native parties. Instead, they have emphasized issues including local government, housing and sanitation, and economic development. With recent media attention on justice, this issue may come to the fore. Reporting on a 1987 symposium on Cree justice, the Grand Council of the Cree Annual Report indicated that the focus had been on redefining the justice system to:

start establishing Cree social control while respecting traditional and modern values, and to incorporate these values in a Cree justice system. The total control of the judicial powers by non-natives does not respect the goal of self-government and is coming to an end.[55]

HOUSING AND MUNICIPAL SERVICES

Sections 2.11 and 2.12 of the James Bay and Northern Quebec Agreement and s.2.9 and s.2.10 of the Northeastern Quebec Agreement, provide that the Inuit, Crees and Naskapi continue to be entitled to existing federal and provincial programs, including those about housing and municipal services. Jurisdictional responsibility for housing and municipal services is mentioned in s.28 and s.29 of the James Bay, and s.20 of the Northeastern Quebec agreements. For the Cree, both Canada and Quebec are responsible for providing a community centre, essential sanitation services and fire protection, "subject to the extent of financial participation possible, and to the priorities set by Canada, Quebec, and the Crees." No explicit mention is made of housing for the Cree.

For the area north of the 55th parallel, s.29.0.40 of the James Bay Agreement indicates that the existing provision of housing and municipal services shall continue "until a unified system, including the transfer of property and housing management to the municipalities" is arranged between Kativik, the northern village municipalities, and the provincial and federal governments.

While the Naskapi were assigned Category IA lands under the Northeastern Quebec Agreement, they retained the option to relocate to another site if, after considering the report of a relocation committee, a majority of the Naskapi favoured the move (s.20, NEQA). The costs of relocation were to be shared by the federal and provincial governments, with the specific contribution of each government depending on the site chosen.

The agreements also contain provisions for transportation infrastructure. Both governments are to continue negotiations with the Cree regarding access roads, and to study the establishment of seaplane bases, public wharves, airstrips, navigational aids, docking facilities and access roads.

Implementation

Bill 23: An Act concerning Northern villages and the Kativik Regional Government (Kativik Act) gave Kativik and the northern village municipalities competence in the areas of housing and municipal services. The direct administrative responsibility for Inuit housing and infrastructure was assumed by Quebec in February of 1981, under the terms of the Northern Quebec Transfer Agreement. Under the terms of this agreement, Canada was to pay Quebec $72 million at the rate of $8 million per year for nine years, and to transfer $30.2 million in assets to the province. The ownership and responsibility for provision of housing, electricity, water, sanitation and municipal services was transferred to Quebec. Since then, housing construction has been carried out by the Quebec Housing Corporation, with cost-sharing through CMHC, mainly under CMHC's non-profit and co-operative housing, and rent supplement programs.

With respect to the Crees, Quebec maintained that it was responsible only for Category IB land (containing Cree corporations under provincial jurisdiction), and that housing and municipal services on Cree Category IA lands were a federal responsibility. There are no settlements on Category IB lands.

The 1982 Tait Report indicated that both the Crees and Inuit felt the federal government had abrogated the spirit and letter of the agreement with respect to housing and infrastructure. The report contended that, during the negotiation process, all parties agreed that the native communities required major programs to upgrade housing and infrastructure, and that, while government representatives rejected a notion of providing for a "catch-up" program in the agreement, they assured the native parties that the necessary improvements could be accomplished through the application of ongoing programs. While the agreement and related documents contain no provision which clearly commits Canada to a catch-up program, the Cree and Inuit interpreted s.28.11.1 and s.29.0.40 to indicate provincial and federal government commitments to a special, federally-funded program for improved housing and infrastructure, in addition to regular programs and services for which they continue to be eligible under s.2.11 and s.2.12.[56]

The Department of Indian Affairs and Northern Development's position was that Cree and Inuit communities were entitled to the same programs as those enjoyed by other Indian and Inuit communities in Canada.[57] On this basis, the Department carried out construction of housing and sanitation services in accordance with existing programs established for that purpose. The Department's interpretation was that while s.28.11.1 recognized the special needs of Cree communities, it created no obligation with respect to increased levels of expenditures or a time within which expenditures must be made.

Evaluating these disagreements, the Tait Report concluded:

> That the overall results anticipated in 1975 have not been achieved seems to be a result more of budgets that have decreased in relation to costs than a failure to respect the Agreement or the justified expectations of the native parties.[58]

However, the report declared that provisions like those contained in s.28.11 were not just lists of possible initiatives to be fitted into existing programs:

> although sections like 28.11 may not contain precise legal commitments, they imply an intention by Canada to make its "best efforts" to assist in the accomplishment of the goals referred to in the Agreement.[59]

And it concluded that federal and provincial governments should explore initiatives to improve housing and infrastructure as quickly as possible.[60] In response to the Tait Report the federal government announced on July 8, 1982, an expenditure of $52.6 million, equally divided by the Crees and the Inuit, part of which was to be used for the accelerated construction of housing for the Cree and Inuit. This accelerated construction program does not appear to have satisfied the housing needs of the Cree, and housing is on the agenda for the implementation negotiations with the federal government. Quebec still appears to take the position that it is not responsible for housing and municipal infrastructure on Cree Category IB lands, although the Cree are at present negotiating with the province. With respect to Quebec's expenditures for the Inuit, Axford indicates:

> Quebec is now responsible for the number of houses built in Northern Quebec and for the type of housing that is built. On both of these fronts there seems to have been an impressive commitment of financial and human resources even though considerable financing for these project comes from CMHC.[61]

Section 29.0.36 respecting various transportation infrastructure issues is being partially implemented under the terms of a federal-provincial northern Quebec airport agreement, signed on

September 27, 1983. Under this agreement, Canada agreed to finance 100 per cent of the costs related to three Cree airports and 60 per cent of the costs for 12 Inuit airports. Canada will also install, operate and maintain all navigational aids. While s.29.0.36 also commits the federal government and Quebec, together with the Inuit communities, to undertake studies concerning public wharves and docking facilities in each community, it does not appear to have been implemented.

The Cree report that the issue of access roads is still subject to jurisdictional dispute, with Quebec maintaining that roads on Category I lands are solely a federal responsibility and not subject to cost-sharing agreements. The federal government, on the other hand, has in the past taken the position that its responsibilities with respect to Cree access-roads are fulfilled by its participation in negotiations, with no obligation to finance road construction.[62]

When the Naskapi chose to relocate from their original Category IA lands, Canada and Quebec were committed, under the Northeastern Quebec Agreement, to training Naskapi personnel in the construction of a new village. The Naskapi Relocation Committee, incorporated in 1980, directed the construction work, and the 1987 December issue of *Recontre* indicated that the work was near completion, with most of the Naskapi community living in houses on the new site.

CONCLUSION

The James Bay and Northern Quebec Agreement and the Northeastern Quebec Agreement are important land-claims settlements, and represent new chapters in aboriginal-federal-provincial relationships. Negotiation of the agreements, complementary agreements and the enacting legislation demonstrated high levels of commitment and co-operation on the part of the native signatories and the federal and provincial governments. The result has been an increase in the control which the native peoples of the James Bay area have over their lives and their cultures. Testimony of the native groups themselves indicates that many of the provisions of the agreements have been successfully put into practice. However, areas not yet implemented threaten to overshadow what has been accomplished.

One of the important features of the James Bay and the Northeastern Quebec agreements is that they are dynamic agreements—the various sections set out principles governing future circumstances and developments. In this sense, the agreements will never be completely implemented: instead, negotiations between the Cree, Naskapi and Inuit, and federal and provincial governments will continue to be necessary and important.

However, this dynamic element has not been the most important source of negotiations and contact between the native parties and governments since the agreements were signed. Instead, it is basic implementation issues which have been the focus. The Cree indicate that:

> What the Crees and Inuit have learned over the last 11 years is that negotiation of a claim settlement is only half the battle and implementation is the other half.[63]

For the native parties, implementation has involved more than a decade of lobbying, injunctions and negotiations which have diverted time, energy and financial resources.

The lack of formal implementation structures and processes with sufficient resources, or the mandate and authority to legally bind other departments and ministries, has frequently been identified as a major source of implementation problems at the federal level.[64] The mediation/negotiation process now in place at the federal level may be a first step toward resolving this difficulty. The federal negotiator speaks on behalf of the federal government and not just the Department of Indian Affairs and Northern Development, and a mediator is available to facilitate the negotiation process (see Appendix, "Implementation and Remedial Steps").

Nevertheless the Cree have expressed some serious reservations about the possibility of negotiating in good faith with the federal government, and about obtaining legally binding commitments from Canada. Moses' address to the Dene and Metis before they signed their agreement in principle, cited violations to the Manitoba Flood Agreement and the COPE Agreement as well the James Bay and the Northeastern Quebec agreements before concluding:

> It might seem that all of this could be solved if there was some kind of arbitration mechanism in place that could assist in implementation and help to resolve disputes and matters of interpretation ... The Manitoba Flood Agreement contains a binding arbitration mechanism. But there are now over one hundred arbitration decisions against the Federal government which Canada continues to ignore. Canada claims

> it cannot be bound by an arbitrator... [In addition,] no matter what you negotiate, *Cabinet may by unilateral decision reinterpret and revoke the benefits to which you are entitled by treaty. And you will never know what they decided because Cabinet decisions are secret.* [65]

Clearly, the absence of a formal implementation mechanism is not the only source of the problem. Comparing the history of the Cree, Naskapi and Inuit dealings with both the federal and provincial governments, it appears that part of the formula has to be the political will to make the provisions on paper a reality in aboriginal communities. There have been serious conflicts between the native parties and the provincial government, both over the provisions of the agreements and over the transfer of services to provincial jurisdiction. J. O'Reilly, writing about Indian-provincial relations in Quebec and Alberta, maintained that:

> [O]n the whole, the implementation of the James Bay and Northern Quebec Agreement by the Quebec government cannot be categorized as satisfactory. What is alarming is that it is probably the best existing model of Indian-provincial co-operation. [66]

Nevertheless, Quebec seems to have been more prepared than the federal government to take the necessary steps to implement the agreement, even though there was no formal, provincial implementation mechanism in place. LaRusic's evaluation of arrangements for the Cree income security program is a case in point.

> The flexible implementation policy of Social Affairs in getting the ISP off the ground was not a chance event. The policy of the Quebec government after the signing of the James Bay Agreement was to use transitional procedures until the legislative packages could be developed and enacted ... The process certainly contrasts with the performance on [sic] the Federal agencies. There is little doubt in my mind that had the ISP been a programme involving the Federal authorities, there would have been no benefits in the hands of the beneficiaries before 1980. [67]

Two important factors which appear to affect Quebec's strategy with respect to the agreements are the potential economic costs of major disagreements with the native parties, and the province's desire to extend its jurisdiction over the northern half of the province. Hydro-Québec, and therefore the Province of Quebec, has an interest in seeing that implementation is pursued in a business-like manner, because serious conflicts might lead to a disruption of hydro-electric power production. The question of sovereignty remains important. As a result, the Province of Quebec has showed much less resistance to the devolution of responsibility for aboriginal peoples from the federal to the provincial government, and much more of a commitment to working out the details of the James Bay and the Northeastern Quebec agreements. Thus, while a number of implementation issues are still outstanding with the provincial government, the legacy of distrust which characterizes relations between the federal government and the Cree especially, does not appear to have emerged.

Concern with setting a precedent appears to have influenced the federal government's approach to implementing the agreements. Clearly there are some areas where the agreements conflict with emerging federal policy. This seems to be the case with the type of funding mechanism negotiated by the Cree in the statement of understanding, and with the commitments concerning economic development. To avoid having the agreements taken as a model for other aboriginal negotiations, the approach of the federal government has, in the past, included ignoring its commitments, meeting minimum legal obligations rather than implementing the agreements in their "spirit and intent," and actively attempting to renegotiate various sections.

These strategies have their own costs. In the first place, they reinforce the notion that governments routinely make promises to obtain surrender of aboriginal lands, with no intention of living up to agreements. The Cree-Naskapi Commission, studying the impasse which had arisen with respect to the statement of understanding regarding funding for Cree local government, wrote:

> In the course of Canadian history, a notion persists that governments make promises to induce natives to surrender their lands and other rights and then routinely break these promises. Regrettably, the evidence supporting this notion is extensive ... The Commissioners hope that the Statement of Understanding will not become one further instance of the unfortunate notion borne true. [68]

This legacy of distrust threatens to affect other negotiations between aboriginal peoples and the federal government. Ted Moses' address to the Dene and Metis at Yellowknife earlier this year demonstrates that aboriginal peoples are beginning to discuss negotiation strategies and the implications of different approaches among themselves. The way in which the James Bay and the Northeastern Quebec agreements are implemented, therefore, have implications for the relationship between the federal government and aboriginal peoples other than the Cree, Inuit and Naskapi.

Finally, federal government strategies have diverted attention from the successes which have been achieved to the problems which remain. Many of the structures and programs created by the agreements are innovative and represent unique ways of approaching various aspects of aboriginal self-government. The atmosphere and attitudes created by continuing implementation problems have frequently meant that the achievement the agreements represent has been overshadowed. Clearly another approach to implementation is required.

Notes

1. D.C. Hawkes and E.J. Peters, *Implementing Aboriginal Self- Government: Problems and Prospects*, Workshop Report (Kingston: Queen's University, Institute of Intergovernmental Relations, 1986).
2. I.E. LaRusic, *Negotiating a Way of Life: Initial Cree experience with the administrative structures arising from the James Bay Agreement* (Ottawa: Research Division, Policy, Research and Evaluation Group, Department of Indian Affairs and Northern Development, 1979).

    B. Richardson, *Strangers Devour the Land* (Toronto: Macmillan, 1975).

    R.F. Salisbury, *A Homeland for the Cree: Regional Development in James Bay 1971-1981* (Kingston: McGill-Queen's University Press, 1986).
3. T. Moses, Address by Chief Ted Moses, Eastmain Band, James Bay, Yellowknife, Northwest Territories, June 13, 1988.
4. The Hon. John Ciacca, "Opening remarks to the Standing Parliamentary Committee of the National Assembly of Quebec convened to examine the Agreement with the James Bay Crees and the Inuit of Quebec prior to its signature, 5 November, 1975," *The James Bay and Northern Quebec Agreement*, éditeur officiel du Québec (1976), pp. xi-xxiv.
5. N. Bankes, *Resource-leasing Options and the Settlement of Aboriginal Claims*, (Ottawa: Canadian Arctic Resources Committee, 1983).

    R. Bartlett, *Subjugation, Self-Management and Self- Government of Aboriginal Lands and Resources*, Background Paper No. 11. (Kingston: Queen's University, Institute of Intergovernmental Relations, 1986).
6. I would like to thank Marsha Smoke, Bob Epstein, Michael Barrett and Don Axford for answering questions and providing background materials for some sections of this chapter. Any inaccuracies which remain are, of course, my responsibility.
7. J.P. Rostaing, "Native Regional Autonomy: The Initial Experience of the Kativik Regional Government," *études / Inuit / Studies* 8(2) (1984), p. 16.
8. *Ibid.*, 1984, pp. 16-17.
9. *Ibid.*, 1984, p. 17.
10. *Ibid.*, 1984, p. 19.
11. Cree-Naskapi Commission, *1986 Report of the Cree-Naskapi Commission* (Ottawa: K.G. Campbell Corporation, January 1987), p. 24.
12. *Ibid.*, 1987, p. 27.
13. *Ibid.*, 1987, p. 27.
14. Grand Council of the Crees (of Quebec) and the Cree Regional Authority, *Annual Report*, Val D'Or, Quebec, 1987-88, p. 24.
15. Canada, Department of Indian Affairs and Northern Development, Letter of the Hon. W. McKnight to Grand Chief Coon-Come, dated July 7, 1988.
16. Rostaing, *op. cit.*, note 7, p. 23.
17. Michael Barrett, Head, Environment and Resource Management, Kativik Regional Government, Remarks to the conference on "Defining the Responsibilities: Federal and Provincial Governments and Aboriginal Peoples," Carleton University, Ottawa, Ontario, October 4, 1988.
18. *Ibid.*

19. Canada, Department of Indian Affairs and Northern Development, *James Bay and Northern Quebec Implementation Review,* (Tait Report), (Ottawa, 1982), p. 5.
20. Grand Council of the Crees, *Annual Report,* Val D'Or, Quebec, 1982-83; 1983-84; 1984-85.
    Makivik Corporation, *The James Bay and Northern Quebec Agreement: Ten Years of Disagreement,* Montreal, 1985, pp. 24-25.
21. Makivik, *ibid.,* p. 25.
22. D. Axford, *The Application of Federal Programs to the Inuit Communities of Northern Quebec,* submitted to Makivik Corporation, Ottawa, July 1987b, p. 55.
    Makivik, *op. cit.,* note 20, p. 25.
23. LaRusic, *op. cit.,* note 2, p. 166.
24. I.E. LaRusic, *Income Security for Subsistence Hunters: a review of the first five years of the operation of the Income Security Programme for Cree Hunters and Trappers,* (Ottawa: Research Branch, Corporate Policy, Department of Indian Affairs and Northern Development, 1982), p. 68.
25. LaRusic, *ibid.,* p. 67.
26. R. Ames, D. Axford, P. Usher, E. Werck and G. Wengel, *Keeping On the Land: A Study of the Feasibility of a Comprehensive Wildlife Support Programme in the North-west Territories,* (Ottawa: Canadian Arctic Resources Committee, 1988), pp. 284-285.
27. Ames *et al., ibid.,* p. 285.
28. Kativik Regional Government, *Annual Report, 1987,* Kuujjuac, Que. p. 39.
29. Makivik, *op. cit.,* note 20, p. 21.
30. LaRusic, *op. cit.,* note 2, p. 174.
31. W. Moss, "The Implementation of the James Bay and Northern Quebec Agreement," in B.W. Morse, *Aboriginal Peoples and the Law: Indian, Metis and Inuit Rights in Canada* (Ottawa: Carleton University Press, 1985), pp. 688-689.
32. Tait Report, *op. cit.,* note 19, p. 13.
33. Makivik Corporation, *The Future of Inuit in Canada's Economic Union: Northern Partnership or Neglect?* Brief to the Royal Commission on the Economic Union and Development Prospects for Canada, (Montreal, October 14, 1983).
34. Makivik, *ibid.,* note 33.
    Makivik, *op. cit.,* note 20.
    Makivik Corporation, *Employment and Income Patterns in Northern Quebec: "Colonized in Our Homeland,"* (Montreal, 1986).
35. Peat, Marwick et Associés, *Financial Analysis: Study of Federal Spending Toward the Crees of Northern Quebec,* prepared for the Grand Council of the Crees (of Quebec), (Montreal, May 1980), pp. III-18.
36. D. Axford, *Government Spending on the Inuit Communities of Northern Quebec—A Comparative Analysis,* submitted to Andrew Croll and Mark R. Gordon, Implementation Negotiations on the James Bay and Northern Quebec Agreement, Ottawa, 9 February 1987a, p. 13.
37. Tait Report, *op. cit.,* note 19, p. 66.
38. Grand Council of the Crees, *Annual Report,* Val D'Or, Que., 1987-88.
    Mativik, *op. cit.,* note 20.
39. Makivik, *Annual Report,* 1986-87, p. 80.
40. Moses, *op. cit.,* note 3, pp. 4-6.
41. LaRusic, *op. cit.,* note 2, p. 175.

42. D. Axford, "Native Claims Policy in Canada", unpublished paper, Ottawa, 1987c, p. 80.
43. Grand Council of the Crees, *Annual Reports*, Val D'Or, Que., 1984-85, p. 6.
44. Tait Report, *op. cit.*, note 19, p. 84.
45. B. Diamond, "The Cree Experience," in J. Barman, Y. Hebert, and D. McCaskill (eds.) *Indian Education in Canada: The Challenge*, Nakoda Institute Occasional Paper No. 3, (Vancouver: University of British Columbia Press, 1987), p. 91.
46. See also McCue, H.A., Director of Education, Cree School Board, "Self-Government in Education: the Case of the Cree School Board," paper presented to the Workshop on Implementing Self-Government, Institute of Intergovernmental Relations, Queen's University, Kingston, May 27-30, 1986.
47. *Ibid.*, p. 5.
48. Diamond, *op. cit.*, note 45, p. 92.
49. Grand Council of the Crees (of Quebec), Reply of the Grand Council of the Crees (of Quebec) to the Report on the Implementation of the Provisions of the *James Bay and Northern Quebec Native Claims Settlement Act* Tabled in the House of Commons on November 18, 1980, pp. 23-24.
50. Grand Council of the Crees, *Annual Reports*, Val D'Or, Que., 1984-85, p. 7.
51. Cree-Naskapi Commission, *op. cit.*, note 11, p. 15.
52. Makivik, *op. cit.*, note 20, p. 24.
53. Cree-Naskapi Commission, *op. cit.*, note 11, pp. 14-15.
54. *Ibid.*, p. 15.
55. Grand Council of the Crees, *Annual Report*, Val D'Or Que., 1987-88, p. 11.
56. Tait Report, *op. cit.*, note 19, pp. 27-28.
57. *Ibid.*, p. 33.
58. *Ibid.*, p. 46.
59. *Ibid.*, p. 13.
60. *Ibid.*, p. 47.
61. Axford, *op. cit.*, note 22, p. 13.
62. Moses, *op. cit.*, note 3, p. 17.
63. Grand Council of the Crees (of Quebec), The Cree Regional Authority, The Cree Bands of Quebec, *Brief Presented to the Standing Committee of the House of Commons on Aboriginal Affairs and Northern Development Respecting Bill C-93, The Sechelt Indian Self-Government Act*, May 13, 1986, p. 3.
64. Canada, Auditor General of Canada. *Report of the Auditor General of Canada to the House of Commons* (Fiscal year ended 31 March 1986), paragraphs 11.107-11.109.
    Axford, *op. cit.*, note 42.
    Cree-Naskapi Commission, *op. cit.*, note 11, pp. 32-34.
    Grand Council, *op. cit.*, note 63.
    Tait Report, *op. cit.*, note 19, p. 101.
65. Moses, *op. cit.*, note 3, pp. 3-8 and 19.
66. J. O'Reilly, "Indian Land Claims in Quebec and Alberta," in J.A. Long and M. Boldt (eds.), *Governments in Conflict? Provinces and Indian Nations in Canada* (Toronto: University of Toronto Press, 1988), p. 145.
67. LaRusic, *op. cit.*, note 24, pp. 68-69.
68. Cree-Naskapi Commission, note 11, p. 36.

APPENDIX I

Cree and Naskapi Local Government

Source	Description	Responsibility
JBNQA 9.01 NEQA 9.01	recommend to Parliament, legislation concerning local government, under federal jurisdiction, on Category IA and IA-N lands	Canada
JBNQA 10.0 NEQA 10.0	incorporate Cree and Naskapi village municipalities, under provincial jurisdiction, on Category IB and IB-N lands	Quebec
JBNQA 28.15	subject to Departmental directives, provide CORE funding for internal administration and administration of delegated programs, for Cree local governments	Canada
Bill 24	approve council of village municipality's by-laws concerning the environment and natural resources	Quebec
Bill C-46 s.45 s.48(5) s.66 s.67, 87 s.93 s.98 s.100 s.122 s.151	may regulate local taxation by-laws; may disallow certain by-laws concerning hunting and trapping; approve election by-laws; may make regulations for elections, special band meetings and referenda; may appoint auditor and seek renumeration if band fails to do so; may regulate long-term borrowing; may appoint administrator if affairs of band are in serious disorder; compensate band for expropriated land; may regulate land registry system;	Canada

216

s.156	may regulate band expropriations;	
s.198	may regulate fine or sentences for breaking band by-laws;	
Part XII	establish and fund a commission to hear submissions regarding, and report to Parliament on, the implementation of the Act.	
1988 Letter	negotiate five-year financial agreement with Cree bands	Canada

Inuit Local Government

JBNQA 12.0.1	submit to the National Assembly, bills incorporating northern village municipalities under provincial jurisdiction	Quebec
JBNQA 7.1.2	incorporate Inuit landholding community corporations to receive title to Category I lands for Inuit community purposes	Quebec
Bill 23 s.113	may appoint person to fill vacancy on municipal council;	Quebec
s.160	may disallow council by-laws;	
Ch.II	may raise local taxation levels;	
Ch.III	may authorize loans.	

Cree Regional Government

Source	Description	Responsibility
JBNQA 11A	introduce legislation to incorporate the Cree Regional Authority, a public corporation with its corporate seat in the Cree Category I lands	Quebec
JBNQA 28.15	provide CORE funding for the internal administration of the Cree Regional Authrity, as well as for the administration of delegated programs	Canada
JBNQA 11B.0.2	introduce legislation to establish the James Bay Regional Zone Council, with Cree representatives, to exercise the powers of the James Bay Municipality on Cree Category II lands	Quebec
JBNQA 11B.0.9	approve by-laws enacted by the Council	Quebec

| JBNQA 11B.0.17 | fund the administration of the Council; approve annual budgets | Quebec |

Inuit Regional Government

Source	Description	Responsibility
JBNQA 13	establish a regional government with respect to the area north of the 55th paralle. The regional government shall be a corporation with its seat in the territory	Quebec
JBNQA 13, Schedule 2.14	approve by-laws passed by the regional government	Quebec
JBNQA 13 Schedule 2.89	approve ordinances requiring approval according to the Agreement	Quebec
JBNQA 13 Schedule 2.156	if there is disagreement, determine the amount Kativik should pay from its compensation funds for municipal services and local improvement works	Quebec

Hunting, Fishing and Trapping Regime: Cree, Naskapi and Inuit

Source	Description	Responsibility
JBNQA 24	establish and administer a hunting, fishing and trapping regime for native people as specified in the Agreement	each for areas under their jurisdiction
JBNQA 24.5.1 NEQA 15.5.1	establish quotas, regulate and manage and protect wildlife resources, subject to the hunting, fishing and trapping regime established by the Agreement	each for areas under their jurisdiction
JBNQA 24.4 NEQA 15.4	with the Crees, Naskapi and Inuit, participate on, and consult with, a co-ordinating committee to review and make recommendations concerning the administration of the hunting, fishing and trapping regime	each for areas under their jurisdiction each pays own members and experts called
JBNQA 24.4.18	fund secretariat for co-ordinating committee	Quebec
JBNQA 5.2.6b; 7.2.6b	take into account rights of native people under hunting, fishing and trapping regime before authorizing exploration, pre-development activities and studies	Quebec

218

JBNQA 24.3.20 NEQA 15.3.19	obtain recommendation from co-ordinating committee before permitting non-natives to trap in an area where native people have exclusive rights	Quebec
JBNQA 24.3.24	take all reasonable measures, within scope of existing or future programs, to assist in establishing trappers associations and a native controlled and run trapping industry	both
JBNQA 24.9.3 NEQA 15.9.1	for thirty years from the execution of the Agreement, provide native people with the right of first refusal for seven out of ten applications, to operate as outfitters on Category III land, within their respective areas of primary and common interest	Quebec
JBNQA 24.10 NEQA 15.10	provide for the training of a sufficient number of native conservation officers	both
JBNQA 24.3.29	modify the *Wildlife Conservation Act* to avoid conflicts with s.24	Quebec
JBNQA 24.14	amend the Migratory Birds Convention to prevent conflict with the hunting, fishing and trapping regime, and with the right of native people to harvest at all times of the year	Canada

Cree, Naskapi and Inuit Income Security Programs for Hunting, Fishing and Trapping

Source	*Description*	*Responsibility*
JBNQA 30	establish and fund, through the Cree Hunters and Trappers Income Security Board, an income security program for Cree hunters and trappers	Quebec
NEQA 19	establish and fund, through the council of the Naskapi band, or the Naskapi local authority, an income security program for Naskapi hunters and trappers	Quebec
JBNQA 29.0.5	establish and fund a program, administered by Kativik, of support for hunting, fishing and trapping activities	Quebec

Environmental Regime for the Cree

Source	*Description*	*Responsibility*

Joint

JBNQA 22	comply with the stages of environmental and social impact assessment review procedures; send committees all relevant information necessary; consult with the Advisory Committee on major issues about implementation of the environmental and social protection regime; decide whether or not to assess a development not subject to assessment under the Agreement; decide whether and under what conditions developments proceed	both; each for areas under their jurisdiction
JBNQA 22.3	participate with the Crees on James Bay Advisory Committee on the Environment to review and make recommendations about the environmental and social protection regime established by the Agreement	both; each pays own members and experts it calls; equally fund secretariat
JBNQA 22.5.6 to 22.5.9	with the Cree, participate on and consult with an evaluating committee to make recommendations regarding requirements for and extent of an impact statement required	both; each for areas under their jurisdiction; each pays own members; adv. com. funds secretariat

Provincial

JBNQA 22.6.1 to 22.6.3 JBNQA 22.6.17	with the Cree, participate on an environmental and social impact review committee to review and make recommendations about developments under provincial jurisdiction; consult committee about modifications to rejection of their recommendations	Quebec; pays own members; funds staff; adv. com. pays for Cree members

220

Federal

JBNQA 22.6.4 to 22.6.6	participate with Crees on Environmental and Social Impact Review Panel to review and make recommendations about developments under federal jurisdiction; consult panel about modifications to or rejection of their recommendations	Canada; pay for own and Cree members; fund staff

Environmental Regime for the Inuit and Naskapi

Source	*Description*	*Responsibility*

Joint

JBNQA 23 NEQA 14	comply with the stages of environmental and social impact assessment and review process; send committees all relevant information necessary for discussion	each for areas under their jurisdiction
JBNQA 23.5	participate, with members of Kativik, on environmental advisory committee to review and make recommendations about the environmental and social protection regime outlined in the Agreement	both; each pays own members and experts calls; equally fund secretariat
NEQA 14.1.2.6	consult the Naskapi local authority before authorizing future development subject to assessment under the Agreement	both

Provincial

JBNQA 23.3; NEQA 2,sch.3	with Kativik representatives (including) two Inuit, or one Inuit and one Naskapi) participate on an environmental quality commission (EQC) to decide whether or not to assess a development not subject to assessment under the Agreement; to decide whether or not a development is to proceed and under what conditions; obtain permission from the minister before modifying the decision of the EQC	Quebec; each pays for own members; Quebec funds staff

Federal

JBNQA 23.4.25	decide whether or not to assess projects not subject to assessment under the Agreement; decide whether or not development should proceed and under what conditions; consult with review panel before modifying or rejecting its recommendations	Canada
JBNQA 23.4.2 to 23.4.10	with Kativik representatives participate on a screening committee to make recommendations about the requirement of impact statements for projects under federal jurisdiction;	Canada; each pays for own members
JBNQA 23.4.10 to 23.4.22	with Kativik representatives participate on an environmental and social impact review panel to review and make recommendations about developments under federal jurisdiction; consult panel about modifications to, or rejection of, their recommendations	Canada; pays for own and Kativik members; fund staff

Compensation and Economic Development: Cree

Source	Description	Responsibility
JBNQA 26.0.1	by a special act, incorporate a Cree corporation to receive the compensation payable to the Cree	Quebec
JBNQA 25	pay $135 million compensation to the Cree	Que 56.333% Can: 43.667%
JBNQA 25.5	pay the Cree $2.2 million for costs of negotiation	Quebec
NEQA 16.4.2	pay the Cree $150 000 for costs of negotiating the Northeastern Quebec Agreement	Que 75 Can 25
JBNQA 28.1.1	continue to make available to the Cree programs, funding and assistance available to other Indians in Canada and in Quebec	both
JBNQA 28.1.2	subject to paragraph 28.1.1, assist and promote the efforts of the Cree within the terms of such programs and services in operation from time to time	both

JBNQA 28.2	establish and finance a James Bay native economic development corporation	Quebec
JBNQA 28.4-7	subject to the conclusion of a feasibility study and to the availability of funds, assist in establishing a trapper's association, an outfitting and tourism association and a native arts and crafts association	both
JBNQA 28.8	participate on a joint economic and community development committee to review and make recommendations about programs related to Cree economic and social development	both
JBNQA 28.9.1	on proposals from the Cree and within budgetary constraints, provide the training programs and services the Cree require to qualify for employment in developments in the Territory	both
JBNQA 28.10	take measures to increase Cree employment in government positions; establish Cree priority in government employment and contracts, and in contracts and employment created by development in the Territory	both
JBNQA 28.11.2	subject to the extent of financial participation possible, and to the priorities set by Canada, Quebec and the Crees, provide for each community an economic development agent and community affairs services	bopth
JBNQA 28.12	within the scope of services and facilities existing from time to time, provide assistance to Cree entrepreneurs	both

Compensation and Economic Development: Naskapi

Source	Description	Responsibility
NEQA 17	by a special act, incorporate a Naskapicorporation to receive the compensation payable to the Naskapi	Quebec
NEQA 16	pay $9 million compensation to the Naskapi	Que 56.333% Can: 43.667%
NEQA 16.4	pay the Naskapi $650 000 for the cost of negotiations	Que 65.333% Can: 43.667%

223

NEQA 18.1.1	continue to make available to the Naskapi programs, funding and assistance available to other Indians in Canada and in Quebec	both
NEQA 18.1.2	subject to paragraph 28.1.1, assist and promote the efforts of the Naskapi within the terms of such programs and services in operation from time to time	both
NEQA 18.2 to 18.8	to the maximum extent possible, pursuant to existing and future programs, train appropriate Naskapi for the construction and maintenance of the Naskapi community; participate for five years, with the Naskapi, on a Naskapi manpower development co-ordinating committee for that training	both
NEQA 18.9	pay for a development agent to establish a development plan for Naskapi manpower	both
NEQA 18.11	within the scope of existing programs, assist the Naskapi in establishing a Naskapi arts and crafts association	both
NEQA 18.13 to 18.15	within the scope of services and facilities existing from time to time, provide assistance to Naskapi entrepreneurs	both
NEQA 18.16	provide economic and technical assistance for establish Naskapi commercial fisheries operations in the Territory	both

Compensation and Economic Development: Inuit

Source	Description	Responsibility
JBNQA 27.0.2	by a special act, incorporate an Inuit development corporation to receive compensation payable to the Inuit	Quebec
JBNQA 25	pay $90 million compensation to the Inuit	Que: 56.333% Can: 43.667%
JBNQA 25.5	pay the Inuit $1.3 for costs of negotiations	Quebec
NEQA 16.4.2	pay the Inuit $150 000 for costs of negotiating the Northeastern Quebec Agreement	Que 75% Can: 25%

JBNQA 29.0.2	continue to make available to the Inuit programs, funding and assistance available to other Indians and Inuit in Canada and in Quebec	both
JBNQA 29.0.3	subject to paragraph 29.0.2, assist and promote the efforts of the Inuit within the terms of such programs and services in operation from time to time	both
JBNQA 29.0.4	whenever appropriate, transfer the above programs to the administration of Kativik	both
JBNQA 29.0.25	on proposals from Kativik and in accordance with criteria established from time to time, provide the Inuit with the training programs and facilities they require to qualify for employment in developments in the Territory	both
JBNQA 29.0.29 to 29.0.31	develop a plan to train and employ, and establish priority for employing, Inuit staff within the bureaucracy of the Territory	both
JBNQA 29.0.27 JBNQA 29.0.33	create and participate on interim joint committees to co-ordinate manpower and training programs, and programs of socio-economic development	both
JBNQA 29.0.39	support Inuit entrepreneurs by providing technical and professional advice and financial assistance	both

Cree Health and Social Services

Source	Description	Responsibility
JBNQA 14.0.2	delivery of health and social services for Category IA and IB lands through a a Cree regional board of health services and social services (CRBHSS)	Quebec
JBNQA 14.0.19 14.0.20	to maximum extent possible, provide employment for native people in health and social services, and budget for the impact of a northern location	Quebec
JBNQA 14.0.20	to maximum extent possible, provide health and social services through the CRBHSS	Quebec

JBNQA 14.0.22	provide funding for existing programs available to native people but not to the provincial population	Quebec
JBNQA 14.0.28	provide funding which "at least" maintains existing scope, range, extent and conditions of health and social services	Quebec
Mercury Agreement	participate on a mercury committee, pay for the costs of the Mercury Program pertaining to health; contribute to the expenses of the committee chair; participate in a joint review of the implementation of the Mercury Program	Quebec

Naskapi Health and Social Services

Source	*Description*	*Responsibility*
NEQA 10.3 to 10.5	delivery of health and social services on Category IA-N lands, upon Naskapi establishing permanent residence on their Category I-N lands; consult the Naskapi Health and Social Services Consultative Committee before modifying any program relating to the health and social services offered to the Naskapi	Quebec
NEQA 10.6	authorize Schefferville hospital to deliver the full range of provincial health services to the Naskapi	Quebec
NEQA 10.10	until the Naskapi establish permanent residence on their Category IA-N lands, continue to provide the health and social services currently available	both
NEQA 10.13	provide funding for existing programs available to native people but not to the provincial population	Quebec
NEQA 10.15	if the Naskapi decide to relocate, share in the establishment of physical facilities to be used by health and social services personnel	both

226

| NEQA 10.20 | progressively encourage the training of Naskapi personnel for health and social services for Naskapi on Category IA-N lands | Quebec |

Inuit Health and Social Services

Source	Description	Responsibility
JBNQA 15.0.1;2	delivery of health services and social services for the area north of the 55th parallel through the Kativik Health and Social Services Council	Quebec
JBNQA 15.0.21	to maximum extent possible, provide employment for native people in health and social services, and budget for the impact of a northern location	Quebec
JBNQA 15.0.19	provide funding for existing programs available to native people but not to the provincial population	Quebec
JBNQA 15, sh1(1)	preserve and improve the scope, extent, conditions and availability of existing health and social services;	both
sh1(3)	set up a working group to organize a broad range of support services;	Quebec
sh1(4)	improve health and social services for Aupaluk, Port Burwell, Akulivik, and any new communities established;	both
sh1(5)	review health, staff, facilities and equipment at Kuujjuaq and Povungnituk	Quebec

Cree Education

Source	Description	Responsibility
JBNQA 16.0.2 JBNQA 16.0.6	management and overseeing of elementary, secondary and adult education on Category IA and IB lands, through the Cree School Board (CSB)	Quebec
JBNQA 16.0.22	fund educational services	Canada 75% Quebec 25%
JBNQA 16.0.24	ensure continuation of existing educational services and programs	joint

| JBNQA 16.0.23 | consult with the Cree regarding the funding formula for the CSB | joint |
| JBNQA 16.0.27 | take unique features of location and needs of student population into account in annual budgets | joint |

Naskapi Education

Source	Description	Responsibility
NEQA 11.1 to 10.5.6	establishment of a Naskapi school; to 10.5.6 management and overseeing of elementary, secondary and adult education on Category IA-N lands, in consultation with the Naskapi Education Committee	Quebec
NEQA 11.18	make available special courses to qualify Naskapi beneficiaries as teachers	Quebec
NEQA 11.20	ensure the continuation of existing services and programs presently available	both
NEQA 11.15 NEQA 11.24	fund educational services; budgets to include the costs of translation, residences for postsecondary students, cost of training teachers in special programs for Naskapi schools, adult education program, administration and operation of school	Canada 75% Quebec 25%

Inuit Education

Source	Description	Responsibility
QA 17.02	management and overseeing of elementary secondary and adult education for the area north of the 55th parallel through the Kativik School Board	Quebec
JBNQA 17.0.84	maintain adequate funding for educational joint services and programs presently available	

| JBNQA 17.0.85 | fund educational services | Canada 25%
Quebec 75% |

Cree Policing

Source	Description	Responsibility
JBNQA 19.1.1 to 19.1.13	establish Cree units of the provincial police force (two constables per 1000 Crees); establish them in the more populated Cree areas and communities	Quebec
JBNQA 19.1.6	consult with the Crees before establishing standards for recruiting members of the Cree units	Quebec
JBNQA 19.1.12	establish a police advisory committee	Quebec
JBNQA 19.2	adopt legislation allowing Cree village corporations to appoint Cree special constables (one per 500 Crees), initially with duties in Category I lands; pay for training these special constables	Quebec
JBNQA 19.3	negotiate cost-sharing agreement for direct costs of policing services, and costs of training	both

Naskapi Policing

Source	Description	Responsibility
NEQA 13.1.1 NEQA 13.1.9	adopt legislation allowing Naskapi village corporations to appoint Naskapi special constables (one per 500 Naskapi), initially with duties in Category IA-N lands; pay for training these special constables	Quebec
NEQA 13.1.5.1	allow for representation on the Police Advisory Committee for Naskapi Matters	Quebec
NEQA 13.2	negotiate cost-sharing agreement for direct costs of policing services, and costs of training	both

Inuit Policing

Source	Description	Responsibility
JBNQA 21.0.5	approve ordinances of Kativik providing for the discipline of members of the regional police force	Quebec
JBNQA 21.0.10	consult with the regional government before making by-laws qualifying admission of Inuit to the regional police force	Quebec
JBNQA 21.0.16	establish and pay for training programs for candidates	Quebec

Cree Justice System

Source	Description	Responsibility
JBNQA 18.0.1,2	administration of justice	Quebec
JBNQA 18.0.7 18.0.9	appoint persons to dispense justice who are cognizant with the customs, and ways of life of the Crees	Quebec
JBNQA 18.0.15 JBNQA 18.0.17 JBNQA 18.0.31 JBNQA 18.0.36	establish rules of practice, sentencing and detention to take into consideration, and train non-native persons working in the system about, the particular circumstances of the district, and the customs, usages, way of life of the Cree	Quebec
JBNQA 18.0.19	amend the *Code of Civil Procedure* to adapt it to Cree usage and way of life, and the circumstances of the district	Quebec
JBNQA 18.0.19	amend the *Criminal Code* and the *Canada* Canada *Evidence Act* to adapt them to Cree usage and way of life and the circumstances of the district	Canada
JBNQA 18.0.20 JBNQA 18.0.22 JBNQA 18.0.32 JBNQA 18.0.33 JBNQA 18.0.34	establish programs to recruit, train and hire Cree in the greatest number of possible positions in the justice system	Quebec

Source	Description	Responsibility
JBNQA 18.0.25	modify the criteria of Quebec Legal Services Commission to take into consideration the cost of living, distances involved, and other factors in determining the eligibility of the Crees for legal services	Quebec
JBNQA 18.0.26 to 18.0.29	establish detention centres in the district	both
JBNQA 18.0.23 JBNQA 18.0.28 JBNQA 18.0.30	make all aspects of the judicial system available in Cree	Quebec
JBNQA 18.0.35	establish and fund information programs for the Crees	Quebec
JBNQA 18.0.37	establish an advisory committee regarding the administration of justice in the area	Quebec

Naskapi Justice System

Source	Description	Responsibility
NEQA 12.1	administration of justice	Quebec
NEQA 12.2.1	appoint persons to dispense justice who are cognizant with the customs, and ways of life of the Naskapi	Quebec
NEQA 12.2.5 NEQA 12.2.5 NEQA 12.7.5 NEQA 12.9.4	establish rules of practice, sentencing and detention to take into consideration, and train non-native persons working in the system about, the particular circumstances of the district, and the customs, usages, way of life of the Naskapi	Quebec
NEQA 12.8.1	amend the *Criminal Code* and the *Canada Evidence Act* to adapt them to Naskapi usage and way of life and the circumstances of the district	Canada
NEQA 12.3.4 NEQA 12.3.5 NEQA 12.4.1	establish programs to recruit, train Quebec and hire Naskapi in the justice system	Quebec
NEQA 12.6.1	modify the criteria of Quebec Legal Services Commission to take into consideration the cost of living, distances involved, and other factors in determining the eligibility of the Naskapi for legal services	Quebec

NEQA 12.7	establish detention centres in the district	both
NEQA 12.3.3	make all aspects of the judicial system available in Naskapi	Quebec
NEQA 12.9	establish and fund information programs for the Naskapi	Quebec

Inuit Justice System

Source	*Description*	*Responsibility*
JBNQA 20.0.1 JBNQA 20.0.2	administration of justice	Quebec
JBNQA 20.0.8 JBNQA 20.0.12 JBNQA 20.0.16 JBNQA 20.0.18 JBNQA 20.0.23	appoint persons to dispense justice who are cognizant of the usages, customs and psychology of the Inuit	Quebec
BNQA 20.0.7 BNQA 20.0.11 BNQA 20.0.22 BNQA 20.0.24	establish rules of practice, sentencing and detention to take into consideration the particular circumstances of the district, and the customs, usages and ways of life of the Inuit	both
JBNQA 20.0.11	upon demand from the Inuit party, translate judgments into Inuttituut	Quebec
JBNQA 20.0.13	establish programs to train Inuit for positions in the justice system	Quebec
JBNQA 20.0.15	station information officers in designated municipalities	Quebec
JBNQA 20.0.19	modify the criteria of Quebec Legal Services Commission to take into account the cost of living, distances involved and other factors in determining the eligibility of the Crees for legal aid services	Quebec
JBNQA 20.0.20	amend the *Code of Civil Procedure* to adapt it to Inuit usage and way of life, and to the circumstances of the district	Quebec
JBNQA 20.0.20	amend the *Criminal Code* and the *Canada Evidence Act* to adapt them to Inuit usage and way of life, and to the circumstances of the district	Canada
JBNQA 20.0.25	establish detention centres in the district	both

232

Housing and Infrastructure

Source	Description	Responsibility

Crees

JBNQA 28.11.1	subject to the extent of financial participation possible, and to the priorities set by Canada, Quebec and the Crees, provide for each community funding and technical assistance for a community centre, essential sanitation services, and necessary fire protection	both
JBNQA 28.14.1	continue to fund facilities and services outside Cree communities, which assist Cree persons	both
JBNQA 28.16.1	continue negotiations regarding roads both between certain communities	both

Inuit

JBNQA 29.0.40	continue the existing provision of housing and municipal services until a unified system, including transfer of property and housing management to the municipalities, can be arranged between the Kativik, the northern village municipalities and Canada and Quebec	both
JBNQA 29.0.41	decide the allocation of Inuit houses in consultation with the Inuit, until the program is transferred	Canada
JBNQA 29.0.36	study the establishment of seaplane both bases, public wharves, airstrips, navigational aids, docking facilities, community access roads and streets	both
JBNQA 29.0.42	provide new housing at Chisasibi	Canada

Implementation and Remedial Steps

Source	Description	Responsibility

Implementation

JBNQA 2.5	recommend forthwith, upon execution of Agreement, suitable legislation to give effect to the Agreement	both

233

JBNQA 2.7	during the transitional period of two years, put into force the transitional measures referred to in the Agreement	both
JBNQA 2.9.6	during the transitional period, implement the provisions relating to health and social services, education, justice and police to the extent possible within existing legislation	both
JBNQA 2.14	negotiate with other Indians and Inuit who are not beneficiaries of the Agreement, in respect to claims they have in the Territory	Quebec

Enrollment

JBNQA 3.4.5	hear and determine appeals for eligibility for enrollment as a beneficiary	Quebec
JBNQA 3.5.1 JBNQA 3.7.1 NEQA 3.5.1 NEQA 3.7.1	maintain a Cree register, a Naskapi register and an Inuit register of persons eligible to be enrolled	Quebec; Canada and Quebec to split cost

Remedial

JBNQA 8.9	establish non-profit Quebec corporation with Cree representation (SOTRAC), to study, plan and execute remedial measures during the construction and operation of Le Complexe La Grande	Quebec; provide funding of $30 mil.

Relocation

JBNQA 6.4	assist the Inuit of Kuujjuarapik (Great Whale River) if they decide to move to Umiujaq (Richmond Gulf)	both
NEQA 20.3 to 20.5	participate on a relocation committee with the Naskapi, to study sites for possible relocation of the Naskapi	both; each contributes $20 000
NEQA 20.11 to 20.12	contribute to the costs of relocation, amounts depending on the site chosen	both

Other

JBNQA 5.4.1	guarantee a supply of wood to Paint Hills sawmill	Quebec

| JBNQA 6.1.2 | pay all costs of survey and monumentation for Inuit Category I lands | Quebec or Canada |

APPENDIX II

Legislation to Implement the Agreement

Federal

July 14, 1977	Billl C-9—*The James Bay and Northern Quebec Native Claims Settlement Act*
June 8, 1984	Bill C-46—*An Act respecting certain provisions of the James Bay and Northern Quebec Agreement and the Northeastern Quebec Agreement relating principally to Cree and Naskapi local government and to the land regime governing Category IA and Categoty IA-N land*

Quebec

June 30, 1976	Bill 32—*An Act approving the Agreement concerning James Bay and Northern Quebec* Bill 40—*An Act modifying the Act on Social Aid*
November 17, 1977	Bill 10—*An Act to amend the Act respecting health services and social services*
June 8, 1978	Bill 2—*An Act to amend the Education Act*
June 23, 1978	Bill 23—*An Act concerning Northern villages and the Kativik Regional Government* Bill 24—*The Cree Villages Act* Bill 25—*An Act respecting the Cree Regional Authority* Bill 26—*An Act to establish the James Bay Regional Zone Council* Bill 27—*An Act to establish the Makivik Corporation* Bill 32—*An Act to create the La Grande Complex Remedial Works Corporation* Bill 33—*An Act to incorporate the James Bay Native Development Corporation*

	Bill 34—*An Act respecting Cree and Inuit Native Persons*
	Bill 42—*An Act approving the Northeastern Quebec Agreement*
December 22, 1978	Bill 28—*An Act respecting hunting and fishing rights in the James Bay and New Quebec territories*
	Bill 29—*An Act respecting the land regime in the James Bay and New Quebec territories*
	Bill 30—*An Act to again amend the Environment Quality Act*
June 21, 1979	Bill 12—*An Act respecting Income Security for Cree hunters and trappers who are beneficiaries under the Agreement concerning James Bay and Northern Quebec*
	Bill 38—*An Act respecting the Police Force of the Cree villages and of the Naskapi villages*
June 22, 1979	Bill 26—*An Act respecting the legislation provided for in the Northeastern Quebec Agreement and amending other legislation*
	Bill 27—*An Act to establish the Naskapi Development Corporation*
December 16,1982	Bill 83—*An Act respecting the support program for Inuit beneficiaries of the James Bay and Northern Quebec Agreement for their hunting, fishing and trapping activities*

Complementary Agreements

January 31, 1978	James Bay and Northern Quebec Agreement, Complementary Agreement No. 1 (Naskapi Agreement)
	James Bay and Northern Quebec Agreement, Complementary Agreement No. 2 (Port Burwell)
	James Bay and Northern Quebec Agreement, Complementary Agreement No. 3 (Fort George)
July 4, 1979	James Bay and Northern Quebec Agreement, Complementary Agreement No. 4 (Chisasibi)
	James Bay and Northern Quebec Agreement, Complementary Agreement No. 5
November 6, 1986	James Bay and Northern Quebec Agreement, Complementary Agreement No. 6 (Inuit Category I lands)
	James Bay and Northern Quebec Agreement, Complementary Agreement No. 7

BIBLIOGRAPHY

Government Documents

Canada. Auditor General of Canada. *Report of the Auditor General of Canada to the House of Commons*: Ottawa, fiscal year ended 31 March 1986, paragraphs 11.107-11.109.

Canada. Department of Indian Affairs and Northern Development, *James Bay and Northern Quebec Implementation Review,* (Tait Report). Ottawa, 1982.

───── *James Bay and Northern Quebec Agreement, Northeastern Quebec Agreement; Annual Report.* Ottawa, 1982-87.

───── *The Northern Quebec Agreements: Government of Canada Involvement,* Supply and Services. Ottawa, 1985.

Canada. House of Commons, "Reply of the Grand Council of the Crees (of Quebec) to the Report on the Implementation of the James Bay and Northern Quebec Native Claims Settlement Act," Session 33-1 A18A1, Reference No. J10347, 26 March 1981.

Canada. Quebec. *The James Bay and Northern Quebec Agreement,* Éditeur officiel du Québec, Quebec, 1976.

Ciacca, The Hon. John, "Opening remarks to the Standing Parliamentary Committee of the National Assembly of Quebec convened to examine the Agreement with the James Bay Crees and the Inuit of Quebec prior to its signature, 5 November 1975," in *The James Bay and Northern Quebec Agreement,* Éditeur officiel du Québec, Quebec, 1976, pp. xi-xxiv.

Québec. Secrétariat des Activités Gouvernementales en Milieu Amérindien et Inuit, *Recontre,* Quebec, 1980-87.

Aboriginal Documents

Grand Council of the Crees (of Quebec), Reply of the Grand Council of the Crees (of Quebec) to the Report on the Implementation of the Provisions of the James Bay and Northern Quebec Native Claims Settlement Act Tabled in the House of Commons, Ottawa on November 18, 1980.

Grand Council of the Crees (of Quebec), Cree Statement to the Standing Committee of the House of Commons on Indian Affairs and Northern Development, Ottawa, March 26, 1981.

Grand Council of the Crees (of Quebec), Cree Brief to the Standing Committee of the House of Commons on Health, Welfare and Social Affairs, Ottawa, May 19, 1981.

Grand Council of the Crees (of Quebec) and the Cree Regional Authority, *Annual Reports*, 1982 to 1988, Val D'Or, Que.

Grand Council of the Crees (of Quebec), The Cree Regional Authority, The Cree Bands of Quebec, *Brief Presented to the Standing Committee of the House of Commons on Aboriginal Affairs and Northern Development Respecting Bill C-93, The Sechelt Indian Self-Government Act*, Ottawa, 13 May 1986.

Grand Council of the Crees (of Quebec), The Cree Regional Authority and The Eight Cree Bands of Quebec, *Brief Presented to the Standing Committee of the House of Commons on Indian Affairs and Northern Development*, 3 December 1985.

Kativik Regional Government, *Annual Reports*, 1981, 1986, 1987, Kuujjuaq, Que.

Makivik Corporation, *Annual Reports*, 1982 to 1988, Montreal and Kuujjuaq, Que.

——— *Employment and Income Patterns in Northern Quebec: "Colonized in Our Homeland"*, Montreal, 1986.

——— *The Future of Inuit in Canada's Economic Union: Northern Partnership or Neglect?*, Brief to the Royal Commission on the Economic Union and Development Prospects for Canada, Montreal, 14 October 1983.

——— *The James Bay and Northern Quebec Agreement: Ten Years of Disagreement*, Montreal, 1985.

Other Published Materials

Ames, R., D. Axford, P. Usher, E. Werck and G. Wengel, *Keeping On the Land: A Study of the Feasibility of a Comprehensive Wildlife Support Programme in the Northwest Territories.* Ottawa: Canadian Arctic Resources Committee, 1988.

Axford, D., *Government Spending on the Inuit Communities of Northern Quebec—A Comparative Analysis,* submitted to Andrew Croll and Mark R. Gordon, Implmentation Negotiations on the James Bay and Northern Quebec Agreement, Ottawa, 9 February 1987.

—— *The Application of Federal Programs to the Inuit Communities of Northern Quebec,* submitted to Makivik Corporation, Ottawa, July 1987.

Bartlett, R., *Subjugation, Self-Management and Self-Government of Aboriginal Lands and Resources,* Background Paper No. 11. Kingston: Queen's University, Institute of Intergovernmental Relations, 1986.

Bankes, N. *Resource-leasing Options and the Settlement of Aboriginal Claims.* Ottawa: Canadian Arctic Resources Committee, 1983.

Cree-Nakapi Commission, *1986 Report of the Cree-Naskakapi Commission.* Ottawa: K.G. Campbell Corporation, January 1987.

Diamond, B., "The Cree Experience," in J. Barman, Y. Hebert and D. McCaskill (eds.) *Indian Education in Canada: The Challenge,* Nakoda Institute Occasional Paper No. 3. Vancouver: University of British Columbia Press, 1987, pp. 86-106.

Gourdeau, E., "Quebec and Aboriginal Peoples," in A.J. Long and M. Boldt (eds.) *Governments in Conflict? Provinces and Indian Nations in Canada.* Toronto: University of Toronto Press, 1988, pp. 109-126.

Hawkes, D.C. and E.J. Peters, *Implementing Aboriginal Self-Government: Problems and Prospects,* Workshop Report. Kingston: Queen's University, Institute of Intergovernmental Relations, 1986.

LaRusic, I.E., *Income Security for Subsistence Hunters: a review of the first five years of the operation of the Income Security Programme for Cree Hunters and Trappers.* Ottawa: Research Branch, Corporate Policy, Department of Indian Affairs and Northern Development, 1982.

—— *Negotiating a Way of Life: Initial Cree experience with the administrative structures arising from the James Bay Agreement.* Ottawa:

Research Division, Policy, Research and Evaluation Group, Department of Indian Affairs and Northern Development, 1979.

Moss, W., "The Implementation of the James Bay and Northern Quebec Agreement," in B.W. Morse, *Aboriginal Peoples and the Law: Indian, Metis and Inuit Rights in Canada*. Ottawa: Carleton University Press, 1985.

O'Reilly, J., "Indian Land Claims in Quebec and Alberta," in J.A. Long and M. Boldt (eds.) *Governments in Conflict? Provinces and Indian Nations in Canada*. Toronto: University of Toronto Press, 1988, pp. 139-148.

Peat, Marwick et Associés, *Financial Analysis: Study of Federal Spending Toward the Crees of Northern Quebec*, prepared for the Grand Council of the Crees (of Quebec), Montreal, May 1980.

Richardson, B., *Strangers Devour the Land*. Toronto: Macmillan of Canada, 1975.

Rostaing, J.P., "Native Regional Autonomy: The Initial Experience of the Kativik Regional Government," *Études / Inuit / Studies*. 8(2) 1984, pp. 3-39.

Salisbury, R.F., *A Homeland for the Cree: Regional Development in James Bay 1971-1981*. Kingston: McGill-Queen's University Press, 1986.

Unpublished Materials

Axford, D., "Native Claims Policy in Canada," unpublished paper, Ottawa, 1987.

Barrett, Michael, Head, Environment and Resource Management, Kativik Regional Government, Remarks to the conference on "Defining the Responsibilities: Federal and Provincial Governments and Aboriginal Peoples," Carleton University, Ottawa, Ontario, October 4, 1988.

Canada, Department of Indian Affairs and Northern Development, Letter of the Hon. W. McKnight to Grand Chief Coon-Come, dated July 7, 1988.

Grand Council of the Crees (of Quebec) and Makivik Corporation, "A Working Paper on Machinery of Government to Implement the James Bay and Northern Quebec Agreement," unpublished, April 16, 1986.

———— "Draft Joint Position Concerning a Formal Implementation Procedure for the James Bay and Northern Quebec Agreement," unpublished, April 7, 1986.

Malone, M., "The James Bay and Northern Quebec Agreement: the search for an Implementation Process," unpublished, prepared for the Grand Council of the Crees (of Quebec) and Makivik Corporation, June 29, 1986.

McCue, H.A., Director of Education, Cree School Board, "Self-Government in Education: the Case of the Cree School Board," paper presented to the Workshop on Implementing Self-Government, Institute of Intergovernmental Relations, Queen's University, Kingston, May 27-30, 1986.

Moses, T., "Address by Chief Ted Moses, Eastmain Band, James Bay," unpublished, Yellowknife, NWT, June 13, 1988.

———— "Parameters, Principles, Objectives and Framework for Negotiations on the James Bay and Northern Quebec Agreement Between Canada and the Grand Council of the Cree," signed on March 2, 1988 by Matthew Coon-Come, Grand Chief, Grand Council of the Crees (of Quebec) and The Hon. William McKnight, Minister, Indian Affairs and Northern Development.

Statement of Understanding of Principal Points Agreed to by the *Cree-Nashapi (of Quebec) Act* Implementation Group, signed August 9, 1984, by the Hon. D. Frith (DIAND), Billy Diamond, Grand Chief of the Cree, Chief Joe Guanish, Nashapi Band Council.

CHAPTER 7

FEDERAL AND PROVINCIAL RESPONSIBILITY IN THE METIS SETTLEMENTS OF ALBERTA

Fred V. Martin

INTRODUCTION

1988 marks the fiftieth anniversary for Metis settlements in Alberta. Legislation passed in 1938 created five geographical areas in Alberta almost equal to Prince Edward Island in total size that are occupied by Metis collectively exercising rights of land ownership and self-government. The geographical blocks are divided into eight Metis Settlement Areas, each set aside for a Metis Settlement Association created under the *Metis Betterment Act* of Alberta. The settlements are home to about 5,000 Metis.

As the only lands in Canada held and "governed" by Metis, the Metis Settlements of Alberta have a unique and interesting history. Although both the federal and Alberta governments have accepted responsibilities with respect to settlement Metis, neither has done so because of a clear legal obligation. In general the progress made by the settlements is a result of pragmatic leadership intent on getting results rather than on achieving specific legal rights. This does not mean, however, that the settlement Metis do not assert the existence of rights essential to their survival as a people. Those rights have origins in British and Canadian history, and in the new Constitution of Canada.

This chapter investigates the roles of the federal and provincial governments in enabling the Metis in Alberta to develop a land base on which to maintain their cultural identity. It surveys the responsibilities that each government has assumed and analyzes the sources of those responsibilities. The settlements came about because of dedicated and capable Metis leadership in the 1930s and because the Alberta government was sensitive to their concerns. This discussion reviews that period in history and then looks at the events that have produced profound changes in the economic and political life of the settlements in the half-century since their creation. It looks at the legal framework in which the settlements developed and at the new legislation being proposed to entrench Metis land in the Constitution and to create a new framework for self-government. Some of the jurisdictional problems involving the federal and provincial governments are examined in that context. Finally it provides some examples of how, in spite of unclear jurisdiction, the settlements, the province and the federal government have been able to work together to produce real development on the settlements.

PHILOSOPHY

Recognition and Responsibility

Both the federal and provincial governments have recognized that the Metis have special rights with respect to the Settlement Areas. Provincial recognition is contained in the *Metis Betterment Act* which provides the basic legislative framework for land management, membership and local self-government on the settlements. Federal recognition appears, for example, in regulations under the *Fisheries Act* which provide for special fishing rights for the Metis members in a Settlement Area. There is thus statutory evidence that both governments recognize special land-related rights for Metis settlement members, and consequently special government responsibilities—if only to ensure that those rights are respected.

In considering federal and provincial responsibilities some care should be exercised in defining what we mean by a "responsibility" and to whom it is owed. Normally a responsibility implies a mandate to do something. For a government the source of the mandate may be conscience or constitution. Here "conscience" is used broadly to refer to the forces that drive a government to do something because it "ought to be done" whether the motivation is morality or Machiavellia. The mandate of the constitution is the hard edge—the legal framework that requires the government to act, whether it wants to or not.

Rights Versus Results

A person seeking government action can develop a strategy focused either on rights or results. The "results" orientation means that the paramount concern is to achieve a specific result without much attention paid to the government's motivation. The source of the government's mandate is not critical; the only real concern is that it accept some responsibility. The "rights" orientation is quite different, with paramount attention concentrated on the source of the government's mandate, since the mandate of the constitution conveys a legal right. Clearly the most successful strategy is the one that relies on both constitutional and conscience mandates. The task of native leaders in Canada for the past hundred years has been to mix the rights and results components in their political strategies to meet most effectively the needs of their present and future constituents.

The history of the Metis settlements is one of pragmatic, results-oriented leadership. Rights have been asserted and assiduously protected, but the driving concern has been results. Metis leaders have not insisted that the government recognize a right and act in response to that right. Rather the emphasis has been on the action, leaving the government to sort out for itself whether its mandate was conscience or constitution. Because of this history, this chapter focuses more on the role assumed by the federal and provincial governments in relation to the Metis settlements, than on the obligations they have at law.

There are two other good reasons for concentrating on assumed roles rather than on strict legal responsibilities:

1. the question of whether or not Metis are "Indians" under s.91(24) of the *Constitution Act, 1867* is unsettled; and
2. the province and the Metis settlements are currently in court on a major claim to proceeds from the sale of oil and gas found in the Settlement Areas.

Section 91(24) of the *Constitution Act, 1867*, part of Canada's Constitution, provides that "the exclusive Legislative Authority of the Parliament of Canada extends to ... Indians, and Lands reserved for the Indians." The term "Indians" is not defined. The current prevalent legal opinion appears to be that the term probably includes Metis, although the matter has never been judicially determined.[1] Notwithstanding this, the system of Metis settlements in Alberta has functioned under provincial legislation for 50 years, and, in co-operation with the Metis, the government has introduced bills in the 1988 spring sitting of the legislature to update this legislation and constitutionally protect Metis settlement lands.

At the same time that the province and the Metis have been co-operating in developing new Metis settlements legislation, they have also been engaged in litigation over the oil and gas revenues flowing from the Settlement Areas. This matter has been before the courts in one form or another since 1968. The current expectation is that the matter will go to trial in 1989. In more than 10 years of discoveries, an enormous amount of material has been collected relating to the legal responsibilities, or lack thereof, of the province. The judicial determinations in that case will no doubt go a long way in defining the legal components of the federal and provincial governments' relationship with the Metis on the settlements. It would be impossible in this discussion to provide a detailed exposition of the arguments involved in that case. It may be useful, however, to highlight a rationale for contending that in the case of the Metis settlements, government responsibility derives from the Constitution as well as from conscience.

Communal Rights

Canada's Constitution recognizes existing aboriginal and treaty rights. Section 35 of the *Constitution Act, 1982* provides:

> (1) The existing aboriginal and treaty rights of the aboriginal peoples of Canada are hereby recognized and affirmed.
>
> (2) In this Act, "aboriginal peoples of Canada" includes the Indian, Inuit and Metis peoples of Canada.
>
> (3) For greater certainty in subsection (1) "treaty rights" includes rights that now exist by way of land claims agreements or may be so acquired.

The *Constitution Act* also provided for a series of constitutional conferences to define just what is meant by "existing aboriginal and treaty rights." Although most aboriginal peoples did not get much help from the conferences in defining their constitutionally protected aboriginal rights, there have been positive developments in the courts.

Probably the most significant recent judicial determination in the area of aboriginal rights was the decision of the Supreme Court of Canada in the *Guerin* case.[2] There the Court confirmed that the common law recognizes a source of aboriginal rights outside of statute or executive order. The *Guerin* decision and the new Constitution provide a more solid foundation for defining aboriginal rights in general. A recent paper by Brian Slattery[3] provides an excellent exposition of that environment and there is no need to duplicate it here. However a brief overview will be helpful in examining the legal implications of events surrounding the establishment of the Metis settlements.

The fundamental problem when discussing aboriginal rights is the difficulty in distinguishing the rights of an individual and the rights of a people. This dichotomy was evident in the recent Manitoba Court of Appeal decision in *Dumont et al v. A. G. Canada*.[4] In a majority decision with one dissent the Court rejected an application by Manitoba Metis for a declaration that amendments to the *Manitoba Act* between 1871 and 1886 were unconstitutional. In the view of the Metis the amendments had made it impossible to establish a land base for the Metis people as distinct from the Metis individuals. Twaddle, J.A., writing the decision for the majority said:

> The argument is purely speculative of what might have been. It offers no justification for a finding that the plaintiffs have a community of interest in some unspecified land or that their own rights are at issue.

> What the court is being asked to consider in this case is the constitutional validity of spent legislation which does not affect anyone's current rights. The rights affected by the impugned legislation were the statutory rights of individuals who are now deceased. These rights are not being pursued individually by the legal representatives of the persons whose rights they were, but generally by descendants whose degree of relationship is not even stated.[5]

O'Sullivan, J.A. also dealt with the person versus people problem in his dissent, stating,

It is difficult for common lawyers to understand what the rights of "a people" can mean. Indeed, at a hearing before a parliamentary committee on The 1987 Constitution Accord (of Meech Lake) held August 27, 1987, the distinguished constitutional expert, the Right Honourable Pierre Elliott Trudeau said:

> "In my philosophy, the community, an institution itself, has no rights. It has rights by delegation from the individuals. You give equality to the individuals and you give rights to the individuals. Then they will organize in societies to make sure those rights are respected."

This is an approach with deep roots in the British tradition and was probably the outlook adopted by the legislators who, following 1870, interpreted s.31 of the *Manitoba Act* as establishing individual rights in the immense tract of land referred to in the section. Indeed, it seems clear that the authorities of the time took painstaking care to count the individuals with rights under the section and did their best to see to it that each claimant received, so far as practicable, his aliquot share of the tract.

But, as far as I can see, what we have before us in court at this time is not the assertion of bundles of individual rights but the assertion of the rights and status of the half-breed people of the western plains.

The problem confronting us is how can the rights of the Metis people as a people be asserted. ... In my opinion, it is impossible in our jurisprudence to have rights without a remedy and the rights of the Metis people must be capable of being asserted by somebody. If not by the present plaintiffs, then by whom?[6]

The problem of communal identity, enabling rights of the people as well as rights of the person, is an essential Metis problem because of their loss of a land base. The existence of a communally held land base puts the Metis on Alberta's settlements much more on the plane of the Indians when asserting aboriginal rights. The Indians, through the reserve system have maintained a land base, i.e., lands held by the community rather than the individual. As a result it has been possible to develop legal theories of self-government and to press in the courts for protection of the rights of Indian peoples (tribes) as well as the rights of Indian persons. The problem of developing an aboriginal citizenship model without a communal land base has been accurately analyzed by Noel Lyon in a background paper, *Aboriginal Peoples and Constitutional Reform.*[7]

The Components of a Nation

Nations are more than aggregates of political entities and geographical areas. They are made up of peoples. Some tend to be homogeneous, recognizing only one essential culture. Others incorporate the recognition of diversity in their legal foundations, a recognition that creates an added dimension to the nation, a recognition of its "people" origins as well as its political origins. World powers adopt different philosophies in their treatment of indigenous peoples when they first exercise dominion over new territory acquired by military or economic conquest. Rome endeavoured, to the extent that it did not threaten its power, to honour the rights of the peoples it conquered. Such recognition allowed them to survive as a people, to maintain their customs, laws and identity. Great Britain followed a similar course. That philosophy had important consequences for the constitutional framework of Canada.

The recognition of the rights of indigenous peoples has ancient historical roots. O'Sullivan in his dissent in the *Dumont* case[8] cited the Papal bull *Sublimis Deus* issued in 1537. Slattery in his recent article states:

> A review of the Crown's historical relations with aboriginal peoples supports the conclusion that the Crown, in offering its protection to such peoples, accepted that they would retain their lands, as well as their political and cultural institutions and customary laws, unless the terms of treaties ruled this out or legislation was enacted to the contrary. Native groups would retain a measure of internal autonomy, allowing them to govern their own affairs as they found convenient, subject to the overriding authority of the Crown in Parliament. The Crown assumed a general obligation to protect aboriginal peoples and their lands and generally to look out for their best interests—what the judges have described as a fiduciary or trust-like obligation. In return, native peoples were required to maintained [sic] allegiance to the Crown, to abide by her laws, and to keep the peace.[9]

In short, the principle appears to be that when the Crown exercised its dominion over new lands, it did so by providing a legal framework that recognized and respected the right of indigenous peoples to maintain their identity as a people.[10]

The principle appears to have been followed in the formation of Canada. The *British North America Act of 1867* (now the *Constitution Act, 1867*) established the country of Canada. In combining existing provinces and peoples, the Act operated in two dimensions—a horizontal dimension relating to government, and a vertical dimension relating to nation building. The horizontal dimension contained the components of the new government, the institutions and systems providing a framework for future political life. The vertical dimension contained the components of the new nation, the recognition of the indigenous peoples comprising the new nation. The recognition of the "indigenous" British citizens was implicit. However the Act also recognized the two other indigenous peoples of the confederation provinces—the French and the Indians. The French were recognized and guaranteed cultural survival rights such as language and education. The Indian peoples were recognized by assigning responsibility for them and their lands to the new national government.

RECOGNITION OF THE METIS

Manitoba and the Northwest

The constitutional recognition of indigenous people occurred again at the time of the creation of the Province of Manitoba. The history of that event is summarized in the *Dumont* decision.

> Rupert's land was granted to the Hudson's Bay Company by Charles II in 1670. By 1867, the effective authority of the company in Rupert's Land was on the decline. The United Kingdom Parliament was thus able to foresee, and provide for, the eventual union of Rupert's Land with Canada. Provisions for this union are to be found in the *Constitution Act, 1867* and the *Rupert's Land Act, 1868.*

> Included in Rupert's Land was the territory which was to become Manitoba. Many of those who lived in the territory in the years immediately preceding union were persons of mixed native and European blood, their European ancestors having come to North America after 1670. These persons were then known as "half-breeds". Some half-breeds occupied small areas of land and all used unoccupied land freely. The area of land used by them lacked definition.

> In anticipation of the union of Rupert's Land with Canada, the Parliament of Canada enacted the *Rupert's Land Act*, S.C. 1869, c.3, by which it made provision for the future government of the territory. Also in anticipation of the union, the Government of Canada sent survey teams into the territory.

> In August, 1869, a number of half-breeds, fearful of the effect the proposed union would have on their use of land, opposed the making of surveys. What followed was, from Canada's viewpoint, rebellion. A number of local inhabitants openly disputed Canada's right to annex the territory, although others were anxious for union. A state of unrest prevailed. The authority of the Company had been weakened by its own inaction. In the absence of an effective ruling power, a provisional government was formed by some of the people.

> The Provisional Government (as it styled itself) sent delegates to Ottawa to negotiate the terms on which the territory might be united with Canada. A draft bill resulted from the negotiations. Before its enactment as the *Manitoba Act*, it was approved by what was known as the Assembly of the Provisional Government. This Act, assented to in May, 1870, preceded the effective date on which legislative authority for the government of the territory was vested in the Parliament of Canada by the Order of Her Majesty in Her Imperial Council dated June 23, 1870.

The decision goes on to quote several sections of the *Manitoba Act* dealing with land, including s.30 and s.31:

> 30.   All ungranted or waste lands in the Province shall be ... vested in the Crown, and administered by the Government of Canada for the purposes of the Dominion, subject to ... the conditions and stipulation contained in the agreement for the surrender of Rupert's Land by the Hudson's Bay Company to Her Majesty.

> 31.   And whereas, it is expedient, towards the extinguishment of the Indian title to the lands in the Province, to appropriate a portion of such ungranted lands, to the extent of one million four hundred thousand acres thereof, for the benefit of the families of the half-breed residents, it is hereby enacted, that, under regulations to be from time to time made by the Governor General in Council, the Lieutenant-Governor shall select such lots or tracts in such parts of the Province as he may deem expedient, to the extent aforesaid, and divide the same among the children of the half-breed heads of families residing in the Province at the time of the said transfer to Canada, and the same shall be granted to the said children respectively, in such mode and on such conditions as to settlement and otherwise, as the Governor General in Council may from time to time determine.

In short, the Dominion retained public lands and resources in Manitoba subject to the conditions of the surrender by the Hudson's Bay Company, and recognized the Metis as an indigenous people with unextinguished land rights. Thus in the first expansion beyond the founding provinces, Canada maintained the approach of nation building by recognizing the vertical component, indigenous peoples, as well as the horizontal component of political structures for the newly added territory.

Initially the Province of Manitoba was a small area of land about 100 miles by 140 miles. However, at the same time as Manitoba was added as a province, the vast area north and west to the boundary of British Columbia, known as Rupert's Land and the North-Western Territory, was transferred to Canada. The Order-in-Council that transferred the land provided that,

> ... upon the transference of the territories in question to the Canadian Government, the claims of the Indian tribes to compensation for lands required for purposes of settlement will be considered and settled in conformity with the equitable principles which have uniformly governed the British Crown in its dealings with the aborigines. [11]

All of the land given up by the Hudson's Bay Company had been surrendered on the condition that,

> Any claims of Indians to compensation for lands required for purposes of settlement shall be disposed of by the Canadian Government in communication with the Imperial Government; and the Company shall be relieved of all responsibility in respect of them. [12]

To summarize, following the creation of Manitoba on July 15, 1870, the Dominion government held the public lands of Manitoba, and the lands that would later become Alberta and Saskatchewan. It held those lands, subject to the commitments made to the Metis in the *Manitoba Act*, and subject to the claims of the Indians.

Following its acquisition of the western territory, the Dominion government set out to resolve the claims problem by signing treaties with the Indians. The government recognized that the Metis also had claims in this territory and developed a strategy of dealing with these concurrent with its efforts to negotiate treaties. To that end the *Dominion Lands Act, 1879*, s.125 gave the Governor General in Council authority

> e.   To satisfy any claims existing in connection with the extinguishment of the Indian title, preferred by half-breeds resident in the North-West Territories outside of the limits of Manitoba, on the fifteenth day of July, one thousand eight hundred and seventy, by granting land to such persons, to such extent and on such terms and conditions as may be deemed expedient...

In other words, the federal government recognized that it had an obligation to satisfy Metis land claims not only in Manitoba, but also in what is now Alberta and Saskatchewan.

The basic situation was summarized in a memorandum dated October 4, 1934, prepared for the Alberta Resources Commission by a Mr. Cohoon, a senior official in the Department of the Interior. The memorandum states:

> The policy of issuing scrip to half-breeds was adopted in consideration of the interference with the aboriginal rights of this class by the extension of trade and settlement into the territories, and it was felt that an obligation devolved upon the State to properly and fully extinguish these rights to the entire satisfaction of the half-breeds.

> The rights of half-breeds were recognized by the Government by reason of their Indian blood. Indian and half-breed rights differed in degree, but they were obviously co-existent.
>
> The general policy was to extinguish the half-breed rights in any territory at the same time the Indian rights were extinguished. ...
>
> The claims were investigated by Commissioners appointed by the Governor in Council, and where allowed, scrip was issued under the authority of Orders in Council passed in pursuance of the statutes in that behalf.

The memorandum goes on to give·a synopsis of each of the relevant Orders-in-Council providing for the issuance of Metis scrip and identify as nearly as possible from the records how much half-breed land-scrip was still outstanding.

Alberta, and the St. Paul des Metis Colony

The Metis had established themselves as a people requiring recognition when the Red River settlement area joined Canada in 1870. The rest of the great plains had been added to Canada at the same time. The railway opened the area to a flood of new arrivals more interested in wheat than buffalo, leading to the inevitable destruction of the old way of life for the Indians and Metis. The reaction was the uprising, the Northwest Rebellion of 1885, that saw major battles at Fort Pitt[13] in west central Saskatchewan, near Fishing Lake, as well as the Frog Lake Massacre less than 20 miles from Fishing Lake.

Following those violent confrontations between the old and new powers of the plains there had been a more peaceful experiment at providing the Metis with a communal land base at St. Paul, about 40 miles northwest of Fishing Lake.[14] Ten years after the end of the Rebellion, Father Albert Lacombe approached the federal government in an effort to set up a farming colony for the Metis. As a Catholic priest famous for his work with native peoples in Alberta, Father Lacombe had some credibility. He also had a willing listener in A. M. Burgess, the Deputy Minister of the Department of the Interior, who had himself done a report on the Metis in North West Territories in 1889.[15] The result was the creation in 1895 of the colony of St. Paul des Metis.

By 1898 there were 50 families of Metis living on the colony. Control of the colony was in the hands of the Catholic church, although two of the five members of the managing board were federal politicians.[16] Along with training in agriculture, the major focus of the management appeared to be religious instruction and education.[17] After 10 years, the managing board decided that the effort had been a failure and on April 10, 1909 the colony lands were opened to homesteading. On that day, in what was apparently an orchestrated effort, 250 French Canadian settlers registered claims on most of the land.[18] Most of the Metis left to find another home.[19]

The colony had been established on public lands before the creation of the province. When Alberta was created by *The Alberta Act* of 1905 the Dominion, as it had in the case of Manitoba, kept the natural resources and public lands.[20] Although its actions had assisted in the loss of communally held lands at St. Paul des Metis, the federal government continued to issue scrip to half-breeds resident in Alberta to extinguish claims.[21] Individual claims were settled by grants from the retained lands.

The Natural Resource Transfer Agreement—Accepting a Trust

The western provinces were galled at the Dominion's retention of Crown lands and resources. Unlike the original parties to Confederation they felt like second-class citizens among the provinces. Pressure for equality led to the Natural Resources Transfer Agreement of December 14, 1929 which gave Alberta the Crown lands and resources within its boundaries, "subject to any trusts existing in respect thereof, and to any interest other than that of the Crown in the same."[22] This agreement subsequently achieved constitutional status by being incorporated into *The British North America Act, 1930* which in turn became part of the *Constitution Act, 1982*.

While the government in Edmonton had been pressuring Ottawa for land, they had been receiving similar pressure from the province's Metis. It is not surprising that the pressure began in the eastern part of central Alberta, at a Metis community at Fishing Lake; most of the major events in the struggle to define Indian and Metis roles in the new Canada occurred within a hundred mile radius of Fishing Lake.

By the mid-1920s there was a fair sized community of Metis on forest reserve land at Fishing Lake, many of whom had lived in the St. Paul des Metis Colony.[23] In 1929, worried that the land was to be transferred to the province and opened for settlement,[24] the Metis, led by Charley Delorme, began organizing to seek some protection of the land before the transfer took place. Although they failed in securing their land before the transfer, they continued to organize, and to lobby the federal and provincial governments for land and aid in general.

As the full force of the Depression hit the Metis, they began organizing throughout the province. They had the good fortune of attracting very capable leadership, the three best known being Jim Brady, Malcolm Norris and Joseph Dion.[25] By 1931 they were able to submit a petition of more than 500 names to the provincial government calling for land, education, health care and free hunting and fishing. This led to the circulation of a questionnaire among the Metis by the province's Department of Lands and Mines. The topics dealt with in the questionnaire seem to indicate that the provincial government was already considering some kind of land scheme in response to Metis concerns.[26] By late in 1933 those concerns had made it to the Legislature where the leader of the Conservatives moved a resolution that a special committee be appointed to investigate Metis concerns and consider "some plan of colonization of the half-breed population."[27]

Arguments over Responsibility

Early in 1934, the provincial government began making arrangements for a commission to investigate "the half-breed question," and asked the federal government to participate. Ottawa refused. The scope of issues that was to be considered is unknown. In public, the province made it clear that the proposed commission would consider the "half-breed question" only from the perspective of the need for social relief. Land was relevant only indirectly, as one component of relief. However, it is probably legitimate to assume that the government was concerned about the broader scope of land-related issues.

In the summer of 1934, Alberta's *Minister of Telephones and Public Health*, George Hoadley, planned a visit to Ottawa for talks with federal authorities. One of the topics for discussion was the "half-breed problem." On July 23, 1934, before he went, his Deputy Minister, J. Harvie, sent him a memo stating,

> ... I am informed by the Premier it is your intention to discuss with the Federal authorities the question of representation by them on the Commission to be set up to investigate *the claims of the half-breeds*.[28] [emphasis added]

It is not clear whether the Deputy Minister was simply referring to the claims of poverty and destitution made by Metis leaders, or whether there was an intention to discuss broader land-related matters with federal authorities.

When Hoadley returned, he sent a memorandum, dated September 7, 1934, to Premier Reid:

> RE: HALF-BREED PROBLEM
>
> I am returning your file in connection with the above subject.
>
> I took this matter up while I was in Ottawa and found that the Dominion Government declined to appoint a representative on the proposed Royal Commission to investigate this problem. They considered it wholly a matter for the Province to deal with, as all half-breeds are citizens and do not come under the Department of Indian Affairs or any other federal Department. [29]

The Superintendent General of Indian Affairs, T. G. Murphy, confirmed this in a letter to the provincial Minister of Telephones and Public Health, George Hoadley, on October 10, 1934. He referred to their telephone conversation that morning regarding "the appointment of a commission by the Government of Alberta to investigate the half-breed question." He indicated that under the provisions of the *Indian Act* the purview of his department was restricted to Indians as defined in that Act. He set out the definition and concluded:

> In these circumstances, it is my opinion that half-breeds are not the responsibility of the Dominion Government and that the problem of relief for half-breed settlers is a matter for the consideration of the municipality or the Province concerned. [30]

Immediately following this there was an exchange of correspondence between the Premier of Alberta, R.G. Reid, and the Member of Parliament for Athabasca, Percy Davies who wrote to the Premier on October 18, 1934:

> Replying to yours of the 12th instant, I understood that the Federal Government asked that the question of legal liability should be referred to the Courts for a decision before the Dominion would undertake any responsibility in respect of the Halfbreed population. Furthermore, I also understood that the Federal Government was willing to abide by the decision of the Courts and if the courts should find that there was any legal liability resting with the Dominion, that the Dominion would shoulder it. [31]

In short, the federal government was not prepared to assume any responsibility for the Metis unless ordered to do so by the Courts. Apparently the possibility of seeking such an order was discussed between the governments of Alberta and Saskatchewan, but it was never pursued.

In their telephone conversation on October 10, Murphy and Hoadley had discussed the proposed commission but whether they discussed a mandate for the commission that would deal with Metis issues beyond health and welfare is unknown. However, the briefing memo dated October 4, 1934, and prepared by A.A. Cohoon of Murphy's department, certainly focused on the legal issues respecting responsibility for redeeming Metis land-scrip. [32]

Mr. Cohoon indicated that the Dominion position was that before 1930 the Crown's duty to redeem Metis scrip was a trust encumbering Crown lands in Alberta. This duty arose by virtue of the conditions in the Hudson's Bay Company surrender and in the subsequent transfer of lands to the Dominion. However, clause 1 of the Natural Resources Transfer Agreement had provided that

> In order that the Province may be in the same position as the original Provinces of Confederation are in by virtue of section one hundred and nine of the British North America Act, 1867, the interest of the Crown in all Crown lands, ... shall ... belong to the Province, subject to any trusts existing in respect thereof ....

The "subject to any trusts existing" component meant that the province was now responsible for those trusts. The Privy Council had considered the scope of the term "trusts" as used in s.109 in *Attorney General of Canada v. Attorney General of Ontario*, (1897) AC 199 at 210. In the Dominion's view that decision clearly implied that the existing trusts would include responsibility for redeeming Metis scrip.

By late in 1934, there were apparently two Metis land-related issues before the provincial government. The government appeared ready to consider the possibility of enabling the Metis to exercise some form of communal ownership of land. It also had to consider its responsibility for enabling individual Metis land ownership through scrip redemption. To deal with the first issue the province established a royal commission on December 12, 1934, to look into the problems of health, education and general welfare of the "halfbreed" population of the province. The Commission was headed by the Honourable A. F. Ewing, an Alberta Supreme Court Justice, and came to be known as the Ewing Commission.

The second issue was dealt with by a provincial Order-in-Council on June 18, 1935 which began:

> Whereas land scrip notes were issued from time to time by the Government of Canada to half-breed grantees properly entitled thereto, in satisfaction of their claims arising out of the extinguishment of the Indian title, and to be used in connection with vacant and available Dominion lands; and
>
> Whereas there are no regulations providing for the redemption of any such scrip, which might be applicable to the Province; and
>
> Whereas it is proper and convenient that regulations be established in respect thereto;[33]

The Order-in-Council then went on to provide for the locating of land-scrip "on any vacant and available Provincial lands."

By mid-1935, it appears that the province had accepted total responsibility for the Metis. For what it apparently considered an obligation of conscience, it had set in motion a mechanism that would consider the propriety of protecting the Metis as a people by setting aside communal lands. It had also acted, from what it apparently considered a legal obligation, to enable the satisfaction of individual Metis land claims by redeeming land-scrip with provincial Crown lands. Through all of this there is no indication of any concern that the Metis might be "Indians" for the purposes of s.91(24) of the *Constitution Act, 1867*, and consequently within "the exclusive Legislative Authority of the Parliament of Canada."

HISTORY OF THE METIS SETTLEMENTS

The Ewing Commission Recommends Communal Lands for the Metis

The Ewing Commission held hearings throughout Alberta in 1935 and submitted its report on February 15, 1936.[34] To no one's surprise the Commission recommended the establishment of Metis Colonies—lands to be held by the Crown but set aside for the exclusive use and occupation of associations of Metis. The Commission made it clear that in so doing they were not responding to Metis claims regarding rights to land. In its report the Commission briefly discussed the extinguishment of Indian title claims by "half-breeds" through the issuing of scrip and went on to say,

The story of this scrip and its final outcome is still vivid in living memory. The precautions of Parliament were easily circumvented and the scrip passed readily and cheaply into the hands of speculators. The resultant advantages to the half-breeds were negligible. The policy of the Federal Government, however, extending over a period of thirty years, and these issues of scrip, throw a strong light on the present problem.

In the first place, the scrip was issued in extinguishment of any supposed right which the half-breed had to special consideration. But *the Government of this Province is now faced, not with a legal or contractual right, but with an actual condition of privation, penury and suffering.* The right to live cannot be extinguished and the situation as revealed to your Commission seems to call for Governmental guidance and assistance. [emphasis added]

Two points are worth making with regard to this part of the report: the Commission made it clear that the land rights issue was not on the table, and the Metis leadership did not insist that it be dealt with. Rather, the Metis leaders focused on Metis needs and on the economic advantages for the government of a self-supporting colony system. In other words the approach was results rather than rights oriented.

Douglas Sanders makes the following comments in this regard:

The assumptions in Alberta in 1933 would seem to have been:

1. Metis claims to Indian title had been extinguished by the Half-breed grants under the Manitoba Act and the Dominion Lands Act.

2. Metis and non-status Indians were the responsibility of the provinces either because they were not "Indians" within the meaning of that term in the British North America Act of 1867, or because the federal government had chosen to exclude them from the exercise of federal legislative jurisdiction over "Indians".

3. The Metis of northern Alberta were not asserting rights but needs.

4. The understood response to the Metis situation in Alberta was going to be some kind of allocation of land (and land was now under provincial ownership and jurisdiction).

The Ewing Commission operated on these assumptions. The Metis colony system in Alberta has operated on them ever since. In contrast the Metis in Saskatchewan in the 1930s sought provincial support in order to present claims to the federal government. In response the Saskatchewan government commissioned the study by Hodges and Noonan which suggested that Metis claims were not of a legal character and, in any case, had been settled. Manitoba Metis in the same period also asserted land claims which would presumably have involved petitioning the federal government.[35]

From the vantage point of history, it now appears that the Metis leadership in Alberta better read the climate of the time, and consequently were able to employ a more effective strategy to secure a land base.

The Ewing Commission recommended setting aside land for the Metis. However, it might have been more accurate to describe the intended beneficiaries as landless natives rather than Metis. The Commission's mandate was with respect to the "Half-breed population of the Province," and it had a problem defining just who that was. The Commission's report stated:

> It may be well to define here the term "half-breed" or "Metis". We are not concerned with a technically correct definition. We merely wish to give a clear meaning to the term as used in this report. By either term is meant a person of mixed blood, white and Indian, *who lives the life of the ordinary Indian*, and includes a non-treaty Indian. It is apparent to everyone that there are in this Province many persons of mixed blood (Indian and white) who have settled down as farmers, who are making a good living in that occupation and who do not need, nor do they desire, public assistance. The term as used in this report has no application to such men. [emphasis added][36]

The Commission recognized that Metis formed an identifiable group linked by aboriginal ancestry and life style. However, it refused to discuss the rights of the group but recognized that some such rights might exist:

> The Commission is of opinion that as the Metis were the original inhabitants of these great unsettled areas and are dependent on wild life and fish for their livelihood, they should be given the preference over non-residents in respect of fur, game and fish.[37]

Pocklington comments on the Commission's report as follows:

> The basic problem is that a fundamental ambiguity permeates the Commission's treatment of the relationship between the Metis and the government, and thereby the dominant society as a whole.
>
> The core of the ambiguity has to do with the Commission's recognition of the uniqueness of the Metis. Throughout much of the report of the Commission the uniqueness of the Metis is seen to consist in their poverty, poor health, and lack of education. But of course the Metis were not really unique in these respects. On the one hand, plenty of white settlers shared these debilities. And on the other hand, many persons of mixed Indian and white ancestry did not. If the Metis were in fact just victims of the Depression, they could have been dealt with by the same measures of relief granted to other citizens. That the Commission did not recommend that they be treated in the ordinary way of people ravaged by the Depression was at least an implicit recognition

that the Metis had something else in common. Part of what they had in common is made explicit in the report. The Commissioners mention frequently the propensity of the Metis to pursue a common style of life. Only this commonality could justify the recommendation that colonies be established exclusively for the Metis. The striking ambiguity here is that the Metis are characterized as both ordinary and special. Clearly, the Commissioners, while steadfastly opposed to granting the Metis special status like that of the Indians, were constrained to admit that the Metis were unique. This ambiguity emerges most clearly in the recommendation that, while the Metis should not be compelled to join colonies, they would have no other claim to public assistance if they did not.[38]

In summary, the Ewing Commission focused on a social problem and recommended a pragmatic solution. It saw a group of suffering people of aboriginal ancestry and "Indian" life style for whom the federal government disclaimed any responsibility. It recognized them as "Metis" and as "original inhabitants of these great unsettled areas." It concluded,

> ... your Commissioners are of the opinion that some form of farm colonies is the most effective, and, ultimately, the cheapest method of dealing with the problem.

It did not concern itself with the question of whether or not the Metis had any legal right to demand such lands. From its perspective the rights issue was simply not relevant. The Metis leaders did not demand that the rights issue be discussed. As a result the work of the Ewing Commission is of historical and social interest, but probably of little significance in the discussion of the legal rights of the people who were the focus of its efforts.

The Metis Betterment Act — A Start to Land and Self-Government

The provincial government responded positively to the report of the Ewing Commission. The federal government had disclaimed any responsibility for the people whose needs the Commission sought to address. Probably because of its recent success in negotiating the Natural Resources Agreement, the province was unwilling to take the responsibility issue to the Courts. Instead it accepted what it saw as its social obligations and began setting up the machinery to reserve land for the Metis and provide for a limited form of local government on the reserved areas.

In a rather unique co-operative approach, Metis leaders apparently prepared drafts of the enabling legislation[39] and worked with representatives of the provincial government on subsequent revisions until a mutually acceptable draft was complete.[40] *The Metis Betterment Act*, was passed and received assent on November 22, 1938. A joint Metis/government committee was established to identify suitable Metis settlement area sites and land areas were set aside by Orders-in-Council commencing late in 1938. By the end of the next year settlement associations had held organizational meetings in eight of the areas and adopted a common constitution and by-laws.[41]

The preamble to the original Act referred to the recommendations of the Ewing Commission and recognized the Metis role in developing the Act by acknowledging that it was in the public interest,

> ... that the ways and means of giving effect to such recommendations should be arrived at by means of conferences and negotiations between the Government of the Province and representatives of the metis population of the Province;

The scheme agreed to in the Act and settlement constitutions would certainly not satisfy any contemporary proponent of self-government. The Act was three short pages of bare bones legislation. It made possible four key elements:

1. the Minister could help the Metis organize settlement associations;
2. by Order-in-Council unoccupied provincial lands could be set aside for settlement by the members of the associations;
3. the associations could develop a constitution and by-laws providing the basic framework for local self-government; and
4. the associations and the Minister could co-operatively formulate schemes for bettering the members and settling them on the reserved lands.

The only means of putting legislative flesh on these bare-bones principles appears to have been by co-operatively developing schemes for the betterment and settlement of members. That these schemes were intended be something more than departmental programs seems to be indicated by the requirement in the Act that

> Every scheme formulated pursuant to this Act shall be submitted by the Minister to the Lieutenant Governor in Council for approval, and upon the same being so approved, shall be laid upon the table of the Legislative Assembly ...[42]

From a legislative drafting viewpoint, the preferable approach today would probably be to enable the skeleton legislation to be filled out by regulations. In the original Act, however, the only regulation-making powers were with respect to hunting, fishing and trapping.

The Act provided a sparse framework for local government by stating that the "control of the business and affairs of the association shall be in a Board," and by enabling the associations to develop constitutions and by-laws providing for "the election of the members of the Board." The provisions of the original constitution, and all changes, were subject to ministerial approval, and the aims and objects of the associations had to include co-operation with the Minister.

The constitution adopted by the settlement associations, and approved by the Minister, outlined minimal requirements for membership, elections, board meetings and other details of managing the settlement association. It provided a rather vague power enabling the board to pass by-laws "... pertaining to the management and governing of the Settlement Association and the reserved area occupied by their Settlement Association." The by-laws had to be consistent with the provisions of the constitution and approved by the Minister.

Changes in the Act Create Problems

The skeletal legislative framework provided by the original Act was adequate for the purpose at hand. It made possible the setting aside of lands and the establishment of a means for residents to govern them, subject to the ultimate authority of the provincial government. The goal of Metis leaders such as Brady and Norris was to create a land base. They did not seem overly concerned if a few concessions had to be made to reach that goal. The legislation was adequate, and that was enough.

The Act was amended on February 16, 1940[43] to what is essentially its present form. The preamble was dropped, but new provisions roughly tripled the size of the Act. The most significant new provisions enabled regulations to be made by Order-in-Council governing most aspects of settlement life, particularly the allocation and use of land and resources;[44] made it possible to convert Settlement Areas into Improvement Districts — the standard rural "local government" entities for non-natives;[45] enabled descent of an individual's interest in land to his family;[46] and prohibited the use of a settlement member's property as security.[47]

The last substantive change to the Act was made in 1952. The original Act, and each subsequent version, had stated that the constitution and by-laws of a settlement association

> shall provide that the control of the business and affairs of the association shall be in a Board consisting of not more than five persons and shall make provision for election of the members of the Board ...[48]

The 1952 amendment stripped the settlements of any clear legal basis for self-government. The words "control of the business and affairs of the association shall be in a Board" were removed. The power to provide constitutionally for election of all five board members was also removed. In its place were added two new sections:

> (2a) A Settlement Association shall have a Local Board consisting of a chairman who shall be the local supervisor of the area appointed by the Metis Rehabilitation Branch of the Department of Public Welfare and four members who shall be *bona fide* members of the Settlement Association.
>
> (2b) The Minister shall appoint two of the members of the Local Board and the members of the Settlement Association shall elect two of the members of the Local Board by secret ballot.

These changes weakened the mandate of the board and changed it from an elected to a mainly appointed body. The current Act still contains these provisions.[49]

This is just one example of the provisions that, over the past 30 years, have made the Act and Regulations increasingly unworkable because of internal inconsistencies, uncertain legitimacy, anachronisms and inadequacy. Despite the wording of the Act, a regulation replacing previous regulations on the same topic, *Regulations Governing the Constitution of Settlement Associations* (A.R. 56/66), was approved in 1966.[50] It specified that "The affairs and business of an association shall be transacted by a Board consisting of 3 members ..."[51] and "The Board shall consist of three members all of whom shall be elected by the members of the Colony." These provisions clearly contradict the five-member board requirement in the Act.

The contradiction has led to practical problems. For example, oil companies negotiating with settlement councils for access to settlement lands have questioned the legitimacy of the elected councils on the basis that the five-member elected council is not properly constituted under either the Act or the regulations. The issue has never gone to court, however. As with other parts of the Act and Regulations, because these provisions have become unworkable they have been largely ignored by the Metis and the government. Today, as in 1939, settlement members elect all five members of their board, and the government deals with the council as the proper representatives of the settlement.

The 1960s and the End of Isolation

By the end of the 1960s the focus of settlement leaders began to change. For 30 years the leaders of each settlement had concentrated primarily on the problems of survival on their particular settlement. At the beginning of the 70s, the focus shifted outward, and settlement leaders became actively concerned about the collective interests of all the settlements and their prospects for the future. The most significant event leading to this new focus on collective action was the loss of Wolf Lake.

Land surrounding Wolf Lake in northeastern Alberta was set aside for the Wolf Lake Settlement Association in 1939. By the late 1950s there were 11 to 12 families living on the settlement. [52] However, in 1960 a provincial Order-in-Council was passed eliminating the settlement area. [53] The resident families were moved to nearby communities or other settlements. The reason given by the province for the closing was essentially that the area could not be adequately serviced. Others have expressed the view that a factor in the decision was the federal government's need for a bombing range for the nearby Cold Lake Air Force base. [54] The legitimacy of the province's action is still the subject of litigation between the Metis and the province. [55] Whatever the reason, the news that a settlement area had been eliminated caused considerable concern among Metis leaders as to the security of their own settlement areas.

This concern for land security was heightened by a review of the settlement situation initiated in 1969. At the instance of the Metis Association, the provincial government set up a Metis Task Force, including representatives of the Metis Association, to conduct a review of *The Metis Betterment Act*, the Metis Settlements and the Metis Rehabilitation Branch. In 1972 the Task Force presented its report. [56] The report stated that "it is incumbent upon the Committee to suggest it was not necessarily the feeling of the [Ewing] Commission that Crown lands for the Metis people should be a perpetual commitment." [57] It went on to recommend that the Settlement

Areas should become Improvement Districts and suggested the possibility of enabling individual settlers to own their own land. In fairness it should be noted that the main thrust of the report was to create a better legislative and policy environment for community development. It should also be noted that the report stated that "We can foresee that some or all of the Metis Settlements could, if desirable, take over all the Crown Lands as corporate bodies under the Improvement Districts."[58] In spite of its apparent good intent, the report caused grave concern on the settlements where it was taken as an indication that the government was considering "lifting the boundaries."

A third significant event in the late 1960s also had to do with land. Regulations under the *Metis Betterment Act* provide for a common trust fund shared by all eight settlements.[59] The regulations specify that the Trust Fund[60] is to be credited with "all moneys accrued or hereafter accruing from the sources hereinafter set out," and includes in the list of sources:

> moneys received by way of compensation from oil companies for use of surface rights on unoccupied lands, and all moneys received from the sale or lease of any other of the natural resources of the said areas.[61]

During the 1960s, oil and gas resources began to be developed on a number of settlements. Settlement leaders took the view that the mines and minerals were part of the land set aside for their benefit, that oil and gas were natural resources of the settlement areas and consequently that money from the sale of these resources should go to the Trust Fund. The province disagreed and settlement leaders filed a statement of claim[62] demanding that the monies be paid to the Trust Fund. Without ruling on the merits of the case, the Court rejected the claim on procedural grounds.[63]

When settlement leaders in the early 1970s looked at their collective situation, they were concerned. The settlement at Wolf Lake had been eliminated by the provincial government. A government task force had raised fears that "lifting the boundaries" might be considered for other settlements. An initial effort to secure the benefit of subsoil resources had failed. It became apparent to settlement leaders that an ongoing co-ordinated effort was required to ensure land security, legislative authority and adequate financing.

Brady had realized the need for an organized common front as early as 1940 and with Norris had endeavoured to establish a coordinating organization for the settlements.[64] They were unsuccessful. Thirty years later, in 1971, Metis settlement leaders again began an effort to "federate" the settlements. A group of settlement leaders[65] visited the settlements, met with settlement councils and members, and discussed common concerns and the need for a co-ordinating body. In 1975 the eight settlement councils created such a body by formally incorporating the Alberta Federation of Metis Settlement Associations (commonly referred to as the Federation). The governing board of the Federation consisted then, and now, of the chairperson of each settlement council and four executive members elected at large. The Federation's mandate was to provide the settlement councils with a mechanism for sharing information, co-ordinating efforts and developing policies on matters that required co-operation, such as the sharing of the common Trust Fund.

The 1970s—Settlement Leaders Reorganize

In essence the goals of the settlements were the same in 1975 as they had been in 1939, and still are today: land security, local legislative authority and adequate finances. With the long-term achievement of the first and third goals in mind the Federation immediately began work on legal action to secure the revenue from oil and gas resource development in Settlement Areas. A new statement of claim was filed in 1977.[66] The major short-term focus of the Federation's efforts, however, was on the second goal—developing local legislative authority.

The Metis Task Force had reported in 1972 that the function of the settlement councils was "more consultative than administrative." Some settlements had no office, all administrative functions being handled by staff of the Metis Development Branch. All purchasing was done by purchase order, and wages on settlement projects were paid by the branch. Settlement councils generally had no bank accounts of their own and no direct financial authority. One of the top priorities of the Federation was to begin building real local governments with adequate administrative capability.

Although settlement concerns about the Metis Task Force recommendations had helped create the Federation, the Task Force and the Federation did agree on the importance of developing local self-government. The Task Force had emphasized the importance of this goal in its report, which while recommending that the settlements be established as Improvement Districts in the near future, went on to say of this approach,

> It is not a final objective, but merely a transitional stage of development with some specific date in mind to move into complete self-government. [67]

The Task Force report had also pointed out the problems created by having all programs for the settlements delivered by one government agency—the Metis Rehabilitation Branch. [68] The Federation also saw this as a problem. In essence the single agency approach provided a single line of communication and program delivery between the province and the settlements. That channel could be easily blocked or overloaded, with the result that developmental efforts were stymied. The settlements had to open new channels to those in power to communicate their needs and establish new ways to meet those needs.

The most important new route was to the federal government. After disclaiming responsibility for the Metis in the 1930s, the federal government had finally begun reassessing its role in the 1960s, and in the early 1970s began assisting Metis organizations through the Department of the Secretary of State. There were no direct links with the settlements, however, until the Secretary of State agreed to participate with the province in a local government development effort spearheaded by the Federation. This involved a number of projects extending over three years from 1976 to 1979. In essence the projects enabled the Federation to hire trained field workers to help settlement councils get organized and do the kind of research and writing necessary to tap external development resources.

A change in policy by the Metis Development Branch in the early 1970s aided this effort. The policy aimed at reducing the branch's administrative role and developing the capacity of settlement administrations. This meant that every settlement would have an office, office equipment and a clerk. It also meant that the real decision-making would move from the branch to the council.

The new policy, combined with offices, information and support staff led to a rapid growth in council responsibilities in the late 1970s. The Federation and individual councils became directly involved with a broad range of federal, provincial and private agencies. Where in 1969 a settlement turned to the branch for information and development assistance, by 1979 many of the settlements had direct contractual or program delivery links with several federal government departments, with half a dozen provincial departments and with corporations in the private sector. [69] Some settlement councils began to feel overwhelmed as the limitations of the single agency were replaced by the problem of managing links with a multitude of agencies.

The problems were exacerbated by anachronistic legislation and paranoia surrounding the natural resources litigation. Alberta had agreed with the settlements that issues related to ownership of the natural resources of the Settlement Areas should be determined by the courts. Since a change in the legislative framework could prejudice the litigation, the government and the settlements agreed that there should be no changes to the *Metis Betterment Act*, or its regulations, while the matter was before the courts. As a result, while the responsibilities of the settlement councils grew rapidly, the legislative framework in which they operated was frozen. The Task Force report in 1972 had recommended that the Act be rewritten.[70] That was at a time when a council's function was, in the words of the report "more consultative than administrative." By 1979 most councils had major administrative responsibilities.

The Act had been essentially static since 1940. The only significant change was the amendment in 1952 that replaced fully elected councils by a board with a branch employee as chairman, two members appointed by the Minister and two elected members. That amendment had been unworkable and by the mid 1970s, although unchanged, was universally ignored; the council continued to be elected as it had been under the original Act. By 1979 the legal system provided by the Act and regulations had become increasingly unworkable because of internal inconsistencies, uncertain legitimacy, anachronisms and inadequacies. As more parts of the system became unworkable they were ignored; the more the system was ignored, the more unclear the legal framework for local government became. The resulting uncertainty tended to increase the inherent friction accompanying the change in roles of the settlement councils and the branch.

In addition to locking in existing legislation, the natural resources litigation contributed to other developmental problems by hampering innovation and limiting trust. Provincial employees had to check constantly with the Attorney General's department before agreeing with any proposal from the settlements or undertaking any initiative. There was a constant concern that some well-intentioned action would prejudice the province's position in the litigation. Having taken the position in its Statement of Defence that the settlement associations were not "persons at law," the province found itself unable to enter into normal contractual relations with the settlements. That made it impossible to transfer funds to the settlement association in order to develop local administration. With the increasing direct links between federal agencies and the settlements, it also led to an interesting source of potential friction between the federal and provincial governments. Federal government departments had no qualms about entering into contracts with the settlement associations and did so regularly.[71] The province was faced with the argument that the Queen having contracted with the settlement associations on behalf of Canada could hardly deny, when acting on behalf of Alberta, that the associations lacked the capacity to contract.

In 1979 the paranoid atmosphere finally produced a political problem for the provincial government. Early one morning, representatives of the Metis Development Branch and other departments simultaneously appeared at all settlement offices, seized settlement and government files that were in their opinion relevant to the natural resource litigation, and removed the files to Edmonton. The Metis and the public were incensed by the action. The story made the front pages and an embarrassed government sought talks with the settlements. Negotiations between the Federation and the government led to an investigation by the Alberta Ombudsman.

The Ombudsman carried out an investigation of the file raids and tabled his report in the summer of 1979.[72] It called for the creation of a joint committee of settlement and government representatives to, among other things, review the *Metis Betterment Act*. It also recommended that responsibility for the settlements be transferred from the Department of Social Services and Community Health to the Department of Municipal Affairs. The transfer was effected in October of 1980,[73] but it was not until March 31, 1982 that the recommended committee was finally established.[74]

In a sense the Ombudsman's report marked the end of an era. At the start of the 1970s most settlement councils had no staff, no offices and no administrative responsibility. In most cases the only channel for information and developmental resources was through the branch. By the end of the 1970s the councils had the offices, equipment and staff to administer local programs. They had established links with provincial government departments, federal government departments and private sector corporations and agencies. They had begun managing housing programs, economic development projects, and local educational and cultural projects. This decade saw settlement leaders realize the goal of Brady and Norris in developing the capacity to co-ordinate their efforts province-wide. In the 1980s the scene became national.

The 1980s and the Constitution

The Joint Committee created on the recommendation of the Ombudsman, was chaired by the Honourable Dr. Grant MacEwan, a former Lieutenant Governor of Alberta. It included the President and past President of the Federation, [75] a Member of the Legislature and an Assistant Deputy Minister of Municipal Affairs. The committee's mandate was "to act in an advisory capacity and in particular to review the *Metis Betterment Act* and Regulations and make recommendations to the Minister of Municipal Affairs which would allow for political, social, cultural and economic development on Metis Settlements." The committee held hearings on the settlements and, based on the concerns expressed in the communities, suggested provisions for a new *Metis Settlements Act*. The committee's report, consisting of the provisions and explanatory comments, was transmitted to the Minister on July 12, 1984. [76]

The committee carried out its work in the new legal environment created by the recognition of Metis aboriginal rights in the Constitution of Canada. The entrenchment of those rights was a major achievement for the Metis, and not achieved without effort. Although there was no mention of these rights in the federal government's constitutional package proposed late in 1980, by January of 1981 a Special Joint Committee of the Senate and House of Commons unanimously agreed that recognition of Metis aboriginal rights should be included. [77] Alberta, and other provinces, objected to the patriation process, Prime Minister Trudeau threatened to proceed without their consent, and the legality of the unilateral approach was referred to the Supreme Court of Canada. The Court's decision forced a new round of negotiations between Ottawa and the provinces resulting in an agreement on an amended package on November 5, 1981. The recognition of aboriginal rights was gone from the new package, reportedly due to pressure from western Premiers.

In Alberta, settlement leaders were extremely upset by the prospect of a patriated Constitution with no recognition of Metis aboriginal rights. The president of the Federation, Elmer Ghostkeeper, led a quiet protest that burned sweetgrass along with the permanent flame at the Alberta Legislature. As public pressure mounted,

Premier Lougheed agreed to meet with settlement leaders to discuss the matter. At the meeting Ghostkeeper argued that recognizing the Metis in the Constitution was essential if there was to be real equality in Canada between the West and the East. He stated that in the east, the two indigenous peoples subsumed into the new nation in 1867, the French and the Indians, had been recognized as unique peoples. The French were assured language protection and the Indians the special status of federal jurisdiction. The nation now included the west, and the new Constitution for the nation should accord the indigenous peoples of the west, the Metis, the same sort of recognition. Whether Premier Lougheed was persuaded is not known, but he did begin encouraging the recognition of the "existing aboriginal rights" of the Metis in the Constitution.

The new Canadian Constitution not only recognized existing aboriginal rights, but also required the First Ministers to meet to define the scope of those rights. This led to considerable soul searching by aboriginal groups in preparation for the First Ministers Conference. Of particular concern to the Metis was the question of whether they came under federal or provincial jurisdiction. This issue was addressed by the settlements in a position paper on aboriginal rights, "Metisism: A Canadian Identity," presented to Premier Lougheed on June 30, 1982. The paper noted that the settlements might be better off under federal jurisdiction since the federal government did not contest the right of Indians to benefit from the subsurface resource revenues of their lands. The paper then went on to say:

> This is not to suggest that we are seeking an exclusive relationship with the federal government. We believe that the province can be more responsive to the needs and aspirations of Metis settlers than a distant federal government. A case in point is the establishment of the Settlements at a time of federal neglect and indifference towards the Metis people. Provincial jurisdiction over education, municipalities, and health and welfare, reinforces our need to deal with the province. Perhaps the most compelling reason for us opting out of an exclusive relationship with the federal government is that, while it might enhance our political status, it does not fit with the Metis way of doing things. More than any other Canadians, we recognize the importance of western provincial rights: our ancestors formed two provisional governments to defend them. We are proud to be western Canadians and proud to be Albertans.

The settlements have consistently maintained this preference for working with the province. Certainly they are affected by the question of whether Metis are "Indians" under the *Constitution Act, 1867*. However, in talks between the settlements and Alberta the issue is generally ignored on the basis that it is a question for the courts and not something either party can do anything about.

The first First Ministers' Conference on Aboriginal Constitutional Matters was held in Ottawa in April of 1983. Federation representatives attended with the Alberta government delegation. Although by the standards of future such conferences this one was a success, settlement leaders left with a feeling of unease. Their primary objective was the constitutional protection of their existing land base and they saw the national process as one way of achieving that objective. However, it became clear in Ottawa that getting agreement on any position further clarifying aboriginal rights would be extremely difficult. The settlements began looking for other options.

The settlements began to consider the possibility of protecting settlement lands in the Constitution by an amendment to the *Alberta Act*. [78] It was felt that such an amendment could be made under s.43 of the *Constitution Act, 1982* by a "made in Alberta" process involving simply the settlements and the province. After the disastrous 1984 First Ministers' Conference, the Federation proposed the idea to Premier Lougheed who said he would look into its feasibility. There was no more communication with the Federation on the subject until the 1985 First Ministers' Conference. Premier Lougheed did not support the federal initiatives at that conference and became upset with what he felt was the media's efforts to paint the Alberta position as "redneck." He indicated to the president of the Federation that he would proceed with the *Alberta Act* amendment approach if he could be assured that the settlements would adopt fair and democratic procedures for membership and land allocations. [79]

The Premier's commitment was a tremendous boost for settlement leaders. It meant that there was finally a realistic possibility of achieving the fundamental goal of protecting their land base. All of the settlement councils met on April 28, 1985 at the town of Westlock, north of Edmonton. A resolution ("the Westlock Resolution") was passed adopting basic principles to govern the granting of membership and the allocation of interests in Metis settlement lands. It also committed the settlements to "continue to work with the Government of the Province of Alberta to complete and implement the recommendations of the Committee and the principles of this Resolution."

The province accepted the principles adopted in the Westlock Resolution as meeting the "fair and democratic" criteria, and on June 3, 1985, Premier Lougheed introduced "A Resolution Concerning an Amendment to the *Alberta Act*" to the Alberta Legislature. It was passed unanimously. In supporting the resolution the Legislature committed itself to "introduce, once a revised *Metis Betterment Act* has been enacted, a resolution to amend the *Alberta Act* by proclamation issued by Her Excellency the Governor General under the Great Seal of Canada to grant an estate in fee simple in existing Metis Settlement lands to the Metis Settlement Associations or to such appropriate Metis corporate entities as may be determined on behalf of the Metis people of Alberta, in accordance with this resolution."

This resolution firmly committed the province to pursue two objectives, the entrenchment of Metis land through an amendment to the *Alberta Act*, and the passage of a new *Metis Settlements Act* that would provide a modern framework for local self-government on the settlements. On January 13, 1986, the Federation met with the new premier of Alberta, Don Getty, to discuss the possibility of a joint effort aimed at producing a new *Metis Settlements Act* and an amendment to the *Alberta Act* before the 1987 First Minister's Conference. Following meetings on all the settlements the Federation, in July of 1986, presented a proposal for such legislation in a document entitled "By Means of Conferences and Negotiations We Ensure Our Rights."

Negotiations on the new legislation proceeded through the end of 1986 and into 1987. The main sticking point was the principle of "territorial integrity." To the Metis, this principle was absolutely basic. In essence it meant that the Metis would own the surface[80] of all the land within a specified boundary. The province was not prepared to concede ownership of the road allowances and the beds and shores of the lakes and rivers. The matter had still not been resolved when the First Ministers' Conference opened on March 26, 1987. However, in his opening statement, Premier Getty discussed the negotiations and stated, "With regard to outstanding matters, we understand and agree with the concept of territorial integrity." With that obstacle removed, discussions proceeded rapidly and on June 17, 1987, a discussion paper entitled "Implementation of Resolution 18" was tabled in the Legislature. The paper included drafts of a *Metis Settlements Act*, an *Alberta Act* amendment and letters patent to transfer the province's interest in settlement lands.

The draft *Metis Settlements Act* provided a comprehensive framework for local self-government for the settlements. It established the existing settlements as bodies corporate, gave by-law making powers to councils, created a central land-holding body with the power to make policies binding on settlement councils and created a tribunal to adjudicate disputes on land, membership and other matters. It also provided criteria for membership and rules for land allocation. Compared to the sparse and inadequate 22 sections of the existing Act, its 212 sections overwhelmed most settlement members.

The Federation held meetings on the settlements to discuss the paper. Although there was general support for the proposal, there was also concern that it was too much too soon. After discussions with the province it was agreed that a better approach might be to begin with bare-bones legislation and implement the rest of the package, as modified in consultation with the communities, over time. The result was the introduction to the Legislative Assembly on July 5, 1988, of Bill 64, *Metis Settlements Act*, and Bill 65, *Metis Settlements Land Act*, and the tabling of a resolution to amend the *Alberta Act*.

A NEW LEGISLATIVE FRAMEWORK

There were two major differences between the discussion draft "Implementation of Resolution 18" that had been tabled in 1987 and the bills actually introduced in 1988. The first was that matters relating to the transfer of land were separated from local government matters and introduced as a separate *Metis Settlements Land Act*. The second was that the *Metis Settlements Act* providing the framework for local government was of an enabling rather than a comprehensive nature. In other words, where the earlier document had spelled out the details of membership, land allocation and resolution of disputes, Bill 64 proposes that these matters be dealt with later by making regulations in co-operation with the Metis.

It is anticipated that the regulations brought in over time will maintain the structures and essential components of the more comprehensive document tabled in June of 1986. Given that, the four cornerstones of the contemplated new legislation are:

1. Constitutionally protected Metis lands set aside as settlement areas;
2. Settlement councils responsible for local government in the Settlement Areas, with additional powers to make decisions on membership and land allocation (subject to appeal);
3. A central land and trust fund holding body (the General Council) responsible for addressing common concerns of the settlement councils—such as the administration of the Trust Fund and the establishing of common policies with respect to land-use planning, resource development, etc;
4. Provincial jurisdiction, consistent with the protection of the Constitution, over the lands and institutions.

The first and fourth cornerstones are to be placed in the Constitution of Canada by an amendment to the *Alberta Act*. The second and third will be put in place by the *Metis Settlements Act*[81] and regulations made under that Act.

The guiding principles in drafting the *Metis Settlements Act* were to respect the traditions of the settlements, to remedy the problems created by current legislation, and as far as possible, to keep in the new Act the institutions and processes that had been found to work in the past.

The *Metis Settlements Act* establishes the eight existing Metis settlement associations as corporations with the powers and privileges of a natural person.[82] It provides for elected five-member councils[83] with the power to make by-laws governing the Settlement Area.[84] The by-law making process is rather unique for local governments in that no by-law can become effective unless it is approved by the members at a public meeting.[85]

Settlement councils have many common concerns, including the use of the Trust Fund shared by all settlements. Over the years they have developed a mechanism for dealing with those concerns called the "All Council." This is a meeting of all council members from the eight settlements to discuss common policy on matters such as surface rights, Trust Fund sharing, and land use. Although the All Council has no legal status, the policies it develops, and the decisions it makes, are generally respected by all settlement councils. In line with the philosophy of legislating what has worked, the new

Act creates an incorporated central body called the "Metis Settlements General Council"[86] which is simply the All Council given legal authority to continue its common policy-making role.

The traditional policy-making role of the All Council is preserved with the new Act recognizing General Council Policies as having legal effect. A General Council policy requires the support of three-quarters of the settlements[87] but once adopted is binding on all settlements to the extent that a settlement council cannot pass a by-law contrary to the policy.[88] In addition to making policies, the General Council will also provide a single entity to hold the Metis settlement lands and possibly act as trustee of the Trust Fund. At present the Crown fulfils these responsibilities.

Another culturally based component of the discussion paper is the use of a Metis Appeals Tribunal for resolution of local problems, especially with respect to land and membership. The Tribunal is made up of seven persons, three appointed by the General Council and three appointed by the Minister. The chairperson of the Tribunal is appointed by the Minister from a list of candidates submitted by the General Council. It is hoped that by the use of this Tribunal, made up mostly of Metis people and enabled to hear matters at the local level without formal court procedures, expensive and time consuming appeals to the courts can be avoided. Bill 64 does provide directly for the Appeals Tribunal, but enables the Minister to make regulations to bring it into existence.[89]

The "Implementation of Resolution 18" discussion paper contained detailed land management provisions. Under the existing Act the highest interest that can be held in settlement land is the Certificate of Occupancy. It can only be held by a member, grants exclusive use, and can be passed on to next of kin on death. The discussion paper preserved this means of land holding but limited the number of certificates any one member could hold. However, there were provisions for the General Council to establish policies providing for other forms of land holding. In Bill 64 these land management provisions are left to be brought in by regulations made by the Minister.[90] Like the discussion paper, Bill 64 does, however, contain prohibitions on the use of land for security and protection from seizure.[91]

The discussion paper contained detailed provisions governing the qualifications for membership and the process for membership application, approval and appeal. However, as with land management, Bill 64 leaves membership matters to be dealt with in regulations.[92] It simply requires that regulations recognize the principles that existing members are entitled to be members and that members must be Metis.[93]

In order to develop a complete legislative package over time, Bill 64 provides the Minister with broad powers to make regulations on substantive matters such as membership and land management. However, these powers must be exercised in conjunction with the General Council: the substantive regulations may only be made or amended at the written request of the General Council, unless the regulation is required to protect the public interest.[94] This is defined as meaning that the regulation "is essential for the peace, order and good government of a settlement area," or "necessary to prevent harm to the general public."[95]

The second component of the legislative package, Bill 65,[96] provides for the transfer of the Crown's interest in Metis settlement lands to the General Council. Included in the transfer are the road allowances and the beds and shores of the rivers and lakes.[97] Not included are mines and minerals and water.[98] The Crown may acquire an interest less than fee simple in settlement lands, but only with the consent of the General Council, or the approval of the courts.[99]

The final part of the package presented to the legislature is a draft "Motion for a Resolution to Authorize an Amendment to the Constitution of Canada." This provides for an amendment to the *Alberta Act*. The proposed amendment prohibits the Crown in right of Alberta from expropriating the fee simple estate in settlement lands, altering the letters patent transferring the land, amending the *Metis Settlements Land Act* or dissolving the General Council, except with the agreement of the General Council. The amendment also emphasizes that the Legislature of Alberta maintains its jurisdiction over the lands.

Nowhere in the materials presented to the Legislature is there a mention of "aboriginal rights." There are two reasons for this. It was felt that any definition of aboriginal rights would have to take place at the national level and involve all the parties interested and affected by the definition. The process in Alberta has only involved the province and the settlements. The second, and collateral reason, is that the *Alberta Act* amendment is sought under s.43 of the *Constitution Act, 1982*. This section allows an amendment to the Constitution of Canada if it is authorized by resolutions of the Senate, House of Commons and the legislative assembly of the affected province—in this case Alberta.[100] It was felt that if aboriginal rights were specifically mentioned, other governments or aboriginal groups would take the position that the general amendment procedures of s.38, involving all provinces, would have to be followed.

In summary, the package presented to the Legislature takes a unique "made-in-Alberta" approach to the constitutional protection of Metis lands. It draws on existing Alberta legislation and existing settlement practice to synthesize a unique set of institutions to meet the challenge of providing fair, democratic and effective government of the settlements and to protect the land as a Metis homeland for the future.

CURRENT JURISDICTIONAL PROBLEMS

Membership

The proposed new legislation limits membership in the settlements to Metis and adopts a definition of Metis based on aboriginal ancestry and cultural identification.[101] At the moment, however, the membership problem has been complicated by the Bill C-31 amendments to the *Indian Act*. The *Metis Betterment Act* employs essentially the same definition of Metis as was used in the 1938 Act, except that to qualify, a person must have at least one-quarter Indian blood. It excludes anyone who is "either an Indian or a non-treaty Indian as defined in the *Indian Act* (Canada)".

The *Indian Act* provides that

> "Indian" means a person who pursuant to this Act is registered as an Indian *or is entitled to be registered as an Indian.*[102] [emphasis added]

In one of the more arcane provisions of the legislation outside of the *Income Tax Act*, the Act in subsequent sections[103] spells out who is entitled to be registered as an Indian. The "Bill C-31" changes in the Act considerably expanded the class of persons entitled to register by removing some of the patriarchal membership criteria and by allowing a woman and her children to register if she had lost status through marriage.

In the past, an Indian woman commonly lost her Indian status by marrying a white man. In Alberta, her descendants were "Metis" for the purposes of the *Metis Betterment Act*, which specifies,

"Metis means a person of mixed white and Indian blood having not less that one-quarter Indian blood, but does not include either an Indian or a non-treaty Indian as defined in *The Indian Act* (Canada).[104]

The descendants were Metis by virtue of their mixed blood and non-Indian status. Given the fact that many status Indians have white ancestors somewhere in the family tree, the woman herself could often satisfy this definition of "Metis."

The changes in the *Indian Act* now enable the woman and potentially several generations of descendants to register as Indians. Estimates by Metis settlement leaders are that over half the members on some settlements are entitled to be registered as Indians under these new provisions. Most of these settlement members consider themselves Metis and have no desire to be on the Indian Register. The fact that they could register, however, means they are "Indians" as defined in the *Indian Act*. Because the definition of "Metis" in *The Metis Betterment Act* excludes anyone who is "either an Indian or a non-treaty Indian as defined in the *Indian Act* (Canada)" they are not "Metis" under the provincial Act. As a result, they are ineligible to be members of the settlement to which many have belonged all their adult life. Needless to say this has created a very awkward situation.

The situation is made worse because the changes to the *Indian Act* also removed the enfranchisement provision[105] that made it possible for a person voluntarily to renounce Indian status. Consequently there are now Metis settlement members[106] who have become "involuntary Indians" — they cannot remove themselves from the definition of "Indian" under the *Indian Act*. Technically, under the *Metis Betterment Act* they are not "Metis" and consequently not eligible for membership in a settlement association. The same problem occurs for infant children of a woman on the settlement who decides to regain her Indian status, and puts the names of her children on the Register at the same time. Her children could technically be barred from settlement membership for life.

There are interesting jurisdictional problems here if one assumes that Metis are not "91(24) Indians"[107] and that the province has exclusive competency to legislate with respect to Metis and land reserved for Metis. In passing legislation conferring rights on a group, and prohibiting an "Indian" as defined by the federal government from becoming a member of the group, is the province legislating with respect to Indians? Conversely if the federal government adopts a definition of "Indian" that results in a loss of membership rights for Metis under provincial legislation, is the federal government legislating with respect to Metis? Can the federal government unilaterally, and without the consent of the individual, deprive a Metis of status recognized by the province?

Fortunately the province and the settlements have adopted a pragmatic rather than legalistic view of the problems created by the *Indian Act* changes. To date no one has lost membership in a settlement because of becoming an "involuntary Indian." There is a different attitude, however, toward members who apply for Indian status. The general feeling is that under the Constitution of Canada there are three mutually exclusive classes of aboriginal peoples, Indians, Inuit and Metis, and people have to decide which class they belong to. This approach has been adopted in the membership provisions of the new Metis settlements legislation. In addition, an effort has been made to enable individual settlements to resolve hardship cases where the eligibility of an individual could be affected by actions outside that person's control.

Hunting and Fishing[108]

The Canadian Constitution gives the Alberta government jurisdiction over game in Alberta, including hunting and trapping, and over the proprietary interests in fisheries.[109] The federal government has jurisdiction over non-proprietary interests in fisheries.[110] Alberta exercises its jurisdiction over hunting and trapping largely through the *Wildlife Act*[111] and its attendant regulations. Section 7 of the *Metis Betterment Act*, however, enables the making of regulations governing "the hunting, trapping and killing of any game bird, big game or fur-bearing animal" on the settlements "[n]otwithstanding anything to the contrary contained in *The Wildlife Act* or any other Act."

Two such regulations are in effect, A.R. 115/60, *Regulations Governing Fishing*, and A.R. 116/60, *Regulations Governing Trapping and Hunting of Game and Fur-Bearing Animals Upon Lands Set Aside for Occupation by a Metis Settlement Association*. The fishing regulations prohibit non-members from fishing in a settlement area but allows members to fish for food in the area and in any adjoining water, subject to the *Fisheries Act*.[112] The hunting regulations prohibit non-members from hunting, trapping, killing or taking any game in the settlement. These regulations must mesh with federal legislation governing migratory birds and fisheries.

Although the provinces have jurisdiction over game, the federal government has the power to enter into treaties[113] and has passed the *Migratory Birds Convention Act*[114] establishing closed seasons on migratory birds. Unlike the Indians and Inuit, there are no specific exemptions for Metis taking food, and at least one settlement member has been convicted of violating this Act. That was before the constitutional entrenchment of aboriginal rights, however, and since then the matter has never been raised in the Courts.

The resolution of jurisdictional problems in the case of fisheries is interesting. Section 34 of the federal *Fisheries Act* gives the Governor General in Council broad regulatory powers. The *Alberta Fisheries Regulations*[115] made under this section contain specific provisions dealing with settlement Metis. The regulations adopt the *Metis Betterment Act* definition of "Metis" involving mixed white and Indian blood[116] and provides for the issuing of a "Metis domestic license" to enable settlement members to fish for food on their settlement. It seems clear that although the federal government has the jurisdiction on these matters, it makes regulations based on the advice of the affected province. Consequently negotiations between the settlements and the province on fisheries matters can eventually be reflected in regulations made by the federal government.

CO-OPERATION AND RESULTS

Meeting the Need for Housing

As in most native communities, housing has been a perennial and pressing problem on the Metis settlements. In the early days of the settlements, housing assistance was provided by the province in the form of nails and basic hardware—the settler supplying the logs and labour. Eventually the log cabins were replaced by frame houses, with some loan assistance from the province. In a Christmas radio address in 1955, the province's Minister of Welfare proudly described the provincial program of assistance to the settlements. He also proffered some (probably unappreciated) advice to the federal government. After opening greetings to his radio audience, the Minister dealt summarily with federal/provincial responsibility for native affairs:

> Publicity in recent weeks regarding the care of Indians and Metis or half-breed people, has created confusion in the minds of people as to who is responsible for the care of these groups.
>
> So that there will be no doubt: The Indians are the sole care of the Federal Government; care of the Metis or half-breed people is the responsibility of the Provincial Government. [117]

The Minister then proceeded to outline how the province was meeting its responsibility:

> All roads in the colonies have been built at no cost to the general public. Roads up to the colony boundaries were built by the Department of Highways, who have been paid in the amount of seven thousand dollars from the Metis Trust Fund. Five thousand dollars has also been paid to the Department of Forestry for fire fighting. Medical accounts and nurses wages have been paid, as well as many other services.
>
> You see folks, the Metis under proper supervision are doing an excellent job, and are paying their own way. This is a record of which they may well be proud.
>
> I am pleased to note that the Federal Government, at last, have come to realize the soundness of our program and are now taking steps to institute such measures at Fort Vermilion. The Federal Government yet has much to learn from the Province of Alberta, particularly in the care of their Indians.

The Minister described the housing program as follows:

> Those established on the colonies are now leading contented, happy, healthful and self-supporting lives. Regulations call for the erection of permanent houses of frame construction, well ventilated, with lots of light, and of the proper size to accommodate the family which is to occupy them.
>
> ....
>
> Assistance is given to the settlers by means of a loan to purchase building material such as hardware, doors, windows, and other materials that cannot be secured on the Colony. A loan of $100.00 is provided for breaking land which the settler has cleared.

By today's standards the housing program certainly appears more limited than the Minister's enthusiasm.

By 1975 the housing assistance program had grown to a provincial grant of $28,000 per settlement to use as the council saw fit to meet their housing needs. [118] Since the amount was clearly inadequate, settlement councils began to look for other sources of assistance, one of which was the federal government as represented by the Central Mortgage and Housing Corporation (CMHC). The councils contracted CMHC officials and after some discussions the Residential Rehabilitation Assistance Program (RRAP) was made available to the settlements. In 1975 and 1976, the program enabled some much needed repair work to be done on existing settlement houses. Funding for new houses, however, still came from the $28,000 per settlement grant provided through the provincial Metis Betterment Branch.

In 1976, responsibility for settlement housing was transferred to the Department of Housing and became part of the province's Rural Housing Assistance Program (RHAP). The funding remained at the same level. However in 1977, following a tour of the settlements by the Minister of Housing, program funding was increased sharply to $50,000 per settlement. The increased funding was made possible by a special warrant passed in response to the Minister's concern over housing conditions. The actual funding then doubled to $100,000 per settlement by matching federal funding through the Alberta North Agreement. Under this cost-sharing arrangement the province's Department of Housing funded the RHAP housing programs on the settlements and then reclaimed 50 per cent of the costs from the federal Department of Regional Economic Expansion (DREE).

From 1978 to 1982, significant progress was made in improving housing on the settlements. The housing program on each settlement was a complex amalgam of federal and provincial programs combined with settlement council co-ordination and individual effort and equity. Each settlement established a Waskayigan Association[119] to co-ordinate the local housing effort. Materials were purchased with RHAP funds and equity from the prospective home owner. Construction was carried out by the home owner, his family, and settlement apprentices enrolled in a carpentry training program. Their training allowances, and consequently the labour component of the houses, were paid by the federal Department of Manpower and Immigration. Construction was supervised by trainers paid by the provincial Department of Advanced Education. The apprentices also received classroom instruction at the Alberta Vocational Colleges in Grouard and Lac La Biche. In all, about 35 journeyman carpenters were trained and close to 200 houses built.

In 1982 the Alberta North Agreement expired and was not renewed. The province, however, assumed the federal share of the RHAP funding and continued the program. The federal government continued to provide labour funding via the carpenter training program, but that assistance ended in 1986. Since then there has been no federal assistance for new home construction. However, to bring matters a full circle, CMHC is once again providing assistance to carry out emergency repairs to existing houses.

The housing programs on the settlements represent the power of pragmatism, co-operation and a problem-solving attitude. The program was not created in one piece by planners. It developed over time as representatives of the settlements, the province and the federal government sought to combine resources to solve a problem. The focus was not on "Whose legal responsibility is this?" but rather on "What role can we realistically play in developing a solution?" If any of the participants had insisted on first clarifying the issue of legal responsibility, the result would almost certainly have been fewer houses and carpenters and more conferences and litigation.

Capitalizing Development—Settlement Investment Corporation

Notwithstanding the rosy picture painted by the Minister of Welfare in his Christmas message of 1955, the facts of life in the early 1970s were that the settlements were economically depressed areas. There was little cash in the local economies. Unemployment was high. Most settlement residents depended on odd jobs off the settlement for cash and on their own subsistence farming operations for food. The Metis Task Force Report in 1972 saw little hope that the farming operations could become viable businesses without new means of accessing capital. It summarized the problem as follows:

> The Metis Settlement Areas have reserved land ownership to the Crown in order to protect their land claim. However, the agricultural resources of Western Canada have been developed largely through land mortgages; but this source of capital has not been available to the residents of Metis Settlements. No alternative source of capital has ever been arranged for the Settlements to replace the mortgage system. [120]

Creating some mechanism to solve this problem was a major priority of the Federation and individual settlements. The Metis Betterment Branch and other provincial agencies were approached for assistance. None was forthcoming. The Federation then approached the federal Department of Regional Economic Expansion (DREE) in an effort to gain access to the native economic development programs available in other provinces. Because of the frosty federal/provincial relationship at the time, DREE representatives indicated that they could not become directly involved in funding native economic development in Alberta. The Department could only respond to initiatives from the province. In other words, the Federation would have to convince a provincial agency to support an economic development proposal and persuade the agency to approach DREE on its behalf. Efforts to do that were not productive.

Early in 1979, the settlements finally saw an opportunity. Before the provincial election Premier Lougheed announced a Municipal Debt Reduction (MDR) Program under which the province would make a $500 per capita grant to each municipality for the purpose of reducing municipal debt. Richard Poitras, one of the founders of the Federation, approached his MLA, the Honourable Al Adair, to find out whether the settlements would qualify for the program. Adair took the matter to Cabinet and it was agreed that the settlements should qualify, the same as other local governments. Because the settlements had no debt, however, the grant provided a new source of capital for settlement development.

In the summer of 1979 the Federation developed a detailed proposal[121] for an economic development mechanism for the settlements, using the MDR grants as seed financing to leverage additional development capital. The mechanism included a finance arm to provide capital and a development support arm to provide expertise. The proposal called for the settlements to invest their MDR money as initial equity in an economic development corporation, with the province to provide assistance in meeting operating costs until the corporation became self-supporting. Additional capital was to be sought from the federal government and the private sector.

In 1980 the settlements incorporated Settlement Sooniyaw Corporation. In 1975 each settlement had contributed $5,000 to get the Federation started as an on-going operation. The same approach was used in launching Settlement Sooniyaw Corporation, each settlement purchasing $75,000 in shares to provide the initial capitalization for the corporation. The corporation then set about looking for additional assistance to implement the overall economic development strategy. NOVA, An Alberta Corporation, agreed to lend the Federation a young manager with some expertise in economics and business development to assist in evaluating economic development opportunities. The province, however, was less helpful. It could not be convinced to provide the funding required to create a real source of economic development capital. At the federal level there simply was no program available that could enable the financing mechanisms envisioned in the Federation's economic development proposal.

The situation changed in 1984 when the federal government announced the Native Economic Development Program (NEDP). The program made capital available to native businesses and financial institutions such as Settlement Sooniyaw Corporation. The NEDP provided some initial funding in 1984 to assist the corporation in developing a more detailed proposal for its proposed economic development mechanism. A complete proposal was presented to the NEDP in May of 1985, and following a year of negotiations a funding agreement was signed in May of 1986. Settlement Sooniyaw created a wholly owned subsidiary, Settlement Investment Corporation (SIC), and the NEDP agreed to provide SIC with $4,220,000 in financing over three years, conditioned on acceptable performance. SIC has performed well and has so far received $3,140,000 of the earmarked funds.

To date SIC has provided debt financing to about 50 settlement businesses and 70 farms. The businesses range from small stores and service stations to heavy equipment contracting. Most are owner operated. About 150 jobs have been created as a result, and by creating community stores and services there has been an improvement in internal settlement cash flow—some of the money that in the past was spent for products and services off the settlement now goes to building a commercial base on the settlement. Some provincial assistance is provided to individual businesses via grants made under the Canada Alberta Northern Development Agreement, a federal/provincial cost sharing arrangement. The province, however, still has not joined the federal government in supporting Settlement Investment Corporation.

Innovations In Agriculture—The Kikino Wildlife Ranch

With the exception of Paddle Prairie, the Metis Settlement Areas contain little land well suited for traditional agriculture. The lands were set aside out of public lands and by that time most of the good farm land in the province was already in private hands. The settlement areas tended to bush, muskeg and "moose pasture." Over the years settlers cleared the better land for subsistence farms or seeded native pasture for cattle ranching operations, but much of the land simply was not amenable to traditional farming and ranching practices. In the past it naturally supported moose, elk and buffalo. It took some effort, however, to make the same land support a viable farming operation based on cattle or grain. In the rougher bush lands or muskeg it was simply not possible.

In the mid-1970s the Intensive Wildlife Production section of the provincial Department of Fish and Wildlife began to explore the possibility of intensifying the production of wildlife on Indian and Metis lands. The effort was spearheaded by a provincial wildlife biologist, Gerry Lynch. By 1978, Lynch had outlined the potential of an intensive wildlife ranch on Metis settlement lands at board meetings of the Federation of Metis settlements and with individual settlement councils. The Kikino settlement council was particularly interested, and in 1978, with the assistance of Lynch and Judd Bundidge of the provincial Department of Agriculture, the council had developed a proposal for establishing a combined moose, elk and buffalo ranch in the Kikino settlement area.

The proposed project called for constructing a facility on the Kikino settlement consisting primarily of a heavy duty fence and corrals. Buffalo and elk would be obtained from the federal government through Elk Island Park east of Edmonton. The moose would be collected locally. Settlement members would construct the facilities and manage the operation. The Department of Fish and Wildlife would provide technical expertise on caring for the animals and monitor the project as a large-scale experiment. The Department of Agriculture would provide additional technical expertise on facilities design and construction. The proposal called for initial funding from the Department of Social Services—the department responsible for Metis settlements at the time. The Minister, Bob Bogle, generally considered by the settlements to be the least supportive minister in their history, vetoed the project. The Kikino council, however, carried on.

In 1979, the council incorporated the Kikino Wildlife Ranching Association. They earmarked an area of the settlement that was primarily muskeg and bush, with little potential for traditional farming practices. The settlement's budget was reworked to allocate funds to the purchase of fencing materials. The federal government was approached for help in funding the labour component of the project. The federal Department of Manpower agreed to support the project and by 1980 the settlement was able to begin fencing.

A page wire fence more than seven feet tall was built, and 23 buffalo imported from Elk Island National Park. In subsequent years additional lands were fenced and elk and buffalo brought in from Elk Island and Waterton Lakes National Parks. Local deer and moose were included when new areas were fenced. The fenced-in ranch area now includes more than nine square miles. Rough estimates of the current wildlife population are about 120 buffalo, 80 elk, 60 deer and 20 moose. The ranch employs three people full time and 15 to 35 on a seasonal basis. In 1987, 24 settlement residents were employed in various ranch projects.

The ranch appears to be a viable operation. Unlike a cattle ranching operation, the mix of indigenous animals makes full use of the natural vegetation—grass, browse and branches. Bison are sold as seed stock and for meat. Elk antlers are sold to brokers for eventual resale in the orient as an aphrodisiac. Some elk are sold as seed stock, but none as yet for meat. The moose population is still being developed, but the objective is eventually to create a sufficient moose population to meet the traditional settlement demand for moose meat as dietary staple.

In addition to the practical contribution of the ranch in the form of food, cash and employment, the project has made a scientific contribution. The original goal of the wildlife biologists was to study the possibilities of "extensive" versus "intensive" animal husbandry. Intensive husbandry relies on extensive intervention—picking the right animals and constantly modifying their environment so they will produce marketable products with efficacy and efficiency. Extensive husbandry prefers minimal intervention, leaving the natural landscape essentially intact and waiting until the animals that survive in that environment can be harvested for commercial use. In the rough areas of Kikino where farming is difficult, the extensive approach seems to be more productive.

CONCLUSION

The current legislative regime of the settlements is deeply flawed. It is paternalistic, anachronistic, inconsistent and inadequate. Nevertheless, for 50 years the settlements have functioned in a way that meets the primary objectives of the original founders. The land has provided a base on which the Metis have achieved some level of individual economic security. The *Metis Betterment Act*, for all its imperfections, has provided a legal structure within which elected Metis representatives have exercised some recognized powers of local self-government. Although short of the ideal, it has been a first for the Metis in Canada. The provisional government of the Red River Settlement in Manitoba had received some recognition by the Canadian government in 1869, but had been replaced almost immediately in 1870 by an exercise of federal political and military force.

In Alberta, however, elected representatives of the Metis have been "governing" lands reserved for Metis use for almost half a century. The province has maintained ultimate legal authority, but outside of a period during the 1950s and early 1960s, it has generally respected the locally elected councils as the final decision-makers on settlement matters. The councils of the settlements certainly do not have full self-governing powers, but for all practical purposes they have in fact governed the settlements, making decision on land allocation, membership and the other key issues of settlement life.

The proposed new package of legislation, federal and provincial, should provide the basis for achieving the long-range goals of land security and local autonomy. The remaining goal of adequate financial resources probably awaits the resolution of the natural resources litigation. The package presented to the legislature in 1988 represents the culmination of eight years of effort by the Metis and the province. Meetings on the settlements, with the All Council, with the Federation board and with appointed representatives have produced a range of documents and reports including "Metisism" in 1982, the MacEwan Report in 1984, "By Means of Conferences and Negotiations" in 1986, "Implementation of Resolution 18" in 1987 and finally the package presented to the Legislature.

The nagging question is "What happens to all these negotiations between the province and the settlements if Metis and lands reserved for Metis are exclusively federal jurisdiction?". The only reasonable answer is that the negotiations having been carried out in good faith will be respected. Perhaps the *Fisheries Act* approach provides a solution—the federal government could simply incorporate into federal legislation the legislation developed by the province and the settlements.

Notes

1. See P. Hogg, *Constitutional Law of Canada*, (2nd ed. 1985) p. 553.
2. *Guerin v. The Queen*, [1984] 2 S.C.R. 335, (1984) 13 D.L.R. (4th) 321 (S.C.C.).
3. Brian Slattery, "Understanding Aboriginal Rights," 66 *Canadian Bar Review* (1987), p. 727.
4. *Dumont et al v. A. G. Canada*, [1988] 5 W.W.R. 193 (MCA).
5. *Dumont, supra*, p. 207.
6. *Dumont, supra*, p. 196.
7. Noel Lyon, "Aboriginal Self-Government: Rights of Citizenship and Access to Government Services," *Aboriginal Peoples and Constitutional Reform*, Background Paper Number 1 (Kingston: Queen's University, Institute of Intergovernmental Relations, 1984).
8. *Dumont, supra*, note 4.
9. Slattery, *op. cit.*, note 3, p. 736.
10. In this context, "peoples" means an organized cultural group exercising some control over a geographically definable area.
11. Schedule 9, *Order of Her Majesty in Council Admitting Rupert's Land and the North-Western Territory into the Union*, June 23, 1870.
12. Paragraph 14 of the Imperial O.C. of June 23, 1870.
13. See for example Beal and Macleod, *Prairie Fire: The 1885 North-West Rebellion* (1984).
14. For a detailed description of the St. Paul des Metis settlement see J. Sawchuk, Sawchuk and Ferguson, *Metis Land Rights in Alberta: A Political History* (Edmonton: Metis Association of Alberta, 1981), ch.5.
15. *Ibid.*, p. 166.
16. *Ibid.*, p. 167.
17. *Ibid.*, p. 170. A large part of the colony's budget apparently went to building a Catholic boarding school, church and presbytery.
18. *Ibid.*, p. 178.
19. After the St. Paul des Metis experience, there appears to have been a shared wariness by Metis and provincial government leaders respecting the role of the church on future Metis colonies. As a result, when land was set aside under the *Metis Population Betterment Act* 30 years later, regulations were made (now A.R. 110/60, s.13, 14) limiting the use of lands leased for church purposes and prohibiting the use of these lands for a school or residence.
20. Section 21 of the *Alberta Act*, S.C. 1905, c.3 provided: "All Crown lands, mines and minerals and royalties incidental thereto ..., shall continue to be vested in the Crown and administered by the Government of Canada for the purposes of Canada ..."
21. For example in conjunction with negotiations on Treaty No. 10, including land in Alberta, P.C. 1459 was issued on July 20, 1906 and P.C. 326 was issued on February 15, 1908. These P.C.s are discussed in a report by one of the Claims Commissioners, N.O. Cote, dated December 3, 1929.
22. Clause 1 of the Memorandum of Agreement.
23. Sawchuk, *op. cit.*, note 14, p. 187.

24. Sawchuk, *op. cit.*, note 14. The land at Fishing Lake was part of the Crown lands to be transferred to the province under the *Natural Resources Transfer Agreement* of 1929.
25. For details of the lives and work of Brady and Norris, see Murray Dobbin, *The One-and-a-half Men* (Vancouver: New Star Books, 1981).
26. Sawchuk, *op. cit.*, note 14, p. 187. For example the questionnaire asked whether they owned livestock or machinery and whether they had ever received scrip or taken homestead.
27. See T. Pocklington, *Our Land—Our Culture—Our Future: The Government and Politics of the Alberta Metis Settlements*, unpublished manuscript, University of Alberta, 1988, p. 11.
28. Alberta government archival document.
29. *Ibid.*
30. *Ibid.*
31. *Ibid.*
32. *Ibid.* Cohoon was a senior official in the Department of the Interior. It is not known if there is any connection between this memo, which is apparently a briefing memo, and the letter six days later from Murphy, the Superintendent General of the Department of Indian Affairs.
33. O.C.706-35, Regulations Respecting the Locating of Half-Breed Land Scrip in the Province.
34. A thorough discussion of the events surrounding the hearings is contained in a paper by Judith Hill, "The Ewing Commission, 1935: A Case Study in Metis-Government Relations," Unpublished Honours Essay, Department of History, University of Alberta, 1977. See also Sawchuk, *op. cit.*, note 14, pp. 190-196. For political aspects of the Commission's work see T. Pocklington, *op. cit.*, note 27. For a legal analysis see Douglas Sanders, "A Legal Analysis of the Ewing Commission and the Metis Colony System in Alberta," in H. W. Daniels, *The Forgotten People: Metis and Non-Status Indian Land Claims*, (Ottawa: Native Council of Canada, 1978) p. 22.
35. Sanders, *op. cit.*, note 34.
36. An interesting aspect of this definition is that it made life style a factor in the definition of "Metis." This cultural identification approach has been adopted in the definition of "Metis" for national aboriginal rights discussions, and in the new Metis legislation in Alberta. It was not present, however, in legislation passed as a result of the report—*The Metis Population Betterment Act*, S.A. 1938, ch. 6. There the definition adopted (s.2(a)) was

    "Metis" means a person of mixed white and Indian blood but does not include either an Indian or a non-treaty Indian as defined in *The Indian Act*, …

37. Report of the Royal Commission on the Half-Breed Population (Known as the Government of Alberta, 1936, Ewing Commission), p. 13.
38. Pocklington, *op. cit.*, note 27.
39. The original drafts of the Act were reportedly prepared by Pete Tompkins and Joe Dion.
40. Sawchuk, *op. cit.*, note 14, p. 198. Other Metis elders confirm this.
41. This constitution and by-laws were adopted by the government as O.C.285/40. It was modified slightly by the settlements shortly thereafter, and the mod-

ification adopted as O.C.947/41. These two O.C.s became Alberta Regulation 634/57.

42. *The Metis Betterment Act*, S.A. 1938, c.6, s.5.
43. *The Metis Betterment Act*, 1940, S.A. 1940, c.6.
44. *Ibid.*, s.8.
45. *Ibid.*, s.9.
46. *Ibid.*, s.14.
47. *Ibid.*, s.18.
48. *The Metis Betterment Act*, S.A. 1938, c.6, s.4(2).
49. Only the name of the responsible department has been changed.
50. The settlements and the government disagree on the legitimacy of this regulation. The settlements contend that Minister's powers are limited to approving or disapproving a change in a settlement's constitution and by-laws once it has been approved by a settlement. That was the process followed on the original constitution and by-laws of the settlements adopted in 1940 (O.C.285-40), and an amendment approved in 1941 (O.C.947-41). The original constitution as amended became A.R.634/57. The settlements contend that they were not consulted on the changes that led to A.R.56/66.
51. *The Metis Betterment Act*, s. 3.
52. Sawchuk, *op. cit.*, note 14, p. 200.
53. O.C.192-60, dated February 10, 1960, rescinded the O.C.s that had set aside land for the Wolf Lake settlement. Many of the Metis who were living on the settlement at the time were moved to other settlements. Some are currently residents of the Fishing Lake Settlement.
54. Sawchuk, *op. cit.*, note 14, p. 200.
55. The Metis in their statement of claim in the action *Keg River Metis Settlement Association et al v. Her Majesty the Queen in Right of Alberta*, No. 83520, Court of Queen's Bench of Alberta, Judicial District of Edmonton, maintain that the action was contrary to the wishes of the members of the settlement association and was not within the authority provided by the *Metis Betterment Act*, c.202, R.S.A. 1955, in force at the time.
56. Alberta, *The Report of the Metis Task Force Upon The Metis Betterment Act, Metis Settlements and the Metis Rehabilitation Branch*, (Research & Planning Division, Human Resources Development Authority, Province of Alberta, February 1972).
57. *Ibid.*, p. 8.
58. *Ibid.*, p. 13.
59. The relevant regulation was, and still is, A.R.112/60.
60. The proper name for the fund under the regulation is the "Metis Population Betterment Trust Account Part I." It is commonly referred to simply as the "Trust Fund."
61. A.R. 112/60, s.1(a).
62. The statement of claim in *Poitras et al. v. Attorney-General for Alberta* was filed on July 29, 1968.
63. *Poitras et al. v. Attorney-General for Alberta* (1969) 7 D.L.R.(3d) 161(A.S.C). The Court held that the plaintiff had not complied with the requirements of the *Proceedings Against the Crown Act*, 1959 which required that permission be obtained from the Lieutenant-Governor in Council before an action could be

brought. The judge was critical of this requirement and the legislation was subsequently changed.

64. Sawchuk, *op. cit.*, note 14, p. 200.
65. The early leaders were Lawrence Desjarlais, Maurice L'Hirondelle, Adrian Hope, Sam Johnson, and Richard Poitras.
66. A statement of claim on behalf of the eight settlement associations was filed on February 5, 1974 in the Supreme Court of Alberta (*Keg River Metis Settlement Association et al v. Her Majesty the Queen in Right of Alberta*, Action No. 83520). On July 6, 1977, a second statement of claim was filed as a class action by Maurice L'Hirondelle on behalf of the settlement associations and their members (*Maurice L'Hirondelle et al v. Her Majesty the Queen in Right of Alberta*, Action No. 100945). The two actions have been joined and amended several times since the initial filing.
67. Report of the Metis Task Force, *supra*, note 56, p. 12.
68. The name of this agency was subsequently changed to the "Metis Development Branch," and more recently to the "Metis Settlements Branch." It has also made the transition from a branch of the Department of Social Services to the Department of Municipal Affairs.
69. The main federal sources were what are now the Department of Employment and Immigration and the Department of the Secretary of State. Most settlements also worked directly with half a dozen provincial departments and agencies responsible for housing, for roads, for social services, for cultural development, for grade school education and for advanced education. In addition most settlements contracted directly with oil and gas companies for work related to oil and gas exploration and development in their settlement areas.
70. In the Task Force report's summary, the third recommendation was "Rewrite the *Metis Betterment Act* to emphasize development at all levels of Metis Society."
71. The two main departments involved directly with the settlements were the Department of the Secretary of State which assisted most settlements with history- and culture-related projects, and the Department of Manpower and Immigration, which assisted in employment creation and training projects.
72. Report by the Provincial Ombudsman, Dealing with the Removal of Files from Metis Settlements on Monday, June 18/1979. For more details on the report see Sawchuk, *op. cit.* , note 14, p. 209.
73. O.C. 718/80.
74. O.C. 422/82 established the "Joint Committee to Review the *Metis Betterment Act*," gave it a mandate, named the government's representatives and the chairman, and specified that the "deliberations and recommendations of the Committee shall be without prejudice" to the litigation between the settlements and the province.
75. The President of the Federation throughout the work of the committee was Elmer Ghostkeeper. Although Mr. L'Hirondelle, the past President, served on the committee for some time, he had other obligations as the chief witness for the settlements in the litigation and eventually the current President of the Federation, Randall Hardy, took his place.
76. *Foundations for the Future of Alberta's Metis Settlements*, Report of the MacEwan Joint Metis-Government Committee to Review *The Metis Betterment Act* and

Regulations to the Honourable J.G.J. Koziak, Minister of Municipal Affairs, Government of Alberta, Edmonton, July 12, 1984.

77. The events relating to aboriginal rights and the patriation of the Constitution are well documented. See for example David C. Hawkes, "Negotiating Aboriginal Self-Government: Developments Surrounding the 1985 First Ministers' Conference," *Aboriginal Peoples and Constitutional Reform*, Background Paper No. 7 (Kingston: Queen's University, Institute of Intergovernmental Relations, 1985); or Douglas E. Sanders, "Aboriginal Peoples and the Constitution," *Alberta Law Review*, XIX No. 3, 1981, p. 410.

78. Originally *The Alberta Act*, 1905, 4-5 Edw.VII, c.3, (Can.), this Act is identified as part of the Constitution of Canada by s.52(2)(b) of the *Constitution Act, 1982.*

79. For details of the 1985 conference see Hawkes, *op. cit.*, note 77. The comments respecting Premier Lougheed are based on personal discussions at the time with the President of the Federation, Joseph Courtepatte.

80. Matters relating to the mines and minerals were to be left to the Court's decision in the natural resources litigation.

81. *Metis Settlements Act*, 1988 Bill 64, The Legislative Assembly of Alberta.

82. *Ibid.*, s.2.

83. *Ibid.*, ss. 4,8.

84. *Ibid.*, s.66.

85. *Ibid.*, s.69.

86. *Ibid.*, s.44.

87. *Ibid.*, s.54.

88. *Ibid.*, s.55.

89. *Ibid.*, s.64.

90. *Ibid.*, s.83.

91. *Ibid.*, ss.79,80,81.

92. *Ibid.*, s.77.

93. *Ibid.*, s.77(2).

94. *Ibid.*, s.96.

95. *Ibid.*, s.98.

96. *Metis Settlements Land Act*, 1988 Bill 65, The Legislative Assembly of Alberta.

97. *Ibid.*, s.2(2).

98. *Ibid.*

99. *Ibid.*, s.7.

100. The Meech Lake Accord, if ratified, should not affect the proposed approach. It provides in s.46 that an amendment under s.43 can be initiated by the legislative assembly of a province, and in s.47 that such an amendment can be made without the approval of the Senate.

101. Bill 64, s.1(h) defines a Metis as "an individual of aboriginal ancestry who identifies with Metis history and culture."

102. *Indian Act*, R.S.C. 1970, c.I-6, s. 2(1).

103. *Ibid.*, s.5, s.6, s.7.

104. *The Metis Betterment Act*, R.S.A. 1970, c.233, s.2(a).

105. Under the "old" Act, (*The Indian Act*, R.S., c.149) on application by an Indian and report by the Minister, the Governor General in Council could issue an enfranchisement order (s.109). On the effective date of the enfranchisement

order the Indian was "deemed not to be an Indian within the meaning of this Act or any other statute or law" (s.110). These sections were repealed by S.C. 1985, c.27, s.19.

106. *The Metis Betterment Act* provides for the formation of settlement associations composed of members of the Metis population of the province (s.4(1)), and the setting aside of lands (settlement areas) for occupation by the association and its members (s.6(1), s.8(a)). In practice "settlement" is used for both the association and the land. Consequently it is common to refer to a member of a settlement association both as "living on the settlement," and as a "member of the settlement."

107. The expression "91(24) Indians" is commonly used to refer to the class of people defined as Indians for the purposes of s.91(24) of the *British North America Act, 1867*, now incorporated in the Constitution as the *Constitution Act, 1867*.

108. Much of the material in this part is taken from an unpublished paper "Control of Hunting, Trapping, Fishing and Gathering on Metis Settlements" by David Covey.

109. Jurisdiction over game is dealt with in the *Constitution Act, 1867*, ss.92(13), 92(16). The proprietary interest in fisheries is provided for in *Constitution Act, 1930*, Schedule, s.9.

110. *Ibid.*, s.91(12)

111. S.A. 1987, c.W-9.1

112. R.S.C. 1970, c.F-14

113. *Constitution Act, 1867*, s.132

114. R.S.C. 1970, c.M-12. This was held to be valid legislation in *R. v. Sikyea*, (1964) 46 W.W.R. 65 (N.W.T.C.A.), affirmed 49 W.W.R. 306 (S.C.C.).

115. C.R.C. 1978, c.838

116. In s.2 the regulations define "Metis" as "a person of mixed white and Indian blood having not less than one-quarter Indian blood, but does not include an Indian or a non-treaty Indian as defined in the *Indian Act*." Is this the only operative federal government definition of "Metis"?

117. Transcript of a public affairs broadcast made December 21, 1955 by the Honourable R.D. Jorgenson, Minister of Welfare.

118. Information on the housing program is based on personal experience and on notes from discussions with Mr. Rick Beaupre, Executive Director of Rural Housing, Alberta Department of Municipal Affairs. Mr. Beaupre has played a key role in improving Metis housing in northern Alberta since the mid-1970s.

119. Waskayigan is the Cree word for "house."

120. The Report of The Metis Task Force, *supra*, note 56, p. 6.

121. *An Economic Development Mechanism for the Metis Settlements of Alberta*, Federation of Metis Settlements, September, 1979.

CHAPTER 8
FEDERAL/PROVINCIAL RESPONSIBILITY AND THE SECHELT

John P. Taylor and Gary Paget

INTRODUCTION

On June 24, 1988, the Sechelt Indian Band hosted a ceremony commemorating the achievement of self-government, a day marking the symbolic conclusion to a long fight. They celebrated freedom from the *Indian Act*, the establishment of their own band constitution, achievement of control of band lands and the establishment of relatively autonomous self-government with a wide range of powers. The provincial government praised the Sechelts for pioneering a form of self-government which can become a model for other Indian bands, particularly because it enables the Sechelts to take their place at the table with other local governments in the province. Saul Terry, President of the Union of British Columbia Indian Chiefs, countered with his concern that native Indian government structures were being cast aside in favour of municipal type arrangements, governed entirely by provincial government legislation.[1]

Clearly, there are many perspectives on Sechelt Indian self-government reflecting the diversity of views on the complicated issue of aboriginal self-government in both British Columbia and other parts of Canada. Unfortunately, the larger debate has a tendency to overshadow and to distort perceptions of what is, in fact, a unique experiment in aboriginal self-government.

The primary focus of this chapter is on the design and implementation of the Sechelt self-government model. Viewing the model from the outside, the authors assisted the Province of British Columbia in the implementation of its responsibilities with respect to the Sechelts. Consequently, the primary focus is on the federal and provincial context and the legislative, political, administrative, financial and service structure implications for the Sechelt Indian government. Others undoubtedly will examine the Sechelt model from other perspectives.

We wish to emphasize that the Sechelt model is one of a number of approaches to achieving self-governance for aboriginal peoples. In David Hawkes' terms it can be described as an ethnic, local form of aboriginal self-government, with a high degree of autonomy.[2] Aboriginal self-government is well adapted to the unique characteristics of the Sechelt and their environment. This model was developed for a highly urbanized, strategically located, relatively prosperous band, holding lands with immense development potential. However, since the Indian community in Canada represents a diversity of values, aspirations and situations, the Sechelt model may not be applicable to other aboriginal peoples, for example, a more traditional band, with a weak economic base, located some distance from an urban area. We concur with David Hawkes' observation:

> What is clear is that no single approach or model will meet the needs or aspirations of all aboriginal people. A "universal formula" is doomed to failure.[3]

We believe that each native community will have to determine for itself what form of self-governance it wishes. It is our hope that this chapter, which describes, analyzes and evaluates the Sechelt's model of self-government, will contribute to the development of understanding and dialogue and the furtherance of native self-governance in Canada.

This chapter is organized into seven parts. After the introduction, section two provides essential context for a discussion of the Sechelt model. It examines aboriginal issues in British Columbia, the unique nature and situation of the Sechelts and their quest for local self-government. It also outlines the objectives of the key participants; the band, the Government of Canada and the province. The third section depicts the legislative framework for Sechelt self-government. Section four analyzes the political and administrative structure of the Sechelt model, and section five describes the functioning of the Sechelt model in terms of federal and provincial fiscal relations, the provision of services, and land and resource issues. Section six examines the implications of the Sechelt model for the Sechelt Band, the Government of Canada, the Province of British Columbia, local governments and other Indian bands. Section seven provides the conclusion.

NATIVE ISSUES IN BRITISH COLUMBIA, THE SECHELT AND SELF-GOVERNMENT

Introduction

The Sechelt Indian self-government model represents a unique response to the desires of a particular Indian band for increased autonomy. In order to appreciate the model, it is vital to understand the context in which it was developed, as well as the unique features and situation of the Sechelts. While the development of the model was spearheaded by the band itself, implementation required action by both federal and provincial governments. Clearly, in order for it to be successfully implemented, it had to be well adapted to its context. This section studies the current aboriginal issues in British Columbia, examines the unique characteristics and situation of the Sechelt people and draws these threads together by considering the objectives of the Sechelt band, the federal government and the province in pursuing self-governance for the Sechelts.

Native Issues in British Columbia

British Columbia has been engaged for many years in a debate with the native community in two areas: native/provincial/local government fiscal relations and aboriginal self-government. Provincial objectives in each of the two areas have established constraints and created opportunities for the development of self-government for the Sechelts. However, on balance, a combination of these have created a magnificent opportunity for the Sechelts to achieve a form of self-government which is well adapted to their unique situation.

The Native Presence

Native people are a significant component of the province's population base, social life and political culture. The native population in British Columbia, approximately 93,000 persons, is second only to Ontario's in size. It comprises approximately three per cent of the provincial population a percentage exceeded only by Manitoba and Saskatchewan. The native population is made up of approximately 194 Indian bands occupying some 1,628 reserves located in all parts of the province but concentrated in the southwest, along the coast and along the major river systems.[4] In comparison to other provinces, more of the native population is urbanized and resides in close proximity to urban areas. This spatial pattern has led to a unique set of service relationships and political problems.

Native/Provincial/Local Fiscal Relationships

The provision of local services and the recovery of costs are contentious issues in British Columbia between Indian bands, the provincial government and local government. The large number of bands and their relatively small size make it difficult for all but the largest to provide a full range of services for themselves. Consequently, bands have either joined in co-operative arrangements with other bands or the non-native community to provide services.[5] The latter arrangement has been facilitated by the close spatial proximity of the native and non-native communities. Over the years a complex pattern of inter-dependent services has developed between the Indian bands, local government and the province.[6] In some cases Indian reserves have actually been incorporated within municipal boundaries; 26 municipalities have some 45 Indian reserves within their boundaries. More commonly, services are provided to bands by local governments on a service contract basis.

While these arrangements have been of practical advantage they have also been contentious.[7] From the province's perspective, the primary source of conflict has been non-Indian occupiers of band lands. In a highly urbanized province, it is inevitable that urban development will spill over municipal boundaries onto Indian lands. British Columbia has jealously guarded provincial and local government prerogatives to levy property taxes on non-Indian occupiers of band lands, while respecting the non-taxability of Indians on band lands. It argues that all real property owners in the province should be treated the same and be subjected to general taxation. The Indian bands, in turn, see the imposition of provincial taxes as an intrusion into federal or Indian jurisdiction. Moreover, Indian bands argue that non-Indian occupiers pay for services they do not receive, that they have no influence over the level of services provided, yet must make the required payment. Bands have achieved full taxing authority over reserve lands through Bill C115. They have also attempted to remove external taxation. In some cases, Indian bands have argued that they lack access to the full benefits of provincial financial programs, particularly those directed at local government.

Over the years the province and Indian bands have attempted to find solutions to these problems. In the late 1960s the province amended the *Municipal Act*, to enable Indian reserves to incorporate as "Indian municipalities." The province's intent was to create the opportunity for Indians to enjoy the benefits of municipalization without jeopardizing their special federal status, in particular, the federal responsibility for their land. To date, no Indian band has chosen to embark on this path, although in 1972, the Cape Mudge Band voted 71 per cent in favour of incorporation. The statutory requirement for success was 75 per cent at that time. Indians generally were fearful of losing their special relationship with the federal government.[8] Also, many were fearful that a "public government" could lead to political domination of Indians by non-Indians.

In the early 1980s, the province was involved with the Government of Canada and Indian organizations in the Tripartite Local Government Committee which examined Indian government in British Columbia. The report of the committee suggested a number of alternate approaches to the resolution of outstanding problems, including tax revenue sharing, a local services commission and full local government status.[9] While there was no immediate result from the work of the committee, it was significant in that the Sechelts participated directly in the committee and strongly influenced the recommendations, in particular, the full local government status option. More recently a series of "Indian Issues Forums," sponsored by the Union of British Columbia Municipalities, has attempted to develop a better understanding of native issues as they relate to local government.[10]

Attempts to solve native/provincial fiscal and servicing problems have usually focused on solutions rooted in local government as opposed to Indian government institutions. This is not surprising because the natural tendency of provincial governments will be to focus on familiar solutions which will dominate the province's perception of both the larger issue of Indian self-governance and the particular issue of self-governance for the Sechelt. However, municipal-type solutions have been resisted, for the most part, by Indian bands.

Native Land Claims

The second major issue which provides a critical context for the discussion of Sechelt self-governance, is aboriginal land claims. The dominance of this issue in the province is a consequence of the fact that the federal government did not negotiate treaties with aboriginal peoples, except on Vancouver Island and a portion of northeastern British Columbia.[11] The issue was brought to a head by the 1973 Calder case, in which the judges of the Supreme Court of Canada split evenly on whether the aboriginal title continued to exist. The result was a federal policy statement advocating negotiated settlement of land claims in non-treaty areas.

Since 1984, the Government of Canada has accepted 18 comprehensive land claims in British Columbia while a further 11 claims are under review or are expected to be filed.[12] These claims are based on aboriginal use that the claimants state has never been extinguished. The federal government has accepted these claims but, as a condition of their acceptance, insists that the province also negotiate and provide a land base. The province has refused to do this, partly because of the fear of the consequences: 260 of the 360 million square miles in the province are under some type of comprehensive claim. The question of aboriginal title is now before the courts with the Gitskan-Wet'suewet'en. Also, the province's position has consistently been that aboriginal title does not exist; if it did, it was extinguished; and if not extinguished, it is a federal responsibility pursuant to the *Terms of the Union* and the *Constitution Act, 1867*.[13]

Clearly, the aboriginal land claims issue has an importance and prominence in British Columbia unlike any other province. It provides a back-drop for the discussion of all native issues in the province; it places the province in contention with the Government of Canada and the native Indian leadership; and it has placed pressure on the provincial government to substantiate its good will towards native people and to demonstrate its commitment to resolving outstanding grievances of native peoples.

Native Self-Governance

Section 37 of the *Constitution Act, 1982,* indicates that a constitutional conference will be convened by the Prime Minister to consider matters that directly affect aboriginal peoples, including the identification and definition of their rights. At the first conference in 1984, the federal government proposed the constitutional entrenchment of the aboriginal "right to self-governing institutions." However, British Columbia and five other provinces rejected constitutional entrenchment. The British Columbia government argued that natives within the province could achieve self-government by becoming regular provincial municipalities. [14]

The British Columbia government has continued to reject constitutional entrenchment to the right of self-government. The major concern has been the lack of definition of the concept, and an absence of a thorough analysis of its implications. A further fear of the province was that it would create a third level of government. Nonetheless, the provincial government has indicated its willingness to deal with individual Indian bands on suitable self-governance arrangements.

The Sechelt Indian Band

The Sechelt model of self-governance can only be understood in the context of the particular situation of the Sechelt. The favorable location of the band lands, the demographic mix on band lands, the cultural characteristics of the Sechelt people and the strong economic base of the band have together resulted in a particular model of self-governance. Although the Sechelt model is well adapted to the particular circumstances of a unique Indian band, it may not be the perfect model for bands with different circumstances. This section explores the band and its environment.

Location

The Sechelt band is located on the Sechelt Peninsula, approximately 58 kilometres (36 miles) by road and ferry from Vancouver (Figure 1). Sechelt is a native word denoting "place of shelter from the sea." The band's tribal base, the former Sechelt Indian Reserve No. 2, is located at the head of Sechelt Inlet immediately adjacent to the primary non-native community, the District of Sechelt which

303

Fig

**LOCATION OF THE
SECHELT INDIAN BAND**

has a population of 4,900 (Figure 2). The band has extensive land holdings comprising 32 former reserves totalling 1,000 hectares, or 2,532 acres, scattered throughout the region (Figure 3). The majority of the lands are located within the Sunshine Coast Regional District, a region which is physically attractive, and possesses a moderate climate with considerably more sunshine and less rainfall than Vancouver. One site is located in the adjacent Powell River Regional District. As a consequence of the location and environment, the Sunshine Coast attracts considerable development, particularly to accommodate retired people, second home owners and recreation development.

People

The Sechelt band is of the Coast Salish ethnic division and the Sechelt linguistic division; it comprises part of the northwest coast cultural complex, typified by totem poles and the potlatch. The current population of the band is about 700 persons, of which 568 live on Sechelt lands. In 1986, these lands were also home to about 500 non-Indians, making a total population of 1,000 living on Sechelt lands. The fact that non-Indian occupiers are such a predominant proportion of the population on the Sechelt band lands has significance for the political structure of the band today, and in the future; the non-Indian population is anticipated to grow significantly as land is developed. The Sechelts are socially, economically and politically well integrated into the surrounding community.

Economy

The Sechelts have a thriving band economy particularly in comparison to other bands in the province. Band enterprises play a predominant role in this prosperity. Possessing a rich land and resource base, the band is engaged in land development; specialty forest products manufacturing; gravel extraction; forestry; aquaculture; and also has a controlling interest in a commuter airline, Thunderbird Air. A marina/hotel complex and condominiums are planned. In addition, there are beginnings of individual enterprise. Finally, these lands offer a high level of off-band employment.

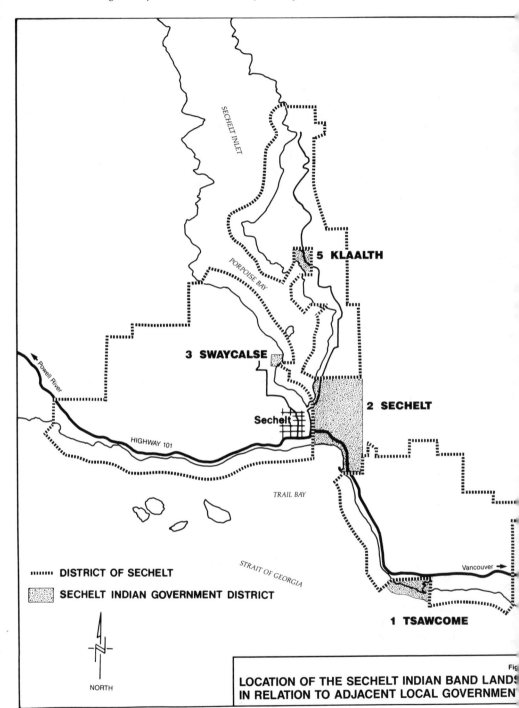

LOCATION OF THE SECHELT INDIAN BAND LANDS IN RELATION TO ADJACENT LOCAL GOVERNMEN

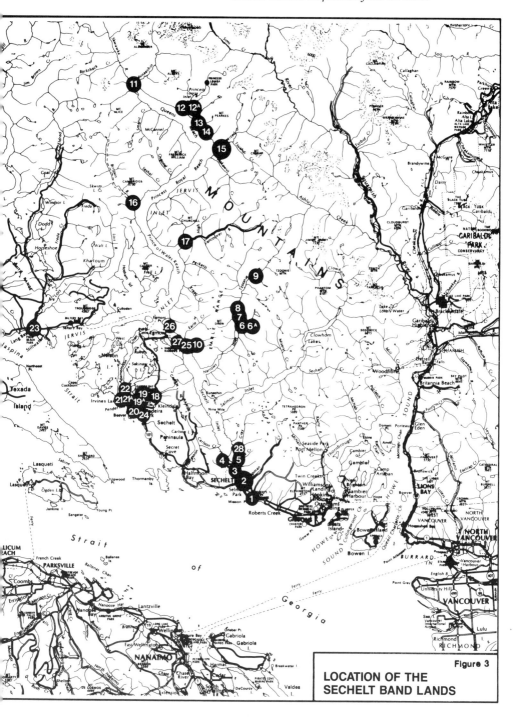

Figure 3

LOCATION OF THE SECHELT BAND LANDS

Objectives in the Pursuit of Self-Governance

The Sechelt self-government model, which ultimately manifested itself in both a federal and provincial statute, can only be understood in the context of the objectives of three parties: the Sechelt band; the Government of Canada; and the Province of British Columbia. The Sechelt band took the initiative and pushed diligently for self-governance over a 15-year span. Intense negotiations between the three parties, from 1983 to 1988, led to substantial conclusions. The success of these discussions was a consequence of a commitment by all parties to a favourable outcome.

Sechelt Objectives

The primary motivating factor for the Sechelt in seeking self-governance, has been the frustration they experienced in developing band lands. They felt crippled by the restrictions of the *Indian Act* and the lack of direct control over band lands. The band had achieved the maximum authority or autonomy within the context of the *Indian Act*. Nonetheless, the Sechelts saw the solution to their problems in autonomous band government, totally in control of its land base. While the band was supportive of the efforts of the national aboriginal leadership to achieve constitutional entrenchment of the rights to self-government, they did not want to wait for the conclusion of the First Ministers' Conferences on the Constitution mandated by the *Constitution Act, 1982*. Consequently, they negotiated directly with the federal and provincial governments to achieve a legislated form of self-government.

Moreover, the Sechelts had a unique objective in the pursuit of self-governance rooted in their particular local history. Former Chief Stanley Dixon described his objective as: "the acceptance of responsibility for our community's well-being to increase both community and individual opportunity, to work with our neighbour communities to improve the quality of life for all citizens."[15] The Sechelts wished to achieve self-governance within the fabric of the larger society at the local, regional and provincial scales. In other words, they wanted the benefits of integration into the local, regional and provincial system, without jeopardizing their own independent status, their special relationship with the federal government, or gains that might be realized at a later date through settlement of aboriginal land claims or constitutional entrenchment of the right to self-government.

Over a 15-year period, the Sechelts participated actively in a number of forums pursuing their particular model of self-governance. The full local government status alternative of the Tripartite Local Government Committee was largely the product of Sechelt participation; Chief Gilbert Joe and Graham Allan, legal advisor, were members of the committee. Failure to achieve substantive changes, as a result of the work of the committee, led the Sechelts to seek solutions in federal forums. Although the Sechelts made a major submission to the Penner Committee,[16] they were not successful until there was a dramatic shift in federal objectives in pursuit of self-governance.

Federal Government Objectives

The federal government's objectives, with respect to the Sechelt, reflect a larger policy agenda to embrace Indian self-government. The present government has built upon the overall thrust of the Penner Report, in an attempt to create a new relationship between Indian First Nations and the federal government.[17] The federal government has supported efforts to entrench local self-government in the Constitution. Simultaneously, however, it has attempted to establish the meaning of self-government through practical experimentation at the local level. Inherent in this approach, appears to be a belief that self-government is a local event with different meanings for different communities. Consequently, they felt that attempts at self-government have to be flexible in order to recognize the diverse needs, traditions and cultures of native people.[18]

The federal government articulated their philosophy in the *Policy Statement on Indian Self-Government in Canada*, issued in April 1986. This statement placed the emphasis on measured approaches to self-government, based on community by community negotiation:

> I want to emphasize that those communities which do not feel ready to move toward greater self-government need not feel under pressure to do so. In the end it will be up to each of Canada's Indian communities to decide whether or not it wishes to undertake the journey. We will help those which wish to move towards self-government but will continue to provide services, as we have in the past, for those which are not yet ready to change.[19]

With the Sechelts, the federal government saw an opportunity to respond to a community which had a clear idea of the form of self-governance it wanted, and which was quite prepared to move quickly towards a maximum degree of autonomy. In this respect the Sechelts provided a concrete opportunity to demonstrate the government's self-government policy. The minister was careful to caution that "The Sechelt proposal reflects that community's aspirations; it is not a model for others."[20]

Provincial Government Objectives

The province's objectives in facilitating local self-government for the Sechelts, were in direct relationship to the stance it was taking on native/provincial fiscal relations, native land claims and the question of constitutional entrenchment of the right to self-governance. The Sechelts provided the province with an opportunity to demonstrate, at the band level, what it was attempting to achieve in its overall provincial policy. Specifically, it wished to demonstrate that self-governance could be achieved without the necessity of constitutional entrenchment. Moreover, it has seen the Sechelts as a model that can form the basis for self-government proposals and initiatives from other bands across the province. It is also clear that a provincial objective was to set a precedent for resolving native grievances through self-government, rather than through the framework of comprehensive land claims settlements. The province's objective was to signal to other bands its willingness to discuss self-government rather than land claims.

Finally, it was the province's objective, that the Sechelt Indian self-government be integrated within the provincial system of local government and property taxation. The government explicitly sought to avoid creation of a third level of government, with a separate constitutional status derived from the federal government. It sought instead a municipal or local form of self-governance for Indian bands. This would mean that Indian bands would receive the benefits that municipalities in the province would normally receive, while being under the supervision of provincial statutes, in particular the *Municipal Act*. As we shall see, the province pursued this objective even though it lacked the full constitutional authority to see it fully realized.

THE LEGISLATIVE FRAMEWORK FOR SECHELT SELF-GOVERNMENT

The legislative structure of the Sechelt Indian government is illustrated in Figure 4. This section dissects this legislative framework into its three most significant components: the *Sechelt Indian Band Self-Government Act* (Canada); the *Sechelt Indian Government District Enabling Act* (British Columbia) and ancillary legislation; and the Sechelt Band Constitution. The purpose is to demonstrate the complex constitutional interrelationships which lie behind the Sechelt model, and explore its unique constitutional nature.

Figure 4

Legislative Structure of Sechelt Indian Self-Government

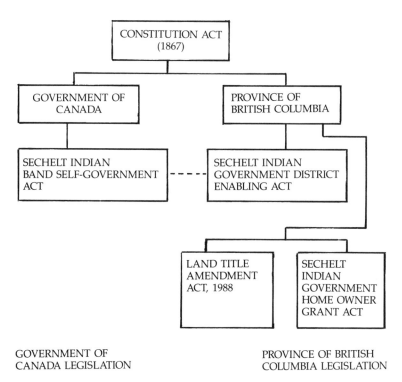

GOVERNMENT OF
CANADA LEGISLATION

PROVINCE OF BRITISH
COLUMBIA LEGISLATION

Sechelt Indian Band Self-Government Act (Canada)

The cornerstone of the Sechelt model is the *Sechelt Indian Band Self-Government Act*, which was given Royal Assent on June 17, 1986. In this Act, the Government of Canada has exercised its exclusive jurisdiction under s.91(24) of the *Constitution Act, 1867* for "Indians, and lands reserved for the Indians." The *Sechelt Indian Band Self-Government Act* is an enabling statute: it creates the Sechelt Band and its form of self-government, and delegates authority and responsibilities to that end. The purpose of the Act is to "enable the Sechelt Indian Band to exercise and maintain self-government on Sechelt lands, and to obtain control over and the administration of the resources and services available to its members." The Act establishes the Sechelt Indian Band as the primary government body on Sechelt lands [s.5(1)]. It specfies that the powers and duties of the band are to be carried out in accordance with a band constitution, the contents of which are specified and which must be approved by referendum of the band and the federal Cabinet. The Act provides for a further transfer of band powers to a quasi-local government body, the Sechelt Indian Government District, but only if the transfer is approved by a referendum of the band, and only if the Legislature of British Columbia has passed legislation relating to the District. This, as we shall see, is in deference to provincial responsibilities in the fields of local government, property and civil rights.

The federal statute effectively removes the Sechelt Band from the purview of the *Indian Act*. According to s.35(1), the *Indian Act* applies, except to the extent that it conflicts with the *Sechelt Indian Band Self-Government Act*, the constitution of the band, or a law of the band. In other words, if the band wishes, it can override the *Indian Act*. In addition, the federal Cabinet may specify that portions of the *Indian Act* do not apply. Clearly, the intent is to create every opportunity for the Sechelt to operate with a high degree of local autonomy and minimal federal intervention. Federal controls on the band are largely restricted to approving the constitution, establishing rules for referenda, and approving procedures relating to the transfer of lands from the federal government to the band. Nonetheless, the Sechelt Indian Band is a federal creature; s.37 indicates that "all federal laws of general application in force in Canada are applicable to the band, its members and its lands." Consequently, while the band has an unprecedented degree of local autonomy it most emphatically is not fully autonomous.

The *Sechelt Indian Band Self-Government Act* gives the Sechelts effective control of Sechelt lands. All lands which were previously Indian reserves, held in trust by the federal government, are transferred to the Sechelt band "for the use and benefit of the band and its members." These lands cease to be "Indian reserves" and become band lands. The band has the full power to dispose of band lands, provided that it is done within the context of rules established in the band constitution. This solidifies band control of one of the critical economic strengths of the Sechelts, its considerable land base, and further reinforces the political and administrative autonomy of the band. Moreover, the statute authorizes band registration of estates or interests in Sechelt lands, and for that purpose the band may make any laws of British Columbia applicable to those lands. Nonetheless, s.31 of the Act indicates that band lands remain "Indian lands" within the meaning of s.91 of the *Constitution Act, 1867*. As we shall see, this is of critical importance when considering the province's role with respect to Sechelt Band lands.

Section 33 of the *Sechelt Indian Band Self-Government Act* provides an additional degree of financial independence for the band. It enables the Minister of Indian and Northern Affairs, with permission of Cabinet, to enter into agreements with the Sechelt Band to facilitate the provision of grants. This section gives the band and the federal government the flexibility to negotiate block grant funding for the Indian band, providing the band with unprecedented budgetary flexibility, which should contribute to the achievement of the benefits of fiscal federalism.[21] Consistent with the principles of fiscal federalism, an autonomous band will receive a fair share of federal fiscal resources while having a maximum degree of freedom to allocate its monies where it sees fit. In this way, the services provided by the band can more closely match the needs and desires of band members.

In conclusion, the *Sechelt Indian Band Self-Government Act* provides the legislative framework for the exercise of self-government by the Sechelt Band. In this respect, it falls short of the Penner Committee's ultimate recommendation of "constitutional entrenchment," but is consistent with the committee's evolutionary approach to the achievement of self-government.[22] The Sechelts statute explicitly states that "nothing in this Act shall be construed so as to abrogate or derogate from any existing aboriginal or treaty rights of the members of the Sechelt Indian band, or any aboriginal peoples of Canada, under section 37 of the *Constitution Act, 1982.*" The significance of this section is two-fold. On one hand, the Sechelt Band and all other bands are free to pursue aboriginal land claims without prejudice. The Sechelts have submitted a comprehensive land claim as well as seven specific land claims. On the other hand, the Sechelt Band's choice of self-government will not detract from the efforts of aboriginals at large to achieve constitutional entrenchment of aboriginal rights to self-government through the constitutional process mandated by s.37 of the *Constitution Act, 1982.*

The Sechelt Indian Band Constitution

The band constitution is the primary legislative instrument of the Sechelt Band. The federal statute sets out the substantive elements of the constitution, and the process for adopting and amending the band constitution. Substantively, the provision for the band to develop and maintain its own constitution differs greatly from the *Indian Act*, where the organization of band government is highly prescribed and uniform.[23] The concept of a constitution provides the Sechelt Band with considerable latitude in determining how it is to be governed. Although the constitution is a delegated authority from the federal Parliament, it also expresses the will of the local people; the constitution must be developed by the band and ratified by a band referendum.

The functions of the Sechelt Band constitution are set out in s.10 of the federal statute, and are summarized in Figure 5. Many of these elements—for example, procedures, financial accountability measures and the specifics of tenures and elections—are common to conventional constitutions of parliamentary democracies, or of local governments. More interesting, from the native perspective, are the powers to establish a membership code and to establish rules and procedures to be followed, in respect of the disposition of rights and interests in Sechelt lands. These two elements go to the heart of native self-government. The ability to establish a membership code means that band members can define themselves in tribal terms, while the ability to control the disposition of Sechelt lands means that the land and resource base, which form the foundation of the band economy, are under effective local control. The only constraints set out in the legislation are that the constitution reflect the matters set out in the statute. In addition, the rights of

Figure 5

Functions of the Sechelt Indian Band Constitution

- establishes composition of band council, term of office, tenure of members and election procedures;
- establishes band council procedures;
- provides for financial accountability of the council to band members including audits and reports;
- mandates a membership code;
- establishes rules for referenda;
- establishes rules and procedures for disposition, rights and interests in Sechelt lands;
- sets out legislative powers of the council selected amongst a set of general powers contained in the statute;
- provides for other matters relating to the government of the band.

Source: *Sechelt Indian Band Self-Government Act, s.10 and 2.11*

Indians who were members of the Sechelt Band prior to the establishment of the membership code, are protected; they are declared members of the band.

The band constitution was adopted by band referendum on September 26, 1986, and in turn, was approved by the federal Cabinet. The constitution is a flexible and powerful instrument for the Sechelts. It provides them with the opportunity to choose collectively how to define themselves, govern themselves and manage their resources. This can be done with minimal interference from the federal government. Moreover, the band constitution can be a significant constraint on provincial actions. Significantly, the legislative actions of the band under its constitution are laws, not by-laws. Furthermore, these laws have the status of federal laws.

The Sechelt Indian Government District Enabling Act (British Columbia)

The *Sechelt Indian Government District Enabling Act*, proclaimed on July 23, 1987, is a companion piece of legislation to the federal *Sechelt Indian Band Self-Government Act*, but considerably more modest in scope; while the federal statute has 61 sections running eight pages, the provincial statute is a modest eight sections, covering three pages. In enacting this statute, the province is exercising its exclusive powers granted under the *Constitution Act, 1867*. These are, specifically: s.92(2), direct taxation; s.92(8), municipal institutions; and s.92(13), property and civil rights. However, provincial powers with respect to the Sechelt Indian Band are relatively limited. Nonetheless, the provincial statute is significant for a number of reasons: it recognizes the Sechelt Indian Government District; it clarifies provincial powers with respect to the Sechelts; it establishes an appointed advisory council; it ensures that provincial laws apply; it confers provincial benefits on the band; it suspends direct provincial property taxation; and it enables the delegation of provincial responsibilities to the band. Each is considered below.

The primary purpose of the provincial statute is to recognize the federally mandated government, the Sechelt Indian Government District, which "shall have jurisdiction over all Sechelt lands." This is a significant provincial action because the Indian Government District has jurisdiction over non-band occupiers of Indian lands, as well as band members. Traditionally, the Province of British Columbia has recognized federal jurisdiction over Indians and Indian lands. However, it has consistently maintained its authority over non-Indians and non-Indian occupiers of Indian lands. It is significant that the federal statute provides that the federal Cabinet cannot declare sections of the Act relating to the District in force, or transfer powers, duties or functions of the band or council to the District, unless the Legislature of British Columbia has passed legislation respecting the District, and the legislation is in force. In effect, the Government of Canada is asking the provincial legislature to assent to the creation of the Sechelt Indian Government District, to the transfer of municipal type powers to the District, and to granting jurisdiction over all Sechelt lands to the District. Clearly, the federal government was reluctant to embark on such a significant venture without the consent of British Columbia. This is understandable given that the federal statute deals with laws for non-Indians, and creates a quasi-local government jurisdiction.

The Province of British Columbia deferred to the interests of the Sechelt Band and the Government of Canada. The *Sechelt Indian Government District Enabling Act* enables the provincial Cabinet to recognize the district council as the governing body of the Sechelt Indian Government District. This was done by a Proclamation issued July 23, 1987. By these actions, the province has accepted the creation of the Indian Government District, and its jurisdiction over all Indian lands.

The second purpose of the *Sechelt Indian Government District Enabling Act* is to clarify matters of provincial jurisdiction with respect to the Sechelt Band. Section 1(2) of the provincial statute indicates that "Nothing in this Act shall be construed as a conferral on or authorizing the conferral on the District Council or the Advisory Council of legislative powers." This is because it is only the federal statute, the *Sechelt Indian Band Self-Government Act*, which can accomplish this. Section 3 of the provincial statute provides further clarification of the role of the province with respect to the Sechelts. It indicates that where the district council enacts laws or by-laws that a municipality has the power to enact under a provincial statute, these by-laws shall, for the purpose of the *Sechelt Indian Government District Enabling Act*, be deemed to have been enacted under the authority of that provincial statute. In other words, the Sechelt Indian Government District is free to use provincial statutes such as the *Municipal Act*, and this use is recognized by the province. However, this does not mean that the Sechelt Indian Government District is compelled to follow the *Municipal Act*. On the contrary, the Sechelt Band, to a large extent, is free to choose from a menu of provincial statutes, and adopt them for its own purposes.

These observations on the provincial statute can be confirmed by re-examining the companion federal statute. Section 14(3) of the *Sechelt Indian Band Self-Government Act* enables the band to adopt any law of British Columbia as its own law, if its constitution authorizes the band to make laws in relation to the subject matter of those laws. Furthermore, s.15 and s.22 of that Act indicate that the band council and the district council, respectively, may exercise any power granted to it by a provincial statute. Finally, and most critically, s.38 of the federal statute indicates that: "Laws of general application of British Columbia apply to or are in respect of the members of the band except to the extent that those laws are inconsistent with the terms of any treaty, this or any other Act of Parliament, the constitution of the Band or a law of the Band." In conclusion, the band and the Indian Government District have a maximum degree of autonomy from the provincial government consistent with their federal status but there are opportunities in taking advantage of provincial statutes.

A third function of the provincial statute is to provide for the creation of an advisory council, the roles and functions of which are discussed in more detail below. The significance of the council in the legislative framework is its provincial genesis; it is created by provincial statute, is appointed initially by the provincial Cabinet, and is subsequently elected under rules established by that Cabinet. The advisory council is the province's window on the Sechelt Indian Government District, and the primary mechanism for the non-Indian occupiers of Sechelt lands to participate directly in the affairs of the District. Consequently, it is a fundamental mechanism for protecting provincial interests in the Sechelt Indian Government District.

Another function of the provincial statute is to create the possibility for *quid pro quo* financial arrangements. It provides the opportunity for the District to participate in the benefits that are normally available to all municipalities in the province. This responds to a major objective of the province and a history of complaints by Indian bands in the province that they do not receive the full benefit of provincial programs. Section 4 enables the province to provide the District with provincial benefits associated with full municipal status. More critically, this section explicitly recognizes the Sechelt Indian Government District as a municipality, not unlike other municipalities in the province, at least in terms of receiving the benefits of being a municipality. As we have already seen, the direct provincial jurisdiction over the Sechelt Indian Government District is largely lacking, but s.4 means that the province will treat Sechelt as a "municipality," even though this is a municipality of quite a different order than the conventional municipality in the province. Nonetheless, the provincial statute provides the province with considerable leverage; the province can specify requirements to be met by the district council in order to be entitled to, or eligible for, the benefits of provincial municipal programs. In fact, this becomes the basis for implementation of a series of *quid pro quo* financial arrangements between the province and the band.

In addition, the provincial statute provides the opportunity for the provincial Cabinet to suspend the provincial property taxes on non-Indian occupiers of band lands. Consequently, a perennial irritant to the Sechelts is removed. In theory, the province's concession in this area provides the band with complete freedom to raise all property taxes on the Sechelt lands in order to provide local services to band members and non-Indian occupiers. However, in practice this concession allowed for negotiation of an appropriate fiscal regime between the band and the province.

The final feature of the legislation is its 20-year life span; the Act is repealed on June 30, 2006, unless a referendum of the band and the provincial Cabinet approve a continuation of the Act. Clearly, this clause commits the province and the band to review and evaluate the legislation after the benefit of 20 years of experience. In this sense, the province's legislation is experimental. In particular, this gives the Province the opportunity to consider whether the interests of non-Indian occupiers are being well looked after.

In conclusion, the *Sechelt Indian Government District Enabling Act* lays bare the provincial context for the Sechelts to exercise self-government. It is clear that the District is a federal creature created by federal statute; the province's role with respect to the district is limited since it explicitly concedes federal jurisdiction over Indians and non-Indians. However, the provincial statute does provide the opportunity for the province to treat the District as a conventional municipality, as if it were created under the provincial statute, and to confer the benefits on the Sechelts that would normally accrue to such a municipality. In turn, this creates the opportunity for negotiation of *quid pro quo* fiscal arrangements.

Other Provincial Enabling Legislation

Implementation of the Sechelt self-government model required the provincial legislature to adopt two other pieces of legislation: *The Land Title Amendment Act, 1988* and the *Sechelt Indian Government District Home Owner Grant Act*.

The *Land Title Amendment Act, 1988* is a complex, technical amendment to the *Land Title Act*. It provides for the registration under the *Land Title Act* of the title to Indian lands held by or granted in fee simple. While initiated to facilitate the achievement of self-governance for the Sechelts, it is not specifically referenced to them. In fact, the legislation could be used by any other band in the province that wishes to gain access to the Torrens land registration system.

The Sechelts wanted the opportunity to place title to lands leased to non-Indian occupiers, within the provincial land registry system in order to give security to lessees of Indian lands, thereby facilitating necessary financing. At present, it is difficult for an Indian band, an Indian or a non-Indian leasing Indian land, to borrow from a bank, using the security of the land. As a consequence of this amendment, Sechelt Band lands will be more marketable.

Furthermore, it will contribute to the increase in the value of Sechelt lands, thereby strengthening the economic base of the community.

It is the intent of the Sechelt Band that only leased band lands be registered in the provincial system, and although the leased lands are within the provincial system, they still are Indian lands pursuant to the *Constitution Act, 1867.* The band has been brought into the provincial system for a specific purpose with no loss of autonomy or status.

The *Sechelt Indian Government District Home Owner Grant Act* is a relatively simple piece of legislation, making members of the Sechelt Indian Band eligible for the provincial Home Owner Grant. Although this grant is provided to all homeowners in the province, typically, Indians living on reserves do not qualify for it while non-Indian occupiers of band lands do. This statute ensures that Indian and non-Indians residing on Sechelt band lands, each qualify for the Home Owner Grant.

Conclusion

The Sechelt Indian Band self-governance model represents a unique achievement for the Sechelts. It gives them almost complete political and administrative autonomy, freedom from the scrutiny of the *Indian Act,* control of band lands, considerable financial independence and their own band constitution. At the same time, the achievement of this model has been accomplished with the acquiescence, and, in fact, the active participation of the provincial government. The resulting legislative structure is a complex mixture of federal, provincial and band legislative instruments which mirror the complex constitutional status of native people in Canada.

THE POLITICAL AND ADMINISTRATIVE STRUCTURE OF SECHELT SELF-GOVERNMENT

The political and administrative structure of Sechelt self-government is established in the *Sechelt Indian Band Self- Government Act* (Canada) and the *Sechelt Local Government District Enabling Act* (British Columbia). The structure, illustrated in Figure 6, has four components: the two federally mandated institutions, the Sechelt Indian Band and the Sechelt Indian Government District, are

Figure 6

Political and Administrative Structure of Sechelt Self-Governance

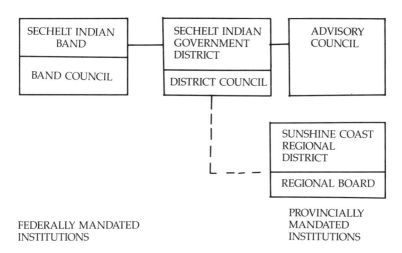

predominant. Each is an autonomous legal entity with a broad range of corporate powers. The governing body of the Sechelt Indian Band, the Sechelt Indian Band Council, can exercise a broad reach of legislative powers but at the same time, a process is established whereby the band can transfer these powers to the district council. This creates the possibility for an effective division of powers between what could be described as a "band government" and "local government." In turn the province, through the *Sechelt Indian Government District Act*, solidifies the local government component by providing for an advisory council to the district council and enabling the District to be a member of the Sunshine Coast Regional District.

The Sechelt Indian Band

The *Sechelt Indian Band Self-Government Act* establishes the Sechelt Indian Band as an independent, autonomous body, replacing the *Indian Act* band. It has "the capacity, rights, powers and privileges

321

of a natural person." This resolves a serious problem that inhibited the development of acceptable contractual relationships between local government, non-Indians and Indian bands; the Indian band, in the eyes of the common law, is not a legal entity. The Sechelt Indian Band Council is declared to be the governing body of the band. Band council members are elected according to the band constitution which indicates that council ers must be band members and that only band members can vote.

The band council's powers encompass matters which are commonly thought to be federal, provincial and municipal responsibilities (Figure 7). In fact, a similar but not identical, melange of powers exists in the *Indian Act*. One crucial difference relates to the addition of several critical powers relating to the devolution of real property of band members on Sechelt lands, taxation of occupants

Figure 7

Legislative Powers Potentially Exercisable by the Sechelt Band Council

1. access to and residence on Sechelt lands
2. zoning and land use
3. expropriation of lands for community purposes
4. building regulation
5. assessment and taxation
6. administration of band lands
7. education
8. social and welfare services
9. health
10. preservation and management of natural resources
11. management of fish and wildlife
12. public order and safety
13. road construction, maintenance and regulation
14. regulation of businesses and professions
15. liquor regulation
16. imposition of fines
17. devolution of band lands
18. financial administration
19. conduct of band elections/referendum
20. creation of administrative bodies
21. matters related to good government
22. power to adopt any law of the Province of B.C. as its own law
23. exercise any power assigned to it by the province

of band lands, and expropriation powers. A further critical difference is that all of these powers can be exercised with virtually no federal discretion. In addition, both the federal and provincial statutes enable the Sechelts to exercise any legislative power granted to it by, or pursuant, to an Act of the provincial legislature.

At first glance the powers of the Sechelt Band Council seem to intrude into provincial jurisdiction. However, where there are conflicts, it is apparent that these already exist because the *Indian Act* deals with these subjects using as its authority s.91(24) of the *Constitution Act, 1867*. The areas where the authority of the province and *Indian Act* presently overlap include education, health services, preservation of natural resources, management of fish and game, laws regarding public order and safety, control of intoxicants and taxation powers. Social and welfare services are not specifically mentioned in the *Indian Act* but are covered by a federal-provincial agreement and, in some cases, the province delegates responsibility for child welfare to Indian bands.

The federal statute establishes a process whereby the federal Cabinet can transfer any powers, duties or functions of the band council, under the *Sechelt Indian Band Self-Government Act*, to the Sechelt Indian Government District. Significantly, the federal statute does not permit the transfer of two important powers to the District: control of membership in the band; and authority for the disposition of the rights and interests in Sechelt lands. Clearly, this is because these are inviolate rights and responsibilities of the Indian band which should not be transferred to a quasi-local government entity. Moreover, with respect to those powers that can be transferred, any transfers are subject to two conditions: a band referendum must be held; and the Legislature of British Columbia must pass legislation respecting the transfer of the powers to the District.

Sechelt Indian Government District

The proclamation of the *Sechelt Indian Government District Enabling Act* (British Columbia) on July 23, 1987 was followed by a Sechelt Band referendum on March 5, 1988, overwhelmingly approving the transfer of certain powers of the Sechelt Band Council to the district council; the vote was 94 per cent in favour. Subsequently, on March 17, 1988, the federal Cabinet passed an order declaring the provisions of the *Sechelt Indian Band Self-Government Act* relating to the District in force, and transferring a set of powers of the band council to the district council. This in effect solidified the two most critical governing components of the Sechelt model.

The Sechelt Indian Government District has jurisdiction over all Sechelt lands, which include both Indian and non-Indian occupied lands. Like the Sechelt Indian Band, the District is an autonomous corporate entity with a full range of corporate powers. However, the district council consists of the members of the council of the Sechelt Indian Band. Consequently, the rules for election are the rules that govern the band council elections. Specifically, non-Indian occupiers of band lands cannot vote in elections, or hold elected office on the district council.

The powers of the Sechelt Indian Government District are set out in the federal order incorporating the District, which transfers authority for a class of services from the band constitution to the District. These powers are exercisable through the adoption of laws and are as follows:

- general government;
- zoning and land-use planning;
- regulation of buildings;
- assessment and taxation of real property;
- regulation of noise, animals, waste disposal and places of amusement;
- road construction, maintenance and regulation;
- regulation of businesses, professions and trades;
- imposition of fines or imprisonment for contravention of laws; and
- the right to make fair and reasonable laws.

This extensive transfer of band council powers provides the District with a set of responsibilities which resemble those of a typical local government corporation in British Columbia. In fact, it is the band's intention that the District resemble and behave like a conventional local government.

The provincial statute governing local government operations in the province, the *Municipal Act*, does not automatically apply because the District is a federal creature. Nonetheless, the architects of the model have ensured that a policy vacuum was not created. The drafters were concerned that adequate standards of fairness and procedural justice be in place. Consequently, the federal order transferring powers to the District specifies that the District adopt such provisions of the laws of British Columbia as it may require to exercise those powers. Furthermore, the order indicates that such provisions and laws include and contain standards at least equivalent to those prevailing in the Province of British Columbia. For example, in the case of land use planning, the procedures for adopting zoning by-laws must provide for the holding of public hearings. These provisions were contained in the federal orders on the instigation, and with the full support, of the band.

The band's rationale for acquiescing to provincial legislation and standards was twofold. First, the band did not want to create what, in effect, was a law-free haven where non-Indian occupiers or Indians would not be subject to prevailing provincial laws and standards in areas such as public health and fire protection. In fact, this corrects an existing jurisdictional ambiguity as to the applicability of provincial laws for non-Indian occupiers. Second, the band wished to provide the protection of provincial standards, or their equivalents, in the areas of fairness and justice to non-Indian occupiers.

In practice, it is the band's intention to adhere strictly to the *Municipal Act* and other provincial legislation relating to local government operations. The District employs the Ministry of Municipal Affairs, Recreation and Culture's *Municipal Administration Manual*. Moreover, it has borrowed by-laws from neighbouring municipalities as models for its own enactments. The band has recruited a capable, experienced, municipal administrator from the British Columbia local government system. Consequently, at this stage in its evolution, the band has chosen to follow conventional practice in the province. Significantly, this is done without compulsion and with the freedom to adapt provincial statutes to its own needs where they are inconsistent with local wishes. The band recognizes the unique nature of the Sechelt model and understands that the eyes of the outside world are on it. It is, therefore, very concerned that it exercise its powers responsibly, particularly as these relate to non-Indians.

Advisory Council

Section 2(2) of the *Sechelt Indian Government District Enabling Act* provides for the provincial Cabinet to establish "an Advisory Council to represent all the residents of the Sechelt Indian Government District." The advisory council is a provincial creature which is not recognized in the federal statute. It represents an attempt by the province to provide an opportunity for non-Indians occupying band lands to be heard and given consideration. The order establishing the advisory council, adopted by the Cabinet on June 23, 1988, provides for an initial appointment of four persons, with elections on a ward, or area, basis to follow in the fall of 1990. The election will be held using the provisions of the *Municipal Act*, which means that both Indians and non-Indians will be able to vote and hold office. However, in practice it is anticipated that the advisory council will become the vehicle for non-Indian participation in District affairs.

The advisory council does not have legislative powers. It is strictly an advisory body to the district council. Moreover, the provincial order restricts its advisory powers to a defined set of activities unless the district council specifies otherwise. The order establishing the council indicates that the advisory council is responsible for the following:

• planning the services program for the District;
• estimating the costs of the servicing program;
• recommending a servicing program including proposed financing to the district council; and
• receiving and considering petitions relating to the provision of a service in the District.

The order also provides a mechanism whereby the advisory council can act as a conduit for residents of the District to present petitions to the council arguing for provision of a service. Clearly, the advisory council represents the interests of District residents as occupiers of land and consumers of services only, but not as citizens in the fullest governmental sense. Experience to date indicates that the advisory council will be an active, rather than a passive, body and will be dealing in many respects with the real business of local government.

Sunshine Coast Regional District

In its desire to remain an integral part of the larger Sunshine Coast social, economic and political culture, the Sechelt Indian Band asked that the Sechelt Indian Government District become a member municipality of the Sunshine Coast Regional District. The regional district is an upper tier local government which provides region-wide services to both municipal and rural members, as well as local services to rural members. On June 16, 1988, using authority contained in the *Sechelt Indian Government District Act*, the provincial Cabinet made the District a member of the regional district. Now the District must pass a law enabling it to participate in the regional district and appoint a director. Once this is accomplished, the band, through the District, will take its place at the regional table, participate in the politics and government of the region and avail itself of the services of the regional district.

Conclusion

The Sechelt Band has achieved a high degree of political and administrative autonomy within the context of its constitution. While effective political authority is focused on the band council, the federal enabling statute allows for the further delegation of powers to a district council. The band has exercised this power and created an effective division between band government and local government. Figure 8 summarizes the division of legislative powers between the band and the District.

Indian band government is paramount. Although the fact that effective political control rests with the band council has been criticized as disenfranchising the non-Indian population, it would be unacceptable for the band to do otherwise. Non-native occupiers could outnumber band members on Sechelt lands. If the franchise were universal, and non-Indians could vote and hold office, there would be the constant threat that political control of the Sechelt Band and its lands would fall out of Indian hands. This is the criticism that has been effectively levelled at the *Alaska Native Claims Settlement Act*[24]. The Sechelts would argue that the creation of the district council and the advisory council are improvements over the status quo where non-natives have neither influence nor control. The Sechelt self-government model opens up the process and gives non-natives influence, if not control, over their environment. Clearly, this is the most controversial aspect of the Sechelt self-government model. In fact, one observer has speculated on whether the *Sechelt Indian Band Self-Government Act* goes beyond the powers granted the federal government under s.91(24) of the *Constitution Act (1867)* and on whether it could be challenged under s.15 of the *Charter of Rights and Freedoms*[25]. While a court challenge is a possibility, it is highly unlikely because the federal, provincial and band governments are in substantial agreement on the concept. Any challenge would have to come from the non-Indian occupiers,

Figure 8

Summary of the Division of Legislative Powers Between the Sechelt Indian Band Council and the Sechelt Indian Government District Council[1]

	Exercised by	
Legislative Power	Band Council	District Council
1. access to and residence on Sechelt lands	x	
2. zoning and land use		x
3. expropriation of lands for community purposes	x	
4. building regulation		x
5. assessment and taxation		x
6. administration of band lands	x	
7. education	x	
8. social and welfare services	x	
9. health	x	
10. natural resources of preservation and management	x	
11. fish and wildlife management	x	
12. public order and safety		x
13. road construction, maintenance and regulation		x
14. regulation of business		x
15. liquor regulation		
16. imposition of fines		x
17. devolution of band lands	x	
18. financial administration	x	
19. conduct of band elections/referenda	x	
20. creation of administrative bodies	x	
21. matters related to good government	x	s
22. power to adopt any law of the Province of B.C. as its law	x	x
23. power to exercise any power assigned to it by the province	x	x

Note: [1] includes powers exercisable and potentially exercisable

which is only a threat to the extent that non-Indian occupiers are dissatisfied. It is the band's intention that good government be exercised for both Indian and non-Indian residents.

Perhaps the most interesting aspect of the model is the advisory council, which warrants monitoring in the coming years. The political framework provides for built-in, creative tension between the district council, representing the band members, and the advisory council, representing residents at large. It is here that the tensions between tribal or ethnic government and public government will be most evident.

THE FINANCIAL AND SERVICE STRUCTURE OF SECHELT SELF-GOVERNMENT

This section examines the financial and service structure of Sechelt self-government: reviews fiscal relationships between the Indian band, and the federal and provincial governments; analyzes the means by which the band provides a wide range of services to its members; and discusses how the band manages its land and resources.

Federal Fiscal Relations

Existing mechanisms for the provision of funding to Indian bands seem to work well for assuring ministerial responsibility that monies are properly spent. However, the ways in which the Government of Canada provides monies to Indians would have to be altered dramatically if the benefits of band self-governance were to be achieved.[26] Band self-governance requires that individual bands receive a fair share of federal monies destined for Indians and that bands have the maximum freedom to choose how to spend monies consistent with local needs and priorities. The federal government has increasingly recognized that the structure of its financial programs inhibits the achievement of the benefits of self-governance.[27] One response has been a more flexible approach to funding through negotiation of Alternative Funding Arrangements which provide for the allocation of funds to fixed categories of expenditures, for a five-year period, but with flexibility to reallocate monies where appropriate.

The *Sechelt Indian Band Self-Government Act*, s.33, provides another mechanism by which the band and the federal government can negotiate special multi-year funding. A five-year agreement has been successfully negotiated between the band and the Department of Indian Affairs and Northern Development, with payments of $2.3 million in the current year. The band in turn augments these funds from its own source revenues. These monies are allocated to six categories of expenditure: administration, local government infrastructure, social assistance, health, education, and economic development. For three of the six categories of funds, the band may allocate funds as it sees fit, subject only to budgeting and auditing requirements. However, for three categories—health, education and social services—the restrictions are imposed by the band constitution to ensure that a basic level of service is provided to the band members. The agreement provides for the adjustment of grants on an annual basis, taking into account inflation and population changes, and does not preclude negotiation of agreements with other federal or provincial agencies.

The Sechelts' agreement represents a significant breakthrough for the Sechelt Band. By providing a higher degree of flexibility than the Alternative Funding Arrangements would, it offers the band many options in choosing where to allocate these revenues. Consequently, it is probable that band expenditures will more closely reflect the needs of band members.

Provincial Fiscal Relations

The Sechelts and the Province of British Columbia had a common interest, or objective, to integrate the Sechelts into the provincial fiscal system without jeopardizing the independence and unique status of the band. Consequently, the two parties negotiated a unique set of *quid pro quo* fiscal arrangements grounded in the particular constitutional relationship between the band and the province.

The province's retreat from applying its rural service levy, the *Taxation (Rural Area) Act* levy, on non-Indian occupiers of band lands, removed a perennial irritant to the Sechelt Band, and provided room for it to tax all occupiers of its lands for the recovery of the costs of local services. This was executed through an order issued under the *Sechelt Indian Government District Enabling Act*. In addition, the province agreed to treat the Sechelt Indian Government District like any other municipality in the province. Specifically, it agreed to offer the Sechelts the full benefits of all provincial grant programs available for municipalities. In particular, provincial basic and unconditional grants from the Revenue Sharing Program have been provided, as well as benefits of the Provincial-Municipal Partnership Program. Finally, through the *Sechelt Indian Government District Home Owner Grant Act*, the province made the Sechelts eligible for this property tax reduction program. These concessions are significant; in 1988 revenue sharing will provide $54,000, and the Home Owner Grant $80,000, while rescinding the *Taxation (Rural) Act* levy has provided a further benefit.

In return for these concessions, the band has agreed to subject both band members and non-Indian occupiers of band lands to the property taxes which normally would apply within a municipality in the Sunshine Coast Regional District. These include the provincial non-residential school tax; the residential school tax of the local school board; the regional district general tax; the regional hospital district tax; and the B. C. Assessment Authority levy. The Sechelt Indian Government District levies these taxes and remits the proceeds to the appropriate government agency. While non-Indian occupiers would have paid these taxes in previous years, band members would not have. Consequently, this represents a significant concession on their part. With these tax concessions, the band can normalize its relationships with the province, the Regional District, the Regional Hospital District, the School District and the B.C. Assessment Authority. With respect to the latter, this enables the band to have its assessment roll prepared by the B.C. Assessment Authority, an independent, objective agency of the provincial government.

Figure 9 summarizes the resulting provincial/band fiscal regime in comparison to other Indian bands in the province; clearly, the Sechelts have an unprecedented fiscal relationship with the province.

Service Structure

The creation of the Sechelt Indian Government District will enable an existing complex service delivery pattern to be solidified and new service relationships developed. As is common with many Indian bands in the province, local services are provided by a variety of methods, often involving adjacent local governments. Local service provision arrangements, currently in place, are summarized in Figure 10. The Sechelt Indian Government District provides general government, local roads, community planning, sewerage

Figure 9

Application of the Provincial Property Tax Regime to the Sechelts in Comparison to Other Indian Bands

CATEGORY OF TAXPAYERS	SECHELT INDIAN GOVERNMENT DISTRICT	OTHER INDIAN BANDS*
A. Indians	• Sechelt Indian Government District tax • Provincial non-residential school tax • Local residential school tax • Regional District tax • Regional Hospital District tax • BCAA • Full eligibility for Provincial Home Owner Grant	• no provincial or local taxes • No eligibility for the Provincial Home Owner Grant
B. Non-Indian Occupiers	• Sechelt Indian Government District Tax • Provincial non-residential school tax • Local residential school tax • Regional District tax • Regional Hospital District tax • BCAA • Full eligibility for Provincial Home Owner Grant	• Municipal general or Provincial Taxation (Rural Area) Tax • Provincial non-residential school tax • Local residential school tax • Regional District tax • Regional Hospital District tax • BCAA/MFA • Full elibigility for Provincial Home Owner Grant

* includes all indian reserves whether located in municipalities or rural areas.

LEGEND

BCAA = B.C. Assessment Authority
MFA = Municipal Finance Authority

collection, recreation/culture and economic development. However, non-Indian governments also play a significant role in providing services on a contract basis. The Sunshine Coast Regional District provides treatment for sewerage collected on band lands, and also

Figure 10

Local Service Provision Responsibilities in the Sechelt Indian Government District

SERVICE	SERVICE PROVIDER				
	SIGD	SCRD	SFPD	PROV	PRIV
General Government	X				
Police				X	
Fire			X		
Building Inspection[3]		X			
Transportation	X				
Waste Collection/Disposal					X
Community Planning	X				
Recreation/Culture	X				
Economic Development	X				
Water Distribution[1]		X			
Water Supply[1]		X			
Sewerage Collection	X				
Sewerage Treatment[2]		X			

LEGEND

SIGD = Sechelt Indian Government
SCRD = Sunshine Coast Regional District
SFPD = Sechelt Fire Protection District
PROV = Province
PRIV = Private

NOTES

[1] Lesees charges collected by SCRD; band members receive free of charge in return for granting of right-of-way.
[2] Band made capital contribution and pays annual per unit charge.
[3] Building inspection provided by SCRD but only in the context of band laws.

supplies and distributes water on the Sechelt lands. Negotiations are anticipated on a contract to provide building inspection services. The Sechelt Fire Protection District provides fire protection for the Sechelt Band, on a contract basis, as well as for the District of Sechelt and the adjacent rural areas.

The establishment of Sechelt self-governance will facilitate the continued provision of existing local services to band members, as well as allow for the efficient provision of new services. Specifically, the band now has, by virtue of s.14(e) of the *Sechelt Indian Band*

Self-Government Act, full taxing powers over band members and non-Indian occupiers. Until the recent adoption of Bill C115, amending the *Indian Act*, Indian bands lacked the clear authority to tax non-Indian occupiers. Furthermore, the *Sechelt Indian Band Self-Government Act*, makes the band and the District corporate entities, eliminating common law problems as to the legal status of an Indian band. This will make it easier for the band, or the district council, to enter into contractual agreements with adjacent local governments for the provision of services.

While the Sechelt Indian Band is empowered to provide education services on band lands, its objective has been to become integrated, to the maximum extent possible, into the normal provincial and regional school system. Under the Canadian Constitution, the federal government has primary responsibility for educating Indians, while the province looks after the educational needs of non-Indians. In most cases, this has meant negotiation of a Master Tuition agreement whereby the federal government compensates the provinces for the costs of educating Indians.

The Sechelt Indian Band has developed a unique approach to the financing of education services provided to band and non-band members on Sechelt lands. In their case, the federal government provides the Sechelt Band with an annual grant, as part of the five-year block funding agreement. The Sechelt Indian Government District levies the provincial, non-residential school tax and the school district residential school tax on both Indian and non-Indian occupiers, and remits the funds to the province and the local school board respectively. In this respect, the District is behaving like a typical municipality in the province. The province in turn treats the school district like every other provincial school district, by forwarding operating grants in proportion to its expenditure requirements and relative fiscal capacity. However, the Indian band, not the District, provides the province with an annual contribution from its budget to compensate the province for its financial contribution to the education of Indians. This is calculated as that portion of the province's grant to the school district, which is directed to the education of Indians. The funds for this grant come from the block funding agreement between the band and the federal government. These arrangements are an attempt to create normal fiscal relations between the band, the school district, and the province.

Perhaps the most critical aspect of this relationship is the integration with the local school board. The board will receive property taxes from band lands, and will also receive grants from the province for educating band members. Both Indians and non-Indians residing on Sechelt land will be able to vote in school board elections, although the elections are held "at large" rather than on an areal or ward representation basis.

Creation of self-governance for the Sechelts will not radically change the way in which health services are provided to the band. Currently, Sechelt Band members have full access to the provincial health care system. In turn, the province bills the Government of Canada for its costs. Self-governance will bring only two small changes to this pattern. The federal/band block funding agreement, facilitated by s.33 of the *Sechelt Indian Band Self-Government Act*, provides for federal funding of a community health worker, and an alcohol and drug counselling program managed by the band. In addition, as part of the *quid pro quo* arrangements with the province, the Sechelt Indian Government District will levy the Sunshine Coast Regional Hospital District tax on both band members and non-Indian occupiers. The tax is used by the hospital district to recover the costs of hospital construction. A representative of the Sechelt Indian Government District will sit on the hospital District Board.

Land and Resource Issues

The band has achieved full control of its land base in fee simple. Its objective is that all lands continue to be held in trust for the benefit of present and future generations of band members. On the one hand, this means that the band will not issue certificates of possession for band lands to band members. This will ensure that the benefits of the development of band lands will accrue collectively to the band, and not to individual members. On the other hand, it is band policy not to sell land to non-Indians even though the statute gives them that right. The band constitution provides that a band referendum, with 75 per cent of the band members' approval, is required to sell land. This clause prevents a future band council from acting unilaterally without regard to the interests of band members. The band is determined not to allow its resource base to be dissipated. In this regard, they are mindful of the defects of the *Alaska Native Claims Settlement Act*.[28] The band has an active land development program, but land is leased only on a leasehold basis, with the most common term being 99 years. This means that the land itself is inalienable, but that the interest in the land is marketable.

The *Sechelt Indian Self-Government Act* provided the band with control of natural resources on band lands including minerals, forests, fish and wildlife. However, this statute does not override the *British Columbia Indian Reserves Mineral Resources Act* (Canada) and the *Indian Reserve Mineral Resource Act* (British Columbia), which in combination, call for 50/50 sharing of royalties between the province and the band, on minerals mined on Indian lands. The Sechelt Band was unsuccessful in negotiating exemption from the provincial statute, but renegotiation has been in process for the past three years. Regardless, at the present time there are no mineral resources being developed or planned for development.

The band has a number of resource projects underway. A valuable gravel resource is being developed through a joint venture with a multi-national construction material company. The band also collects a transportation fee for gravels extracted by the company on adjacent fee simple lands held by the company. Forestry activities are restricted to some small-scale harvesting by a band member-owned company. However, a major silviculture project is being planned to reforest depleted resources. Finally, the band has a successful salmon hatchery.

IMPLICATIONS OF THE SECHELT MODEL

This section returns to the basic objectives of the participants in the Sechelt process, and asks what has been achieved, and at what cost, if any. The discussion focuses successively on: the Sechelt Indian Band; the Government of Canada; the Province of British Columbia; and the native community in Canada.

The Sechelt Band

In embarking on the path to self-governance, the Sechelt Band has achieved everything it set out to achieve. It has full control of a substantial land base from which to govern. It has a highly autonomous form of self-government, through an Act of the federal Parliament. It has a wide range of legislative powers, delegated by the federal government, but exercisable within the context of its own constitution. The legislation provides for tribal or ethnic government, under almost total control of the Sechelt people.[29] At the same time, a form of public government is provided, which is modelled after municipal government in British Columbia. The interests of non-Indian occupiers are protected through election of an advisory council. The Sechelts have almost totally removed themselves from the purview of the federal *Indian Act*, and are not bound statutorily by provincial laws, particularly those supervising local governments. The enabling legislation, in effect, creates a third level of government exclusively for the Sechelts. In turn, the Sechelts have been able to negotiate effectively with the federal, provincial and local governments on a unique fiscal framework, for the exercise of self-government.

While the Sechelts have achieved self-government, they have also realized their objective to remain an integral part of the larger local, regional and provincial community. At their wish, the Sechelts will participate politically in the regional district, hospital district and school board, receive relevant local services, and pay all relevant regional property taxes. At the same time, the band is integrated with the provincial system, paying relevant provincial taxes, receiving the benefits of provincial programs for local government, and taking advantage of the provincial property assessment and land registration systems. The Sechelts have achieved all of this, without prejudice to their aboriginal status, aboriginal land claims or whatever benefits are achieved through the constitutional entrenchment of aboriginal rights to self-governance.

The Government of Canada

The creation of self-government for the Sechelts ranks with the Cree-Naskapi settlement of 1975, and the Inuvialuit Claim Settlement of 1984, as the most significant achievements in self-governance for native people in Canada. The Sechelts prompted the Minister of Indian and Northern Affairs at that time, to seek a radical shift in how the federal government approached the Indian governance issue. The Minister saw the Sechelt approach, not as a threat, but an opportunity. The Sechelt model provided the federal government with a practical opportunity to demonstrate its willingness to seek self-governance through negotiation from the bottom up, as well as through constitutional entrenchment from the top down. Nonetheless, the Sechelts' scheme is not seen as an inflexible model for other communities. According to the previous Minister of Indian and Northern Affairs, "The Sechelt proposal reflects that community's aspirations; it is not a model for others."[30]

The federal government has achieved its objectives with little cost to itself. While the direct scrutiny of the *Indian Act* is removed, the federal government is still responsible for monitoring the application of the legislation, particularly through its approval of the band constitution, and the transfer of powers to the district council. Moreover, the federal government has not had to concede jurisdiction to the provincial government. On the contrary, the federal and provincial governments have come to a unique accommodation in the area of legislative authority over non-Indian occupiers.

Province of British Columbia

The Province of British Columbia sees the creation of self-governance for the Sechelts as a significant achievement. From its perspective, the Sechelt model responded to the needs of the Sechelts but also demonstrated to the larger native community that the province was willing to negotiate self-government with individual bands outside the framework of a comprehensive land claims settlement, or constitutional entrenchment of the right to self-government. In this respect the province feels that it has a model which it can offer to other Indian bands in the province. Although the province's Indian leadership has rejected the model, a number of individual bands have expressed interest. It remains to be seen how many proceed to implementation.

The province did not fully achieve its objective of native self-governance being kept totally under the umbrella of provincial statutes governing local government institutions. This clearly was beyond its constitutional prerogatives. The province has had to accept the Government of Canada's prerogative to create a "local government" with federally delegated powers. Nonetheless, while the province does not have control, it is able to exercise influence on the Sechelts through *quid pro quo* financial relationships. In other words, it can achieve desired behaviour or outcomes through the provision of financial incentives. At the same time, the Government of Canada, conscious of the sensitivity of its relationship with the province, has constrained the exercise of the District's powers such that it does not offend provincial sensibilities, particularly in the areas of fairness and due process. Consequently, the province has achieved its self-governance objectives through indirect rather than direct means.

In terms of costs, the province has had to concede jurisdiction it has historically claimed over non-Indian occupiers of Indian lands. It has recognized that the Sechelt Indian Government District has jurisdiction over all Indian lands and has withdrawn direct taxation of non-Indian occupiers. However, offsetting the apparent loss of jurisdiction, the province has achieved a fuller integration of the Sechelts into the provincial system. Specifically all band lands are assessed by the province; band members pay provincial and regional property taxes through the District; any band lands can be placed in the provincial registry system; the band participates directly in the regional district; and all taxpayers on Sechelt lands share in the benefits of provincial programs such as the Home Owner Grant and Revenue Sharing. All of these actions represent an unprecedented integration of an Indian band, and its land base, into the larger provincial system.

In conclusion, directly and indirectly, the province has accomplished what it set out to achieve. Moreover, the province has the opportunity, in twenty years' time to review the Sechelts experiment and determine whether it continues to meet its objectives.

Local Government in British Columbia

The Sechelt model has been well received by neighbouring local governments and the Union of B.C. Municipalities because the Indian Government District will be integrated into the local government system. Band members will pay taxes like typical municipal electors, receive normal provincial benefits and participate directly in local government institutions. The District has become a member of the Union of British Columbia Municipalities and will avail itself of its many services, in particular for preparation of a tax roll and tax notice.

Other Indian Bands

The major Indian organization in the province, the Union of British Columbia Indian Chiefs, is highly critical of the Sechelt model because it falls short of what the chiefs have attempted to achieve at the First Ministers' Constitutional Conferences. Their objective continues to be constitutional entrenchment of the right to self-government and constitutional recognition of aboriginal title. The Sechelt model is rejected because it achieves a form of self-government through an Act of Parliament rather than through constitutional recognition of "inherent jurisdiction."[31] Furthermore, the Indian critique alleges that the Sechelt model undermines tribal government structures, making them municipal institutions, and subjecting them to provincial laws.

The Sechelt model presents some significant innovations for native self-government which deserve careful scrutiny. Perhaps the most significant innovation is the removal of the authority of the *Indian Act* and its replacement by a band constitution. This represents an unprecedented attempt to replace externally imposed authority with internally legitimized tribal authority. Furthermore, the Sechelt model gives the Sechelts control of their land and resource base. Again, this is unprecedented and worthy of attention. Finally, the separation between "band government" and "local government" represents a unique attempt at dealing with the dilemmas associated with non-native occupiers of band lands. All the above can be seen as experiments, the results of which can be scrutinized by other bands.

In addition, the worst fears of the native leadership are unfounded. The Sechelt Indian model of self-government is, most emphatically, *not* just a replication of a typical British Columbia municipality under the umbrella of the provincial *Municipal Act*. It is a federal, not a provincial creature; provincial laws apply only insofar as they are consistent with the *Sechelt Indian Band Self-Government Act*, any other Act of Parliament, the constitution of the band, or any law of the band. Furthermore, the powers of the Band Council go well beyond the conventional powers of either municipal, or in some cases, provincial governments.

CONCLUSION

The Sechelt model is a legislated and negotiated form of self-governance. As such, it falls short of the objectives of the native leadership in this country—constitutional entrenchment of the right to self-government, and aboriginal title. Nonetheless, it is not inconsistent with an evolutionary approach to self-governance articulated in the Penner Committee's report. The Sechelts take their place alongside the Cree-Naskapi and the Inuvialuit as the most notable achievers of self-governance for aboriginal peoples. The Sechelts provide the native community with a concrete, practical demonstration of a band-focused, tribal, autonomous form of self-government. Moreover, they have achieved this without prejudice to aboriginal land claims, or rights to self-government.

A significant feature of the Sechelt model has been the degree to which it is integrated institutionally into a larger, local, regional and provincial community. Most emphatically, this has been done voluntarily and at the discretion of the Sechelt. This is in recognition of the close proximity of the native and non-native occupiers of band lands, the close servicing relationships with adjacent local governments, and a history of co-operation with non-natives. The band has not subjected itself to provincial law, becoming just another provincial municipality, nor has it lost the benefits of tribal government. On the contrary: the Sechelt model is a federal, not a provincial creature, and is subject to provincial law only if the band so chooses. Moreover, it is a judicious mixture of tribal and municipal type institutions, in recognition of the inescapable fact that natives and non-natives live and work side-by-side on band lands. Finally, while it is a federal creature, it has a high degree of autonomy. In fact, it could be argued that the Sechelt represent a third level of government.

The most critical test of any self-governance proposal is whether it meets the needs of the community for which it is designed. In this regard, the Sechelt model is a resounding success; the Sechelts have achieved virtually everything they have pursued so relentlessly over a 15-year period. The Sechelt model is well adapted to the unique needs, values, aspirations and situation of the Sechelt people. This does not mean that it is an approach to self-governance which should be transferred and become a model for other native communities in British Columbia or Canada. It is vital that each community look carefully at its own unique values, aspirations and situation before adopting a particular model. The consequences of not undertaking this kind of assessment can be disastrous for the community. In conclusion, the Sechelt model should be seen as a significant experiment in native self-governance, which provides an opportunity to learn about the practical significance of self-governance for native people. The objective should be to encourage a variety of approaches to the achievement of self-governance.

CHRONOLOGY OF EVENTS LEADING TO THE ESTABLISHMENT OF SECHELT BAND SELF-GOVERNMENT

1985

February 5, 1985   Bill C-93 *Sechelt Indian Band Self-Government Act* introduced

March 15, 1985   Sechelt Indian Band votes 70 per cent in favour of legislation

1986

March 15, 1986   Band referendum on exercising self-government and transfer of lands from Canada to Sechelt Band

May 3, 1986   Bill C-93 *Sechelt Indian Band Self-Government Act* passed

June 17, 1986   Royal Assent given to Bill C-93

September 26, 1986   Referendum on Band Constitution successful

October 9, 1986   *Sechelt Indian Band Self-Government Act* proclaimed

1987

March 11, 1987   *Sechelt Indian Government District Enabling Act* (B.C.) introduced in Legislature

April 3, 1987   *Sechelt Indian Government District Enabling Act* adopted by Legislature

May 26, 1987   *Sechelt Indian Government District Enabling Act* given Royal Assent

July 23, 1987   *Sechelt Indian Government District Enabling Act* proclaimed, OIC 1466

Notes

1. Terry Glavin, "Politicians, Sechelt Indian Band Celebrate Self-Government," *Vancouver Sun* [Vancouver], June 25, 1988.
2. David C. Hawkes, *Aboriginal Self-Government: What Does It Mean?* (Kingston: Queens University, Institute of Intergovernmental Relations, 1985).
3. *Ibid.*
4. *The Canadian Encyclopedia* (Edmonton: Hurtig Publishers, 1985).
5. Paul Tennant, "Local Community: Indian Self-Governance in Perspective," in Union of British Columbia Municipalities (ed) *Indian Issues Forums: A Summary of Oral Presentations.* (Vancouver: Union of British Columbia Municipalities, 1987).
6. Robert Bish, *Property Taxation and The Provision of Government Services on Indian Reserves in British Columbia.* Report prepared for the Department of Indian Affairs and Northern Development (Victoria: University of Victoria, School of Public Administration, 1987).
7. Union of British Columbia Municipalities, (ed) *Indian Issues Forums: A Summary of Oral Presentations* (Vancouver: Union of British Columbia Municipalities, 1987).
8. Nirmala Devi Cherukapelle, *Indian Reserves as Municipalities: Problems and Prospects, the British Columbia Case.* Papers on Local Government, Volume 1, No. 3 (Vancouver: University of British Columbia, Centre for Continuing Education, 1972).
9. Tripartite Local Government Committee, *Report of the Tripartite Government Committee Respecting Indian Local Government in British Columbia* (Victoria: Tripartite Local Government Committee, 1981).
10. Union of British Columbia Municipalities, *op. cit.,* note 7.
11. Douglas Sanders, "The Aboriginal Title Question in British Columbia," (Vancouver: Continuing Legal Education Society, 1986).
12. Ruth Montgomery, "Provincial Government Policy on Indian Issues," in Union of British Columbia Municipalities (ed) *Indian Issues Forums: A Summary of Oral Presentations, op. cit.,* note 7.
13. *Ibid.*
14. Paul Tennant, "Indian Self-Government: Progress or Stalemate," X, *Canadian Public Policy,* (1984), pp. 211-215.
15. Canada, House of Commons, *Minutes of Proceedings and Evidence of the Standing Committee on Aboriginal Affairs and Northern Development* 1984-85-86 (Ottawa: Queen's Printer).
16. Canada, House of Commons, *Indian Self-Government in Canada: Report of the Special Committee* (Ottawa: Queen's Printer, 1983).
17. *Ibid.*
18. David Crombie, *Policy Statement on Indian Self-Government in Canada. Minister of Indian Affairs and Northern Development* (Ottawa: Department of Indian Affairs and Northern Development, 1986).
19. *Ibid.*
20. *Ibid.*

21. Robert Bish, *Financing Indian Self-Government Practice and Principles*. Report Prepared for the Department of Indian and Northern Development (Victoria: University of Victoria, School of Public Administration, 1987).
22. Canada, House of Commons, *Indian Self-Government in Canada: Report of the Special Committee* (Ottawa: Queen's Printer, 1983).
23. J. Anthony Long, Le Roy Little Bear and Manno Boldt, "Federal Indian Policy and Indian Self-Government in Canada: An Analysis of A Current Proposal, VIII," *Canadian Public Policy* (1982), pp. 189-199.
24. Thomas Berger, *Village Journey: The Report of the Alaska Native Review Commission* (New York: Hill and Wang, 1985); Shannon D. Work, "The Alaska Native Claims Settlement Act: An Illusion in the Quest for Self-Determination," LVI *Oregon Law Review,* (1987) pp. 195-218.
25. Sara E. Pope, *The Sechelt Indian Government District: Legal Structure and Policy Implications from a Local Government Perspective*. Unpublished.
26. Crombie, *op. cit.,* note 8.
27. *Ibid*.
28. Berger, *op. cit.,* note 24; Work, *op. cit.,* note 24.
29. Crombie, *op. cit,* note 18.
30. *Ibid*.
31. Frank Cassidy, "On the Inherent Jurisdiction of Indian Governments," prepared for "Creating and Enforcing Local Laws: An Instructional Conference for Indian Governments" (Victoria: University of Victoria, School of Public Administration, 1987).

BIBLIOGRAPHY

Government Documents

Books and Articles

The Canadian Encyclopedia. Edmonton: Hurtig Publishers, 1985.

Berger, Thomas. *Village Journey: The Report of the Alaska Native Review Commission.* New York: Hill and Wang, 1986.

Bish, Robert. *Financing Indian Self-Government: Practice and Principles.* Report Prepared for the Department of Indian Affairs and Northern Development. Victoria: University of Victoria, School of Public Administration, 1987.

————. *Property Taxation and The Provision of Government Services on Indian Reserves in British Columbia.* Report prepared for the Department of Indian Affairs and Northern Development. Victoria: University of Victoria, School of Public Administration, 1987.

Cassidy, Frank. "On the Inherent Jurisdiction of Indian Governments." Prepared for "Creating and Enforcing Local Laws: An Instructional Conference for Indian Governments." Victoria: University of Victoria, School of Public Administration, 1987.

Cherukapelle, Nirmala Devi. *Indian Reserves as Municipalities: Problems and Prospects, the British Columbia Case.* Papers on Local Government, Volume 1, No. 3. Vancouver: Centre for Continuing Education, University of British Columbia, 1972.

Crombie, David. *Policy Statement on Indian Self-Government in Canada: Minister of Indian Affairs and Northern Development,* 1986.

Farley, A.L. *Atlas of British Columbia: People, Environment, and Resource Use.* Vancouver: University of British Columbia Press, 1979.

Gibbons, Roger and J. Rick Pointing. "The Paradoxical Nature of the Penner Report." *Canadian Public Policy,* X, (1984) pp. 221-224.

Glavin, Terry. "Politicians, Sechelt Indian Band Celebrate Self-Government," *Vancouver Sun* [Vancouver] June 25, 1988.

Hawkes, David C. *Aboriginal Self-Government: What Does it Mean?* Kingston: Queen's University, Institute of Intergovernmental Relations, 1985.

Canada. House of Commons. *Minutes of Proceedings and Evidence of the Standing Committee on Aboriginal Affairs and Northern Development.* Ottawa, 1984-85-86.

Long, J. Anthony, LeRoy Little Bear and Menno Boldt. "Federal Indian Policy and Indian Self-Government in Canada: An Analysis of A Current Proposal," in *Canadian Public Policy,* VIII, (1982) pp. 1189-1199.

Montgomery, Ruth. "Provincial Government Policy on Indian Issues" in UBCM (ed) *Indian Issues Forums: A Summary of Oral Presentations.* Vancouver: Union of British Columbia Municipalities, 1987.

Morse, Bradford. *Aboriginal Self-Government in Australia and Canada.* Kingston: Queen's University, Institute of Intergovernmental Relations, 1986.

Pope, Sara E. *The Sechelt Indian Government District: Legal Structure and Policy Implications from a Local Government Perspective.* Unpublished.

Sanders, Douglas. "The Aboriginal Title Question in British Columbia." Vancouver: Continuing Legal Education Society, 1986.

Tennant, Paul. "Indian Self-Government: Progress or Stalemate?" *Canadian Public Policy,* X, (1984) pp. 211-215.

———. "Local Community: Indian Self-Governance in Perspective," in UBCM (ed) *Indian Issues Forums: A Summary of Oral Presentations.* Vancouver: Union of British Columbia Municipalities, 1987.

Tripartite Local Government Committee. *Report of the Tripartite Government Committee Respecting Indian Local Government in British Columbia.* Victoria: Tripartite Local Government Committee, 1981.

UBCM. *Indian Issues Forums: A Summary of Oral Presentations.* Vancouver: Union of British Columbia Municipalities, 1987.

Vander Zalm, W.N. Speech to the Legislature on The Second Reading of the *Sechelt Indian Government District Enabling Act. Hansard*, April 3, 1987, pp. 440-441.

————. Speech to the Legislature concerning First Ministers Conference on Aboriginal Rights. *Hansard*, March 30, 1987, pp. 331-333.

Weaver, Sally. "A Commentary on the Penner Report," in *Canadian Public Policy*, X, (1984) pp. 215-221.

Work, Shannon D. "The Alaska Native Claims Settlement Act: An Illusion in the Quest for Native Self-Determination." *Oregon Law Review*, 66, (1987) pp. 195-218.

Legislation and Regulations

British Columbia: Legislation

Sechelt Indian Government District Enabling Act

Land Title Amendment Act, 1988
Sechelt Indian Government District Home Owner Grant Act, 1988
Municipal Act, RSBC, Chapter 290, 1979

Canada: Legislation

Sechelt Indian Band Self-Government Act

Constitution Act 1867, enacted as *British North America Act, 1867*. 30-31 Victoria C3 (UK) s.55

Constitution Act, 1982
Indian Act

British Columbia: Regulations

Sechelt Indian Government District Proclamation, OIC Regulation, 1466, July 23, 1987

Sechelt Indian Government District Property Taxation Suspension Regulation, OIC 565, March 25, 1988

Sechelt Indian Government District Municipal Benefits Regulation, OIC 1176, June 16, 1988

Sechelt Indian Government District-Sunshine Coast Regional District Participation Regulation, OIC 1177, June 16, 1988

Sechelt Indian Government District Enabling Act, Advisory Council Regulation, OIC 1236, June 23, 1988

Canada: Regulations

Order-in-Council PC 1988-05, March 17, 1988, Proclaims s.17 and s.20 of *Sechelt Indian Band Self-Government Act* in force and establishes powers of the District.

PART III
CHALLENGES AND CONCLUSIONS

CHAPTER 9

ADDRESS BY THE HONOURABLE IAN G. SCOTT, MINISTER RESPONSIBLE FOR NATIVE AFFAIRS AND ATTORNEY GENERAL (ONTARIO)

It is a pleasure to address this conference. I have now been minister responsible for native affairs in Ontario for just three years. Those years have been for me full and rewarding—as we have at long last begun the responsibility of responding to land claims, continued to grapple with the issues presented by the aboriginal desire for constitutional change and set in place in our province some mechanisms within which we may tackle the objectives of our native citizens in the area of self-government.

But I propose tonight simply to say a word about another challenge, a major challenge, which faces aboriginal people and government policy-makers today—the respective responsibility and roles of the federal and provincial governments in their dealings with the aboriginal peoples of Canada.

I well know that one way to make Canadian eyes glaze over (especially after a good dinner) is to threaten an exploration of the federal and provincial roles in relation to any subject whatever. I don't hesitate, however, to raise this question with you tonight because I believe, on the basis of increasingly voluminous evidence, that our failure to make the advances that not only aboriginal peoples, but all Canadians of good will anxiously seek—whether the issue is constitutional change, land claims, self-government or resources co-management—may be traced directly to our willingness or inability to grapple in this federal system with the basic question of jurisdiction and responsibility: What level of government is responsible for what?

In purely human terms, the issue has another more pressing dimension found in the tragic personal circumstances of most aboriginal people today.

We all know the statistics which describe poverty, poor education and health, high levels of criminal conviction and incarceration, shorter-than-average life expectancy, chronic unemployment and mounting suicide rates. These statistical indicators describe people who are excluded from their rightful place in Canadian life, not a privileged group—not citizens plus—but a marginal and deprived class of Canadians.

Almost invariably in my experience when a proposal is being advanced to alleviate some of these unfortunate realities, the issue will at bottom be: Whose responsibility is it to assume the cost? Where does the jurisdiction and the responsibility belong?

I think it is time to grapple with this almost intractable problem, fundamentally and afresh, for at least two reasons.

First, the problem is getting worse, not better, as governments at both levels confront the need for fiscal restraint and face heavily increased demands for finite tax dollars. Second, I believe the development of a new formula for jurisdiction and responsibility is the key without which it will be extremely difficult to approach, let alone resolve, the problems that the challenge of self-government and resource co-management present.

Like all persistent Canadian problems, its origin is the constitutional arrangement on which our federal system is based.

It was perfectly natural in designing a federal system to attempt to divide legislative subject matter in some practical way between the two levels of government. You deal with criminal law and banking for everybody, we will deal with contract law and education for our own provincial citizens. But s.92(24) is odd because it treated Indians as a subject matter—notwithstanding that they live on reserve, off-reserve, in cities and towns, in every province—and might be expected to need and entitled to require the same level of services as any other Canadian.

The traditional federal approach is to view its jurisdiction for Indians as being largely permissive or discretionary. The provisions of the *Indian Act* by definition apply to a narrower class of Indians than the Constitution envisages. It draws the line all too often at the border of the reserve. It likes to believe, as the White Paper of 1969 and the Nielsen Report of 1985 reveal, that it could limit or even terminate its traditional involvement in the provision or financing of services to aboriginal people without legal consequence.

Needless to say, this deeply entrenched attitude, especially when accompanied by actual withdrawal or reduction of services, does nothing but cause fiscal panic in the provinces and, if anything, induces them to take a more conservative, more narrow view of their responsibilities.

The provinces, on the other hand, tend historically to read the constitutional provision both literally when it suits them and broadly when it suits them. Their view has long-standing historical antecedents often fostered by the native peoples themselves founded on the special federal fiduciary relationship. It is also connected with the inability of the provinces to raise revenue by taxing property and economic activity on reserves. There is, of course, nothing in the Constitution that prevents the provinces from providing services to native people—and everything in logic and humanity to require them to do so—for after all, native people on- or off-reserve are permanent residents of the province.

The historical ad hoc compromise has been to regard the reserve as a kind of federal enclave—on-reserve, federal; off-reserve, provincial.

The aboriginal nations historically, and no doubt for very good reasons, attach great importance to their special relationship with the federal government. In my experience, they frequently show an uncertain and ambiguous attitude toward the provinces. The extension of provincial services pursuant to laws of general application is frequently a considerable benefit to their people but is often perceived as a step toward assimilation or the loss of their distinct aboriginal identities.

This was brought home to me early as a new minister when I offered to increase funding for a joint federal-provincial on-reserve program that was very important to the aboriginal people. Our increased funding was offered to replace certain funds that had been withdrawn by the feds. Our offer was promptly rejected. The province was to pay its share; it would not be permitted to pay the federal share.

This historic federal/provincial uncertainty and ambivalence about jurisdiction and responsibility has gone on too long and the price extracted from the native peoples of Canada has been far too high.

It is interesting that only in the case of the aboriginal peoples do questions arise as to the relative obligations of the federal and provincial governments to provide even the basic services which are now taken for granted by all other Canadians. And long protracted disputes produced by the constitutional ambiguity have contributed to chronically low standards of many basic services.

Furthermore, as I have said, the problems are getting worse, not better. As we begin to explore the parameters of aboriginal and treaty rights, self-government, aboriginal economic development and other issues of great current interest, the difficulties in assessing the respective roles of federal and provincial governments become magnified. Without doubt, these uncertainties have contributed enormously both to lack of progress on many aboriginal issues in recent years, and to the frustration and disillusionment which have resulted from the failure of progress.

However, I would like to suggest—albeit in a tentative way—a new approach to these issues. Any new approach must, of course, take into consideration the dynamic nature of Canadian federalism. This dynamism is of course particularly evident in this decade of constitutional patriation, amendment and debate. The fundamental values which define our federation are under intense scrutiny as we re-examine the delicate balancing of federal and provincial interests.

It is also necessary to keep in mind the quite recent constitutional affirmation of aboriginal and treaty rights, and the subsequent and numerous attempts to entrench a right of aboriginal self-government. While those attempts have not yet succeeded, I believe that a positive feature is that the attempts have done away with many outmoded stereotypes and prejudices about the place of aboriginal peoples in our federation.

I believe that perhaps the place to begin, if we wish to look at the question of jurisdiction and responsibility afresh, is with the old, but I think accurate, notion that the aboriginal people of Canada are "citizens plus."

To me, this phrase expresses the idea that the aboriginal peoples enjoy a special place in society *in addition* to their enjoyment of the basic rights of all Canadians. The special character of the aboriginal peoples stems from their being the original occupants of Canada, and it gives them a place in our society that is enjoyed by no other group of Canadians.

The challenge for all of us is of course to narrow that gap between the theory of "citizens plus" and the reality which faces aboriginal people today. For governments, it seems to me that the challenge is to work toward a new consensus as to the appropriate roles of the federal and provincial governments in the lives of the aboriginal peoples, and then to build on that consensus to help secure a healthier future for aboriginal communities. And I should add that this process must involve aboriginal peoples as central participants.

Upon what would this consensus be founded? In my view it must be founded upon a fresh analysis of the place of the aboriginal people within our society and within the federal structure of Canada. Such an analysis raises some basic questions.

First of all, are aboriginal people Canadians? I do not ask this facetiously. There is an implied racism in the view that aboriginal Canadians can be discriminated against through service levels which other Canadians would not tolerate. My answer is that, of course, aboriginal Canadians are Canadians. There must, therefore, be a rejection of any view which places aboriginal people in some conceptual ghetto. We must begin by accepting that aboriginal people are full citizens of our country and our provinces, with the full set of rights, freedoms and responsibilities which this implies.

Second, what then does the special status of aboriginal people entail? I believe that this is a complex matter. At a minimum, it necessitates profound respect and support for the right of aboriginal people to retain and develop their own culture and their own communities free from pressures to assimilate. It also entails, to an as yet undetermined degree, an obligation of both the federal and provincial governments to support the social, political and economic development of native communities in accordance with native aspirations.

I am of course aware of the federal special relationship with aboriginal peoples, and I am also aware of the view held by many aboriginal peoples that they are not subject to provincial laws. My province has no wish to intrude on the special relationship which the Government of Canada has with aboriginal peoples. It is a relationship of high political trust, and it has its roots in the historic policies of the British Crown which were largely embodied in the Royal Proclamation of 1763. The federal government represents the national interest and has consistently held and should retain the responsibility to make special arrangements for aboriginal peoples.

There is, however, no doubt that aboriginal people are, in addition, full citizens of the province in which they live. I certainly regard the aboriginal population of Ontario in this light. The special relationship with the federal government is simply no reason to deprive aboriginal peoples of the advantages of their residence in a province, including all provincial programs and services. The courts have now unequivocally rejected the theory that Indian reserves are enclaves which are insulated from provincial life and provincial laws. It is thus too late to regard reserves as federal enclaves, and their inhabitants as the human equivalent of such enclaves. Nondiscrimination in service delivery to aboriginal people is in fact a cornerstone of Ontario's present native affairs corporate policy, first enunciated in 1985.

Of course, this view has not always been accepted. Until relatively recently, Canadian governments assumed that the aboriginal peoples, and particularly Indians living on reserves, were a separate class of people, existing in federal enclaves, waiting to become assimilated into the general population.

The federal government released its White Paper on Indian policy in 1969, proposing that this pattern of assimilation be completed through the termination of all special arrangements for Indian people. Canadian policymakers—as well as aboriginal people—have rejected the philosophy of the White Paper, and we have accepted the idea that aboriginal peoples have the fundamental right to continue to exist as distinct peoples within Canada. We no longer subscribe to the assumption that aboriginal cultures are primitive while the rest of us are civilized. We accept, in theory at least, that their communities should not be considered as temporary and essentially doomed, but as permanent features of Canadian life—and as features of Canadian life which enrich Canada and all its residents. But this shift in emphasis—and I stress again that it is a major reversal of very old and well-established policies—requires a fundamental reassessment of the federal role.

This exercise has not yet occurred. In a real sense our federal-provincial relations are still governed by the spirit that culminated in the 1969 White Paper.

I would like to suggest a new vision of that role. First of all, the role of the federal government is no longer that of an interim trustee awaiting the disappearance of its beneficiaries into the mainstream of society. It seems to me that the special federal role requires the ongoing support and enhancement of those features of aboriginal life which are uniquely aboriginal. I have no precise formula for this, but at a minimum it requires ongoing and increased federal government support for the social, economic and political develop-ment of aboriginal communities on- or off-reserve toward greater self-reliance and autonomy within Canadian society. For the fore-seeable future, I believe that the federal government will be required to maintain at least the present amount of financial support for ab-original communities to fulfil this permanent role, at least until the goals of self-sufficiency and self-reliance are achieved.

Second, the provinces can no longer stand by, waiting for their aboriginal residents to acquire the full rights of provincial citizen-ship through some type of enfranchisement. It is now clear that those rights already exist. The provinces need to accept their ab-original residents as full and special members of provincial society. It goes without saying that in my view all services—however they are delivered—should be appropriately tailored to aboriginal peo-ples' special needs and circumstances, so that the extension of pro-vincial services cannot inadvertently become an agent of assimila-tion. But the important point to recognise and act on is that natives can no longer be denied a level of services equal to that enjoyed by all other provincial residents.

It is very easy to look at any problem and to do nothing because you believe that the solution to that problem is the responsibility of someone else. Through this conference, and I hope others like it, I would like to issue a challenge, not only to the government of Canada, but to the governments of all of the provinces and indeed to the leaders of the aboriginal peoples of our country, to engage in new discussions leading to a clearer understanding of the place of aboriginal peoples in our society and to a fuller understanding of federal and provincial roles in support of that place in society.

For my part, I look forward to entering tripartite discussions with the aboriginal peoples of my province and with the federal govern-ment toward a resolution of these difficult problems. I look forward to fulfilling Ontario's 1985 native affairs policy, and to ensuring that the aboriginal peoples of Ontario become full members of pro-vincial society as "Ontarians plus."

I am open-minded regarding the discussions I have proposed. They may be specific to our province, or they may be national in scope. They may begin by examining the unique position of on-reserve status Indians, or they may include all of the aboriginal peoples of Canada.

These are political questions. Governments—and I include aboriginal governments in these comments—cannot abdicate their political duty to come to grips with these vital questions. We cannot expect, nor should we desire, answers on these political matters from the courts. Finally, we cannot achieve our desired goals of aboriginal development without the sympathetic and spirited participation of federal, provincial and aboriginal leaders.

Thank you.

CHAPTER 10
CONCLUSION
David C. Hawkes

Despite the wide range of subjects covered in the preceding chapters, a number of common themes emerge. These themes, together with the main lines of argument which dominated the conference on aboriginal peoples and federal/provincial government responsibility,[1] are woven together in this final chapter.

- With respect to government roles and responsibilities, it is important to distinguish between government jurisdiction and government responsibility.

While this point is applicable to any field of government activity, it is particularly important for aboriginal peoples, since they are identified in the Constitution, in s.91(24), as a federal head of power.[2] Federal and provincial government jurisdiction flows from the *Constitution Act, 1867*, which provides these governments with legislative powers—that is, with the legal power to act or to legislate. It is important to note that jurisdiction does not *oblige* governments to act. Jurisdiction allows discretionary performance by government; it does not make such legislation mandatory. For example, although it is clear that the federal government has jurisdiction with respect to Inuit, there is no *Inuit Act* for Inuit as there is an *Indian Act* for Indian peoples. Nor, one should hasten to add, is there any obvious reason—or opinion—encouraging the federal government to develop such legislation. It should be noted in this regard, that s.91(24) ("Indians and lands reserved for the Indians") enables the federal government to legislate only in ways which are preferential to aboriginal peoples, as was argued by Alan Pratt in Chapter 2.

Not everyone accepts this description of government jurisdiction regarding aboriginal peoples. Some First Nations are of the view that the Canadian Constitution does not apply to them, and that they retain their original and inherent sovereignty. The legislative powers of federal and provincial governments are conferred within our legal system, not theirs. Others point to the treaties, which they characterize as nation-to-nation agreements, or international treaties, as recognizing Indian government jurisdiction as opposed to federal government jurisdiction.

Government responsibility is more difficult to define than jurisdiction, as Brad Morse notes in Chapter 3, since its origins can be more numerous. Responsibility generally refers to whether or not some government action or conduct is required. Governments may be legally or morally *obliged* to act because of a duty, trust or debt, or because they are accountable and have the authority to spend public funds, or because they are responsible, in the broadest sense, for the welfare of the public. For example, despite the fact that provincial governments have exclusive jurisdiction in the fields of health care and education, the federal government provides significant funds to provincial governments for these purposes, and even legislates in respect of federal financing in health care (*Canada Health Act*). Although the federal government has no jurisdiction in these areas, few would argue that the federal government has no responsibility for health care and post-secondary education in Canada.

- For many reasons, provincial governments are becoming increasingly important in the lives of aboriginal peoples.

One reason for this development is that provincial governments are now involved in defining the constitutional rights of aboriginal peoples. Since 1979, and throughout the First Ministers' Conferences on Aboriginal Constitutional Matters which ended in 1987, provincial governments have been fully involved in defining the rights of aboriginal peoples in the Canadian Constitution. And since the proclamation of the *Constitution Act, 1982* (and the subsequent amendments in 1983 relating to aboriginal peoples), provincial governments have become involved in the modern treaty-making process in Canada. This has changed the formerly bilateral relationship of aboriginal peoples and the federal government to a trilateral one formally involving the provinces.

The change has not gone unchallenged. Many aboriginal peoples who have treaties with the Crown insist on retaining their direct bilateral relationship with the federal government, which they regard as the Queen's representative in Canada.

Some formal involvement of provincial governments in the lives of aboriginal peoples, however, predates developments surrounding constitutional reform. For many years, provincial governments have sought and achieved the application of some provincial laws to aboriginal peoples living on Indian reserves. Another reason for the increasing importance of provincial governments to aboriginal peoples relates to the federal government's interpretation of its jurisdiction over, and responsibility toward, aboriginal peoples flowing from s.91(24) of the *Constitution Act, 1867*. As the federal government moved to define its responsibility in terms of status Indians on reserves, and as it saw its powers in this regard in more discretionary terms (and hence, able to restrict access to some programs at will), non-status Indians and Metis began to welcome provincial involvement. As Fred Martin concludes in Chapter 7, when special status is denied, and access to many federal programs restricted, few choices were left. Hence, many provincial governments became involved in some aboriginal program areas by default. Provinces remain concerned about the possible federal divestiture of further programs and services for aboriginal peoples.

It would be wrong to characterize provincial involvement in aboriginal affairs as entirely one of "participation by default." As Frances Abele and Katherine Graham point out in Chapter 5, provincial governments are purposefully moving forward to address the needs of aboriginal peoples. This highlights yet another reason why provincial governments are increasingly important in the lives of aboriginal peoples in Canada. Provincial governments have more expertise in program delivery at the community and regional levels than has the federal government. Although most provincial governments are using existing functional programs to provide services to aboriginal peoples, there is room for (and need of) new programs and fresh and innovative approaches. Historically, such program experimentation has occurred more frequently at the provincial, rather than the federal, level of government.[3]

It should be noted, as well, that more aboriginal peoples, including some First Nations, are now ready and willing to deal with the Crown as a whole—that is, to deal with both federal and provincial governments. In Chapter 6, Evelyn Peters documents the history of such a relationship over the past decade in the James Bay region. John Taylor and Gary Paget, in Chapter 8, examine the more recent experience of the Sechelt in British Columbia.

- Although the federal government has jurisdiction over aboriginal peoples, both federal and provincial governments have responsibilities toward them.

As Alan Pratt argues in Chapter 2, both the federal and provincial orders of government are subject to the special relationship between aboriginal peoples and the Canadian state, although the federal government bears the main responsibility. This special relationship constantly changes over time. Since the early 1970s, the federal role has been redefined to accord with the interpretation of this relationship in terms of the empowerment of aboriginal peoples.

Aboriginal peoples are subject to the laws of both orders of government, though this is limited in the case of provincial laws. The collective rights of aboriginal peoples, now entrenched in the Constitution, as well as their rights as individuals (such as equality), entrenched in the *Charter of Rights and Freedoms*, should be accessible to all aboriginal peoples. They do not negate each other. The federal government is the primary guardian of the collective rights of aboriginal peoples, while provincial governments are the primary guardian of their individual rights. The roles of federal and provincial governments with regard to aboriginal peoples should follow accordingly. The federal role is now to affirm and strengthen aboriginal reality, as it is permanent and ongoing. Or, as Ian Scott describes it in Chapter 9, the federal government is responsible for "aboriginality" or the special aboriginal nature, while the provincial governments are responsible to treat aboriginal peoples as full provincial residents. This means that there is a provincial role in the area of programs. Aboriginal persons, as individuals, should receive provincial programs and services equal to those of other non-aboriginal persons.

This in no way detracts from the special rights of aboriginal peoples. The fiduciary, or trust, relationship of aboriginal peoples to the Canadian state remains intact, and is redefined so that the federal government acts only in ways which are positive to the beneficiaries, the aboriginal peoples of Canada. Nor does it alter, for example, the exemption from taxation of Indian lands. This is part of the special relationship, flowing from unextinguished sovereignty and aboriginal rights, which extends to both federal and provincial governments.

It is less clear, however, in what way shared federal and provincial government responsibility might lead to federal-provincial sharing of costs, and on what basis. As with other fields of federal-provincial negotiations on financing, this will be an intensely political decision.

- The drive for constitutionally-based aboriginal self-government at the national level, and the provision of meaningful programs and services to aboriginal peoples at the community level, ought to be viewed as complementary rather than contending objectives.

The constitutional negotiations on aboriginal rights raised the hopes of aboriginal peoples across Canada. When these negotiations ended without agreement, many people—both aboriginal and non-aboriginal—were critical of aboriginal leaders for pursuing constitutional reform at the expense of caring for their own communities. In practicing the "high politics" of constitutional reform at televised First Ministers' Conferences, it was inferred that aboriginal leaders were neglecting the needs of their people at the local level, needs such as education, housing, alcohol and drug counselling, and economic development.

There is a move, according to many observers, toward issues of programs and services at the grass-roots level, rather than high politics at the national, constitutional level. The needs of aboriginal peoples cannot wait, it is argued, until constitutional issues are resolved.

In several senses, this represents a false dichotomy, between enshrining principles of aboriginal self-government in the Constitution, and improving aboriginal peoples' lives at the community level. It is the case that administrative realities must be addressed before constitutional questions of self-government are settled. There must be administrative capacity at the local, grass-roots level, otherwise major changes at the constitutional level may have little meaning. In order for more autonomous aboriginal governments to be effective, they will have to be able to deliver programs and services, to negotiate intergovernmental agreements, to be accountable to their people, and to accept increasing responsibility. This will require more internal administrative capacity than now exists in most aboriginal communities. The renewed concern of aboriginal peoples with programs and services should be seen as a response to this problem. As they become involved in the direct delivery of services, using community-based vehicles, they move closer to self-determination in concrete terms.

There is the potential for matters of program delivery to subvert the larger political questions surrounding constitutional change. As well, program changes at the community level can up the ante for self-government, as Frances Abele and Katherine Graham argue in Chapter 5, providing gains at both levels. There is a relationship here which should not be overlooked. Having the right to aboriginal self-government entrenched in the Constitution could lead, at the local level, to autonomous but inept aboriginal government. On the other hand, a solid administrative structure with increased delivery capacity, but without entrenched rights and powers at the national level, could lead to competent but dependent aboriginal government.

Aboriginal peoples can work on two levels: on systemic change at the constitutional level, and on incremental change at the level of programs and services. Pragmatic change at the local level does not have to impinge on the larger political issues. There are meeting points between the two levels, as John Taylor and Gary Paget describe in Chapter 8 with respect to the Sechelt, in such areas as financing and government powers. The progress required at both levels can be achieved without risking either the rights of aboriginal Canadians, or the well-being of individual aboriginal people.

- A debate is now raging across Canada as to whether a third level of government—aboriginal self-government—is now emerging in the Canadian federal system.

Much of this debate revolves around the Sechelt Indian government experiment, described in Chapter 8. It is argued by some that British Columbia now has, in fact, a third level of government in Sechelt. The proponents of the argument that aboriginal self-government represents a third order of government in Canada make the following points: provincial laws do not apply to the local or district aboriginal governments unless these groups pass a law which accepts the provincial laws (the situation of Sechelt). Moreover, provincial legislation is powerless in the absence of federal legislation: the B.C. self-government legislation cannot stand alone, since it is merely complementary to federal legislation granting self-governing powers to the Sechelt. Provincial and federal laws apply to Sechelt only insofar as they are consistent with Sechelt by-laws, although it is acknowledged that Sechelt powers are limited in this regard.

Although the parties involved in the Sechelt legislation negotiations claim that it is not a model for other self-government arrangements, many of the detractors of the Sechelt experiment feel that it is the model being advocated by federal and provincial governments, despite statements to the contrary.

Since, from a constitutional perspective, the legislation passes no legislative power to the Sechelt government, it is therefore supported by federal and provincial governments, which do not wish to lose any powers. Sechelt is what these governments want, it is argued, since aboriginal peoples come into the political system on the level of municipal governments, without taking more control of resources. If aboriginal peoples begin with municipal-type government, it is concluded, this is where it will end.

Both sides agree that aboriginal self-government is here to stay, that the critical issues are power (or power-sharing) and financing, and that more practical experiments, such as Sechelt, are required.

- At times, it appears that the interpretation of what is the source of power for aboriginal governments is more of a barrier to agreement than the range of such powers.

Few oppose aboriginal peoples from becoming more self-sufficient, and from gaining more control over their lives. Most agree that the federal government, and the Department of Indian Affairs and Northern Development in particular, exercise too much control over these peoples. The view is widely held that it is time for responsibilities to be deemed to be aboriginal, rather than federal or provincial. Aboriginal governments should exercise an increasingly broad range of powers over such matters as resource management, citizenship in their governments, education and culture, law enforcement, child welfare, taxation, economic development ... the list is long.

What is more contentious, however, is the source of these powers. Do they flow from inherent and unextinguished aboriginal sovereignty, from existing treaty and aboriginal rights, or from federal and provincial governments? It was on this very question that the constitutional reform process on aboriginal rights foundered.[4]

Although disagreement continues on such matters of principle on aboriginal self-government, it would seem that there is an emerging consensus regarding the need for aboriginal self-government in practice.

• Aboriginal self-government will be meaningless without a secure fiscal base, which both responds to the need for fiscal independence while at the same time providing a supportive national and provincial framework.

The operation of aboriginal self-government can be greatly affected by the accountability requirements of those arrangements, the term or time during which they are in effect, the conditions attached to the transfer of funds, the flexibility of implementation and other factors. As Allan Maslove and I demonstrate in Chapter 4, these features can limit the scope for decision-making for the recipient aboriginal government, regardless of its formal governmental powers. Put another way, there is a relationship between cost-sharing and leverage. The more that a government relies on transfers or cost-sharing from another government, the more leverage that donor government will have on the recipient government. This is currently the case in federal-provincial fiscal arrangements, as well as in federal-aboriginal and provincial-aboriginal arrangements.

Generally, while aboriginal self-government agreements have become increasingly autonomous, the fiscal arrangements which accompany these have not been adjusted accordingly. The financial arrangements remain predominantly short-term, highly conditional and very inflexible. Progress is evident, however, in the Alternative Funding Arrangements of the Department of Indian Affairs and Northern Development and in the Sechelt government experiment. In this case, the band government has the fiscal flexibility to move funds among six program areas, and local Sechelt officials are directly responsible and accountable for these expenditures.

The questions which these new developments pose for aboriginal peoples are these: Are the new fiscal arrangements, such as those for Sechelt, the floor or the ceiling regarding aboriginal self-government and fiscal arrangements? Are federal and provincial governments willing to negotiate fiscal arrangements which, in terms of autonomy, match the self-government agreements to which they are attached?

366

Notes

1. The conference was held on the campus of Carleton University during October of 1988.
2. Aboriginal peoples are the only group of people to be identified as a federal head of power, that is, as a subject of federal jurisdiction in the Constitution.
3. For example, major experiments in the field of health care, such as community doctors and clinics, and the first medicare program in Canada (the basis of our current health care system), were initiated by the Government of Saskatchewan.
4. Named the section 37 process after its constitutional parentage, this included a series of four First Ministers' Conferences on Aboriginal Constitutional Matters, which ended in 1987 without agreement. See David C. Hawkes, *Aboriginal Peoples and Constitutional Reform: What Have We Learned?* (Kingston: Institute of Intergovernmental Relations, Queen's University, 1989).

THE CONTRIBUTORS

David C. Hawkes is a Visiting Professor in the School of Public Administration at Carleton University in Ottawa.

Alan Pratt is a lawyer with the firm of Blaney, McMurtry, Stapells in Toronto.

Bradford Morse is an Associate Professor in the Faculty of Law at the University of Ottawa.

Allan M. Maslove is a Professor in the School of Public Administration at Carleton University.

Frances Abele is an Assistant Professor in the School of Public Administration and in the School of Social Work at Carleton University.

Katherine Graham is an Assistant Professor in the School of Public Administration at Carleton University.

Evelyn J. Peters is an Assistant Professor in the Department of Geography at Queen's University in Kingston.

Fred V. Martin is a lawyer with the firm of Ackroyd, Piasta and Lennie in Edmonton.

John P. Taylor is a consultant in Victoria, and former Deputy Minister of the Ministry of Municipal Affairs in British Columbia.

Gary Paget is Director of Organizational Policy in the British Columbia Ministry of Municipal Affairs.

Ian G. Scott is the Minister responsible for Native Affairs and the Attorney General of Ontario.